Linguistic Symposium on Romance Languages: 9

William W. Cressey
Donna Jo Napoli
Editors

Georgetown University Press, Washington, D.C. 20057

Library of Congress Cataloging in Publication Data

Linguistic Symposium on Romance Languages (9th :
    1979 : Georgetown University)
    Linguistic Symposium on Romance Languages, 9.

    Bibliography: p.
    1.   Romance languages--Congresses. I. Cressey,
William W. II. Napoli, Donna Jo, 1948-   . III. Ti-
tle.
PC11.L53 1979   440   81-6291
ISBN 0-87840-081-8   AACR2

International Standard Book Number: 0-87840-081-8

CONTENTS

iii

Syntax and Semantics

Contents / v

PREFACE

This volume contains papers from the Ninth Annual Linguistic Symposium on Romance Languages, which was held on the campus of Georgetown University in March, 1979. The Linguistic Symposium on Romance Languages is held each year at a different campus and is devoted to linguistic analyses of the Romance languages within the context of various contemporary, formal approaches to linguistics.

The papers are presented in two parts: (1) papers dealing with phonology and morphology, and (2) papers dealing with syntax and semantics. All bibliographical references in the papers are listed in a combined bibliography at the end of the volume.

The editors wish to acknowledge the contributions of all those who helped make the conference a success and this volume a reality: the authors of the papers, the session chairpersons, the program committee, the editors of Georgetown University Press, the Dean and other administrative staff of the School of Languages and Linguistics at Georgetown University, and many others who generously volunteered their time for various aspects of conference organization.

SUBSEGMENTALS IN SPANISH PHONOLOGY: AN AUTOSEGMENTAL APPROACH

John Goldsmith
Indiana University

1.   One of the more interesting questions being asked in
phonology today goes back directly to the questions being
asked in the 1940s by Bernard Bloch, Zellig Harris, and J. R.
Frith.   Is phonology concerned with simple strings of segments,
with a geometry like a picket fence, albeit a fence made out of
a hodgepodge of pickets of varying width?   Or is the phonologist's soundstream more like a Mondrian, a brick wall made
from bricks with everywhere the same height--so there are
clear rows--but varying width to each brick?   In what ways
is the phonological segment atomic and indivisible?
    Within the framework created by the introduction of distinc-
tive features, it was clear that the segment was divisible in at
least a classificatory sense.   One could say of a p that it was
voiceless, for example, and one could break it down into various
specifications which, taken all together, fully characterized the
segment for the purposes of the language at hand.
    Still, within the general context of American structuralism,
and, until recently, of generative phonology, the phonological
segment was viewed as 'divisible' only in this limited sense.
Feature specifications could not be 'added' or 'taken away' from
a segment; all that could happen, it was supposed, was that
feature specifications could be modified by the effects of phonological rules.
    One generativist who raised doubts about this easy assump-
tion in the generative model was Cressey (1974), who himself
noted James Harris' (1969) earlier discussion of the problem.
The problem, as Cressey formulated it, was this:

(1) Certain subsets of features (tend to, may) cluster
    together in rules involving the Greek variable notation,
    that is, assimilation and dissimilation rules.

1

2 / John Goldsmith

Cressey notes, for example, that a rule like (2), involving
total assimilation of point of articulation, is more natural than
(3), whose point is difficult to imagine.

(2)

$$[\text{+nasal}] \rightarrow \begin{bmatrix} \alpha\,\text{coronal} \\ \beta\,\text{anterior} \\ \gamma\,\text{back} \\ \delta\,\text{distributed} \end{bmatrix} / \underline{\hspace{1cm}} (\#) \begin{bmatrix} \text{+obstruent} \\ \alpha\,\text{coronal} \\ \beta\,\text{anterior} \\ \gamma\,\text{back} \\ \delta\,\text{distributed} \end{bmatrix}$$

(3)

$$[\text{+nasal}] \rightarrow \begin{bmatrix} \alpha\,\text{anterior} \\ \beta\,\text{coronal} \\ \gamma\,\text{voice} \\ \delta\,\text{continuant} \end{bmatrix} / \underline{\hspace{1cm}} (\#) \begin{bmatrix} \text{+ obstruent} \\ \alpha\,\text{anterior} \\ \beta\,\text{coronal} \\ \gamma\,\text{voice} \\ \delta\,\text{continuant} \end{bmatrix}$$

The evaluation metric proposed in *Sound Pattern of English*
fails to achieve this result; Cressey proposed to elaborate the
notational system by introducing a single 'quasi-feature' to be
used in writing rules, called 'PA' for 'point of articulation'.
Thus 'αPA' would mean αhigh, βback, γcoronal, δanterior, and
εdistributed.

Such a notation is quite evidently in order for any language
which, like Spanish, has a rule assimilating nasals to the point
of articulation of a following obstruent. Instead of (2), the
language would have the formally simple Rule (4).

(4) $[\text{+nasal}] \rightarrow [\alpha\text{PA}] / \underline{\hspace{1cm}} \begin{bmatrix} \text{+obstruent} \\ \alpha\text{PA} \end{bmatrix}$

By incorporating Cressey's proposal for the αPA notation in
the theory, a certain level of explanation is achieved, in that
total assimilations of point of articulation are explicitly claimed,
by the notation, to be simple, and simpler than such arbitrary
assimilations as that of (3). The phenomenon has been 'captured', in the sense that it has been isolated, and a place has
been provided for it in the theory. Another level of explanation can be reached, however, if the αPA notation can be
removed from its theoretical isolation--if it can be linked, that
is, to a wider range of otherwise peculiar phenomena. That is
the aim of this paper: to suggest a theoretical basis for the
existence of subsegmental units, like Cressey's point of articulation complex, and to look at various related phonological
phenomena in Spanish. I argue that by simplifying the rule
of point of articulation assimilation in Spanish, one arrives at
an account of the stop/spirant alternation which is simpler and
more revealing than those proposed to date.

2. **Autosegmental phonology.** The starting-point of this
discussion is a view of suprasegmental tone that I have

suggested in a number of papers (see especially Goldsmith
1975, 1976a, 1976b, and 1979). Although I originally considered only tonal phenomena within this framework, which I
called 'autosegmental phonology', convincing proposals along
similar autosegmental lines have been advanced for the treatment of vowel harmony (by Clements 1976 and Chinchor 1978)
and nasal harmony (Goldsmith 1976b, Hart 1978). By considering a phonological representation as a multi-tiered structure,
as in (5), a number of recalcitrant properties of tonal systems
could be accounted for for the first time.

(5) nontone   V   C   V   V   C   V
     features   =   pitch

    tone features [+high]   [-high]

First, one could account for single segments (e.g. the second
vowel in (5)) which had consecutive internal components, such
as a vowel with a falling tone which was composed of a High
tone plus a Low tone. The problem was serious, it was clear,
because it was often easy to show that the vowel was a single
segment, not a long vowel composed of two short vowels, and
the falling tone was actually composed of two parts, an initial
High and a final Low. By postulating structures where different features were present on parallel, but co-equal, rows, this
lack of one-to-one correspondence between vowel specification
and tone specification turned from being anomalous to being
expected.

    Similarly, the phenomenon of 'tone stability' became trans-
parent. Phonological rules affecting vowels in most tone languages fail to affect the tone of the vowel, even when the rule
deletes the entire vowel segment. This follows naturally if the
tone composes a separate segment itself. By the same token
(and this foreshadows the case from Spanish), total assimilation
of two consecutive vowels virtually never is so 'total' that the
tones of the two vowels are changed. Rather, the oral gesture
features of one of the vowels totally assimilates to the other,
leaving the tonal segment to which it was associated unchanged.

    3.   Nasal point-of-articulation assimilation. Rather than pro-
ceeding with the account of autosegmental analysis of African
tone languages, let us return to the matter at hand, Spanish
phonology. There are parallels here, I would like to suggest,
to these two common tono-phonological processes in African
tone languages.

    3.1   One of these parallels is the spreading of a tonal 'auto-
segment' to neighboring tone-bearing units (generally, vowels).
This assimilation may be so 'overwhelming' that the original
tonal specification of the assimilating segment is lost; or it may
be partial, in that a level tone becomes a contour tone by

assimilation. A Low-toned vowel may become Falling-toned by assimilation in this sense to a High-toned vowel on its left, as in (5). This phenomenon gives the effect of all the tonal features on one vowel assimilating en bloc to those of another vowel, the kind of en bloc assimilation to which Cressey's notation addressed itself.

3.2 In the case I have mentioned, it is possible that the tone derived from the assimilation is a contour tone, as noted, and this in itself is a peculiarity to be noted.

Now both of these phenomena are matched in the behavior of nasal segments in Spanish. The spreading of tonal autosegments is parallel to the spreading of a segment specifying the oral point of articulation. This is illustrated in (6), where only the features of nasality and point of articulation are indicated.

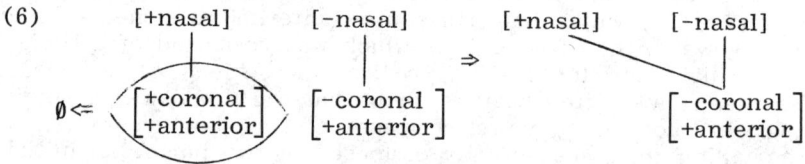

(6)

$$
\begin{array}{ccccc}
[+\text{nasal}] & [-\text{nasal}] & & [+\text{nasal}] & [-\text{nasal}] \\
\end{array}
$$

$$
\emptyset \Leftarrow \begin{bmatrix} +\text{coronal} \\ +\text{anterior} \end{bmatrix} \quad \begin{bmatrix} -\text{coronal} \\ +\text{anterior} \end{bmatrix} \Rightarrow \begin{bmatrix} -\text{coronal} \\ +\text{anterior} \end{bmatrix}
$$

Is there a parallel to the contour-specified segments as in (5)? That the answer is 'yes' is, in fact, well known. Harris, for example, notes (1969:15-16):

> ... (M)any Cubans pronounce *enfermo* as [e$\overset{\sim}{\underset{\eta}{m}}$fermo], where the first nasal, presumably systematic phonemic *n*, is realized with no alveolar contact at all, but rather with a labio-dental articulation superimposed on a dorso-velar articulation. Current phonological theory includes no device for assigning a feature specification that would reflect the auditory and articulatory properties of the segment represented as [$\overset{\sim}{\underset{\eta}{m}}$] and capture in some way the phonological process involved, namely, the [ŋ] component as a prejunctural phenomenon and the [m̃] component as an assimilation to the following [f]. It must be left to future research to explore the significance of such data.

The problem Harris noted in the segmental representation of the then current generative theory is precisely the parallel we are looking for, a parallel to the contour-toned vowels of tone languages. Thus, Harris' example is ultimately to be represented as in (7), with the velar segment specified by a syllable-sensitive rule, to which I return, and an autosegmental assimilation rule, spreading the oral gesture of any consonant leftward onto a nasal segment. (The velar insertion rule must apply first, which follows from the natural assumption that rules whose domain is the syllable apply before rules applying across syllables.)

(7)
$$\begin{bmatrix} +\text{nasal} \\ -\text{continuant} \\ \text{etc.} \end{bmatrix} \quad \$ \quad \begin{bmatrix} -\text{nasal} \\ +\text{continuant} \\ \text{etc.} \end{bmatrix}$$

PA: G   F

I use the symbols 'G' and 'F' as cover symbols for the velar and labio-dental point-of-articulation complexes, respectively. I henceforth assume that the oral point-of-articulation auto-segments are specified for all and only the PA features: anterior, coronal, high, back, and distributed. The rule of nasal assimilation is, then, (8).[1]

(8a)

    [+nasal]   [−nasal]   [+nasal]   [−nasal]

PA: ∅ [   ] [ ] ⇒ [   ] [ ]

or,

(8b)

    [+nasal]   [−nasal]

PA: ∅ [   ] [ ]

Since vowels, presumably, do not have point of articulation autosegments associated with them, the question in fact arises of how to insure that the *n* of *nuevo*, for example, does not assimilate to the following point-of-articulation segment, a bi-labial, turning *nuevo* wrongly into *muevo*. The correct answer, I believe, is that (as Hooper and others have suggested, for radically different reasons) (8) nasal assimilation, like other assimilation processes in Spanish, operates across syllable boundary, which should be indicated in the rule.

The rule creating syllable-final velar nasals is given in (9).

(9) [   ] ⇒ $\begin{bmatrix} -\text{coronal} \\ -\text{anterior} \end{bmatrix}$

    [+nasal] $

(That I indicate syllable boundaries with the symbol '$' should be taken to indicate a theoretical commitment to this notation rather than to that of Kahn (1975) or other notations assigning constituency to syllables and their subparts; on this, more follows directly.

4. s → h̲: 'Aspiration'. Let me summarize where I am at
this point.‾ So far I have simply tried to show that there are
a certain number of suggestive parallels between the anomalous
behavior of the oral gesture features, on the one hand, and
autosegmental tone units, on the other. I have also suggested
that Cressey's notational proposal would follow from a treatment
of segmental phonology in which, at the appropriate stage in
the derivation, the oral gesture features actually formed an
independent (autosegmental) tier or row. This proposal seems
not only desirable, in the sense of providing a more satisfying
explanation of Cressey's proposal, but it seems to be necessary,
in order merely to represent the contour-valued nasal segments
to which Harris refers.

One aspect of anomalous phonological behavior in tone languages was mentioned earlier: recurring processes that delete
only part of a segment. It is frequently found that a vowel
deletes under certain conditions--before another vowel, for
example--though the vowel's tone specification does not delete.
The imperviousness of tone to vowel deletion is, as has been
noted, directly accounted for in a model in which the tonal
autosegment is distinct from the vowel autosegment. This
leads to an additional test for autosegmental status, in addition
to the two tests considered earlier, which were contour specification and simultaneous assimilation of more than one feature.
This third test for autosegmental status is deletion: if a set of
features can undergo deletion as a unit, it must form a segment
on a separate tier.

In fact, there is clear evidence of this sort for a separate
oral tier in Spanish phonology. As suggested in Goldsmith
(1979), the widespread rule of 'aspiration' of *s* to *h* is an example of a rule deleting the oral gesture autosegment, but leaving behind untouched the laryngeal gesture of voicelessness.
For purposes of concreteness, I consider primarily the aspiration process in educated Porteño (Buenos Aires) speech.

In this dialect, /s/ appears as *h* in the environment V__C.
(I improve upon this formulation shortly.) Word boundaries
play no role in this rule, but I overlook the formal nicety of
including word boundaries in what follows.

(10) s → h / V____C (obligatory)

$$\begin{bmatrix} +\text{coronal} \\ -\text{voice} \\ +\text{continuant} \end{bmatrix} \rightarrow \begin{bmatrix} -\text{coronal} \\ -\text{anterior} \\ +\text{low} \end{bmatrix}$$

This rule gives rise to such allophony as that seen in (11).

(11a) más [mas] 'more'
(11b) más tonto [mahtonto] 'more stupid'
(11c) más inteligente [masintelixente] 'more intelligent'

That the left environment is a vowel is illustrated by the interaction of (10) with the optional fast speech rule of vowel
nasalization, as in (12).

(12) V N C → Ṽ C

Rule (12) deletes a postvocalic nasal and nasalizes the preceding vowel. Forms like *conspiración* can be derived either as
in (13a) or (13b), depending on whether (12) applies or not.

(13a) konspirasion	(13b) konspirasion
kõ spirasion (12)	--
kõ hpirasion (10)	not applicable

In the formulation of (10) in terms of features, there is no
clue as to why the change is from s to h rather than z, say,
or t, or any relatively common segment. I should like to say
that the element which the underlying s becomes is not one
specifically marked as having a wide open oral gesture; rather,
to use Y.-R. Chao's words (1963:39), we should say that the
'[h] is simply the feature of voiceless glottal friction and [we
should] leave the other nonsignificant features unspecified'--
even in derived contexts, I would add. This is achieved auto-
segmentally by deleting the oral gesture tier autosegment of
the underlying /s/, leaving only the voiceless laryngeal gesture.

There is, in fact, additional evidence for this treatment of
aspiration. There are other allophones of /s/ that appear in
the context V__C. After the high front vowel i, two allophones are possible, one which would be transcribed as [h],
and one which would be transcribed as [ç]. This allophony
of a word like *mismo* [mIhmo/miçmo] might be accounted for by
means of an optional rule (14), making what was orally unspecified once again specified, following this with the obligatory Rule (15), where I represents a slightly laxer version of
i).

(14) h → ç / i -- (optional)

(15) i → I / h -- (obligatory)

But such a pair of rules misses the point, clearly. The palatal
fricative [ç] occurs after the normal, tense allophone of the
vowel i. In fact, the oral gesture made to produce the [ç] is
nothing more than a continuation, during a period of nonvoic-
ing, of the gesture making the vowel i. The only way that an
h-type sound can be produced after an i in this dialect, in
fact, is if the i is produced in a more lax position, which is
possible, as noted in (15). But the important point to note is
that the variation in the allophone of s produced is not only
determined by the tenseness of the preceding i; it is directly

determined by it. The oral gesture of the preceding vowel
extends through the period of time of the laryngeal voicelessness left from the underlying s.

Let us consider how these various rules actually should be
formulated. I must emphasize that this is the most tentative
part of my suggestion; once one begins to consider the role
that the structure of the syllable may play in the formulation
of phonological rules, one comes to terrain that is not well
charted. All that can be attempted, at this point, is to see
if minimal assumptions about structure will lead to maximally
simple rule formulations.

Let me observe, as is well known, that all s's that delete
are syllable-final, and all n's that are syllable-final[2] are subject to deletion (bear in mind that in both cases, when I speak
of 'deletion', I mean only deletion of oral autosegment). As a
crude approximation, then, one might suggest that the rule
involved in both cases is in fact (16).

(16) oral tier: [+coronal] $

$$\downarrow$$

$$\emptyset$$

Clearly, one could not hope to find a simpler formulation of
the rule or rules involved, and (16) has the curious property
of handling some cases of both s and n deletion.

In several respects, however, it is not entirely adequate.
First, it fails to note that, in the Porteño dialect, the (s and
n) deletion must not only be syllable-final, but it may not be
prepausal. Second, the n which 'deletes' need not be syllable-
final; as was seen in (13), it may precede a tautosyllabic s.
Third, the rule, as it stands, does not express the fact that
s-deletion is essentially[3] obligatory, while n-deletion is optional.
Finally, the s must not be immediately preceded by a consonant.
I return to these questions in a moment.

On the other hand, (16) as it stands predicts that the other
syllable-final coronals will delete. This is partially true: d/č
does delete, as is seen in alternations like verð a/verð a čes
'truth/truths', but l and r do not (as in carcel 'jail'). The
formulation in (16) must minimally be revised, then, to indicate
that the coronal is an obstruent.

(17) oral: ([+coronal]) → $\emptyset$ $
          |
       [-vocalic]

Returning to the initial problems noted, it might be observed
that the failure of Rule (16) or (17) to indicate that it should
not apply to prepausal syllables is a step backwards, it seems,
from the early formulation of this rule as (10), which did not
mention syllable boundaries. In this case, however, I think that

it is probably correct that the Porteño grammar is more complicated than one in which the deletion rules apply to prepausal
syllables as well; again, as is well known, most other Latin
American dialects with such aspiration rules do generalize them
to prepausal position as well.

Second, the fact that *n*-deletion applies to a structure like
(18), as well as to one where the *n* is in fact syllable-final,
suggests that syllable-governed rules should not be formalized
in terms of symbols such as '$', but should, instead, refer to
internal constituency. Borrowing certain apparatus from the
recent work of Liberman, Kiparsky, Halle, and McCarthy, it
might be noted that the condition for coronal deletion is quite
generally 'constituent-final', and then (17) might be written as
(19), where α is a metric constituent.

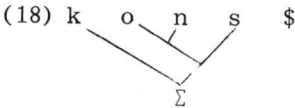

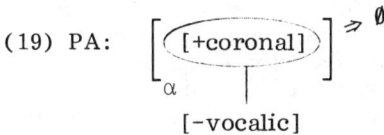

(18) k o n s $

$$\Sigma$$

(19) PA: $\left[\overbrace{[+coronal]} \right]_{\alpha} \rightarrow \emptyset$

[-vocalic]

This extends the rule to all the correct environments, it is
noted, and, of course, blocks the rule from applying to
syllable-initial consonants. If one assumes that at the point
of the derivation where (19) applies, vowels are not associated
with an 'oral' autosegment (not a necessary assumption), then
the bracketing indicated in (19) insures that no consonant
precedes the deleting element. (A single segment is not interpreted as forming a constituent.)

I have not gone into this extended but tentative discussion
of 'metrical phonology' simply in the hopes of simplifying the
rules of Spanish phonology. Actually, whether the specific
formulation in (19) is correct or not as it stands is less important than the fact that formulations of *s*-deletion and *n*-
deletion stated in terms of syllable and subsyllable structure
lead one closer to an account of why the nasal autosegment
left by *n*-deletion, and (though here the facts are less clear)
the *h*-autosegment left by *s*-deletion are both reassociated with
the preceding vowel. On a structural account such as the one
under consideration, this would follow from the natural assumption that reassociation takes place within the domain in which a
rule applies. Such statements are simply not available within
a segmental framework like that presupposed by rule formulation (10).

5. Stop/spirant allophony. I turn now to another, rather different problem in Spanish phonology in which the alpha-point-of-articulation notation has been employed--the formulation of the phonological rule responsible for the stop/spirant alternation. There are, of course, three voiced obstruents in Spanish which are traditionally said to have a stop and a spirant allophone, as illustrated in (20). The stop allophone--[b,d,g]--appears after a nasal; the [d], furthermore, appears after an *l*, though the spirant allophones [β,γ] appear after *l* as well. In short, one may say that the stop versions appear after 'homorganic nasals and liquids', or 'homorganic non-continuant sonorants'.[4]

(20)

After	β/b	ð/d	γ/g
m	ambos	--	--
n	--	mandar	--
ŋ	--	--	teŋgo
l	alba	maldito	alγo
V	aβer	deðo	aγo

There has been extended discussion at various points in the literature as to whether these segments should be considered stops underlyingly, as Harris proposed, for example; under such an assumption, a rule of spirantization much as in (21) would be necessary. Alternatively, the spirants, or continuants, could be considered basic, and a rule of stop formation as in (22) would be posited to account for the allophony.

(21) $\begin{bmatrix} -son \\ +voice \end{bmatrix} \rightarrow [+cont] \; / \; \left\{ \begin{matrix} [-son] \\ [+cont] \\ <[\alpha cor]> \end{matrix} \right\} \begin{bmatrix} \underline{\quad} \\ <-\alpha cor> \end{bmatrix}$

(22) $\begin{bmatrix} -son \\ +voice \end{bmatrix} \rightarrow [-cont] \; / \; \begin{bmatrix} -cont \\ \alpha cor \end{bmatrix} \begin{bmatrix} \underline{\quad} \\ \alpha cor \end{bmatrix}$

(23) $\begin{bmatrix} -son \\ +voice \end{bmatrix} \rightarrow [-cont] \; / \; \begin{bmatrix} -cont \\ \alpha PA \end{bmatrix} \begin{bmatrix} \underline{\quad} \\ \alpha PA \end{bmatrix}$

As Cressey (1974) notes, (22) can be stated using the αPA notation, as in (23), although in the particular case being considered, this introduction of αPA is not necessary--in a sense for accidental reasons, on a segmental view. The only nasals that could precede the spirants would already be homorganic by the earlier effects of the rule making nasals homorganic to a following consonant. The only remaining restriction that needs to be stated along these lines is that the presence of an *l* will trigger the stop formation only of a *d*, not of a *b* or *g*. But that can be stated with reference simply to the feature [coronal], as in (22), rather than PA, as in (23).

I do not argue here that stop formation is in fact a more adequate treatment of the phenomenon than spirantization; a thorough account of various theoretical and empirical (both synchronic and diachronic) factors all indicating a stop formation rule is found in Lozano (1978). For present purposes, then, I take Rule (22), or a slight modification of it, to be the most adequate segmental account of the process, and one which I shall see if I can improve upon.

Before leaving the domain of the facts to be accounted for, one should note that it is generally said that the stop allophones occur initially--that is, after pause. To the extent that this is true, it requires a separate environment of Rule (22) to account for this. In any event, the occurrence of a stop in this position is more optional, I believe, than some of the literature might lead one to think, and contrasts with the obligatory character of the stops after the nasals, as Lozano points out.

$$(24) \quad \begin{bmatrix} \text{-son} \\ \text{+voice} \end{bmatrix} \rightarrow [\text{-cont}] \;/\; \begin{bmatrix} \text{-cont} \\ \alpha \text{PA} \end{bmatrix} \begin{bmatrix} \underline{\quad} \\ \alpha \text{PA} \end{bmatrix}$$

As noted earlier, the sense in which the rule of stop formation is conditioned by the 'homorganicity' of the preceding noncontinuant is somewhat elusive. Since *l* triggers stop formation only of *d*, not *b* or *g*, it is clear that some mention of homorganicity of the noncontinuant and the spirant-turned-stop must be made in the rule. On the other hand, since nasal assimilation precedes stop formation, and insures that all nasals preceding consonants are homorganic to what follows, it then should not be necessary to state explicitly, and redundantly, in the stop formation rule that the preceding nasal be homorganic--the condition that the nasal be already homorganic is implicitly guaranteed by an earlier rule in the derivation.

What I would like to suggest is that the alternative autosegmental account of nasal assimilation can also be extended to a revised account of stop formation which explicitly accounts for the relationship between nasal assimilation and stop formation, and which, in a sense, allows for a grammar of Spanish which has no explicit rule of stop formation at all--the effects of the former rule of stop formation would all result from the structure created by nasal assimilation, under certain conditions, to which I now turn.

The most important conclusion in the study cited by Lozano (1978) is that segments such as *b, d, g* do not, strictly speaking, derive from underlying spirants; she argues rather that the Stop Formation Rule (24) applies (in the cases being examined here) to segments underlyingly unspecified for the feature [continuant]. Rule (24) is, then, supplemented by an 'elsewhere' process, given here as (25).

(25) $\begin{bmatrix} -\text{son} \\ +\text{voice} \end{bmatrix} \rightarrow \begin{cases} [-\text{cont}] \ / \ \begin{Bmatrix} \begin{bmatrix} \overset{||}{-\text{cont}} \\ \alpha\text{PA} \end{bmatrix} \end{Bmatrix} \begin{bmatrix} \overline{\quad\quad} \\ \alpha\text{PA} \end{bmatrix} \\[2em] [+\text{cont}] \qquad (\text{elsewhere}) \end{cases}$

I am not going to review the evidence Lozano adduces, but the argument for this position, within a segmental framework, I find convincing. I might add I find totally unconvincing the arguments that have been put forward to date against segments underlyingly unspecified for certain features; these arguments are almost without exception nonempirical, and rest on additional assumptions which are surely false.

Accepting Lozano's conclusion regarding the underlyingly unspecified status of the feature [continuant] in the voiced nonstrident obstruents, and assuming the account of nasal assimilation suggested earlier, the 'input' stage to 'stop formation' looks roughly like (26).

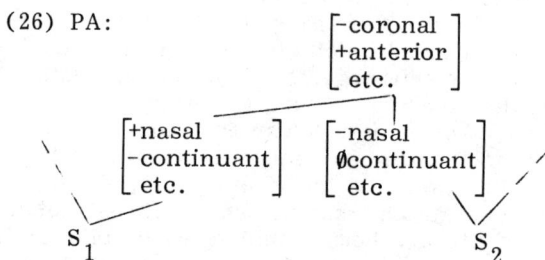

(26) PA:

$$\begin{array}{c} \begin{bmatrix} -\text{coronal} \\ +\text{anterior} \\ \text{etc.} \end{bmatrix} \\[2em] \begin{bmatrix} +\text{nasal} \\ -\text{continuant} \\ \text{etc.} \end{bmatrix} \qquad \begin{bmatrix} -\text{nasal} \\ \emptyset\text{continuant} \\ \text{etc.} \end{bmatrix} \\[2em] S_1 \qquad\qquad\qquad\qquad S_2 \end{array}$$

Now holding aside the case of the phrase-initial stops (see note 3), (26) illustrates an interesting fact: all the voiced obstruent stops are found in precisely a structure like (26), where a [-continuant] segment (here, a nasal) and a nonspecified segment are associated with the same point-of-articulation autosegment. That this holds for the case of the postnasal obstruents should be clear; let us review for a moment the reasons that make clear that the *d* following an *l* appears as well in a structure like (26).

As Harris (1969) observes, *l* is underlyingly alveolar, but before dental (*t, d*) and alveopalatal (*č*) segments, *l* assimilates in point of articulation. Harris in fact suggests that this assimilation is in some sense closely related to the process of nasal assimilation. 'Clearly', he says (1969:19),

> there is a significant linguistic generalization here: non-continuant sonorants become homorganic with a following obstruent, within the limits set by certain constraints (there are no labial, labio-dental, or velar *l*s).

Whether the limitation of *l*-assimilation to only following coronals is actually predictable on theoretical grounds must remain an open question; what is important for my purposes, however, is that the *l* participates in a point-of-articulation process in precisely that case where it induces the stop *d*; or, to put the matter in terms of my theory, the structure *ld* appears, parallel to *nd*, as in (27). One may assume a rule of *l*-assimilation as in (28). Recall that although it is only the feature specification [+coronal] that triggers *l*-assimilation (28), it is the other feature specifications in the oral autosegment that actually affect the *l*.

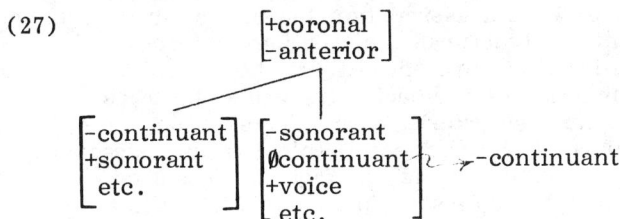

(27)
$$\begin{bmatrix} \text{+coronal} \\ \text{-anterior} \end{bmatrix}$$

$$\begin{bmatrix} \text{-continuant} \\ \text{+sonorant} \\ \text{etc.} \end{bmatrix} \quad \begin{bmatrix} \text{-sonorant} \\ \text{\O continuant} \\ \text{+voice} \\ \text{etc.} \end{bmatrix} \quad l \quad \gamma\text{-continuant}$$

(28) *l*-assimilation

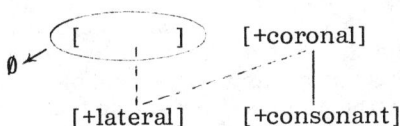

$$\emptyset \leftarrow \quad \big[\quad \big] \quad \text{[+coronal]}$$

[+lateral]   [+consonant]

The obligatory environment for stop formation, then, is precisely that seen in (26) or (27); in all other positions, the equivalent of Lozano's 'elsewhere' rule in (25) inserts a [-continuant] specification (e.g. intervocalically).

The process of stop formation, then, is one that turns (27), for example, into (29). What mechanism could be responsible for this?

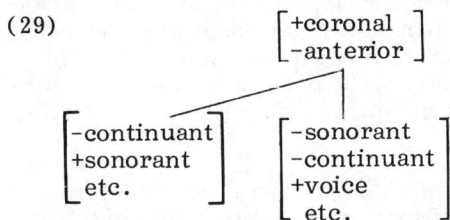

(29)
$$\begin{bmatrix} \text{+coronal} \\ \text{-anterior} \end{bmatrix}$$

$$\begin{bmatrix} \text{-continuant} \\ \text{+sonorant} \\ \text{etc.} \end{bmatrix} \quad \begin{bmatrix} \text{-sonorant} \\ \text{-continuant} \\ \text{+voice} \\ \text{etc.} \end{bmatrix}$$

This mechanism is one by which the [-continuant] specification of the preceding segment is 'contributed' to the segment which itself is not specified for the feature [continuant]. However, it is not sufficient that there simply be a noncontinuant segment to the left; [*futβol*] 'football/soccer', for example, does not contain a stop [*futbol*] in normal speech.

I would like to suggest that features underlyingly unspecified, other things permitting, receive their specification by a 'minimum distance principle' of a rather natural sort. In the case of structures (26), (27), (29), the unspecified feature [continuant] is found in a segment which itself forms a complex unit with the preceding nasal/liquid. The specification [-continuant] in the preceding nasal/liquid is structurally closest to the unspecified continuant feature in that each is associated with the same subsegmental autosegment. Under these conditions, then, (27) becomes (29). It follows, too, that when nasal or lateral assimilation has not applied, the unspecified segment is structurally 'closest' to the vowel which follows (or, more rarely, precedes) it in the syllable, which is [+continuant]; hence, the unspecified segment becomes [+continuant] in this 'elsewhere' case. This renders the 'elsewhere' subpart of the segmental Rule (25) unnecessary.

The principle involved here is, in fact, a special case of a more general principle suggested in Hart (1978), where several languages displaying nasal harmony are investigated. What is of particular interest here is the fact that, on quite independent grounds, Hart concludes that segments alternating in harmony specifications are underlyingly unspecified for the feature [nasal], and he argues that the ultimate nasal specification of these segments is derived or 'inherited' from a more abstract nasalization specification of a larger unit--the syllable, the foot, or the word--in which the unspecified segment is found. Hart's principle, then, says that a segment unspecified for a feature receives the specification of a larger unit in which the segment is found--and in particular, the specification of the 'smallest' larger unit in which the segment is found (thus, an unspecified segment may become [-nasal] in a syllable which itself is marked [-nasal], even though it is in a [+nasal] word).

The result noted in (29) from Spanish appears to be a special case of this more general result, though apparently the sonorant + stop elements do not form a phonological or metrical constituent. If they did, then the application of Hart's principle would be immediate. In fact, such an assumption is not unreasonable, but must be left for future research. In the meantime, we may assume that Hart's principle is itself a subcase of a minimum distance principle which fills in unspecified features.

6. **Conclusion.** In the three cases I have examined from Spanish phonology--nasal assimilation, s-aspiration, and stop formation--the notion of 'point of articulation' has played a crucial role, though in quite different ways. I have suggested several reasons for thinking that the autosegmental approach may allow one to achieve a deeper understanding of the processes involved, processes which to date have not been

adequately described, I believe, within the more traditional segmental framework. One direction for future research that is suggested here is the study of processes that fill in under-lyingly unspecified features, a question which has generally not been addressed in the recent phonological literature.

NOTES

This paper would not have been possible without the lengthy and frequent discussions of Spanish phonology I have had with Carmen Lozano, whose dialect (Porteño) is the one studied here (described in her dissertation, Lozano 1978, as well). I am also grateful for the comments of James Harris, which occasioned most of the notes in the present version.

1. In the 'standard' dialects that do not have 'contour-valued' nasals. In those dialects with a structure like (7), the nasal assimilation will not, clearly, delete the nasal's original point-of-articulation autosegment.

2. There is perhaps some variability in the *n*-deletion pro-cess related to the character of the following consonant, but the *n* can delete not only before *s* but before a voiced stop/ spirant (as in *tengo, ambos,* for example), occasioning a spi-rant allophone. There certainly is cross-dialectal variability regarding the frequency of this process, whose range I have not examined.

3. The rule applies in all normal speech situations, but may be 'overridden' in hypercorrect styles, such as when one is speaking to someone who does not speak the language well.

4. James Harris has brought two interesting observations to my attention regarding this point. He notes, first, that in very careful speech one may pronounce *invitar* [in-bi-tar], where the *n* is presumably in some sense a spelling pronunci-ation. Nonetheless, although the *b* is not homorganic to the nasal, it is realized as a stop.

I believe that the stop character of the *b* here is not due to the effect of the preceding nasal, but is rather due to the intersyllabic pause at this slow speech rate. I would expect, then, that at a rate slow enough to produce the pronunciation [in-bi-tar], one would also find [e-bi-tar].

I assume that a rule exists essentially as in (i), which is in some measure optional in normal speech.

(i) $\begin{bmatrix} \text{+voice} \\ \text{-sonorant} \\ \text{-strident} \end{bmatrix} \rightarrow \text{[-continuant]} \; / \; || \; \underline{\quad}$

Harris also notes that in some dialects, otherwise similar to the Porteño described here, one finds such forms as *ane*[kd]*ota* rather than the Porteño *ane*[kð]*ota*, and such forms as *fu*[tb]*ol*. I have not worked with such dialects, and

leave to future work precisely in what ways dialects may vary
with respect to the rules being discussed here.

ON LOANWORD PHONOLOGY
AS DISTINCTIVE FEATURE PHONOLOGY
IN CUBAN SPANISH

Jorge M. Guitart
State University of New York at Buffalo

I would like to show that the analysis of certain phenomena in the borrowing of English words by Cuban speakers (which occurs also among speakers of other Hispanic dialects) provides strong support for a distinctive feature-based loanword phonology. Some of the same phenomena have been analyzed by Peter C. Bjarkman (1976) in his study of Miami Cuban Spanish and in other writings (Bjarkman 1975, 1977, 1978). Bjarkman adopts a theoretical framework that specifically denies the role of distinctive features in the nativization of foreign words. I am going to show that Bjarkman's proposal is counterintuitive and unrevealing and that the theory of borrowing upon which it is based is too abstract.

When discussing English loanwords in Cuban Spanish, two observations are in order which Bjarkman practically does not take into account. One is that some of the loans he discusses (in Bjarkman 1976, 1977, for example) existed in Cuban Spanish before the Cuban exodus to the United States. They were definitely not borrowed in southeastern Florida in the sixties and seventies. Among these items are [pulóber] for *pullover*, [hambérger] for *hamburger*, and [tán] for *tan* (as in *suntan*), which I can attest were used by middle-class speakers in Cuba before the Revolution. The expression *coger un tan* was part of the lexicon of middle-class speakers at Havana beach clubs in the late fifties.

A second observation--a far more important one--is that the pronunciation of loanwords in Cuban Spanish is not entirely derived from the spoken language but is in some cases influenced by the written version of those words. One must take into account that many Cubans are literate and are bilingual in different degrees.

That it makes a difference whether an English word entered Spanish via speech or script can be illustrated with the case of the borrowing of *sweater*. There are at least two versions of this word: one is [syéter], which is the pronunciation of the item among educated speakers (of Cuban Spanish as well as of other dialects) and the other is [syéra], attested to in United States Hispanic dialects (for example, by Rissel 1976), and originating very probably with speakers who were either illiterate or were at least unaware of the educated borrowing. In [syéra], of course, speakers have perceived the American English flap as /r/, while in [syéter] they have assigned to t the phonetic value that it has in Spanish orthography.

The influence of Spanish spelling may be total, as in [kolgáte] for *Colgate* (the toothpaste) and [palmolíße for *Palmolive* (the soap), or only partial, as in the case of [syéter] itself; an orthographically more faithful borrowing would have shown [ea] for the orthographic sequence *ea*. The borrowing of *sweater* as [syéter] illustrates the fact that literate speakers who are at least minimally bilingual may apply orthographic criteria to portions of the items being borrowed and phonetic criteria to other portions of the same item.

I now show that the pronunciation of certain English words on the part of Cubans supports a distinctive feature-based theory of borrowing. I use in my analysis the set of features proposed by Chomsky and Halle (1968) in *The Sound Pattern of English* (SPE). The fundamental assumption advanced here is that a hearer actively analyzes a foreign segment as a physical signal and on the basis of its phonic characteristics assigns it to a class in his native system, with both the analysis and the assignment being in terms of distinctive features.

The most revealing cases for the theory are those in which borrowers have apparently not been influenced by the spelling, having interpreted the foreign sound as a native sound that would not be represented in the native orthography by the same letter as in the foreign orthography. Such is the case in the nativization of English *man* as [méŋ] in Cuban Spanish, where English /æ/ has been borrowed as /e/. Obviously, the borrowers were not aware of the orthographic shape of the word in English. In Cuba, in the late fifties, less educated speakers included this item in their lexicon and used it in the same way that *man* was used in so-called 'hip talk' in the United States. That is to say, it was a generic form of address in the singular, as in *¿Qué estás haciendo, men?* 'What are you (sing.) doing, man?'[1]

Other examples of borrowing /æ/ as /e/ in Cuban Spanish are [kéčer] for *catcher* (the baseball position) and [sénkju] for *thank you*, both old loans.

Now, /æ/ does not exist in Spanish. This vowel is analyzed in SPE as having the features [-high, -back, +low, -round]. No Spanish vowel phoneme has that particular combination of features. There are only two vowels, /e/ and /a/, that are

[-high, -round]. The problem is that /æ/ is like /e/ in backness and like /a/ in lowness, but is unlike /e/ in lowness and
unlike /a/ in backness. That is to say, it resembles both and
differs from both in one feature. This presents the speaker
with a perceptual dilemma which he apparently solves by valu-
ing more highly the distinctness of one feature over the other.
In assigning /æ/ to /e/, the speaker has valued [back] more
highly than [low]. He has in effect decided that the sound
cannot be /a/ because it is nonback, and because it is also
nonhigh and nonround, he assigns it to the only vowel that
has that particular combination of features in Spanish, /e/.

But the dilemma can be solved the other way. In some instances, the speaker values [low] more highly than [back] and
decides that the sound cannot be /e/ because it is low, and
because it is also nonhigh and nonround, it is assigned to the
only vowel so classified, /a/. Examples are [hámanék] for
ham and eggs, [kác̆] for *cash*, and [kác̆er] as the rendering
of *catcher* by some speakers.

But in [kác̆], [kác̆er], etc., it may be argued that the
borrower has been influenced by the orthography since /a/
is always symbolized *a* in Spanish.

There are, however, other cases of alternative solutions to
a feature dilemma in which neither choice can be imputed to
the influence of spelling, because the orthographic symbol for
the English sound is unlike the symbol for either Spanish
sound. This occurs in the borrowing of stressed schwa, /ʌ/,
as either /a/ or /o/ when it is spelled *u* (which is usually the
case).

English /ʌ/ is [+back, -high], like both /a/ and /o/. It is
also nonround like /a/ in opposition to /o/, but nonlow like
/o/ in opposition to /a/. In some cases, the Cuban borrower
values [low] more highly than [round] and decides that the
segment cannot be [a] because it is [-low]; and because it is
also [-high, +back] it is assigned to the only class of vowels
that has those features, /o/. In other cases, he assigns the
segment to /a/, having decided that it cannot be /o/ because
it is [-round], thus choosing the distinctness of [round] over
the distinctness of [low].

One example is the alternative pronunciation of *Buffalo* by
some bilingual Cubans living in the city of that name. I have
heard both [báfalo] and [bófalo]. Bjarkman (1976) records
l[o]nchear and *fl[o]nquear* as the nativization of the verbs
lunch and *flunk* in Miami Cuban Spanish, but records also
[dáḅalyu] as the adaptation of English [dʌbəlyu] for *double u*
in the rendering of *W.T. Grant*, the name of a Miami store.

Similarly, unstressed schwa, [ə], which being [+back, -high,
-round], is both like and unlike Spanish /a/ and /o/, may be
borrowed as either. Notice the example from Bjarkman just
given, where it is borrowed as /a/; there is also the old loan
[ku̯óra] for *quarter*, probably borrowed from an *r*-less dialect
(compare [su̯éra] for *sweater*). As to [ə] being borrowed as

/o/, Bjarkman records [aƀéilaƀol] as the nativization of *available*, in which the sequence [əɏ] is rendered as [ol]. In this case, the borrower may have been influenced by the 'o-colored' character of [ɏ], the English 'dark' /l/, in the production of which the back of the tongue assumes a configuration similar to the one it has in the production of a rounded nonhigh back vowel. The lateral is perceived as nonback, since there are no back laterals in Cuban Spanish. It may very well be that what is perceived as [ol] in not the sequence but [ɏ] itself. That is to say, the speaker hears the 'o-colored' quality of [ɏ] as Spanish /o/ (probably relying here on scalar gradations of backness, i.e. on /o/ being more back than /a/) and hears the consonantal features [+lateral, +anterior, +coronal] as nonback [l] since, again, Cuban Spanish has no back laterals.

Apparently, something similar occurs in the borrowing of words containing the vowel [ər]. Cubans interpret this vowel as the sequence /er/, thence, for example, [sonderbér] and hambérger] for *Thunderbird* (the auto model) and *hamburger*. [2] According to Ladefoged (1975:71), [ər] is a retroflex vowel which has *r*-coloring (or rhotacization), and some speakers produce it with the tip of the tongue raised but others 'keep the tip down and produce a high bunched tongue position'. Ladefoged adds that the two different gestures cause a very similar auditory effect. Apparently, the Spanish hearer interprets this sound as having been made with the tip raised, since Spanish (including Cuban Spanish) does not have any class of retroflex sounds produced with the tongue bunched up high (in other words, there are no retroflex sounds at the systematic level). Now, any retroflex vowel produced with tongue tip raised would be coronal and nonback (see Chomsky and Halle 1968:308). It would also be nonhigh (as opposed to retroflex consonants, which are high--see Ladefoged 1975:243). We can hypothesize that this segment is perceived as having the features [-consonantal, +syllabic, +sonorant, -nasal, +coronal, -high, -back, -low, -round]. The fact that it is indeed a vowel with the tongue feature values possessed only by /e/ in Spanish explains its being interpreted partially as that vowel. But the fact that it is also coronal--and there are no coronal vowels in Spanish--explains the speaker's 'hearing' also Spanish /r/, which has that value for coronality and in addition has the same values for the other tongue features. (Of course, the fact that the segment is not lateral prevents it from being perceived as /l/, the other coronal liquid occurring systematically in syllable-final position.)

Thus far, I have been analyzing the borrowing of vowels, but the nativization of English consonants that do not exist in Cuban Spanish may also be analyzed revealingly in terms of distinctive features.

For instance, /š/ is borrowed as /č/, for example, [čou] for *show*, [káč] for *cash*, etc. The English segment is [+coronal, -anterior, +delayed release] and /č/ is the only

Spanish consonant that has those features. English [ž], which is also [+coronal, -anterior, +delayed release] is also borrowed as [č], e.g. [béič] for *beige*, [řúč] for *rouge*, etc. Curiously, however, English [ǰ], which shares those features, may be borrowed as either /č/ or /y/, the voiced palatal obstruent phoneme (and rendered as either the affricate [ỹ] or the fricative [ɏ] in the allophonic variation of the latter phoneme), e.g. [dóčers] for *Dodgers* (the baseball team), [mánačer] for *manager*, but [ỹon] for *John*, [niuɏérsi] for *New Jersey*, etc. This can be explained by appealing again to the feature dilemma scheme. English [ǰ], being [+coronal, -anterior, +voiced, +delayed release] is unlike /č/ in voicing and unlike /y/ in coronality, but similar to both in the other features. If the speaker values [voiced] over [coronal], [ǰ] will be borrowed as /y/, whereas if he values [coronal] over [voiced], it will be borrowed as /č/. Seemingly, there is a preference to borrow [ǰ] as /y/ in word-initial position and as /č/ in word-final position. In the latter case, the occurrence of /č/ is absolute since /y/ does not occur in that position in Spanish. I have no explanation at this point for the preference for /y/ in initial position. In medial position either /y/ or /č/ may be substituted; compare [dóčers] for *Dodgers* with [řóɏer] for *Roger*.

I think that the illustrations given in the foregoing provide sufficient evidence in support of a theory of loanword phonology based on distinctive features.

I would now like to contrast my position with that advanced by Bjarkman in his treatment of loanwords in Miami Cuban Spanish. The theoretical framework that Bjarkman adopts is that of natural phonology, his proposals constituting a particular interpretation of the views of David Stampe (1973). In Bjarkman's natural phonology, binary features play no role in loanword phonology. Rather, native substitutions of foreign sounds are entirely due to the application of what Bjarkman calls 'active processes'.

To illustrate, Bjarkman (1978:30) claims that Cubans, in nativizing *discount* as [dihkáũ], have applied to the English phonetic form [dískāũnt] the following paradigmatic processes: denasalization, vowel raising, cluster reduction, and stress shift, resulting in the phonemic (lexicalized) form--the terms are Bjarkman's--/diskawn/. To this, in turn, Cubans apply allophonic processes such as nasalization, aspiration, etc., accounting for the phonetic rendering [dihkáũ].

Now, since Bjarkman (1975:69) holds that processes are 'actual substitutions working upon real segments in the mental and physical performance of the speech act', it follows from his proposal that Cubans first construct a mental representation of *discount* identical to the English phonetic form and then apply to that representation the processes posited by Bjarkman. You cannot, for instance, apply vowel raising unless you have a vowel to be raised and cannot shift the stress to the last

syllable unless it was on another syllable before the process
applied.

There is no evidence, however, that speakers construct such
representations. Instead, there is a great deal of evidence
that, when going only by the physical signal, borrowers perceive segments in terms of their own phonological systems.
Ample proof exists that English phonemic differences that do
not exist in Spanish have no psychological reality for Spanish
untrained speakers, who normally fail to hear the difference
between, for example, *rice* and *rise*, *bit* and *beat*, etc.

Bjarkman's loanword theory, in addition to being too abstract,
is contradicted by the facts.

To contrast his approach with mine, in the nativization of
Rise (the name of a product) as [ráịs] Bjarkman would be com-
mitted to claiming that the speaker has a representation containing /z/ to which he applies a process of devoicing. In the
framework that I have proposed, the Cuban hearer never perceives [z] as [z], but always as [s]. To illustrate further,
when a hearer perceives /ʌ/ as /o/, he has not perceived a
nonround vowel which is subsequently rounded. Rather, he
has perceived a round vowel. The hypothesis that I have advanced here is that the hearer accomplishes this through a
process of elimination. The vowel can be perceived as either
/o/ or /a/. In some cases, the speaker decides that it cannot
be /a/ because it is not low; therefore it must be /o/. In
other cases, he decides that it cannot be /o/ because it is not
round; therefore it must be /a/.

Returning to the borrowing of *discount*, I would like to observe first of all that [dihkág̃] is the pronunciation only in the
most relaxed style of speech. Depending on speed and/or care
of pronunciation, the word may be pronounced [diskáunt],
[dihkáuņt], [dihkáuŋ], or [dihkág̃]. Secondly, I would like
to suggest that in this case borrowers have been guided a
great deal by orthographic considerations, which Bjarkman
ignores. There are in Cuban Spanish the old loans
[paramáuŋ(t)] for *Paramount* (the motion picture company),
[bakgráuŋ] for *background*, and [ráuŋ] for *round* (the boxing
term), which are nonetheless written with the English spelling
by literate Cubans, indicating that they assign the phonetic
sequence [aŭn] to the orthographic sequence *oun* in those
words.

The position of the primary stress on the last syllable of
[diskáuŋ] can be explained by the fact that Spanish words
ending in a consonant are normally stressed on that syllable.
One cannot speak of 'stress shift' in [diskáuŋ] unless it were
the case that Cubans had previously pronounced it as [dískauŋ]
--which is a possibility since there are words ending in a
consonant in Spanish that are penult stressed (e.g. *examen*
'examination'). But most probably the borrowing originated
with bilingual Cubans seeing the word in print and assigning to
oun the pronunciation [aŭn] and placing the stress on the

final syllable in agreement with a general rule of Spanish phonology.

One serious shortcoming of Bjarkman's framework is that it
provides no explanation for why a certain English segment is
perceived as a certain Spanish segment (or alternatively as
two Spanish segments), but not as any other Spanish segment.
In fact, nothing is said in Bjarkman's natural phonology about
perception; his treatment of phonetic borrowings boils down to
describing the production of Spanish sounds in terms of the
behavior of English sounds. For instance, Bjarkman would
have to say that if /ʌ/ is borrowed as /a/ it is because it has
been lowered, but if it is borrowed as /o/ it is because it has
been rounded; if /ǰ/ is borrowed as /č/ it is because it has
been devoiced, but if it is borrowed as /y/ it is because it
has been palatalized, etc.

In closing, I would like to point out that, even though
Bjarkman specifically denies that binary features play a role
in loanword phonology, nowhere in his writings does he give
empirical evidence showing that a distinctive feature analysis
of borrowing is incorrect or unwarranted.

In my opinion, the distinctive feature-based model that I
have offered here provides an explanation for the facts both
of production and of perception in the nativization of foreign
words and is strongly supported by the empirical facts.

NOTES

This is a much revised version of the original paper presented at the Symposium under the title 'How autonomous is the
natural phonology of Cuban Spanish?' I am very grateful to
William Cressey for suggesting a number of revisions. All
errors remain my responsibility.

1. In the fifties, Cubans of low socioeconomic status used
to migrate to the New York City area to work on menial jobs
which were, however, better paying than comparable jobs on
the island. Some of them would return to Cuba and it was
probably they who brought the item into the Cuban lexicon.
But they may not have borrowed it directly from English but
from some non-Cuban dialect of United States Spanish--most
probably Mainland Puerto Rican Spanish, where the word
exists with the same function.

2. I have given the most conservative pronunciations of
Thunderbird and *hamburger*. In more relaxed styles of speech,
the words might be rendered as [hã^mbə́gge] and [sõde^bə́ɖ],
where [ɖ] is a brief retroflex stop and is the realization of
/r/ in absolute final position. The examples also show that
/r/ is realized as a geminate before noncoronal segments (see
Guitart 1978).

ON THE FORMULATION AND INTERACTION
OF CERTAIN PHONOLOGICAL RULES
IN CATALAN

Janet Ann DeCesaris
Indiana University

1. **Introduction.** Among recent attempts to constrain phonological theory, there are various appeals to functionalism. In
one type of functional phonology, a rule's structural change is
directly correlated with its particular effect. For example, it
has been claimed recently by Houlihan and Iverson (1979) that
phonological rules which produce relatively marked segments
are necessarily allophonic, and conversely, rules which produce unmarked segments are necessarily neutralizing. They
argue that this approach can account for those neutralizations
which do occur in natural languages while excluding types of
neutralization which do not occur.

In this paper data from two Catalan dialects, the Standard
Eastern and Barcelona varieties, are adduced as a counter-
example to their hypothesis. I discuss two different possible
analyses of the data: in one analysis, the rule in question is
taken to be neutralizing, in the other, it is considered allophonic. It is shown that no matter which analysis is chosen,
the Houlihan and Iverson proposal cannot account for both
dialects.

Finally, it is suggested that Houlihan and Iverson's claim be
modified so that it applies only to strictly binary oppositions--
rules in which only one feature is affected.

2. **The data and the rules.** Standard Eastern Catalan
exhibits a stop lengthening (or gemination) process before
[l]. Consider the data in (1).

(1) Standard Eastern Catalan[1]

/p/ ~ [bb]
escopir [əskupí] 'to spit'
escup-lu [əskúbblu] 'spit it!'
replicar [rrəpliká] 'to reply'
ample [ámplə] 'ample'

/b/ ~ [bb]
sabem [səβém] 'we know'
saber [səβé] 'to know'
qui sap-lo? [kisábblu] 'who knows?'
biblioteca [biβliutέkə] 'library'
possible [pusíbblə] 'possible'
possibilitat [pusiβilitát] 'possibility'
flexible [fləksíbblə] 'flexible'
flexibilitat [fləksiβilitát] 'flexibility'
problema [pruβlέmə] 'problem'
rambla [rrámblə] 'avenue'

/k/ ~ [gg]
articular [ərtikulá] 'to articulate'
articulista [ərtikulístə] 'one who articulates, writes
    articles'
article [ərtígglə] 'article'
aclarir [əklərí] 'to clarify'

/g/ ~ [gg]
regular [rrəɣulá] 'to regulate'
regla [rrégglə] 'rule, regulation'
englobar [əŋgluβá] 'to enclose'
negligència [nəɣliʒέnsjə] 'negligence'

Dental assimilation
atlas [álləs] 'atlas'
atlantic [əlléntik] 'Atlantic'
fred litre [frèllítrə] 'cold liter'

As forms like [pruβlέmə] versus [pusíbblə] indicate, long
obstruent stops occur immediately after a stressed vowel and
before [l]; otherwise, the voiced stops spirantize (except
directly following a nasal consonant) and the voiceless stops
remain unaltered. The most clear-cut examples are those in
the bilabial series, as alternations obtain across morpheme
boundaries. Although it can be claimed that lengthening also
applies to velar stops, to my knowledge there are no alternations across morpheme boundaries to make such a claim
uncontroversial. There are never any surface alternations
with dentals, as they totally assimilate to the following [l].
The process appears to have no morphological restrictions: it
applies to verbs (escup-lo [əskúbblu]), nouns (regla [rrégglə]),

and adjectives (*possible* [pusíbblə]).[2] I propose the following formulation for lengthening.

(2) Consonant Lengthening (Standard Eastern dialect)

$$\begin{bmatrix} \text{-sonorant} \\ \text{-continuant} \end{bmatrix} \rightarrow \begin{bmatrix} \text{+voice} \\ \text{+long} \end{bmatrix} / \ [\text{+stress}] \ \underline{\quad} \ \begin{bmatrix} \text{+lateral} \\ \text{+anterior} \end{bmatrix}$$

The effect of Rule (2) is to lengthen and voice bilabial and velar[3] stops after a stressed vowel before [l]. The underlying contrast between voiceless and voiced stops is lost in the process--only long voiced geminates result. This can be seen in the following sample derivations.

(3) /eskup + lo/ (underlying /p/, cf. infinitive *escopir*)
eskúplo   stress[4]
eskúbblo   lengthening (2)
əskúbblu   vowel reduction
[əskúbblu]   'spit it!'

/ki # sab + lo/ (underlying /b/, cf. infinitive *saber*)
kisáblo   stress
kisábblo   lengthening (2)
kisábblu   vowel reduction
[kisábblu]   'Who knows?'

On the surface, two changes are affected: voiceless stops become voiced and all stops become long. This is a well-known phenomenon, documented in standard references (e.g. Fabra 1912, Badia-Margarit 1951).

The Catalan spoken in Barcelona is very similar to the Standard Eastern variety just described. With respect to the crucial clusters, however, it differs from the standard dialect in that the result is a voiceless geminate, as shown in (4).[5]

(4) Standard Eastern vs. Barcelonès

escup-lo   [əskúbblu]   vs.   [əskúpplu]   'spit it!'
possible   [pusíbblə]   vs.   [pusípplə]   'possible'
article   [ərtígglə]   vs.   [ərtíkklə]   'article'
regla   [rrégglə]   vs.   [rrékklə]   'rule'

As in the standard dialect, long obstruent stops occur only after a stressed vowel and before [l]; the rule has no morphological restrictions, and (at least for bilabial stops) alternations across morpheme boundaries occur. Thus, I propose the following rule to account for Barcelonès.

(5) Consonant Lengthening (Barcelonès dialect)

$$\begin{bmatrix} -\text{sonorant} \\ -\text{continuant} \end{bmatrix} \rightarrow \begin{bmatrix} -\text{voice} \\ +\text{long} \end{bmatrix} / [+\text{stress}] \underline{\quad} \begin{bmatrix} +\text{lateral} \\ +\text{anterior} \end{bmatrix}$$

In other words, /p, b/ and /k, g/ become /pp/ and /kk/, respectively, immediately following a stressed vowel and preceding [l]. The fact that voiceless geminates occur in Barcelonès is also well documented (Fabra 1912:21; Badia-Margarit 1975:74).

With respect to consonant lengthening, the two dialects differ in the specification for the feature [voice]. Examples similar to this are apparently rare: despite the rather extensive literature within generative phonology, few such cases have been discussed; in some theoretical frameworks, this situation is excluded.[6] Therefore, one might well look for a way other than opposite feature specifications to account for the difference.

Voiced geminates occur across word boundaries, as the result of a rule of voice assimilation.

(6) glutinós   [glutinós]   'gluttonous'
    ric (m), rica (f)   [rrík] [rríkə]   'rich'
    un ric glutinós   [unrrìgglutinós]   'a rich, gluttonous man'
    amic (m), amiga (f)   [əmík] [əmíɣə]   'friend'
    amic glutinós   [əmìgglutinós]   'a gluttonous friend'
    cap   [káp]   'no, not'
    blau (m), blava (f)   [bláw] [bláβə]   'blue'
    cap blau   [kàbbláw]   'not blue'
    rep (cf. INF *rebre*)   [rrép]   'he/she receives'
    les rep blaves   [ləzrrèbbláβəs]   'he/she receives them
       blue' (he receives them and they are blue)

Since this assimilation crucially affects voice in clusters, it might be responsible for the variation between the two dialects. Specifically, assimilation in Barcelonès may have a more restricted application than it has in the Standard dialect.[7]

Regressive voice assimilation is formulated for the Standard dialect in Dinnsen (1978:21) as shown in (7).

(7) Regressive Voice Assimilation

$$[-\text{sonorant}] \rightarrow [\alpha\text{voice}] / \underline{\quad} \begin{bmatrix} +\text{consonant} \\ \alpha\text{voice} \end{bmatrix}$$

Condition: Does not apply to prenuclear tautosyllabic clusters.

As Dinnsen states, 'all heterosyllabic clusters and all tautosyllabic post-nuclear clusters agree in voice' (Dinnsen 1978: 21), and this is true across word boundaries as well as within words. His observation is correct for both dialects, as shown by the data in (8).

(8) Standard Eastern vs. Barcelonès[8]

cap [káp] vs. [káp] 'no, none'	
baix [báʃ] vs. [báʃ] 'low'	
capbaix [kəbbáʃ] vs. [kəbbáʃ] 'crestfallen'	
davall [dəβáλ] vs. [dəβáλ] 'underneath'	
capdavall [kàbdəβáλ] or [kàddəβáλ] vs. [kàbdəβáλ] or [kàddəβáλ] 'at the end'	
girada [ʒiráðə] vs. [ʒiráðə] 'turn, revolution'	
capgirada [kàbʒiráðə] or [kàdʒiráðə] vs. [kàbʒiráðə] or [kàdʒiráðə] 'upheaval'	
sentit [səntít] vs. [səntít] 'sense'	
cap sentit [kàpsəntít] or [kàtsəntít] vs. [kàpsəntít] or [kàtsəntít] 'no sense'	
vuit [bwít] vs. [bwít] 'eight'	
capvuitada [kàbbwitáðə] vs. [kàbbwitáðə] 'octave'	
goig [gɔ́tʃ] vs. [gɔ́tʃ] 'pleasure'	
cap goig [kàbgɔ́tʃ] or [kàggɔ́tʃ] vs. [kàbgɔ́tʃ] or [kàggɔ́tʃ] 'no pleasure'	
llit [λít] vs. [λít] 'bed, couch'	
cap llit [kàbλít] vs. [kə̀bλít] 'no bed'	
manera [mənérə] vs. [mənérə] 'way'	
cap manera [kàbmənérə] or [kàmmənérə] vs. [kabmənérə] or [kàmmənérə] 'no way'	
poc [pɔ́k] vs. [pɔ́k] 'little'	
temps [téms] vs. [téms] 'time'	
poc temps [pɔ̀ktéms] vs. [pɔ̀ktéms] 'little time'	
decent [dəsén] vs. [dəsén] 'decent'	
poc decent [pɔ̀gdəsén] vs. [pɔ̀gdəsén] 'not very decent'	
patriòtic [pətriɔ́tik] vs. [pətriɔ́tik] 'patriotic'	
poc patriòtic [pɔ̀kpətriɔtík] vs. [pɔ̀kpetriɔtík] 'not very patriotic'	
modern [muðɛ́rn] vs. [muðɛ́rn] 'modern'	
poc modern [pɔ̀gmuðɛ́rn] vs. [pɔ̀gmuðɛ́rn] 'not very modern'	
lleig [λétʃ] vs. [λétʃ] 'ugly'	
poc lleig [pɔ̀gλétʃ] vs. [pɔ̀gλétʃ] 'not very ugly'	
lògic [lɔ́ʒik] vs. [lɔ́ʒik] 'logical'	
poc lògic [pɔ̀glɔ́ʒik] vs. [pɔ̀glɔ́ʒik] 'not very logical'	

In both dialects, heterosyllabic obstruent-consonant clusters agree in voice, and the assimilation is regressive. Voice assimilation in Barcelonès cannot be restricted to obstruent-obstruent clusters, as evidenced by the voiced obstruents in *cap llit* [kàbλít], *poc lògic* [pɔ̀glɔ́ʒik], and *cap manera* [kàbmənérə]. Nor can the condition on the rule be altered or eliminated. As proposed by Dinnsen, the condition allows for voiceless obstruent-sonorant clusters in syllable-initial position (e.g. Standard and Barcelona dialects *ple* [plɛ́] 'full', *flor* [flɔ́] 'flower', and *clau* [kláw] 'key'), but in all other positions clusters must agree in voice. This is also true for Barcelonès, as shown by the data in (8). Since both dialects have the same rule, it cannot account for the difference in [voice]. Therefore, I maintain the rules given in (2) for Standard Eastern and (5) for Barcelonès are correct as formulated.

3. 'Functionally constrained phonology'. Houlihan and Iverson (1979) attempt to constrain the structural change of certain types of phonological rules. A rule's structural change is correlated with the nature of its effect--a rule is either neutralizing or allophonic. This hypothesis is bidirectional: within a particular language, the structural change determines the rule's effect and vice versa, i.e. one is a predictable consequence of the other. It is important to note that the Houlihan and Iverson analysis strives to distinguish 'permissible phonological rules ... from impermissible ones by considering only the interaction between a rule's function, i.e. whether it is neutralizing or not, and the relative markedness of the input and output of the rule' (Houlihan and Iverson 1979:67-68). Specifically, they claim that phonologically conditioned rules which produce (relatively) unmarked segments are necessarily neutralizing (the Markedness Constraint) and conversely, rules which exclusively produce (relatively) marked segments are necessarily allophonic (Corollary). Neutralization rules are defined as in (9) (following Kiparsky 1976:169).

(9) A rule of the form A → B / XC ___ DY is neutralizing if and only if there are strings of the form CBD in the input to the rule. Otherwise the rule is non-neutralizing (Houlihan and Iverson 1979:50).

For Houlihan and Iverson, 'input to the rule' is synonymous with 'existing at some level of derivation before the rule applies' (1979:50). Therefore, rules such as terminal devoicing in Catalan or German are neutralizing because both voiced and voiceless obstruents serve as inputs to the rules' structural description, whereas mergers to a third segment which is not a possible input--such as English flapping--are classified as nonneutralizing or allophonic. Rules such as intervocalic obstruent voicing in Korean are also considered allophonic, as voiced stops occur in Korean only between voiced segments and thus no contrast is neutralized.

The notion of a marked versus unmarked segment is based on implicational universals determined by typological studies. One relevant implicational universal is 'the presence of voiced stops implies the presence of voiceless stops but not vice versa' (Houlihan and Iverson, from Jakobson (1968:70)). In terms of markedness, this means that voiced stops are marked with respect to voiceless stops. Additionally, long or geminate obstruents are considered marked relative to single obstruents, as the presence of the former implies the presence of the latter but not vice versa. [9] The outputs of rules (2) and (5) can now be classified with respect to these two parameters.

(10)   Length   Voice

bbl, ggl	marked	marked	most	marked
ppl, kkl	marked	unmarked	?	?
bl, gl	unmarked	marked	?	?
pl, kl	unmarked	unmarked	least	marked

The Houlihan and Iverson claim is a strong one because it excludes two of the four logically possible rule types on principled grounds.

(11a) a phonologically conditioned neutralization rule which produces exclusively marked segments;
(11b) a phonologically conditioned allophonic rule which produces unmarked segments.

Thus an example of either (11a) or (11b) would falsify their proposal.

The rules for Catalan given in Section 2 can be analyzed in two different ways in principle: they are either neutralizing or allophonic, depending on one's acceptance of long consonants as underlying segments and thus potential inputs to the rule. I turn now to a discussion of both possibilities, in order to show that the Houlihan and Iverson hypothesis proves to be incorrect for at least one of the two dialects.

4. Two analyses of Lengthening

4.1 Lengthening as a neutralization rule.
For Rule (2) (Lengthening in Standard Eastern Catalan) to be neutralizing by Houlihan and Iverson's definition, long obstruents must either be underlying segments or must arise somewhere earlier in the derivation. It has been seen that they do arise in a derived context due to regressive voice assimilation, but there is a fundamental difference in the two environments. Lengthening as formulated in (2) crucially depends on the preceding vowel having primary stress; in the examples of long obstruents from assimilation, the preceding vowel has secondary, not main stress.[10] The C of Houlihan and Iverson's A → B / XC __ DY is not the same. So far, it appears that the rule produces relatively marked segments and is nonneutralizing by their definition, thus upholding their proposal.

The argument for underlying geminates is supported by the existence of nonalternating stems, such as /kɔbbl-/ and /teggl-/.

(12) cobla [kɔ́bblə] 'couplet'
coblaire [kubbláirə] 'petty poet'
coblejador [kubbləʒəð ó] 'rhymer'
acoblar [əkubblá] 'to couple, join'
acoblament [əkubbləmén] 'coupling'

tecla [tégglə] 'piano key'
teclat [təgglát] 'keyboard'
teclejar [təgglə3á] 'to rap one's finger'

It is a fact of Standard Eastern Catalan that every instance
of these morphemes (and many others like them) has a voiced
geminate surface output, regardless of stress placement. Evidence of an alternation is one of the primary criteria in anyone's understanding of the concept 'phonological rule',[11] and
in its absence it is quite reasonable to posit the long segments
in the underlying form. With underlying forms like /kɔbbl-/
and /teggl-/ as inputs, Rule (2) must now be defined as
neutralizing; yet the rule uniquely produces segments which
are marked with respect to both length and voice (the *most*
marked output possible). Such a neutralization is by definition
excluded by the Markedness Constraint. It is important to
note that only marked segments are produced by rule (2), for
the Houlihan and Iverson claim is not falsified if both marked
and unmarked segments result.[12]
A parallel argument can be made for underlying voiceless
geminates in Barcelonès. Those morphemes which contain nonalternating voiced geminates in the Standard dialect always have
the corresponding voiceless geminate in the Barcelona dialect.

(13) Standard Eastern vs. Barcelonès

poble [pɔ́bblə] vs. [pɔ́pplə] 'town, people'
poblat [pubblát] vs. [pupplát] 'populated'
poblar [pubblá] vs. [pupplá] 'to populate'
poblament [pubbləmén] vs. [puppləmén] 'settlement'
població [pubbləsjó] vs. [puppləsjó] 'population'
poblador [pubbləðó] vs. [pubbləðó] 'settler (m.)'

With underlying long segments in Barcelonès, possible inputs
to Rule (5) are /pl/, /bl/, and /ppl/; the only possible output
is [ppl], the relatively marked member with regard to length
although unmarked in relation to voice. Once underlying segments are posited, what is defined as a neutralization rule produces exclusively segments which are maximally marked in the
Standard dialect and (partially) marked in the other dialect, a
situation excluded by the Markedness Constraint.

4.2 Lengthening as an allophonic rule. Although the foregoing is a possible analysis, there are several reasons for re-
jecting underlying long obstruents. Other than to account for
data like [pɔ́bblə]-[pubbləsjó], underlying long consonants are
not needed for any other phonological process. Those segments appear, with the exception of the preceding stressed
vowel, in precisely the same environment specified by the
Lengthening rule. The overall regularity--the fact that long
obstruent stops occur only before [1]--is being lost. For all

words belonging to nonalternating stems, there is one form of
the structure [V̆CCl]. Furthermore, it has been extensively
argued by Mascaró (1978) that the transformational cycle is
needed to account for various aspects of Catalan phonology.
With the cycle it is possible to derive all long obstruents, as
shown in (14).

(14)   /póbl+e/   /póbl+a+sjó/

    Lengthening (2)   póbble   póbblasjó
    Destressing   ---   pobblasjó

Mascaró provides much evidence that stress is an underlying
feature of morphemes in Catalan.[13] Destressing, which will
apply when two or more stressed morphemes occur within a
word, destresses all but the last stressed vowel and is formulated as in (15).

(15) Destressing (Mascaró 1978:21)

    $V \rightarrow$ [-stress] / # # X ___ Y [+stress] Q # #

Mascaró states it must apply after Lengthening, in order to
arrive at the correct pronunciations of *població* and *poblar*.
Such an application could be accomplished by extrinsically
ordering Lengthening before Destressing. It is unlikely, however, that Houlihan and Iverson would accept such a position,[14]
nor is it necessary for them to do so: Destressing and Lengthening are in a potentially bleeding relationship and thus the two
rules can apply simultaneously (Koutsoudas, Sanders, and Noll
1974:5).

The two competing analyses may now be outlined. The primary concern here is not to choose between them, but rather
to show that the second analysis, which is the only possibility
given the Markedness Constraint, does not account for the
Barcelonès dialect, even with the transformational cycle.

(16) Output of Lengthening Rule

	Standard Eastern	Barcelonès
Neutralization (underlying long segments)	Length: marked Voice: marked Excluded by Marked-ness Constraint	Length: marked Voice: unmarked Excluded by Marked-ness Constraint
Allophonic (long segments derived by the cycle)	Length: marked Voice: marked Predicted by Marked-ness Constraint	Length: marked Voice: unmarked Excluded by Marked-ness Constraint

If the effect of Lengthening is neutralizing, neither dialect can be accounted for because the output in each is marked: marked for length in Barcelonès and marked for both features in the Standard dialect. If Lengthening is considered allophonic, the Standard dialect result of voiced long stops is predicted by the Markedness Constraint; the Barcelonès result of voiceless geminates, however, is not: [ppl] and [kkl] are marked for [long] but unmarked for [voice]. Since one of the two changes being effected by the rule is toward a less marked specification (i.e. underlying voiced stops become voiceless), the rule's output is unmarked in one respect and thus directly counter to the prediction made by the Corollary to the Markedness Constraint.[15]

This example is problematic for the Markedness Constraint because two parameters--length and voice--are being changed, and therefore two outputs which differ from each other in markedness (e.g. [bbl] versus [ppl]) can result from the same possible inputs (/bl/ and /pl/). Houlihan and Iverson only consider rules in which one potential contrast is lost. However, not all rules affect only one feature specification: in Catalan it has been seen that voicing cannot be separated out from the lengthening process. It would be unfortunate to dismiss the Markedness Constraint because it does correctly predict the function and direction of many phonological rules. If limited to dealing with strictly binary oppositions--rules in which only one feature is affected--it would account for the data originally discussed by Houlihan and Iverson, and would not apply to the Catalan data presented here.[16] Unmodified, their claim is empirically incorrect.

NOTES

This paper has benefited greatly from discussions with John Goldsmith, John Clifton, Marios Fourakis, and Edith Maxwell. I am grateful to Josep Roca-Pons for helping me with the data. Most especially I wish to thank Dan Dinnsen, whose insight and encouragement have been invaluable. All errors are my own.

1. The vocalic alternation in *escopir - escup-lo* is found in a small group of third conjugation verbs (e.g. *collir* 'to catch', *cosir* 'to sew', *sortir* 'to leave', *tossir* 'to cough') and does not affect lengthening in any way.

Also evidenced in the data is a process of vowel reduction in unstressed position. Vowel reduction is an independently motivated rule (see Mascaró 1978:25-30 for discussion) and may be schematized as:

This particular vowel reduction is characteristic of both the Standard Eastern and Barcelonès dialects.

2. For adverbs, two main groups can be distinguished: those which are monomorphemic (e.g. *ara* [árə] 'now') and those which are formed from an adjective plus the stressed suffix *-ment* [mén]. I know of no adverbs of the first type which contain a stressed vowel-obstruent stop-[l] sequence, and therefore none have long stops. The second group, by far the larger, evidences long stops in those words related to adjectives in which the lengthening environment is met; see pages 30–32 for discussion.

3. As I have formulated it, lengthening applies to all obstruent stops. On the surface, however, dental stops completely assimilate, not only in the environment

$$[\text{+stress}] \underline{\quad\quad} \begin{bmatrix} \text{+lateral} \\ \text{+anterior} \end{bmatrix},$$

but to any following sonorant consonant regardless of stress.

(i) setmana [səmmánə] [sədmánə] 'week'
ratlla [rráʎʎə] [rrádʎə] 'stripe'
atmosfera [əmmɔ́sfərə] but careful speech: [ədmɔ́sfərə] 'atmosphere'
admirable [əmmirábblə] [ədmirábblə] 'admirable'
tot l'acte [tòlláktə] [tòdláktə] 'all the act'

By not restricting lengthening to bilabial and velar stops, it applies to all points of articulation, and is followed by a rule of assimilation restricted to dentals in normal speech.

(ii) $$\begin{bmatrix} \text{-sonorant} \\ \text{-continuant} \\ \text{+anterior} \\ \text{+coronal} \end{bmatrix} \rightarrow [\alpha\text{feature}] \ / \ \underline{\quad} \begin{bmatrix} \text{+consonant} \\ \text{+sonorant} \\ \alpha\text{feature} \end{bmatrix}$$

(The item /r/ is specified [-sonorant] due to its articulatory characteristics in Catalan.)

An assimilation rule of this nature is needed in any generative account of the data, and is independent of lengthening. As formulated, the rule does not mention length in the structural description, so that both [+long] and [-long] dentals assimilate. The following sonorant, to my knowledge, is always [-long], creating a surface sequence of $\begin{bmatrix} C \\ \text{-long} \end{bmatrix} \begin{bmatrix} C \\ \text{-long} \end{bmatrix}$. In the absence of counterevidence from an instrumental study, and due to their perceptual equivalence, such a sequence can be specified as one $\begin{bmatrix} C \\ \text{+long} \end{bmatrix}$.

I have found two exceptions, *súplica* [súplikə] and *réplica* [rréplikə].
4. It has been argued that stress is underlying in Catalan (Mascaró 1978). The particular manner of stress assignment is not at issue here. See page 32 for additional discussion.
5. I am not claiming that the two dialects differ in only this respect; another difference is the loss of the voice distinction between [dʒ] and [tʃ] in favor of [tʃ] in certain words.
6. For example, in equational phonology (Sanders 1979).
7. Another possibility is a constraint restricting the nature of long consonants. Thus, if in Standard Eastern Catalan, all long stops before [l] are voiced, the [+voice] marking would be redundant information and therefore could be eliminated from the rule's formulation. Voiceless geminates do occur, however, across word boundaries within phrases such as the following.

cap [káp] 'no, none'
plata [plátə] 'silver'
cap plata [kàpplátə] 'no silver'
pluja [plúʒə] 'rain'
cap pluja [kapplúʒə] 'no rain'

But to my knowledge there are no word-internal [ppl] sequences. Such a constraint not only would have to be restricted to word level, but would also have to be very limited in nature because there are voiceless geminates in words such as *adquirir* [əkkirí] and *adquisició* [əkkizisjó]. The reverse situation is Barcelonès--i.e. a constraint against voiced geminates would also be difficult to formulate as there is at least one word, *capblanc* [kəbbláŋ] 'gray-haired', that contains a surface sequence of [bbl]. Historically, *capblanc* derives from *cap* 'head' and *blanc* 'white'. Synchronically, it should be considered one word as the plural is *capblancs* [kàbbláŋs].
8. Data partially from the *Vox Diccionari Manual* and partially from Yates (1975) for the Standard dialect; Barcelonès data verified with Josep Roca-Pons, a native speaker of the Barcelona dialect.
In cases where two possible pronunciations are given, the first is more formal and the second (which always involves an additional assimilation) is characteristic of more casual speech.
9. Jaeger (1978:21).
10. That the vowel is not completely unstressed is shown by the fact that it does not reduce to [ə].
11. Alternations are not absolutely necessary, however; see Hyman (1975:12-15) for a brief discussion of 'phonological rule'.
12. Note the 'exclusively' in their claim, which enables them to account for assimilatory rules such as Nasal Assimilation in Spanish.

13. For example, underlying stress eliminates the need for diacritic features otherwise needed only for stress assignment; see Mascaró (1978: 15-23) for discussion. Mascaró's analysis of the process described in this paper as a morpheme structure constraint cannot be entirely correct due to the alternations given in (1). Although he transcribes *possible* as [pusiplə] with a single voiceless stop, Standard Barcelonès has [ppl] (cf. Badia-Margarit 1975:74; Josep Roca-Pons, personal communication).

14. At least one of the authors has argued against extrinsic ordering on various occasions (e.g. Iverson 1974; Iverson and Sanders 1978).

15. If only a voice alternation were involved, Houlihan and Iverson would predict voiceless single stops as the output--the rule would be neutralizing because both voiced and voiceless stops are possible inputs. This, in fact, does exist in a style of speech particular to Catalan speakers of Castilian-speaking parents (cf. López del Castillo 1976:55-57). I know of no dialect which neutralizes the distinction in favor of the single voiced obstruent, and this follows from the Markedness Constraint.

16. It would also solve another apparent problem for Houlihan and Iverson, also from Catalan. Dinnsen has pointed out that in Western Catalan the distinction between [a] and [e] is neutralized in favor of [e], the more marked vowel (cf. Dinnsen 1979a: 47).

Kaye (1979) has also adduced counterexamples to the Houlihan and Iverson claim. Although his cases involve binary oppositions, they depend crucially on the acceptance of abstract, underlying morpheme structure constraints.

PORTUGUESE EVIDENCE
FOR THE NON-UNITARY NATURE
OF SYLLABLE PARSING

W. J. Redenbarger
Ohio State University

This study presents a new and much simpler analysis of the problem of Portuguese syllabication. It has two enabling premises: (1) a new insight into the mechanics of parsing a segmental string, and (2) a rejection of the research program adopted in Hooper (1972) and continued by most process phonologists to date. I begin by examining these two issues in detail, proceed to the specifics of the Portuguese data and syllabication solution, and conclude by indicating the parallels between this new solution and other well-known linguistic phenomena.

Although some linguists have recently proposed an auto-segmental type of syllable associating rule based on Goldsmith's (1976a) model, in this study I follow the more usual approach toward a formal definition of the syllable, viz. that of inserting syllable boundaries into the string of phonological segments. This boundary is symbolized with a lowered dot in transcriptions, for example [ab.lə.géj.ʃən] *obligation* and by a '$' symbol in phonological rules.

1. The problem with previous analyses. It is generally recognized today that Hooper (1972) was on track and took a bold first step toward remedying a flaw in the original SPE formalization of generative phonology. Whatever criticism I have to make here of a particular pair of points in her work should not obscure the fact that Hooper's criticism of the notion 'weak and strong cluster' in SPE, and her pointing out the necessity of formalizing the notion 'phonological syllable' in a generative grammar constituted a major contribution.

Hooper's (1972) algorithm for inserting syllable boundaries begins with the explicit assumption that two [+syllabic] phonological segments in a string are necessarily in different syllables. While I am not suggesting this point is in error, this approach has an unfortunate side effect: it puts one in the position of having to look at *all* of the segments intervening between two syllabic segments in order to parse the string. Even with all its formal hardware, it can be seen that what Hooper is looking at is all the material between two consecutive vowels; note the 'V' at each end of the structural description of Hooper's (1972:536) rule.

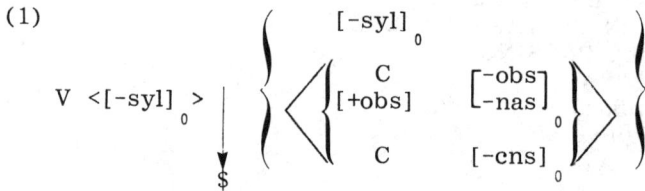

(1)

$$
V <[-syl]_0> \Bigg| \left\{ \left\langle \begin{matrix} [-syl]_0 \\ \begin{matrix} C \\ [+obs] \\ C \end{matrix} \quad \begin{bmatrix} -obs \\ -nas \end{bmatrix}_0 \\ [-cns]_0 \end{matrix} \right\rangle \right\} \longrightarrow \$
$$

Brakel (1977) attempted the same kind of rule for Portuguese. Its labyrinthine form amply illustrates its implausibility; I reproduce his rule exactly since it (1) uses non-standard DFs which I hesitate to reinterpret, (2) has indexed angle brackets with no matching indexes elsewhere in the rule's SD, and (3) is clearly wrong since its minimal expansion--the one with the material in both large parentheses not elected--would put syllable boundaries after every segment of every word in the language if it were ever allowed to operate, or else the parentheses are simply otiose and thus the rule is improperly framed. In short, the rule is cited only to show the impossibility of this approach.

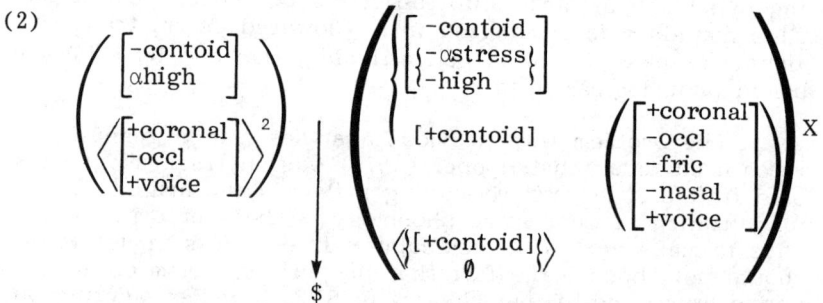

(2)

$$
\left(\begin{bmatrix} -\text{contoid} \\ \alpha\text{high} \end{bmatrix} \left\langle \begin{bmatrix} +\text{coronal} \\ -\text{occl} \\ +\text{voice} \end{bmatrix} \right\rangle^2 \right) \Bigg| \left(\left(\begin{bmatrix} -\text{contoid} \\ \{-\alpha\text{stress}\} \\ -\text{high} \end{bmatrix} \\ [+\text{contoid}] \\ \left\langle [+\text{contoid}] \right\rangle_{\emptyset} \right) \left(\begin{bmatrix} +\text{coronal} \\ -\text{occl} \\ -\text{fric} \\ -\text{nasal} \\ +\text{voice} \end{bmatrix} \right) X \right) \longrightarrow \$
$$

The problem here is that as one reads from left to right in a string of segments, the same syllabication rule may well divide the same subsequence of segments differently in two different words. For example, in Portuguese, the underlying sequence -Vɾ- may be divided in one word as -V$ɾ- and in another as -Vɾ$-, e.g. [ka.ɾə] *cara* 'face' versus [kaɾ.lus] *Carlos* 'Charles'. In short, when reading from left to right, segment by segment, it is simply not possible to know what to do with a -VC- sequence since the syllabication of a post-vocalic consonant obviously cannot be determined by examining the preceding vowel nor can it be determined from the characteristics of the consonant itself.

I suggest that the problem lies in this type of parsing technique itself. Instead, I offer the following insight: 'If one can figure out where each phonological syllable begins, one automatically knows where the preceding syllable ends.' Mechanically, therefore, all that is needed is an algorithm to put a boundary at the beginning of each syllable. While this does not solve the syllabication problems outright, it allows one to home in on the single real problem--defining the notion 'permissible syllable onset'. The indeterminacies of the -VC-situation become a nonproblem under this approach.

To summarize this first section, I am suggesting that one no longer read left to right along strings of segments trying to parse them, but rather that one find a vowel and 'back up' with respect to the speech continuum, i.e. go right to left to find where that vowel's syllable begins. In this regard, I am suggesting that the demarcation of syllables is quite like the demarcation of stress where, for example, in the Romance languages, one starts at the end of the word when counting off syllables, not at the front. Considering the close suprasegmental relationship between syllables and stress, this similarity would suggest that we are on the right track.

2. **The universal / unitary assumption.** The second problem area which until now has obscured the solution of Portuguese syllabication is one of research program rather than of mechanics as was the case in Section 1. Hooper (1972:536) asserts that Rule (1) is 'a universal rule for the insertion of $-boundaries, and as such is included in the metatheory'. As Hooper was aware at the time, there are many systematic counterexamples to her universal rule, some of the most common of which she itemized at the time (p. 535). The mind set illustrated here is, I think, where the problem lies. There is a tacit assumption: 'since all languages undergo syllabication, there must be one universal syllabication rule; therefore, any counterexamples are "exceptions"'. Let us examine that assumption more closely.

The 1972 rule, for the reasons I have suggested, is superseded in Hooper's later work by a Sievers 1893-type sonority hierarchy explanation: $O > L > N > G$. It is important to observe, however, that this hierarchy per se is not capable of parsing the segmental strings in any particular language for two reasons: (1) as Bell and Hooper (1978) note, the occurrence of nearly every combination which violates this order 'is attested in a natural language'; (2) within a given language, this sorting only along major class lines is not sufficient--within the same language, one -OLV- sequence may go into a

single syllable, $OLV, while another sequence identical in terms
of major classes may be split into two separate syllables, O$LV.
See, for example, Portuguese -s$1V- versus -$f1V-, both of
which are OLV sequences and both of which are obligatory
syllabications and different. In other words, the universal-
implies-unitary approach is simply not tenable.

I suggest that it is the belief in a unitary syllabication
principle which is in error. Consider an analogy with stress
assignment. If one were to adopt this universal-implies-
unitary logic, one would argue:

> Every language has a stress rule, there are certain sug-
> gestive surface patterns across languages, e.g. only one
> surface main stress is permissible per phonological word,
> etc. and, therefore, there must exist one universal,
> unitary stress rule which is part of the metatheory.

Although the parallel to the syllabication argument is exact,
this stress assignment case is obviously wrong, as anyone who
contrasts a columnar stress rule with one which counts from
word ends can attest; or one who contrasts the English stress
rule and the French stress rule as well. No one attempts to
write one unitary stress rule for all languages, yet many
authors follow Hooper (1972) in suggesting that anything
which does not fit a single universal, unitary syllabication rule
must be an 'exception'.

I shall now proceed to codify a new solution of Portuguese
syllabication, making use of a mechanically simpler algorithm
for parsing segment strings, as indicated in Section 1, and
based on an intentionally nonunitary syllabication procedure,
as argued in Section 2.

3. Portuguese: The general syllabication rule. Consider
the following data showing the result of Portuguese syllabication of a single prevocalic segment. The data are for the
careful speed speech of an educated paulista, this dialect and
speed being chosen since there are fewer syllable-final phonological phenomena to obscure the underlying data.

V V → V$V   [su.aɾ]
G V → G$V   [saɪ.ə]

L V → $L V   [ka.ɾə] [fa.lə] [vɛ.λu]
N V → $N V   [kɐ.mə] [kɐ.nə] [kɐ.ñə]

  O   V → $O   V   ⎰[ka.fɛ] [pɔ.su] [a.ʃu]
[+cnt]   [+cnt]   ⎱[dɛ.vi] [ka.zə] [a.ʒə]

  O   V → $O   V   ⎰[ʃo.pi] [pa.tu]   [sa.ku][a.kʷo.zu]
[-cnt]   [-cnt]   ⎱[su.bu] [fa.du]   [si.gu] [a.gʷə]

From these data one can see that if a prevocalic segment is
+consonantal, it obligatorily goes in the syllable onset; if it is
not consonantal, it does not.

Let us now consider the Portuguese situation where there is
more than one segment in the onset of an internal syllable.
The first observation to be made is negative: in addition to
not finding –consonantal segments in syllable onsets, one never
finds internal onsets of the following shape.

*LL cf. [aɾ.le.kĩ]
*LN cf. [aɾ.ma.zẽ]
*LO cf. [aɾ.kə]

*NL cf. [ẽ.li.a.du]
*NN cf. [am.nɛ.zi.ə]
*NO cf. [ẽ.tis]

*ON cf. [ab.nɛ.tu]
*OO cf. [ap.tu]

In other words, the only two-segment onsets one finds in
internal syllables are of the shape $OL-, as in the following
examples.

$pɾ–	[a.pɾo.si.máɾ]	$pl–	[a.pli.káɾ]
$bɾ–	[o.bɾáɾ]	$bl–	[a.bla.tí.vu]
$tɾ–	[a.tɾáz]	$tl–	[a.tlẽ.ti.ku]
$dɾ–	[ó.dɾi]		
$kɾ–	[a.kɾé.si.mu]	$kl–	[a.klá.mu]
$gɾ–	[a.gɾés.ti]	$gl–	[a.gló.su]
$fɾ–	[ʀe.fɾẽw̃]	$fl–	[a.flí.tu]
$vɾ–	[la.vɾáɾ]		

In addition, it should be noted that there are no $CCC– onsets
of any shape.

We now have 95 percent of the larger facts before us and
can formalize all the data to this point in one general syllabication rule for Portuguese.

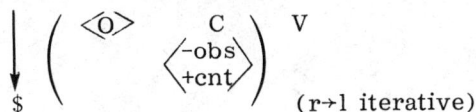

$$\Big|\ \left(\begin{array}{cc} \langle O \rangle & C \\ & \left\langle \begin{array}{c} -obs \\ +cnt \end{array} \right\rangle \end{array} \right)\ V$$
$$\downarrow \atop \$ \qquad\qquad (r \rightarrow l\ \text{iterative})$$

This rule has three expansions.

(a) | O L V   [o.bɾaɾ] [a.tlẽ.ti.ku]
     ↓   [la.vɾaɾ] [a.fli.tu]
     $

(b) |C V   [pa.sə]   [ʃe.gə]
          ↓   [kɐ.mə]   [ka.ɾə]
          $

(c)   ↓V   [saɟ.ə]   [su.aɾ]
           $

The generalizations captured by each expansion are: (a) There is no onset longer than \$CC-. The only permissible two-segment onset type is OL-. (b) No matter what C is to the left of a V, it is in that V's syllable onset. (c) There are no [-cons] segments in onsets.

4. The resyllabication rule. While the general syllabication rule given in Section 3 does codify the larger pattern of Portuguese syllables, it does have one set of systematic counterexamples. Specifically, all *\$sL- sequences are unacceptable syllable onsets.

[des.li.gáɾ]   desligar   'disconnect'
[is.ɾa.ɛ́w]   Israel   'Israel'

Notice the immense difficulty one would have in trying to build this additional information into Rule (3), since there are other acceptable O[+cont]L- onsets, e.g. [a.fli.tu] [la.vɾaɾ], etc.; moreover, there are other acceptable O[+cor]L- onsets: [a.tlẽ.ti.ku] [o.dɾi], etc.

This is an appropriate point, in the face of these problem examples, to stop and consider the several ways that languages resolve segment sequence problems. Consider, for example, the English system which comes into play especially with the /+s/ noun plural and 3sg. verb desinence, and the /+d/ preterite marker. While /kæt+s/, /bɛd+s/, /pæs+d/, /fez+d/, suffer only the results of voicing assimilation, forms like /bʌs+s/, /gəɹaʒ+s/, /weɟt+d/, /disaɟd+d/ undergo the English [ə]-epenthesis rule:

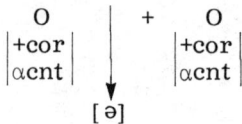

$$
\begin{array}{ccc}
\text{O} & + & \text{O} \\
\begin{vmatrix} +\text{cor} \\ \alpha\text{cnt} \end{vmatrix} & \downarrow & \begin{vmatrix} +\text{cor} \\ \alpha\text{cnt} \end{vmatrix} \\
 & [\text{ə}] &
\end{array}
$$

As the alphas in the structural description make abundantly clear, the rule breaks up only sequences which are too similar; anything else is acceptable.

When one examines the Portuguese situation in this light, the counterexamples to the general rule bear a very striking resemblance to the English case, viz., after the general syllabication rule has operated, the only tautosyllabic unacceptable cluster is:

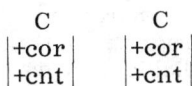

$$\begin{array}{cc} C & C \\ \left|\begin{array}{c} +\text{cor} \\ +\text{cnt} \end{array}\right| & \left|\begin{array}{c} +\text{cor} \\ +\text{cnt} \end{array}\right| \end{array}$$

Having argued in Section 2 that syllabication is probably no more unitary than is stress placement, I suggest we put that observation into effect here. Namely, let us solve this small Portuguese subcase with a language-specific rule which differs from the English epenthesis case only in its manner of resolving the problem: instead of creating an additional syllable by vowel epenthesis, this rule breaks up the cluster by resyllabifying.

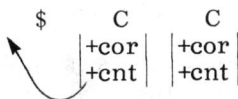

$$\begin{array}{ccc} \$ & C & C \\ & \left|\begin{array}{c} +\text{cor} \\ +\text{cnt} \end{array}\right| & \left|\begin{array}{c} +\text{cor} \\ +\text{cnt} \end{array}\right| \end{array}$$

Like the English [ə]-epenthesis rule, this is phonologically a very well-motivated rule. But more importantly, the benefit to be gained from codifying this language-specific rule is greatest when related to the larger problem of Portuguese syllabication. The general syllabication Rule (3) can remain in its present, elegant form with the resyllabication rule as part of the Portuguese phonological rule set. By separating out the language-specific, the elegance of the general process can be seen for the first time. (Compare these to Brakel's Rule (2).)

The separateness of the two processes is well evidenced in other languages also, e.g. Latin. In authors like Vergil there appears in addition to the normal, general syllabication rule an optional--and therefore obviously separate--cluster simplification rule of the form:

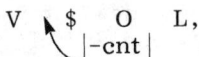

$$\begin{array}{cccc} V & \$ & O & L, \\ & \left|\begin{array}{c} -\text{cnt} \end{array}\right| & & \end{array}$$

thus closing the preceding syllable, making that syllable into one metrically heavy. As Lindsay (1894:129) notes, 'in Vergil *agrum* (with ā) may be scanned with the first syllable long or short as the poet chooses'.

Note that this is not a diachronic change but rather is a synchronically productive rule. One must therefore discount Bell and Hooper's claim (1978:7) that while principles of syllabication can change historically, and though traces of former syllabications are sometimes found in the alternations of a language, no evidence for different productive syllabications has been found, except where distinct speech styles or tempos are involved.

The Latin data constitute counterevidence. Note, moreover, that if one adopts Bell and Hooper's research program, elegant solutions to problems like that of Portuguese syllabication can never be discovered since the starting assumption is that they do not exist.

5. **The word-initial data.** We should deal specifically with one additional prediction made by a syllabication rule of the form which I am proposing. A right-to-left syllabication rule which marks only syllable beginnings has the characteristic of potentially arriving at the initial vowel of a word, marking the beginning of that vowel's onset with a $-boundary, and still having segments left over. Such segments would in effect be in limbo--not a part of the syllable onset, but with no preceding syllable to be incorporated into.
Precisely this situation obtains in Portuguese. Word-initial pnV-, or ptV-, or psV- will all be parsed by the second expansion--$CV--of our left-to-right syllabication rule as:

p.new	p.to.le.maj.ko	p.si.ko.lo.ʒi.ə
pneu	ptolemaico	psicologia
'tire'	'Ptolemaic'	'psychology'

leaving the word-initial /p/ stranded. Compare apto [ap.tu]. These cases are made even clearer when one considers the parallel to the spV-, skV-, and like cases.

#skɔlə#	#spɔɾti#
s.kɔ.lə	s.pɔɾ.ti
[es.kɔ.lə]	[es.pɔɾ.ti]

The synchronically productive rule of *e*-prothesis rescues the stranded /s/ by supplying it with a syllable nucleus. Likewise, in hyper-slow citation form Portuguese pronunciation, one gets for the p.CV cases cited [pi̥.new] (or [pi̥.new] in Lisbon), etc., clearly demonstrating that the /p/ and /n/ of *pneu* are not in the same syllable.
A second language-specific Portuguese phonological rule, observed especially in rapid speech, is the deletion of such stranded stop obstruents, yielding: [new], [tolomajku], and [sikoloʒiə] for the examples cited.
These cases are important for three reasons. First, they bear out the predictions of my suggested right-to-left parsing algorithm; note that Hooper's (1972) rule cannot insert a boundary in these nonpostvocalic cases. Second, they

demonstrate again the kind of language-specific rules which
arise to solve the problems created by the larger, more general
parsing rule, and so prove the two rules' separability and thus
their nonunity. Third, they provide an opportunity to view
the way the language-specific innovations arise diachronically.
If the deletion rule or epenthesis rule cited were to move down
and become part of the obligatory phonology, the system would
have changed by the addition of a new language-specific rule;
this is clearly a more explanatory approach than Hooper's suggestion that syllabication rules just change from one unified
rule to another.

6. **Summary.** To summarize, in this paper I have advanced
a new type of right-to-left parsing algorithm (similar to stress
assignment) which establishes syllable division not by parsing
the entire string of segments intervening between two consecutive syllabic segments, but rather by defining only the beginning of each successive syllable. In addition to solving the
many formal problems of word-internal parsing which had
rendered previous analyses so very awkward, the algorithm
also leads to a natural explanation of the relation between
consonant configurations in word-initial position versus internal
sequences.
Second, it is argued that the assumption tacitly held by Bell,
Hooper, and others that a universal syllabication rule implies a
unified syllabication process is not a priori correct. By positing a general rule of Portuguese syllabication, it is shown that
the very small group of cases which do not fit the larger pattern are precisely a subset of the clusters being broken up by
the English [ə]-epenthesis rule; and thus one deduces the
existence of a well-motivated language-specific phonological rule
of resyllabication in Portuguese. From this the first really
elegant codification of the processes effecting Portuguese
syllabication follows and is formalized.
The theoretical importance is that once one overcomes the
fear of writing language-specific (re)syllabication rules, the
larger general syllabication schema shines through. Moreover,
in Portuguese this larger principle is now without any counter-
example not codifiable by well-motivated rules, and is in perfect harmony with the sonority hierarchy of syllable structure
advanced by Sievers. A more productive research program
then would seem to be suggested: for those languages exhibiting surface counterexamples to the universal syllable sonority
schema, seek to find a well-motivated language-specific, separate, resyllabication rule like the one shown here for Portuguese. Having discarded the unified/universal syllabication
assumption, it may well turn out that the universal involved
can finally be codified and be shown in fact to exist.

FRENCH LIAISON
AS A SOCIOLINGUISTIC PHENOMENON

William J. Ashby
University of California, Santa Barbara

Liaison is the process whereby an orthographically represented word-final consonant which is mute in prepausal and in
preconsonantal position may instead be articulated when followed
by a vowel. Thus, for example, the adjective *grand* 'big' is
pronounced with no final consonant in *le grand bâtiment* but is
pronounced with a final /t/ in *le grand immeuble*, both 'the big
building'.

Diachronically, liaison represents maintenance in prevocalic
position of word-final consonants, which more generally have
been lost. Synchronically, too, linguists usually consider
liaison as an exception to the rule of final consonant deletion
(cf. Schane 1968 and Selkirk 1972), although Klausenburger
(1978) claims that it is instead best accounted for by a rule of
consonant insertion.

Be it deletion or insertion, liaison is clearly not governed
by phonological constraints alone, since it does not invariably
apply except between words of close syntactic juncture (Anderson 1975, Ashby 1975). Traditionally, a distinction is made
between 'obligatory' liaisons, which 'always' occur, and 'optional'
liaisons (Delattre 1947, 1955).[1] It is usually claimed that the
optionality of the second type depends in part on stylistic and
sociolinguistic factors; yet until now, empirical data on how
liaison is actually used by speakers of French have been limited.
Delattre (1947, 1955) relies, apparently, on introspection.
Agren (1973) bases his study on a corpus of radio speech,
which can hardly be taken as representative. Rosoff (1973)
studies liaison only among 'educated' speakers of Montréal
French, noting that optional liaisons were 'nearly non-existent'.
Malécot (1975) has studied liaison empirically, but only among
informants of the 'Parisian upper-middle class'. A socially more
diverse sample is desirable, if one wishes to trace the dynamics

of liaison. None of these studies has used any rigorous statistical operation.

The need for sociolinguistic data is noted by Selkirk (1972:
247).

> The type of investigation that proceeds by asking indi-
> vidual informants questions about their use of language is
> most likely inadequate in the study of ... liaison. A true
> picture of what people actually do can only emerge from a
> sociolinguistic study ...

This paper attempts to provide part of that picture.

The data on which this report is based were extracted from
a corpus of over 100 interviews which I recorded in and around
Tours, an important center of commerce, agriculture, and tour-
ism, 235 kilometers southwest of Paris. According to popular
belief, Tours is the city where 'the best' French is spoken; at
any rate, Tourangeau French is relatively unmarked by regional
peculiarities and can perhaps be considered typical of northern,
central French. To study the question at hand, I selected as
a subsample the interviews of 16 speakers, evenly divided into
two age strata separated by at least one generation. Within
each age group are an equal number of men and women and of
speakers representing two informally defined socioeconomic
classes. The 'higher' class includes speakers with a university
education or the equivalent, who occupy positions of prestige
and importance in business, the professions, and government.
In the 'lower' class are speakers with less than a high school
diploma, who are employed as blue-collar or low-level clerical
workers, artisans, and farmers. Some younger speakers are
categorized according to their anticipated educational and pro-
fessional attainment. In terms of these demographic categories,
eight groups of two speakers each are given in Figure 1.
While this categorization is too broad, and the number of
speakers too small to constitute a representative sample, an
analysis of liaison in this corpus may at least demonstrate the
sociolinguistic constraints on liaison and may suggest something of its statics and dynamics in Modern French.

Since the goal of this study was to analyze liaison as a phenomenon of linguistic variation, I excluded from my data syntactic contexts where liaison was categorically either applied or
not applied. [2]

All other sites of possible liaison were extracted from the
corpus, and were then coded according to whether the liaison
was or was not made. There were 3,182 such sites, and the
relative frequency of liaison in the corpus was 34 percent.

It has often been claimed that liaison is constrained not only
by the social characteristics of the speaker, but also by phonetic, syntactic, and stylistic factors. In order to verify this
assumption, and especially to establish, where possible, the
relative influence of one or another factor on the application of

Figure 1. Grouping and demographic characteristics of speakers.

Age group	Socioeconomic class	Sex	Group number	Speaker	Profession
14–21 years	Lower	Male	1	J.B.	Apprentice waiter
				B.E.	Student, agricultural high school
		Female	2	R.I.	Apprentice technician
				G.E.	Library aide
	Higher	Male	3	P.B.	Student, high school
				B.J.	Student, hotel administration
		Female	4	B.C.	Student, medicine
				V.G.	Student, music
51–64 years	Lower	Male	5	C.H.	Farmer
				B.A.	Plumber
		Female	6	R.E.	Hotel maid
				S.A.	Factory worker
	Higher	Male	7	M.J.	Medical doctor
				J.B.	Architect
		Female	8	J.A.	Hospital administrator
				L.A.	Social Services administrator

liaison, each token was also coded for the factors shown in Figure 2.[3]

Phonetic factors tested include the identity of the liaison segment itself, and that of the segment immediately preceding the site of potential liaison (factor groups A and B of Figure 2). Syntactic factors tested include the context of the potential liaison site (factor group C) and the relative length (in terms of number of syllables) of each word forming the liaison site (factor group D). Since the present corpus consists of individual interviews between the speaker and myself, little style-shifting and its effect on liaison is observable. However, on the assumption that as the interview progressed, the speaker would grow more relaxed and consequently would use fewer liaisons, the effect of the location of liaison sites in the conversation was tested (factor group E). Illustrations of factors in groups A to C are given in Figure 3.

Once each token had been extracted from the corpus and coded for the factors I have discussed, it was then possible to tabulate the observed frequencies and relative frequencies for each factor. The Sankoff variable rule program (Varbrul 2) was then used to determine within each group the relative weight of the various factors. These data are also displayed in Figure 2, where the factors favoring the use of liaison are assumed to be those with a Varbrul 2 probability above .500 (Fasold 1978:93-94).

Several observations about these results can now be made.

1. The segment most favoring liaison is /n/. This finding agrees with that of Malécot (1975). The segment /t/ also favors liaison, while /z/ does not. It is important to remember here that the numerous instances of liaison between the determiner and noun (e.g. les enfants [lezãfã] 'the children') were not included in my data, because in that context liaison was categorical. Had they been included, it is likely that the variable rule probability for /z/ would be higher. In Malécot (1975), /z/ ranks higher than /t/ in relative frequency of application.

2. Not surprisingly, preceding vocalic segments favor liaison, while preceding consonantal ones disfavor it. This pattern is consistent, generally, with that of deletion of final consonants noted in other languages (e.g. Labov 1969). It would be expected, however, that the application of liaison with liquids would be higher than with consonants, since the former are more vocalic than the latter. In my data, although liaison has a higher relative frequency with liquids than with consonants, the variable rule probabilities suggest the opposite ranking. Neither liquids nor consonants have a probability sufficiently high to favor application of liaison, however.

3. The syntactic factors with the three highest relative frequencies and variable rule probabilities are usually said to require 'obligatory' liaisons (Malécot 1975:174). Although the probability of liaison in these contexts is high in my data, it

Figure 2. Factors influencing the use of liaison, ranked
within factor groups by Varbrul probabilities.

Factor	Observed frequency	Relative frequency (% of liaison occurrence)	Varbrul probability
A. Liaison segment			
1. /n/	127/205	.61	0.727
2. /t/	554/1486	.37	0.603
3. /z/	389/1363	.28	0.483
other	2/128	.01	0.210
B. Preceding segment			
1. Oral vowel	714/2117	.33	0.666
2. Nasal vowel	312/781	.39	0.569
3. Consonant	11/137	.08	0.433
4. Liquid	35/147	.23	0.332
C. Syntactic link			
1. Object clitic/__verb	177/181	.97	0.981
2. {ils elles}/__X /T__X	126/158	.79	0.913
3. quand/__X (noninterrogative)	119/142	.83	0.877
4. Adverb+modified element	139/215	.64	0.769
5. Preposition/__X	25/51	.49	0.732
6. être/__X (nonauxiliary)	331/681	.48	0.524
7. Noun+adjective (plural)	9/50	.18	0.382
8. Monosyllabic aux./__X	59/198	.29	0.351
9. Negative/__X	24/142	.16	0.234
10. Verb+complement	39/515	.07	0.177
11. Polysyllabic aux./__X	6/71	.08	0.135
12. Noun+verb	2/52	.03	0.121
13. Other	16/726	.02	0.052
D. Relative word length			
1. Equal length	601/1375	.43	0.640
2. 2nd word longer	436/1030	.42	0.611
3. 1st word longer	35/777	.04	0.264
E. Locus in interview			
1. 1st half	544/1604	.33	0.515
2. 2nd half	528/1578	.33	0.485

N = 3,182; 16 speakers

Figure 3. Examples of phonetic and syntactic factors tested (cf. Figure 2, Groups A-C). Relevant liaisons underlined in transcriptions.

A. Liaison segment
1. *Elle en a parlé* [εlãnaparle]
   'She has spoken about it'
2. *Elle est arrivée* [εlɛtarive]
   'She has arrived'
3. *Elles ont parlé* [εlzɔ̃parle]
   'They have spoken'

B. Preceding segment
1. *Vous m'avez écrit* [vumavezekri]
   'You have written to me'
2. *Elles m'ont écrit* [εlmɔ̃tekri]
   'They have written to me'
3. *Nous sommes arrivés* [nusɔmzarive]
   'We have arrived'
4. *Elles ont parlé* [εlzɔ̃parle]
   'They have spoken'

C. Syntactic link
1. *Je les ai vus* [ʒlezevy]
   'I have seen them'
2. *Ils ont parlé* [ilzɔ̃parle]
   'They have spoken'

3. *Quand elle viendra* [kãtɛlvjẽdra]
   'When she comes'
4. *Très important* [trɛzɛ̃portã]
   'Very important'
5. *Chez une femme* [ʃezynfam]
   'At a woman's house'
6. *C'est un professeur* [sɛtœ̃profɛsœr]
   'He is a teacher'
7. *Soldats américains* [sɔldazamerikẽ]
   'American soldiers'
8. *Vous êtes arrivé* [vuzɛtzarive]
   'You have arrived'
9. *Ce n'est pas un étudiant* [snɛpazœ̃netydjã]
   'He is not a student'
10. *Nous cherchons un stylo* [nuʃɛrʃɔ̃zœ̃stilo]
    'We're looking for a pen'
11. *Vous m'avez écrit* [vumavezekri]
    'You have written to me'
12. *Les français arrivent* [lefrãsɛzariv]
    'The French are arriving'

52/ William J. Ashby

is far from absolute, especially with subject clitics and with
the adverb *quand*. This is discussed further on. The extremely low probabilities of liaison in all but the first six contexts sampled are remarkable.

4. Liaison is favored at the juncture of words of equal
length, or when the second word is longer. It is highly dis-
favored when the first word is longer than the second. This
finding agrees with the claim of Delattre (1955).

5. As expected, optional liaisons are more likely in the first
half than in the second half of the interview. Although the
relative frequencies are identical, the variable rule probabilities
show the first half to be more favorable to liaison. Although
this finding in no way constitutes a serious study of the constraints of style on liaison, it does confirm the expected
existence of such constraints.

Let us now consider the differential application of liaison
among the various groups of speakers. Figure 4 displays the
overall observed and relative frequencies of liaison for each
speaker group.

Figure 4. Observed frequency of liaison per total potential
cases, and relative frequency, by Speaker group.

Speaker group	1	2	3	4	5	6	7	8
n.	$\frac{34}{203}$	$\frac{100}{293}$	$\frac{174}{408}$	$\frac{124}{527}$	$\frac{96}{386}$	$\frac{57}{293}$	$\frac{215}{450}$	$\frac{272}{622}$
%	17	34	43	24	25	19	48	45

N = 3,182; χ^2 = 173.177; d.f. = 7; P < .001

N = total number of tokens; χ^2 = chi-square; d.f. = degrees of
freedom; P = probability that the data displayed are independent of the Speaker groups (here such probability is small).

The following generalizations can be drawn from this distribution: (1) with one exception, the younger speakers make
fewer liaisons than do the older speakers of the same sex and
socioeconomic class; (2) with one exception, the speakers of
the lower socioeconomic class make fewer liaisons than do those
of the higher socioeconomic class; (3) with one exception, the
female speakers make fewer liaisons than the male speakers.

In each case, the one exception to the general pattern is
speaker group 2, which includes the younger, lower class
women. This pattern is displayed in Figure 5, where the
relative frequency of liaison rises with age, with socioeconomic
class, and among male speakers, except where group 2 is involved. Another look at Figure 1 suggest a possible explanation of this phenomenon. A narrower socioeconomic classification than that possible for this study might more appropriately

have called speakers of group 2 'lower middle class', whereas
the other speakers of my 'lower' class (those in groups 1, 5,
and 6) may be more representative of the 'working' class.
Since lower middle class speakers are typically more conservative than those of the working class, and often exhibit, in the
context of an interview, more linguistic conservatism than even
the higher status speakers (Labov 1972), the pattern displayed
in Figures 4 and 5 is not surprising. Since the younger speakers use fewer liaisons than the older speakers, since those of
the 'lower' socioeconomic class use fewer than those of the
'higher' class, and since a conscious conservatism on the part
of the lower middle class speakers is suggested, however
tentatively, by the data, the pattern of distribution which
emerges suggests that of an ongoing linguistic 'change from
below' (Labov 1972). The only surprising aspect of these
findings is that the women appear less conservative linguistically than the men.

Figure 5.   Relative frequency of liaison between homologous
            Speaker groups, by age, SEC, and sex (cf.
            Figure 1).

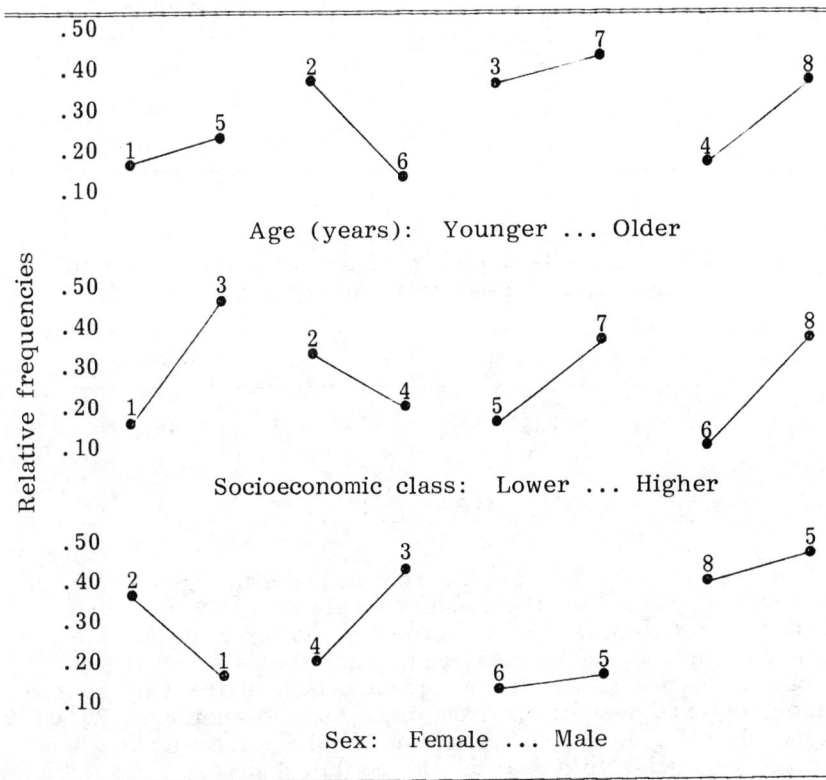

This finding is, nevertheless, consistent with that reported in Ashby (1977). The significance of the variation among the social categories was substantiated by a series of chi-square tests, as reported in Figures 6, 7, and 8.

Figure 6. Observed frequency of liaison per total potential cases, and relative frequency, by age.

	14-21 years	51-64 years
n.	$\dfrac{432}{1,431}$	$\dfrac{640}{1,751}$
%	30	37

$N = 3,182;\ \chi^2 = 14.2665;\ \text{d.f.} = 1;\ P < .001$

Figure 7. Observed frequency of liaison per total potential cases, and relative frequency, by socioeconomic class.

	Lower	Higher
n.	$\dfrac{287}{1,175}$	$\dfrac{785}{2,007}$
%	24	39

$N = 3,182;\ \chi^2 = 71.5662;\ \text{d.f.} = 1;\ P < .001$

Figure 8. Observed frequency of liaison per total potential cases, and relative frequency, by sex.

	Females	Males
n.	$\dfrac{553}{1,735}$	$\dfrac{519}{1,447}$
%	32	36

$N = 3,182;\ \chi^2 = 5.63419;\ \text{d.f.} = 1;\ P < .02$

The frequencies and variable rule probabilities given in Figure 2 are based on the combined data of all 16 speakers. Although the frequencies and probabilities for each speaker group do not, in most cases, contradict the overall pattern shown in Figure 2, the frequency of liaison in the various syntactic contexts does differ from one group to another. Figure 9 shows data for each speaker group, in the six contexts which proved conducive to liaison in the combined data. Some

Figure 9. Syntactic link, by Speaker group.

Speaker group	C1			C2			C3			C4			C5			C6		
1	10/12	.83	.915	11/16	.68	.345	1/5	.20	.804	3/11	.27	.542	0/2	.00	.000	3/50	.06	.119
2	21/21	1.00	1.000	15/20	.75	.307	9/19	.47	.974	24/34	.70	.613	4/5	.80	.836	21/95	.22	.041
3	16/16	1.00	1.000	35/36	.97	.985	24/24	1.00	1.000	28/37	.75	.872	4/9	.44	.732	47/109	.43	.582
4	27/27	1.00	1.000	11/13	.84	.946	20/28	.71	.937	13/30	.43	.608	5/11	.45	.909	39/105	.37	.441
5	19/19	1.00	1.000	22/35	.62	.944	5/5	1.00	1.000	8/17	.47	.781	0/5	.00	.000	28/67	.41	.630
6	11/11	1.00	1.000	12/18	.66	.935	10/11	.90	.983	7/13	.53	.578	0/1	.00	.000	12/47	.25	.257
7	35/35	1.00	1.000	11/11	1.00	1.000	11/11	1.00	1.000	16/20	.80	.902	4/5	.80	.865	95/103	.92	.923
8	38/38	1.00	1.000	9/9	1.00	1.000	39/39	1.00	1.000	40/53	.75	.812	8/13	.61	.704	86/105	.81	.787

Within each cell: observed frequency, relative frequency, Varbrul probability (cf. Figures 1 and 2).

interesting differences among speaker groups can be seen.
The first three contexts (C1, C2, and C3), although generally
strongly favoring liaison, are far from being sites where liaison is 'universally required' (Malécot 1975) for all speakers.
Liaison is categorically applied in all three contexts only for
speaker groups 7 and 8, the older, higher class speakers.
All speakers invariably made liaison in context C1 (at the
juncture of an object clitic and verb), except for speaker JB
of Group 1 (the younger, lower class males). Both examples
in which liaison was not made are in *ils en ont* [izãɔ̃] 'they
have some' for standard /ilzãnɔ̃/. In context C2 (after the
plural subject clitics *ils* and *elles*), liaison was surprisingly
infrequent, especially among the lower class speakers (groups
1, 2, 5, 6), although even the younger speakers of the higher
class sporadically neglected liaison in this context. Examples
are *ils arrivent* [ilariv] 'they are arriving' for [ilzariv], and
ils ont [ilɔ̃] 'they have' for [ilzɔ̃]. In context C3 (after noninterrogative *quand*) liaison is categorical, or nearly so, for
all older speakers (groups 5 to 8). Among the younger speakers, however, this was so only for the higher class males
(group 3).

In contexts C4, C5, and C6, the rate of liaison application
varies widely among the different social groups. The pattern
of this variation is constant in each context, however. The
younger speakers of each socioeconomic class use fewer liaisons
than the corresponding older speakers; and the lower class
speakers of each age group use fewer liaisons than the corresponding higher class speakers. Once again, the only exceptions to this pattern are the speakers of group 2, the younger,
lower class women.

We have seen that the so-called 'optional' liaisons of French
are not used randomly. The usual claim that their use depends
on phonetic, syntactic, stylistic, and social factors has been
substantiated by applying a rigorous statistical operation, the
Sankoff variable rule program, to a corpus of Tourangeau
French. The social patterning of liaison in these data suggests
that liaison is not an example of static, inherent variation, but
that its loss is ongoing.

NOTES

This research was supported by grants from the American
Council of Learned Societies and the Academic Senate of the
University of California at Santa Barbara. Acknowledgment is
also due Helen Neu, who made a pilot study of liaison in my
corpus for William Labov's course in the 1977 Linguistic Institute at the University of Hawaii. A report of her findings was
presented at the 1978 meeting of the Michigan Academy (see
Neu MS).
  1. Selkirk (1972) calls the former 'basic', the latter
'stylistic'.

2. The preliminary study of Neu (1978), together with a perusal of the data, indicated that liaison was virtually always made in the noun phrase after a determiner, or after a preposed adjective. Within the verb phrase, liaison was categorically made after the subject clitics, *on*, *vous*, and *nous*. Also excluded from the data were monosyllabic prepositions ending in a nasal vowel (e.g. *dans*, *en*), since there, also, liaison was nearly always made. Fixed locutions were also excluded (e.g. *c'est-à-dire*, *peut-être*, *de temps en temps*) for the same reason. Contexts where liaison never occurred were at the juncture of a singular noun and a following adjective (*soldat américain*) and following a proper noun, a polysyllabic conjunction, an interrogative adverb, or the conjunction *et*. Note, however, that not all liaisons traditionally called 'obligatory' are excluded from consideration: factors C1, C2, and C3 of Figure 2 are so designated by Malécot (1975), but are contexts in which liaison is variable in my data.

3. Many of these factors are suggested by Delattre (1955).

FRONTING, BACKING,
AND SIMPLICITY IN FRENCH PHONOLOGY

Jean Casagrande
University of Florida

For decades, French phonological studies have been dominated by phenomena at word boundaries. Liaison and elision, the on-again off-again behavior of schwa, the peculiarities of what, in our dependence on orthography, we call mute and aspirate *h*, are among the most studied topics. While these phenomena have continued to fascinate the linguistic world, a relatively new topic has emerged in the wake of the rapid, although perhaps ephemerous, conquest of the field by the proponents of generative grammar. In his work on Russian phonology (Halle 1959) and in articles leading to the oft quoted SPE (Chomsky and Halle 1968), Halle led the way in proposing and formulating structure-relating rules on the basis of morphological alternations. A number of dissertations written at MIT in the mid-sixties echoed for different languages those claims made by Halle. One such dissertation on French was Schane (1968), a scholarly work which has remained an example to emulate for those of us who work in French phonology.

Among the claims made by Schane (1968, 1972), one rule which fronts certain low vowels looms as the cornerstone of his work. This rule is justified on the basis of alternations of front vowels with central and back vowels. The rule, known as Fronting, along with its justification, its scope, and also alternative solutions, constitute the topic of this brief communication. I contend that Schane's solution, while not ideal, is not improved upon by those who argue that instead of Fronting there exists a backing rule whose purpose is to relate the same word pairs.

The problem. French has alternations of the types shown in (1) and (2).

(1) /a/ alternates with /ɛ/

salinité	sel
carnivore	chair
parité	paire
charité	chère
clarté	clairière

(2) /ɔ/ alternates with /œ/

solitude	seulet
ovaire	œuf
horaire	heure
floral	fleuriste
sororal	sœur

Logically, one can argue either that the underscored vowels in the left column are underlying and those in the right column are derived, or that the underscored vowels in the right column are underlying and those in the left column are derived. A priori, there is no reason why one given derivation should supersede the other. Schane opted for the vowels in the left column as primitives and those in the right column as derived. This direction happens to correspond to the historical rules. He supported this position (1972) when he argued that if the morphology of a language is divided between learned and native forms and both sets are issued from a common source, then the language in question will have an abstract phonology and its underlying representations will contain the segments typically found in the learned vocabulary.

In contrast to Schane's position, Dell and Selkirk (1978, henceforth D&S) argue that the proper direction of the derivation is from the front to the back vowels. Their approach is supported by everyday observations of language acquisition. Obviously, children know and use most of the words in the right column before they acquire those of the left. D&S, however, do not argue for a backing rule on grounds of language acquisition but rather on the grounds of simplicity. Their claim is that unlike their backing rule, the Fronting solution requires the use of an ad hoc feature. Consequently, theirs would be the simpler solution.

While the D&S article (1978) is very well documented,[1] it nevertheless leaves some questions unanswered. My purpose here is to address these questions and draw some conclusions on the nature of the opposing viewpoints. Among the topics to be discussed are the relation between the phonetic framework established by phonologists and the phonetic framework determined by phoneticians, the relationship of Fronting and Diphthongization, the relationship of the low vowel alternations of (1) and (2) with alternations in the high vowels. Finally, some conclusion about the theory assumed in D&S and in my reply is drawn.

The phonetic framework. Schane's phonetic framework is as shown in Figure 1.

Figure 1. Schane's phonetic framework.

+FT, -BK		-FT, -BK	-FT, +BK	
i	y		u	+HI -LO
e	ø		o	-HI -LO
ε	œ	ə/a	ɔ	-HI +LO
-RD	+RD			

D&S's proposal is as shown in Figure 2.

Figure 2. Dell and Selkirk's framework.

-BK, -RD	-BK, +RD	+BK, -RD	+BK, +RD	
i	y		u	HI LO
e	ø	ə	o	HI LO
ε	œ	a	ɔ	HI LO

Comparing the two proposals in Figures 1 and 2 suggests that there is no standard framework. There are several differences between the two approaches, some of which have far-reaching consequences in the way rules are written. The one we need to examine here is the Front/Back parameter. Schane distinguishes three degrees of articulation from front to back, while D&S say that there are only two. The picture becomes even more blurred if, in an attempt to corroborate one of the two views, we examine the work of a phonetician such as Delattre (1951), which is shown in Figure 3.
Delattre's vowel triangle contrasts with both Schane's and D&S in that it distinguishes four levels of vowel height. In particular, /a/ is placed on a new, lowest level, which is neither front nor back. From a phonetic point of view, it is instructive then to contrast the two approaches of generative phonology. Schane places /a/ as a central vowel, in agreement with Delattre, whereas D&S claim that /a/ is back. One might argue that in the context of a phonological grammar these

decisions are of little significance, that the main purpose is to simplify the grammar by reducing the feature inventory by one; but it turns out that the difference between these two views is in fact crucial.

Figure 3.   Delattre's work.

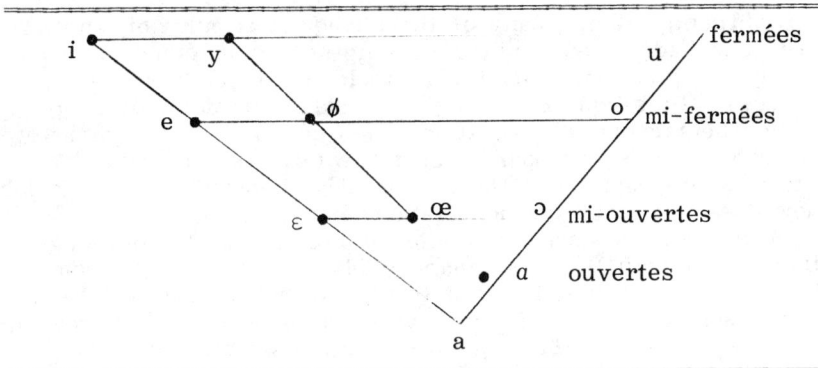

Suppose that we wanted to write a backing rule in the context of the more phonetically oriented system of Schane. The purpose of the backing rule would be to relate the pairs of words in (1) and (2). We would have to say that round vowels become back, and unrounded vowels become [-BK, -FR]. Suppose instead that we wrote a fronting rule in the same phonetic framework. The rule would simply state that vowels are made [+FR]. In both cases the rule would apply only to low vowels.

(a) Backing

$$\begin{bmatrix} +LO \\ +RD \end{bmatrix} \longrightarrow \begin{bmatrix} +BK \end{bmatrix} \text{ / in env. X}$$

$$\begin{bmatrix} +LO \\ -RD \end{bmatrix} \longrightarrow \begin{bmatrix} -FT \\ -BK \end{bmatrix} \text{ / in env. X}$$

(b) Fronting

$$[LO] \longrightarrow [FT] \text{ / in env. X'}$$

The elegance of the fronting rule is inescapable. It is therefore not surprising that the proponents of a backing analysis would slightly stretch the phonetic framework to simplify the rule they propose. D&S's decision to shift /a/ from central to back seems to be motivated solely by phonological factors, and those factors--namely, the relative simplicity of an ensuing rule--are not empirically founded. If, in fact, we do turn our attention to empirical evidence relative to the proper placement

of /a/ in the phonetic chart, we must observe, after Martinet
(1958), that there is a strong tendency to front /a/. Any
attempt to make /a/ back is therefore not empirically supported.
Schane's framework distorts the phonetics of French less than
D&S's. Consequently, I do not see the Backing solution proposed by D&S as an improvement over Schane's.

Diphthongization. Many of the phonological rules of language
are identified as weakening or strengthening tendencies. For
example, reduction is generally considered to be a weakening
process. Diphthongization, by contrast, is thought of as a
strengthening one. A question which can be raised legitimately
regarding D&S's proposal is the following. In what way does
the D&S proposal affect these general tendencies? In particular,
how does it affect Diphthongization?

In his now classical formulation of Fronting and Diphthongization (henceforth DPGN), Schane (1968) underscored the similarity of environment between these two rules. Just as Fronting is sensitive to the native/learned division in French vocabulary, so is DPGN. This can be observed by comparing (1) and
(2) with (3)-(5).

(3) /e/ alternates with /jɛ/ or /je/

pédestre	pied
céleste	ciel
lévrier	lièvre
fébrile	fièvre

(4) /e/ alternates with /wa/

légal	loi
réception	reçois
crédule	crois
sérénité	soir

(5) /i/ alternates with /wa/

épilation	poil
biberon	boisson
fidèle	foi
vision	voyons
trident	trois

In (1) through (5), the segments which in learned vocabulary
(left column) correspond to fronted or diphthongized segments
in native vocabulary, are always in unstressed position. Their
native equivalents can all be found in stressed position. Although stress is not an absolute conditioning factor, the fact
that it does not fall on the underlined vowels of the words in
the left column suggests clearly that the choice of deriving one

from the other of these alternants has unavoidable repercussions on whether the ensuing rule will weaken or strengthen segments.

Since D&S do not address themselves to that question,[2] it is necessary to speculate on what their views might be. Three possibilities come to mind. First, they could claim that neither DPGN nor its presumed reverse (call it De-DPGN) relates the forms of (3) through (5). Second, they could try to derive the vowels from the diphthongs. Third, they could try to derive the diphthongs from the vowels.

The first contention--namely, that the left and right columns of (3)-(5) are not related by application of DPGN or its reverse--is simply untenable. If we chose to pursue it, we would have to assume one of two alternatives: the existence of an alternate rule or the claim that the forms in (3)-(5) are unrelated. Consider the first alternative.

Presumably, one would have to derive diphthongs via Gliding. This would be wrong because Gliding is a weakening rule, one which weakens a vowel contiguous with another vowel by taking away its syllabicity. DPGN is a strengthening rule which adds a glide to a vowel. The two must not be confused. Deriving the glides of diphthongs via Gliding would constitute a fundamental mistake.[3]

Another way of handling the contention that the left and right columns of (3)-(5) are not related by the application of DPGN would be to claim that they are simply not related at all, by any rule. But that can hardly constitute a tenable argument, given that alternations in the more highly valued inflectional morphology can be found between vowels and diphthongs.

(6) V alternates with /jɛ/

venons	viens
tenons	tiens
acquérons	acquiert

(7) V alternates with /wa/

reçevons	reçois
devons	doit
déçevons	déçois

Although these limited alternations can only constitute evidence for minor rules since they are few in number and relate verbs in nonproductive classes, it is nevertheless clear that they must be considered as evidence for a rule, especially by those who would argue that the alternations of (1) and (2) constitute sufficient evidence for the formulation of a rule, be it Backing or Fronting. It is therefore safe to assume that, should they consider the alternatives in connection with the

eventual integration of their system with DPGN, D&S would
rule out the first of the three possibilities envisaged here.

The second contention under consideration is that the left
and right columns of (3)-(5) are to be related by a rule which
weakens the diphthongs of stems occurring in learned words.
This could be referred to as the De-DPGN hypothesis. This
approach, which calls for deriving the segments in learned
vocabulary from the segments in native vocabulary, is absolutely consistent with D&S's Backing hypothesis. One would
expect D&S to be in favor of the De-DPGN hypothesis, even if
it is unconventional and apparently counterintuitive. Unfortunately, De-DPGN is not only counterintuitive, it also causes
complications in the grammar.

The alternations shown in (4)-(5) call for some means by
which the ultimate grammar will distinguish between learned
forms with /i/ and learned forms with /e/. Deriving diphthongs from /i/ and /e/ (cf. Casagrande 1973 and forthcoming
a) gives the grammar a foolproof means of distinguishing between the /i/ and /e/ which alternate with /wa/. They are in
the underlying representation. Deriving /i/ and /e/ from /wa/
is another matter. The only way to insure that the grammar
can derive *épiler* but not **epéler*, or *sérénade* instead of
*sirénade, is to add an ad hoc feature that marks stems as
exceptions to the rule that would raise the proper /e/'s to
/i/'s. Since adding an ad hoc feature is precisely the solution
they take a position against, one can hardly expect that D&S
would embrace the second of the three alternatives we are considering, even if it is so similar to their Backing rule.

The third alternative to the treatment of diphthongs in the
context of a Backing analysis would call for a rule, DPGN,
which would derive /wa/ and /jɛ/ from vowels. This alternative is not consistent with the Backing analysis because it
confers on segments in learned froms a primitive status, a
decision which goes against the intent of Learned Backing.
However, having exhausted the other alternatives, we must try
this last one as the way out of the dilemma facing the proponents of a Backing rule.

DPGN would derive /wa/ from /e/ (which includes the /i/'s
lowered by High Vowel Lowering)[4] and /jɛ/ from /ɛ/ just as
proposed by Schane (1968), except that the environment would
constitute the morphological conditioning so thoroughly documented in D&S (1978). The problem, however, is that DPGN
and Learned Backing are not compatible rules. Consider the
following forms and their UR as listed in (10) and (11).

(10) /sɛkyl-ɛR/   séculaire/siécle

(11) /ʃɛR-ite/   charité/cher

Recall that both DPGN and Learned Backing are dependent on
the learned/native distinction as a conditioning factor. DPGN

can derive the /jɛ/ of *siécle* from /ɛ/ and Learned Backing can derive the /a/ of *charité* from the /ɛ/ in its underlying representation. Reproduced in (12) and (13) are Casagrande's version of DPGN[5] and D&S's version of Learned Backing.[6]

(12) DPGN

$$\emptyset \longrightarrow \left\{ \begin{array}{l} j/\underline{\quad} \quad \left[\begin{array}{l} -RD \\ +LO \\ \hline \quad + NAT \end{array} \right] X \\[2em] w/\underline{\quad} \quad \left[\begin{array}{l} -HI \\ -LO \\ \hline \quad + NAT \end{array} \right] X \end{array} \right\}$$

(13) Learned Backing

$$\left[\begin{array}{l} +SYL \\ +LO \end{array} \right] \longrightarrow [+BK] \ / \ \left[\begin{array}{cc} Y & C_o \\ \hline & +L \end{array} \right] + \left[\begin{array}{l} X \\ +L \end{array} \right]$$

From what precedes, it is clear that DPGN does not apply to vowels in learned forms: they remain unchanged. It is also clear that Learned Backing applies to any low vowel occurring in the specified learned environment. Consequently, Learned Backing applies to /ɛ/ in learned forms which alternate with diphthongs, whereas it is only intended to apply to /ɛ/ in learned forms which alternate with /a/. As a result of this overapplication, the starred forms in (14) can be generated instead of the correct forms in (15).

(14) */a/   (15) /e/ (/ɛ/)
    */sakylɛR/   /sekylɛR/séculaire
    */padɛstR/   /pedɛstR/pédestre
    */salɛst/   /selɛst/céleste
    */fabRil/   /febRil/fébrile

To avoid these nonforms, D&S would have to make use of an ad hoc feature making these forms exceptions to Learned Backing. Since their argument against Fronting hinges on their belief that Fronting requires an ad hoc feature not needed in the Learned Backing analysis, they are unlikely to find this alternative any more appealing than the others.

It appears, therefore, that the Learned Backing analysis cannot be justified over the Fronting analysis when examined in the context of the diphthongs of the language.

High Vowel Fronting. In two of his works (1968, 1972), Schane argued for a Fronting rule. Smith (1969) criticized the 1968 analysis for deriving all /y/ from /u/. In his 1972 paper, Schane brought forth some alternations which, coupled with the Free Ride Principle, would enable him to retain the analysis. As it turns out, the very fact that there are front/ back alternations in the high vowel system constitutes strong grounds for a morphologically conditioned rule, not for Schane's sweeping rule that fronts all /u/'s. High Vowel Fronting[7] is a rule which relates the underlined vowels in (16).

(16) /y/ alternates with /u/

bif<u>u</u>rcation	fo<u>u</u>rche
éb<u>u</u>lition	bo<u>u</u>illant
b<u>u</u>ccal	bo<u>u</u>che
gén<u>u</u>flexion	g<u>enou</u>
p<u>u</u>lsation	po<u>ul</u>
dég<u>u</u>ster	g<u>ou</u>t
s<u>u</u>rd<u>i</u>té	so<u>u</u>rd

Since there is essentially no difference in the types of alternations represented in (1) and (2), on the one hand, and (16) on the other, one would expect that D&S would have included facts such as those of (16) in their analysis. Their silence on this must be attributed to inadvertence. But, were they to incorporate these facts into their analysis, what would be the consequence?

It is obvious that Learned Backing will not do. As Schane (1972) noted, the high front vowels in (16) occur in learned vocabulary, while the back vowels occur in nonlearned vocabulary. High Vowel Fronting, then, is a rule which derives the vowels of learned forms from their equivalents in native forms, just as Learned Backing does. This rule provides a reasonable solution for both Schane's and D&S's position. In the case of Schane's analysis, it eliminates the criticized Free Ride by limiting the fronting of high vowels to those few morphologically defined learned forms such as are found in (16). In the case of D&S's analysis, it completes their learned shift system. Note, however, that the shift is to the front, in the opposite direction. Therefore, while this additional rule completes their system of learned shifts, it supports in no way the direction of the rule they argue for. In fact, it supports equally well the rule they argue against. Once again, we are forced to conclude that D&S's case for a Backing rule is not supported by the evidence advanced.

Conclusion. This paper has focused on the consequences of a proposal by D&S that pairs of words illustrated in (1) and (2) be related by a morphologically conditioned rule which shifts vowels occurring in learned forms from front to back. It has exposed some questionable decisions regarding the phonetic framework of D&S's article. It has suggested a way of making the analysis more complete, by incorporating into the system another learned shift rule, High Vowel Fronting. Most importantly, by demonstrating that the Learned Backing analysis entails complications in the grammar, it has shown that

D&S's proposal does not constitute an improvement on the Fronting solution.

Besides consequences bearing on the phonology of French, some other points must be made in connection with these problems. First, with respect to the phonetic framework, our phonologies should not do violence to the observable facts. The more we move away from empirically observable data, the more we are likely to get tangled up in speculation.

Second, we are weary of arguments based on simplicity, but we still find ourselves using them. This very paper is an example of the narrowness into which such considerations lead us. There is a certain security in the mind of a linguist who can make a point on quantitative grounds. We end up counting features and rules. Yet we have all noticed that simplifying one area of grammar is often done at the expense of another area. Some points ought to be defensible on grounds other than simplicity. In the case of D&S (1978), it may well be that their proposal is indeed worthy of further consideration; but they should have chosen to measure their contribution not on the yardstick of simplicity but on the empirically testable grounds of language acquisition.

Third, what if the whole argument between proponents of a fronting analysis and those of a backing analysis were a non-question? What if it were said that all alternants are related in some way other than by means of a directional rule? The notion of direction is totally theory-dependent, just as the choice of active and declarative structures as primitives rather than passive or interrogative structures is in generative syntax, or the choice of one allophone to represent the phoneme in phonemic theory. We may do well to rethink that theoretical constraint, and possibly reject it, just as relational grammarians have (cf. Perlmutter and Postal 1978, for example), by moving away from ordered rules and directionally defined structures. If we utilized a theory based more on empirical evidence and constrained in such a way as to prevent structural changes such as Fronting or Backing, then D&S's observations about the French data could be couched in a more generally acceptable way.

NOTES

1. My disagreement with D&S is mostly with the argument they advance for the Backing rule. In no way do I wish to cast aspersion on the rest of their fine article. Their main point, namely, their identification of the morphological conditioning, is quite well taken. The wealth of data, even in the list of exceptions they provide, brings forth important facts about French and contributes very positively to the field. Theirs is indeed an important contribution and my purpose is not to tear down, but rather to suggest ways in which their paper could be improved.

2. D&S outline clearly the main lines of the phonology they
postulate for French. They list the rules of that phonology as
Nasalization, Gliding, Vowel Harmony, Closed Syllable Adjustment, Round Vowel Raising, and the rules involving the deletion of schwa. They do not refer to Diphthongization, which,
as Schane showed, operates on an environment based on the
native/learned contrast, just as Fronting does.

3. For a treatment of this topic as it relates to French, see
Casagrande (forthcoming b:Ch. 12).

4. High Vowel Lowering is discussed in Casagrande (forthcoming b:Ch. 10 and 12).

5. DPGN is actually two rules. One applies in the environment of mid vowels to account for alternations like *sérénade/
soir* and *monacal/moine*, while the other applies in the environment of the low front unrounded vowel to relate words like
céleste/ciel. They are collapsed for the purpose of our argument.

6. Learned Backing is predicated on the belief that stems
are not intrinsically native or learned but are 'colored' by the
suffixes which, in turn, are intrinsically native or learned.
For a thorough treatment of this topic and a long list of exceptions, see Dell and Selkirk (1978).

7. This is a fictitious name used for the purpose of the
argument. There is no need to have this as a separate rule.
The grammar of French, if it is stated in terms of movements
like Fronting and Backing (an assumption which I am no longer
willing to make), can be stated in terms of a Learned Shift
rule which accounts for the alternations shown in (1), (2),
and (16).

ROMANCE PHONOLOGICAL EVIDENCE
FOR THE NONCONTINUANT STATUS OF /l/

Pasquale Tatò
Harvard University

The purpose of this paper is to address the question of whether /l/ should be regarded as a [+continuant] or as a [-continuant] phoneme, and to provide evidence for the latter alternative, drawn from the Romance languages.

The problem is not a new one. In *The Sound Pattern of English*, Chomsky and Halle (1968:317) define the feature continuant-noncontinuant (stop) as follows:

> In the production of continuant sounds, the primary constriction in the vowel tract is not narrowed to the point where the air flow past the constriction is blocked; in stops the air flow through the mouth is effectively blocked.

The key words here are 'primary constriction': this specification permits the grouping of nasal stops together with oral stops, affricates, other kinds of stops with secondary articulations, clicks, and the glottal stop under the heading 'noncontinuant'. All other sounds should go under the heading 'continuant', although the liquids pose some problems.

This class of sounds is usually understood to include trills, taps, flaps, and laterals. Of these, trills are assigned by Chomsky and Halle the feature specification [+continuant], while for the 'single tap' and the 'tongue flap' only a vague suggestion is made that the former might be a continuant and the latter a noncontinuant.

Chomsky and Halle (1968:318) further add:

> The characterization of the liquid [l] in terms of the continuant-noncontinuant scale is even more complicated. If the defining characteristic of the stop is taken (as

above) as total blockage of air flow, then [1] must be viewed as a continuant and must be distinguished from [r] by the feature of 'laterality'. If, on the other hand, the defining characteristic of stops is taken to be blockage of air flow *past the primary stricture*, then [1] must be included among the stops.

It is clear, of course, that the best evidence toward a solution of this issue can come from phonological rules or other distributional facts supporting the establishment of continuants and noncontinuants as natural classes. In this connection, the evidence--while it clearly supports assigning, for instance, trills to the class of continuants--is of a mixed nature in the case of /l/.

Chomsky and Halle proceed to offer one example of each. As a case supporting a [+continuant] analysis of /l/, the Chippewyan lateral system is given.[1] The Chippewyan phonemic system includes three manners of articulation for stops and affricates (voiceless, voiced, voiceless glottalized) and two for fricatives (voiceless and voiced). The laterals here are exactly parallel to the sibilants; thus we have:

t	č	tɬ
d	ǰ	dɬ
t'	č'	tɬ'
	š	ɬ
	ž	l

It should be noted, however, that even if we take /l/ to be a continuant here, the correspondence is still only a partial one, since /š/, /ž/, and /ɬ/ are strident while /l/ is nonstrident.[2] In other words, what we really expect in the slot occupied by /l/ is rather the voiced lateral fricative /lʒ/, known to contrast with both /ɬ/ and /l/ in such languages as Zulu. At any rate, there are reported to be voicing alternations in Chippewyan affecting continuants but not noncontinuants, in which /l/ patterns with the former.

On the other hand, a very nice example supporting the noncontinuant status of /l/ is also given by Chomsky and Halle (1968:318). In certain dialects of Scots English, diphthongs are apparently lax before noncontinuants but tense before continuants;[3] cf. ['rʌjd] but ['rajz]. Here /l/ patterns with the noncontinuants, but /r/ with the continuants; cf. ['tʌjl] but ['tajr].

Despite such controversial evidence, the general tendency over recent years has been to regard /l/ as a [+continuant] sound. For instance, Anderson (1974:298) squarely states:

Noncontinuant sounds are made with a complete blockage of the oral tract. Stops, affricates, flaps, and nasals (except nasalized glides, fricatives, etc.) are noncontinuant. Spirants, trills, laterals, vowels, and glides (except ?) are continuant.

Similarly, Ladefoged (1975:246), in his interpretation of the Chomsky-Halle Feature System (which he contrasts with his 'Prime Feature System'), also definitely understands /l/ to be a continuant.

Harms (1968:19,33) specifies /l/ as [+continuant] but /r/ as [-continuant], reflecting here an earlier Jakobsonian usage.

There are even cases in which a phonologist will simply dodge the issue altogether, for example, Schane (1973:28-29).

I should like at this point to present evidence drawn from the Romance languages in favor of a [-continuant] analysis of /l/. The evidence hinges on the fact that in all examples involved, criteria of economy and simplicity support the inclusion of the lateral /l/ in a class with the nasals, identifiable by the feature specifications [-obstruent, -continuant].

The first example, or rather group of examples, comes from the Ibero-Romance languages. It is a case that has already been discussed in the generative literature, particularly in Harris (1969:37-40).[4]

There is a rule in Spanish whereby voiced stops are spirantized in all positions except utterance-initially (as well as word-initially in careful speech) and after a homorganic nasal or lateral; cf. the following examples.

V___V : lo[β]o 'wolf', la[δ]o 'side', la[γ]o 'lake'
V___# : clu[β$^\phi$] 'club', se[δ$^\theta$] 'thirst', zigza[γ^{x}] 'zigzag'
C___ : a[δβ]erso 'adverse', a[βδ]omen 'abdomen', su[βγ]lotal 'subglottal'
V___N : su[β]marino 'submarine', a[δ]miración 'admiration', dia[γ]nóstico 'diagnostic'
V___r : ca[β]ra 'goat', pa[δ]re 'father', a[γ]rio 'sour'
V___l : ha[β]la 'speech', a[δ]látere 'buddy', a[γ]lutinante 'agglutinative'
r___V : ár[β]ol 'tree', ver[δ]e 'green', lar[γ]o 'long'
l___V : cal[β]o 'bald', al[γ]o 'something' but cal[d]o 'broth'
#___V and N___V : [b]om[b]o 'drum', [d]on[d]e 'where', [g]an[g]a 'bargain'; however: el[β]om[b]o 'the drum', de[δ]on[d]e 'from where', una[γ]an[g]a 'a bargain'

The last three forms occur in the Allegretto (and Presto) style, according to Harris.[5]

Harris (1969:40) proposes a rule for the Andante style and one for the Allegretto style, respectively (49) and (50).[6]

(49)
$$\begin{bmatrix} +\text{obstr} \\ -\text{tense} \end{bmatrix} \rightarrow \begin{bmatrix} +\text{cont} \\ -\text{strid} \end{bmatrix} \Big/ \left\{ \begin{matrix} [+\text{obstr}] \\ [+\text{cont}] \\ <[-\alpha\text{cor}]> \end{matrix} \right\} \begin{bmatrix} \\ <\alpha\text{cor}> \end{bmatrix}$$

(50)
$$
\begin{bmatrix} +\text{obstr} \\ -\text{tense} \end{bmatrix} \rightarrow \begin{bmatrix} +\text{cont} \\ -\text{strid} \end{bmatrix} \bigg/ \left\{ \begin{matrix} [+\text{obstr}] \\ [+\text{cont}] \\ <[-\alpha\text{cor}]> \end{matrix} \right\} (\#) \begin{bmatrix} \quad\quad \\ <\alpha\text{cor}> \end{bmatrix}
$$

The only difference between the two rules is that the Allegretto rule may apply across word boundaries, while the Andante rule cannot.[7]

I would have some reservations about the foregoing distinction: Harris' Spanish is perhaps a bit too conservative here. My own experience with speakers of a wide variety of Spanish dialects points rather in the direction of an extension of Harris' Allegretto rule to the Andante style: how many speakers of Spanish would ever say *el*[b]*ombo, de*[d]*onde, una*[g]*anga*, outside of deliberately overprecise speech, i.e. Harris' Largo style?[8]

This brings me to my next point, which is a suggestion that the direction of the rule should actually be reversed,[9] omitting the unnecessary specification of stridency (cf. note 6).

$$
\begin{bmatrix} +\text{obstr} \\ -\text{tense} \end{bmatrix} \rightarrow [-\text{cont}] \bigg/ \left\{ \begin{matrix} || \\ \begin{bmatrix} -\text{obstr} \\ -\text{cont} \\ \alpha\text{cor} \\ \beta\text{ant} \end{bmatrix} \end{matrix} \right\} (\#) \begin{bmatrix} \quad\quad \\ \alpha\text{cor} \\ \beta\text{ant} \end{bmatrix}
$$

This formulation, which would involve a case of Rule Inversion in the sense of Vennemann (1972), is simpler than Harris' in that it requires a two-way disjunction instead of Harris' three-way disjunction (or rather four-way, if we consider the angled bracket notation).

If there were dialects of Spanish that extended the spirant allophones of the lax obstruents also to the utterance-initial position and/or the position after nasal or lateral, the inverted formulation would become even more preferable. At any rate, whether or not such dialects exist, it does seem quite clear that the rule will eventually be reinterpreted in that direction and that that is the further diachronic development to be expected.[10]

For the moment, the situation is as follows. If it is true that the Largo style consists largely in undoing late phonological rules (low-level phonetic rules),[11] then one should probably maintain Harris' formulation, whereas, if that is not necessarily the case or, at any rate, in the case of speakers who never use Largo forms (possibly the majority of speakers), one should perhaps adopt the alternative formulation here proposed.[12]

Whichever formulation is eventually opted for,[13] the generalization remains which can be captured by including the laterals with the nasals in a single class specified by the features [-obstruent, -continuant].[14]

A few words should be added concerning the dialectal variation encountered with reference to this phenomenon in Spanish. First of all, in various parts of the Spanish-speaking world, pronunciation like *fut*[b]*ol, anec*[d]*ota,* perhaps *cat*[g]*ut,* can be heard, with or without voicing assimilation of the tense stop to the following voiced obstruent: in such cases, the noncontinuant allophones of the voiced obstruents occur, instead of their continuant counterparts, after another noncontinuant obstruent (not necessarily homorganic).

Another dialectal (or idiolectal) phenomenon is the occurrence of the stop allophones [b], [d], [g], after all sonorant consonants, whether or not homorganic; e.g. *ár*[b]*ol, ver*[d]*e, lar*[g]*o, cal*[b]*o, al*[g]*o,* as well as *cal*[d]*o.* [15]

Finally, the occurrence of the stop allophones after any consonants (thus including the obstruent continuants in addition to the classes of obstruent noncontinuants and sonorants already mentioned in the foregoing two examples) is reported for two distinct areas of Spanish-speaking America, the Salvador-Honduras-Nicaragua region and Colombia (cf. Castillo and Bond 1972:31-32), e.g. *par*[d]*o, bar*[b]*a, al*[g]*o, des*[d]*e, las*[b]*acas.*

Rather similar rules are found in most dialects of Continental Portuguese, as well as some of the Azorean dialects. The Portuguese spirantization rules, however, tend to be more restricted and more variable than the Spanish ones. [16] For one thing, they always require a right environment, which either excludes all consonants, in the more conservative dialects, or excludes only the noncontinuant consonants, in the more progressive dialects; thus, for instance, such words as *pedra* 'stone' and *objecto* 'object' would have stop [d] and [b] in the former case, but spirant [δ] and [β] in the latter (e.g. Lisbon [p̌εδrʌ] and [ɔβ'ž̌εtᵘ]).

The northern dialects (e.g. Porto) are in general more progressive and spirantize more. Thus, for the dialect of Porto the spirantization rule is identical to that of Standard Spanish with the exception of the right environment mentioned earlier, which has to list disjunctively the features [-consonantal], [+continuant] and the word boundary, in order to exclude just noncontinuant consonants.

In Lisbon, however, the spirantization rule has a more restricted left environment: the spirant allophones of the voiced obstruents do not occur after all sonorant consonants, whether or not homorganic, just as in the Spanish dialectal variants I have mentioned. [17] The right environment of the rule is essentially the same as in Porto, except that, particularly in the case of /d/, the spirant allophone occurs only optionally, i.e. in more or less free alternation with the stop allophone, when immediately followed by a stressed vowel, as in the following examples.

dedo ['deðu] 'finger'
o dedo [u'ðeðu] or [u'deðu] 'the finger'
os dedos [už'ðeðuš] or [už'deðuš] 'the fingers'
idade [i'ðaðᵊ] or [i'daðᵊ] 'age'

In the so-called 'Coimbra literary standard', the spirantization is yet more restricted. It does not normally apply across
word boundaries, or before or after any consonants, or
immediately before a stressed vowel. The rule can be easily
stated as follows.

$$\begin{bmatrix} \text{+obstr} \\ \text{-tense} \end{bmatrix} \rightarrow [\text{+cont}] \ / \ [\text{-cons}] \underline{\quad} \begin{bmatrix} \text{-cons} \\ \text{-stress} \end{bmatrix}$$

It is noteworthy that the Portuguese [β] [ð] [γ] are
occasionally described as 'frictionless continuants' rather than
fricatives stricto sensu; cf. Gonçalves Viana (1903:19).
Furthermore, it appears that the frequency of spirantization
varies with the point of articulation; according to Gonçalves
Viana (1886:75), the spirantization of /g/ is rarer than that
of /b/ and /d/.
In some of the Azorean Islands, e.g. Terceira, no spirantization phenomena are found, as, say, in Brazilian Portuguese.
In others, e.g. St. Michael's, the spirantization rule exists,
but with a rather complicated picture. Waugh's (1979) recent
phonetic study on the dialect of Lagoa, in St. Michael's Island,
yields the following: [β] does not exist; a fricative [ð] may
occur instead of [d] in three cases: after /r/, after /a/, and
after high rounded vowels; finally, a frictionless continuant
[γ] occurs instead of [g] in postvocalic position, although
never syllable-finally (cf. Waugh 1979:36-38). However, the
distribution of the stop and continuant allophones seems to
correlate with a variety of factors, such as speech style, individual preference, etc. Thus, after /r/, which is phonetically
a flapped [ř], only about 50 percent of the speakers have [ð],
the others [d], each particular speaker being consistent in
this regard. On the other hand, after stressed [α], [ð]
occurs about one-quarter of the time, and after the high
rounded vowels, only about one-seventh of the time, with all
speakers varying between [d] and [ð] in the latter two cases
(cf. Waugh 1979:46, note 18).
If we turn our attention to Catalan, we find again a rather
complicated situation with regard to the spirantization of the
voiced obstruents /b/, /d/, /g/. The rule requires a right
environment, in that it is normally restricted to the position
before sonorants and voiced continuant obstruents (although
for several more 'conservative' speakers it applies only before
vowels and /r/, while for others, more 'progressive', it applies
optionally also before the remaining obstruents, continuant and
noncontinuant); it never occurs in word-final position. It
should be noted, however, that certain assimilation rules

'bleed' the spirantization rule by completely assimilating stops
to a following nasal and occasionally to another stop. As far
as the left environment is concerned, the rule is more stable.
Spirantization does apply across word boundaries, but is
blocked by a preceding stop (although not by an affricate),
a nasal (even if not homorganic), or a homorganic lateral.[18]
Following are some examples.

abella [ə'βɛʎə] 'bee', fadiga [fə'ðiɣə] 'fatigue', pagar [pə'ɣa]
   'to pay'
una boira [unə'βɔjrə] 'a mist', pa dur ['pa'ðu] 'hard bread',
   la guia [lə'ɣiə] 'the guide'
bíblia ['biβliə] and ['bibliə] 'bible', troglodita [truɣlu'ðitə]
   and [truglu'ðitə] 'troglodyte'
abril [ə'βriɬ] 'April', pedra ['peðrə] 'stone', agre ['aɣrə]
   'sour'
submarí [summə'ri] and [submə'ri] 'submarine', admirar
   [əmmi'ra] and [ədmi'ra] 'to admire', dogma ['dɔɣmə] and
   ['dɔgmə] 'dogma'
objecció [uβžəksi'o] and [ubžəksi'o] 'objection', adjectiu
   [əðžək'tiu] and [ədžək'tiu] 'adjective', examen [əɣ'zamən]
   and [əg'zamən] 'examination'
observar [upsər'βa] rarely [uβsər'βa] 'to observe', adsorpció
   [ətsurpsi'o] rarely [əðsurpsi'o] 'adsorption'
obtenir [uptə'ni] rarely [uβtə'ni] and [uttə'ni] 'to obtain',
   adquirir [ətki'ri] rarely [əðki'ri] and [əkki'ri] 'to acquire',
   anécdota [ə'nɛgdutə] rarely [ə'nɛɣdutə] and [ə'nɛddutə]
   'anecdote'
pot venir ['pɔdbə'ni] 'he can come', cap desig ['kabdə'zič]
   'no desire', cap gust ['kab'gust] 'no taste'
vaig ballar ['baɉβə'ʎa] 'I danced', vaig dir ['baɉ'ði] 'I said',
   vaig guardar ['baɉɣwər'ða] 'I kept'
més baix ['mez'βas̃] 'lower', més dur ['mez'ðu] 'harder',
   més gros ['mez'ɣrɔs] 'bigger'
arbre ['arβrə] 'tree', perdó [pər'ðo] 'pardon', orgull [ur'ɣuʎ]
   'pride'
alba ['aɬβə] 'dawn', falda ['faɬdə] 'lap', algú [əɬ'ɣu] 'someone'
el barri [əɬ'βaři] 'the quarter', el disc [əɬ'disk] 'the record',
   fil groc ['fiɬ'ɣrɔk] 'yellow thread'
tomba ['tombə] 'tomb', tenda ['tendə] 'shop', languit ['laŋgit]
   'languid'
cinc vides ['siŋ'biðəs] 'five lives', com dits ['kɔm'dits] 'like
   fingers', som grans ['som'grans] 'we are great'

The Catalan facts are certainly very complex and subject to
a great deal of variation, yet our major point can still be made.
Although the parallelism between the nasal stops and the laterals
is not perfect, since the former block spirantization of a following voiced obstruent also when not homorganic, while the latter
have to agree in the feature [±coronal], the contrast between

fal[d]*a* and *ten*[d]*a* on the one hand and, say, *per*[ẟ]*ô* on the other, is very telling. Similarly, as far as the right environment of the rule is concerned, we have observed that in what I have called the more 'conservative', i.e. less spirantizing, variety (which is by no means as unusual as some normalizing grammar books would lead us to believe),[19] only vowels and /r/ allow the spirantization of an immediately preceding voiced obstruent, while /l/, like the nasals, does not. Both of these facts confirm the analysis here supported of a noncontinuant /l/ opposed to a continuant /r/.

The second example comes from a number of distinct areas in central and southern Italy, although my own data are drawn primarily from one of these only, namely, from the dialects of Central Apulia (Puglia Centrale), in southern Italy, specifically from a territory surrounding the city of Bari and including about one-third of the 'Provincia' of Bari.[20] The presentation of these data requires first some background information on the southern Italian dialects. Over a very large part of south-central and southern Italy--leaving out, however, almost all of Calabria and southern Apulia--there is a characteristic low-level phonetic rule that voices (either partially or totally, depending on the specific areas) voiceless obstruents--essentially stops and affricates, since fricatives become affricates in this position over this entire area--when immediately preceded by a (homorganic) nasal (cf. Rohlfs 1949: 425-426 and Tagliavini 1969: 102, Figure 4).[21] The rule applies also across boundary. The 'partial' assimilation can be understood as an assimilation in tenseness, but not yet in voice, which produces a voiceless lax stop, or 'voiceless lenis' (such is the situation, for instance, in the city of Naples). The total voicing is, of course, an assimilation in both tenseness and voicing. The following examples are from the dialect of Bari.

[lɑmbə̣] 'lightning' (cf. It. lampo)
[tɑndə̣] 'so much' (cf. It. tanto)
[bbjɑŋgə̣] 'white' (cf. It. bianco)

The following are examples of the application of the rule across word boundary, again drawn from Barese.

[m#ba:sə̣̃] 'in peace' (cf. It. in pace)
[n#dærrə] 'on the ground' (cf. It. in terra)
[ŋ̣#gɑnnə] 'in the throat' (as if It. in canna)

A formalization of the rule can be the following (for the dialects with only 'partial' assimilation, just delete the specification [+voice]).

$$[\text{+obstr}] \rightarrow \begin{bmatrix} \text{-tense} \\ \text{+voice} \end{bmatrix} / \begin{bmatrix} \text{-cont} \\ \text{-obstr} \\ \text{+nas} \end{bmatrix} (\#) \underline{\quad}$$

The rule, incidentally, does not cause a merger with the re-
flexes of original -mb-, -nd- (although it usually does with
-ŋg-), because another rule, found in a yet larger dialect
area, assimilates -mb- and -nd-, respectively, to -mm- and
-nn- (cf. Rohlfs 1949: 418-422, and Tagliavini 1969: 101-104,
Figures 4,5).[22]

In the aforementioned territory--which includes, in addition
to the city of Bari, a small area to the north (with Bisceglie)[23]
and a larger area to the south and southwest (with Grumo,
Casamassima, Altamura, Gravina), the latter extending marginally into the 'provincie' of Taranto and Matera (with Palagiano,
Ferrandina, Bernalda, Pisticci)--the left environment of the
rule is modified to include /l/, provided that the obstruent
following /l/ is [+coronal], i.e. underlyingly /t/, /¢/, or /č̆/;[24]
the following examples are again from Barese.

['ɑldə̧] 'other' (It. altro)
[n#alda#'vɔldə̧] 'another time' (It. un'altra volta)
[vəl'dæ̃] 'to turn' (It. voltare)
[fəl'du:rə] 'cork, stopper' (from VL *fultōrium)
[al'ʒæ̃] 'to raise' (It. alzare)
['fɑlj̆ə̧] 'sickle' (It. falce)
['fɔlj̆ə̧] 'to clog, stop' (from VL *fulcere for Lat. fulcīre)
['fuldə̧] 'clogged, stopped' (past participle of the foregoing)
   (cf. It folto 'thick, dense')

For a comparison, these forms would be, in Grumese, the
dialect of Grumo Appula: ['aldə̧], [n#alda#'voldə̧], [vəl'dø̸],
[fəl'dɛurə], [al'ʒø̸], ['falj̆ə̧], ['fɔlj̆ə̧], [fəl'j̆ɛutə̧] (cf.Colasuonno
1976).

Exactly the same phenomenon is reported by Rohlfs (1949:
407-409) for various other areas of central and southern Italy.
First of all, it seems to have existed in Neapolitan, as it appears from certain forms culled from D'Ambra's (1873)
Neapolitan-Italian Dictionary: dorge for Italian dolce 'sweet',
curdo for Italian culto 'cult', murdo for Italian molto 'much',
etc. However, in all such forms, the contemporary Neapolitan
dialect has restored the voiceless obstruent, often with loss of
the /l/; e.g. doce 'sweet'. Further, the phenomenon is reported for various localities in Abruzzi, such as Palena, where
we have ['aldə] as Barese ['ɑldə̧], [al'ʒa] as Barese [al'ʒæ̃],
etc.[25]

Other localities referred to by Rohlfs are found in southeastern Umbria (Trevi, Norcia), the southern marches, and
Latium, northeast of Rome (Palombara Sabina), as well as
southeast (Palestrina, Nemi). In many of these localities, /l/
further turns to /r/ (however, original /r/ does not cause the
voicing of a following obstruent) or disappears altogether; cf.
vòrda for Italian volta, ardo for alto 'tall', úrdimo for ultimo
'last', dórgé for dolce, farǵe for falce with the former

development; *ado* for *alto*, *poǵe* for *pulce* 'flea' with the latter. However, forms like *aldo*, *úldimo*, *pulǵe* also occur. What is peculiar about this latter group of localities (in Umbria, the marches, and Latium) is that /l/ voices [-coronal] obstruents as well as [+coronal] ones; cf. *gólbe*, *górbe* for *volpe* 'fox', *sólgo*, *sórgo* for *solco* 'furrow'. The same thing can be said for another group of localities, which are, quite curiously, situated well outside the dialect area over which obstruents are voiced by a preceding nasal—scattered as they are over northern and southern Tuscany (Barberino di Mugello, Montespertoli, Incisa in Val d'Arno, Stia, Radda in Chianti, Montecatini, Pitigliano).

Aside from the Tuscan local dialects just mentioned, where the voicing of obstruents caused by /l/ is obviously an independent development, the claim is here made that the foregoing facts represent a case of Rule Generalization (or Rule Simplification): the left environment of the rule is simplified by deletion of the specification [+nasal], thereby generalizing the rule to the whole class of noncontinuant sonorants. Small adjustments are then necessary to distinguish between the dialects in which /l/ voices only [+coronal] obstruents from those in which /l/ voices all obstruents.

It should be noted that there is yet another little dialect area in the Romance-speaking world where voicing of stops after /l/ is attested; that is the *comarca* 'district' of Sercué in the extreme north of Aragon and neighboring areas, where we find such forms as *aldo* for *alto*, *saldo* for *salto* (cf. Sp. *soto* 'grove'), *algalde* for *alcalde* 'mayor', etc. Here, too, we are dealing with a case of Rule Simplification, since the process involving voicing of obstruents—in fact, only stops—after nasals is attested in a larger dialect area, straddling both sides of the Pyrenees and including the northern Aragonese as well as the upper Bearnese dialects (cf. Menéndez Pidal 1950:296-299, Zamora Vicente 1974:235, 237-239, and Elcock's 1938 impressive study devoted entirely to this area). However, in this particular case, the rule is generalized so as to include /r/ as well as /l/, in other words, all sonorants. Examples of *-rt- → -rd-* are: *suarde* for *suerte* 'luck', *chordiga* for *ortiga* 'nettle', etc. The surprising fact is that the examples of voicing after /r/ seem to be scattered over a wider area than those after /l/. This peculiarity, however, can probably be explained either by the rarity of the sequence /l/ plus stop—a rarity caused in turn by various phenomena of vocalization of /l/ (cf. Aragonese *muito* 'much' from Lat. *multum* (Sp. *mucho*) or *taupa* (but also *tauba*) 'mole' from Lat. *talpa* (Sp. *topo*)) or else in terms of dialect interference.

The third and last example is again drawn from the dialects of central and southern Italy (this time including Sicily) and northeastern Spain and southwestern France. In all of these dialects, phonological rules are found which involve the complete assimilation of a voiced oral stop to a preceding nasal

stop, mostly changing -mb- to -mm- and -nd- to -nn-. As
already mentioned in note 21, the corresponding assimilation
of -ŋg to -ŋŋ- only occurs in parts of Sicily, Calabria, and
southern Apulia (Salento). In Italy, the dialect areas exhibiting the process for the labial and the dental cluster are
roughly coextensive (cf. Tagliavini 1969:101-104, Figures 4,5),
whereas in Spain the assimilation of -nd- to -nn- (appearing
now as -n-) took place in a more restricted area than did -mb-
to -mm- (nowadays -m-); (cf. Menéndez Pidal 1950:286-306).
For the latter, cf. the following forms:[26] Catalan and Aragonese *demanar* vs. Castilian *demandar*; but Catalan *coloma*,
Aragonese as well as Castilian *paloma* vs. Leonese *palomba* and
Portuguese *pomba*; likewise, Catalan *llom*, Aragonese and
Castilian *lomo* vs. Leonese, Portuguese *lombo*. Similarly, in
southern France, the -nd- → -n- rule leaves out northern
Gascony and Foix, which, however, participate in the -mb- →
-m- rule.

Now, always within the boundaries of the assimilation rule
concerning the dental cluster -nd-, a similar assimilation of
-ld- to -ll- may occur. This latter phenomenon is only sporadically attested in the northern Spanish dialects, especially
in Aragonese (cf. Menéndez Pidal 1950:294-296), while it occurs
rather systematically in southcentral Italy and parts of southern Italy (mostly in inner Apulia); cf. even in the modern
Roman vernacular *callo* for *caldo* 'warm, hot', elsewhere *sollato*
for *soldato*. (cf. Rohlfs 1949:400).

Here, too, we seem to have a case of Rule Generalization of
the kind mentioned earlier. Notice that no examples of a
corresponding process assimilating -rd- to -rr- are reported,
at any rate, not for the aforementioned dialect areas.

NOTES

1. Reference is made by the authors to Li (1946).
2. Presumably, /ł/ is also an obstruent, as are /š/ and /ž/,
while /l/ is certainly a sonorant.
3. Reference is here made to Lloyd (1908).
4. See, in addition, Cressey (1978:67-74) and especially
Lozano (1979), which is entirely devoted to the problem of
stop-spirant alternations in Spanish and only very recently
became available in print.
5. Harris (1969:6-8) distinguishes among four styles of
pronunciation: Largo, Andante, Allegretto, Presto, which do
not differ so much in relative speed as in style (although
Harris does not insist on this point and leaves it open to
interpretation). Presumably, the two more common styles are
Andante and Allegretto, while Largo is really only unnatural
overprecise pronunciation (such as when correcting a child or
a foreigner making a mistake, or when clearly enunciating over
a bad telephone connection—cf. Harris 1969:7), and Presto

covers essentially sloppy or otherwise substandard styles of
pronunciation, usually stigmatized by the community at large.

6.   Later in his book, Harris (1969:199–201) claims that all
segments of Spanish are unmarked for stridency and that this
essentially acoustic feature is, in fact, completely predictable
for all Spanish sounds as well as for many others.   He further
suggests (1969:201, note 8) that the feature [+strident] might
be entirely redundant, but leaves the question open (quite
ironically, the note ends in a comma!).

7.   Cressey (1978:36–37) adopts the same view; he further
replaces [+continuant] with its converse [–occlusive] (cf.
Cressey 1978:34, 41, note 7; 65–66, 73–74) and rewrites
(1978:72) Harris' Rule (49) as his (3.10), in which Harris'
unnecessary angled brackets have been deleted and [+cont] in
the left environment has been replaced by [–nas, –lat], presumably to avoid any overlapping in the disjunction.

$$\begin{bmatrix} -son \\ -tns \end{bmatrix} \rightarrow [-ocl] \ / \ \left\{ \begin{array}{c} [-son] \\ \begin{bmatrix} -nas \\ -lat \end{bmatrix} \\ [-\alpha cor] \end{array} \right\} \begin{bmatrix} \overline{} \\ \alpha cor \end{bmatrix}$$

8.   In this connection, cf. the concept of 'hyperemphatic'
speech developed by Lozano (1979:116–118).

9.   The same idea was independently developed by Judith
Aissen; most recently, Lozano (1979) spends as many as 83
pages arguing for the existence of a Stop-formation (Fortition)
Rule in Spanish.

10.   One such dialect seems to be Miami Spanish (as described
by Hammond 1976), and possibly other Cuban Spanish dialects,
in which the spirant allophones of the voiced obstruents may
optionally occur also in the environments requiring the stop
allophones in Standard Spanish; cf. Lozano (1979:72–81).

11.   This line of thinking leads Cressey, for instance (1978:
71–72), to consider the [+occlusive] (i.e. [–continuant]) allophones as basic.

12.   The Spanish rule of nasal assimilation before obstruents
is generally presented as an obligatory rule within the word,
as well as across word boundary (except for the same varieties
of careful speech, in which the voiced stop allophones appear
word-initially); cf. Harris (1969:8–18).   As far as forms like
[inbitar] for *invitar* and other apparent violations of this rule
are concerned, Lozano (1979:116–118) makes the point that such
forms, which occur only in 'hyperemphatic' speech, are very
probably influenced by the spelling.

13.   There is yet a third alternative, entertained but then
rejected by Cressey (1978:70–72) and vigorously propounded
by Lozano (1979:85–110), and that is an archisegmental analysis: the voiced obstruent phonemes would not be specified as

to the feature [+continuant] and bidirectional rules would simultaneously yield both stop and spirant allophones.

14. Or, of course, following Cressey (1978), [+son, +ocl].

15. Lozano (1979:119) cites Malmberg's (1955:63, 70, 77) report of one such case in one of his Argentinean informants. However, rather than invoking--as Lozano does--an unstable [+continuant] behavior of the /r/ phoneme to explain such cases, I would propose simply to modify the left environment of the rule, so as to generate the noncontinuant allophones of the lax obstruents after all [-cons, -obstr] phonemes. Nevertheless, the report made by Jorge Guitart during the discussion of this paper about the existence of a contrast between ver[d]e and lar[γ]o in certain dialects of Costa Rica would pose some problems for my view. Yet, even in such a case, I would prefer to propose different environments of the rule for different points of articulation of the voiced obstruents (something well known from Portuguese dialects) rather than resorting to an ad hoc [-continuant] analysis of /r/.

16. The facts here reported about Portuguese result mainly from my own observations. The standard literature is strikingly poor in useful information on this topic; yet, cf. Gonçalves Viana (1886:69-70) and (1903:7, 19), as well as Barbosa (1965: 169-170).

17. Again, it would be incorrect, in my opinion, to attribute this to a hypothetical [-continuant] status of /r/, as does Lozano (1979:122).

18. For the Catalan data, cf. Badia Margarit (1951:96-113) and (1962:72-106); Wheeler (1974:11-20); Yates (1975:21).

19. I owe this piece of information to my major Catalan informant, Marisa Escribano, who was born and raised in Barcelona, and says only--and hears mostly--: o[p]tenir, a[t]quirir, ane[g]dota, o[p]servar, o[b]jecció, e[gz]amen, su[b]marí, a[d]mirar, do[g]ma, and crucially, bí[b]lia, but, of course, a[β]ril, pe[δ]ra, a[γ]re, etc.

20. The 'provincia' is an administrative unit of about the size of a county in the United States.

21. It should be noted, however, that the exact extension of the rule is not quite the same for the stops as for the affricates, or even, within each of these two classes, for each given point of articulation.

22. On the contrary, the parallel process -ŋg- → -ŋŋ- occurs only sporadically in Sicily, Calabria, and southern Apulia (Salento); cf. Rohlfs (1949:422-423).

23. Interestingly, two other towns, Trani and Molfetta, respectively situated immediately north and south of Bisceglie on the Adriatic coast of Apulia, react to the rule by hypercorrecting original -ld- to -lt-; cf. Rohlfs (1949:408, note 1, 353, note 2).

24. The area in which affricates are voiced by a preceding /l/ is slightly different, in fact larger, than in the case of the stops.

25. For these forms, Rohlfs refers to Merlo (1909:246).
26. The medieval documents cited by Menéndez Pidal show that these assimilation processes once had a wider diffusion than they now have in the languages and dialects of Spain.

GOOD NEWS ABOUT FRENCH NASAL VOWELS

John A. Rea
University of Kentucky

French nasal vowels[1] have been dealt with so often that it would seem foolhardy even to try summarizing the various approaches, let alone attempting to find some new ground. It might take 20 minutes just to read off the bibliography, and it is scarcely conceivable that any unsifted datum would shed sudden new light. Thus I shall be limited mainly to preaching at you, to insisting that one of the already proposed treatments is essentially the correct one. Stealing a line from Halle's already borrowed Russian newspaper joke, I bring you *not* News, but Truth (Halle and Kiparsky 1975).

I would like to expand on this immediately by claiming that truth is not to be found by examining yet again the data of nasalization only in French. This despite the fact that, long before American linguists began basing universal theories of language solely on their own idiolects, French linguists had set an ethnocentric tradition for absolute values which makes Massachussetts monoculites seem Argus-eyed in comparison. For even the finest linguists dealing with French have occasionally failed to avoid the trap of explicating the French language entirely from within itself, and have in fact at times explained or evaluated all other languages by reference to that same umbilical--with perhaps a stray hair or two from Greek or Latin.

Rather, we must first of all determine which data of French, or of any other language, are functions of universal linguistic phenomena, of 'grammaire générale' (see Chomsky 1966, especially 52-53), and which are particular to French--somewhat along the lines of that charming World War I song, 'Mademoiselle from Armentières', one verse of which began with the thrice repeated assertion, 'The French they are a peculiar race', and then went on to specify clearly and unambiguously wherein lay that

peculiarity, in a lambently alliterative last line which the laws
of copyright and public decency prevent my quoting.

Although details of previous publications are too lengthy to
recapitulate here, and although these details are often beside
the point, a general orientation is perhaps necessary. A
fuller summary is available in Tranel (1977b), including a
wealth of pertinent examples, exceptions and counterexamples
(leaving for subsequent investigators a rather inferior list on
which to draw). One may quickly classify the treatments of
nasal vowels of Contemporary Standard French under two major
headings. The most venerable of these for its age (if senility
be a virtue) specifies for French a phonemic inventory including typically four nasal vowels plus an abundance of nonnasal
vowels. Items are listed lexically with these nasal vowels
appropriately symbolized, as, for example, *constipé* with nasal
[õ] in the first syllable, or *cunéiforme* with only nonnasal
vowels, to mention two examples which come randomly to mind.

Morphologically related items are treated either by listing one
under the lemma of another where French orthography facili-
tates this (like *gouine* under *gouin*); or by cross reference to
a morphological appendix, as in the instance of verb conjugations (like *s'abstenir*) displaying forms with and forms without
nasal vowels; or, indeed without indication of phonological and
semantic relatedness (as *parfum-fumiste*). A method such as
this, although attractive to many who are unable or unwilling
to handle anything more abstract than surface allophonic
relationships, gives the lie to Greenberg's (1977) claim that
'After all, no one *tries* to be shallow'.

A second approach to nasal vowel phenomena in French relates
them in a rule-specified manner to sequences of nonnasal vowel
followed by a nasal consonant. Subsumed under this rubric
are several variants. At one extreme, Schane (1968: 45-50)
derived all nasal vowels from abstract sequences of nonnasal
vowel plus nasal consonant, that nasal consonant subsequently
undergoing truncation. Surface occurrences of nonnasal vowels
preceding nasal consonants presume nonapplication of the
nasalization rule when the nasal consonant is in turn followed
by a vowel--various bits of machinery such as schwa and so-
called aspirate-*h* being available for the clever to handle minor
messy details of such items as *mon haschisch* (where nasalization and truncation seem to occur before a vowel) and *la pine*
(wherein a sequence of nonnasal vowel plus nontruncated consonant occurs finally). Nonalphabetic symbols may also be used
alone or in globs for border-line behavior at boundaries, as in
ton anguille, with nontruncated [n] in the possessive, but with
nasalization. It was this treatment Hudson (1975: 215-216) had
in mind when he said:

> Virtually all generative phonologists worthy of the name
> would bar underlying nasalized vowels in French and

derive all these by a rule ... Denial of this analysis would be tantamount to a denial of the basic spirit of generative phonology.

Nevertheless, a variant of this approach as in Selkirk (1972; see also Tranel 1977a) limits rule-derived nasalization just to those instances wherein morphologically related items show nasal vowel alternating with a sequence of nonnasal vowel plus nasal consonant in surface forms--but specifies that nonalternating items with nasal vowel (such as *gonzesse*) have no other form than their surface one. This treatment requires claiming that, in addition to derived nasalization as in Schane, French has nonderived nasal vowels, as was the case in the nonphonological approach first summarized. This permits the timid to avoid specifying which nonnasal vowel underlies a surface nasal vowel in such nonalternating items as *bander*, wherein that underlying nonnasal vowel might be represented by either the first or the fifth letter of the alphabet. On the other hand, those who, with Schane, derive all nasal vowels from nonnasal ones, can make do with a smaller underlying vowel inventory in keeping with some simplicity metric or vow of linguistic poverty.
A quite different solution relating forms with and forms without nasal vowel is the mirror image of that proposed by Schane, taking the nasal vowels as basic both when there is morphological alternation with sequences of oral vowel plus nasal consonant or, indeed, where nasal vowels have no alternants (note Bibeau 1975, Tranel 1974 and 1977b; and Klausenburger 1977a, 1977b). According to this approach, items with a basically nasal vowel, say *con* [kõ] would underlie derivative such as *conasse* [konas] where the nasal consonant and nonnasal vowel are derived, in part by the kinky-sounding process of 'nasal insertion'.
There is no doubt at all that any of these approaches can in fact account for the data, as may be readily determined by reading the articles pleading for one or the other of them. One notes Klausenburger's comment (1977b:158) that, 'since both epenthesis and deletion can account for the facts ... they may both be called true'. The problem is to select among the possibilities and their variants without merely tossing a coin-- nor, for that matter, simple-mindedly choosing an approach just because it seems most like mathematics, or is least abstract (i.e. most superficial), or that it accounts for an infinitesimally greater percentage of the lexical items. On the other hand, as Ruhlen (1978:217) reminds us in speaking of nasalization in languages like French, 'it would seem rather doubtful if language specific considerations would be much use. Rather it will be necessary to discover universal principles ...'
Some years ago, there was considerable noise about a 'simplicity metric', a principle which would select from possible alternative grammars and parts of grammars just that one which specified all-and-only those forms under consideration and did

so in the most parsimonious fashion. It was suggested that
this simplicity might be obtained by perhaps counting symbols,
so that of two rules which both account for all the data, we
would choose the one with the fewest symbols--although we
might also opt perhaps for the least complex rule 'shape', or
even the smallest remainder of exceptions to be swept under
the carpet of the lexicon.

This simplistic approach to simplicity lost appeal as it became
apparent that rules actually occurring in a variety of languages
were often of greater complexity than conceivable rules occurring in no known or possible language. Unvoicing of obstruents contiguous to voiced sounds is just as 'simple' as voicing
when put in rule form: yet all languages and many linguists
seem able to choose between these rules. And assimilation of
nasal consonants to following consonants has as yet not been
reduced to a formula in distinctive features with any paucity
of symbols. Alternatives which would impose some sort of
nonabstractness condition, such as Hooper's (1976) so-called
natural generative phonology, seem either to fail (as nicely
documented by Kenstowicz and Kisseberth 1977 and by Harris
1977) or lead to the reductio ad absurdum alluded to earlier
of simply abandoning rule-governed morphophonemics in favor
of lexical listing.

But there are principled ways of choosing. We do know now
enough facts about enough languages, and about their physiological and psychological bases, so that we may handle processes of any individual language, not simply through narrow
examination of the data of that language. (This was one weakness of those belittled as mere taxonomists by the early generative school.) We may bring to bear what we have learned from
our study of phenomena that are natural and universal: processes present by implication in all languages except where
blocked by rules specific to some individual language. I refer,
of course, to the sort of phenomena and processes discussed
by Jakobson, by Greenberg, by Ferguson, and by Stampe.
Marking conventions were intended to formalize such universals
even in Chomsky and Halle (1968: 400-435) in ways amenable to
the simplicity metric as then conceived, for simple symbol
counting was already recognized as insufficient.

With respect to nasal vowels and nasal consonants, several
processes appear to be natural in human language, and therefore by implication in French--except where French has a
specific mechanism overriding them. First of all, as Ferguson
(1975: 181 and 189) notes, the tendency to nasalize vowels before nasal consonants is 'apparently universal'. In this connection, see also Stampe (1973: 25 etc.), and Greenberg (1966:
514). Thus Schane's (1968) rule nasalizing vowels before
syllable-final and preconsonantal nasal consonants is not a
specifically French rule at all. If we wish to measure the cost
of a 'rule' to a language, French can have this one for free.

One only pays for the optional extras, and such nasalization is standard equipment.

Further, as Stampe has also pointed out (1973), consonants that precede syllable boundary or precede other consonants are subject, both synchronically and diachronically, to weakening processes, so that loss of the nasal consonant under these conditions is a natural process which one expects to find in human languages--not excluding French. English, that universal language, of course exhibits this loss of nasal consonant before other consonants and after the nasalization of a preceding vowel, as exemplified in the normal and natural pronunciation of *can't* [kæ̃t] (Stampe 1973:25), or in a more complex fashion in the fine example of *divinity fudge* (p. 59). To some closer to our hexagonal home, both Italian--in such expressions as *in fatti* (ĩf:at:i)--and Spanish--in words like *ninfa* [nĩfa] (not to mention Caribean Spanish *mismo* [mĩhmo])--show nasalization of vowels before nasal consonant with deletion of syllable-final consonant. It is no more necessary for French to have special rules for such assimilatory vowel nasalization than it is to have rules voicing intervocalic sonorants. In this connection, it is interesting to notice that French nasal vowels are always long, as if filling in the space of the vanished nasal consonant--perhaps seducing the clever into seeing these nasal vowels as double vowels, the second being a total assimilation of the nasal consonant to the preceding vowel, except for the feature nasal, which spreads regressively.

Some areas of Romance have gone even further, and have 'denasalized' vowels subsequent to truncation of syllable-final nasal consonants. In both North Italian and in Catalan, we have morphological pairs such as masculine *fi* beside feminine *fina*, the latter form commonly with some nasalization in anticipation of the following nasal consonant--but with no nasalization in the masculine, apparently in keeping with Stampe's generalization that vowels are naturally nonnasal (1973:17).

If thus I have defended a treatment of French nasal vowels as derived by the natural processes of assimilatory nasalization before following nasal consonant, and of subsequent truncation of syllable-final nasal consonant, I am merely saying that as regards these two, French is doing 'what comes naturally', and is unworthy of remark. Indeed, it scarcely needs rules to accomplish these if they are natural and universal. But I would not want to leave French in such a banal position, subject merely to the mundane processes that all language is heir to. For indeed, each language in the world seems subject to some peculiar rules--all languages are not alike and, as Orwell would put it, 'some are more unequal than others', so that linguistically we must specify this 'inégalité' of French. We must ask ourselves, along with Mark Twain's Jim, if the Frenchman is a man, 'then why don't he talk like a man?'

In fact, what is 'peculiar' about French nasals--their only significant abnormality and therefore the only thing for which

French needs a rule to specify wherein it deviates from what
we know to be normal and natural for human languages--this
sole peculiarity is that in forms like *pine*, French does not
nasalize vowels before pronounced syllable-final and utterance-
final nasal consonants. Delattre (1965)--and before him
Denkinger (1946)--pointed this out long ago, with its implications for those trying to master the French language, especially
in using such words as *mine*, *mène*, *manne*, etc., without sub-
jecting them to the natural but non-French process which would
spread nasalization through the vowel. This, then, is what we
must explain, what we must set up specific rules to account for.
Whatever may be the formalism or the side effects of our treatment of nasalized vowels, or of alternation of nasal consonants
with zero, the essential thing to include in a description of
French is some device or statement that will produce nonnasal
vowels before nasal consonants in syllable-final and preconsonantal positions. French can have assimilatory vowel nasalization for free, but it must be made to pay for such unnatural
couplings.
  It should be remarked that this denasalization rule has not
always been a part of the French language. At an earlier
stage--as in, say, the seventeenth century, vowels were
nasalized not only in words like *tringler*, where the vanished
nasal consonant has left them syllable-final or preconsonantal,
but likewise when they were followed by a pronounced nasal
consonant that was in turn followed by a vowel. In Molière's
time, the past participle of *connaître* was *connu*, unfortunately
pronounced [kõny]. Thus the unnatural rule of contemporary
French denasalizing vowels before nasal consonant has been
added to the language in modern times. I should also point
out that were I to impute inherently nasal vowels to French, I
would be flying in the face of the fact that vowels are naturally nonnasal save when nasalized by assimilation, as remarked
earlier. Ferguson (1975:180) refers to languages with supposed
distinctive nasal vowels as 'less normal' than other languages.
As a matter of principle then, rather than have concreteness as
our initial assumption so that our base form equals the surface
one whenever possible, we should instead give consideration to
assuming a set of natural items to which universal processes
apply.
  It may be noted that I have light-heartedly avoided both a
symbolization of the processes and rules necessary to specify
what is natural and what is unnatural French, and a listing of
still more exceptions to whatever rules and processes I might
symbolize. First, others have provided plenty of rule schemata for us to choose from--once we have found a principled
way to choose--and a stunning array of exceptions and counterexamples are already available. And, as I warned at the beginning, this is not intended as a *tour de force* to produce
cleverer formulae or additional tacks with which to puncture
other people's tires, but is rather what I promised you earlier,

a sermon about sin and about truth. The truth is that vowel
nasalization and nasal consonant truncation in French are
natural, whereas oral vowels before nasal consonants are a
lusus naturae. The sin consists in accepting the deviant behavior as normal, while trying to explain away universal truth,
or concealing it in the archaic void of the lexicon.

NOTE

1. Since this paper speaks against underlying vocalic
nasality, I have left it in its oral form.

A METRICAL ANALYSIS OF SPANISH STRESS

Lawrence Solan
University of Massachusetts, Amherst

In this paper I explore some of the properties of stress in
Spanish, at both the phrase and word levels. Section 1 deals
with phrasal stress in Spanish, taking advantage of Liberman
and Prince's (1977) theory which relates stress and constituent
structure. Section 2 deals with word stress in Spanish, about
which there has been considerable controversy in the literature.
Finally, Section 3 discusses the so-called 'rhythm rule' and
cases of stress shift.

 1. **Nuclear stress in Spanish.** Phrasal stress in Spanish
can be described by a Nuclear Stress Rule similar to the one
used to describe phrasal stress in English (see Chomsky and
Halle 1968 and Halle and Keyser 1971 for descriptions of nuclear
stress within a system of cyclic application). In discussing
these phenomena, I take advantage of insights provided in
Liberman (1974) and Liberman and Prince (1977), making crucial use of the notion of metrical structure.
 According to the theory, nodes in a metrical tree are labeled
S(trong) or W(eak), in relation to each other. That is, if a
node on the tree is strong, it can only be so in relation to a
sister which is weak. Thus, an algorithm which determines
which nodes on the tree are to be labeled strong, also determines automatically which nodes are to be labeled weak, since
all nodes must be labeled one way or the other. As an example, consider (1).

 (1) Carlos comió una manzana.
   'Carlos ate an apple.'

The main stress in this sentence falls on *manzana*, as would be
predicted by a rule similar to the Nuclear Stress Rule (NSR)
found in Chomsky and Halle (1968) (henceforth, SPE). But
let us consider the constituent structure of (1).

(2)

```
                    S
          _____/ _____
        NP                  VP
         |            _____/ _____
       Carlos        V              NP
                     |         _____/ \_____
                   comió     Det           N
                              |            |
                             una        manzana
```

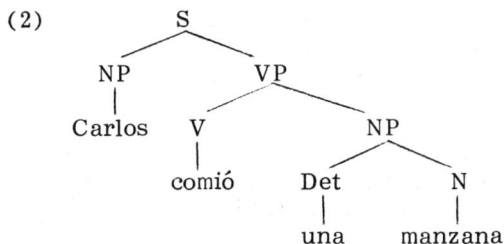

Given a simple SVO structure such as (2), it is the object
which always receives main sentence stress. This fact can be
captured simply by referring to the metrical version of the NSR
as stated by Liberman and Prince (1977) (henceforth L&P).

(3) Metrical Nuclear Stress Rule (MNSR):

In a configuration $[A \quad B]_C$:

if C is a phrasal category, B is strong.

The constituent tree (2) can now be transformed into a metrical
tree (4a), and the nodes labeled according to the MNSR, pro-
ducing (4b).

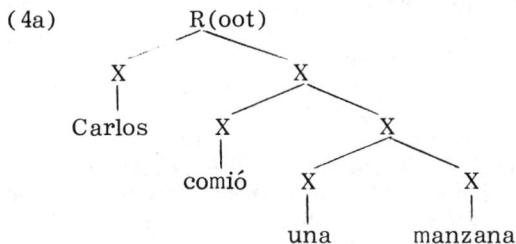

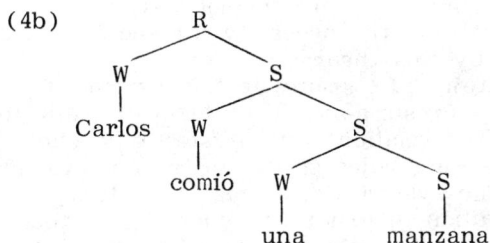

(4a)

```
                      R(oot)
            _____/  _____
          X                    X
          |              _____/ \_____
        Carlos          X            X
                        |       ____/ \____
                      comió    X          X
                               |          |
                              una       manzana
```

(4b)

```
                      R
            _____/ _____
          W                  S
          |            _____/ \_____
        Carlos        W            S
                      |       ____/ \____
                    comió    W          S
                             |          |
                            una       manzana
```

Note that this tree describes only binary relations. That is,
given a pair [S W] or [W S], the metrical tree describes the
relationship only between the two members of the pair. In my
example, the constituent *Carlos* is weaker than the constituent
comió una manzana. Similarly, the constituent *comió* is weaker
than the constituent *una manzana*. The same relationship holds

between *una* and *manzana*, both of these being members of the
final NP. To relate the metrical tree to sentence stress, one
must first define the term 'designated terminal element', also
borrowed from L&P, and restated here.

(5) The Designated Terminal Element of a (sub)tree (DTE)
    is the terminal node whose pathway to the root of the
    (sub)tree passes only through S nodes.

Now it should be clear how phrasal stress in Spanish can be
described using metrical trees. The DTE of the tree contains
the main stress. This can be stated formally using L&P's
Relative Prominence Projection Rule:

(6) Lexical Prominence Projection Rule (LPPR):
    In any constituent on which the strong-weak relation
    is defined, the designated terminal element of its
    strong subconstituent is metrically stronger than
    the designated terminal element of its weak sub-
    constituent.

If, by 'metrically stronger' one means more heavily stressed,
then specific predictions have been made about the entire
phrasal stress system in the language. That is, it should be
possible to take any tree describing the constituent structure
of a phrase, transform it into a metrical tree which is labeled
according to the MNSR, and translate this into relative prominences by the LPPR. In cases such as the ones being discussed here, this works quite well.[1]
    A final feature of the system needs to be mentioned. Given
the MNSR, the cycle becomes irrelevant in the determination of
stress. The prominences are predicted directly from the tree,
which can be labeled in any order. That is, the assignment of
S's and W's can occur simultaneously throughout the tree.
Since most arguments for the cycle on phonology stem from
stress rules, as L&P point out, the necessity for such a device
is brought into question by this theory.
    Thus far I have not attempted to motivate this system of
rules for Spanish stress. Presumably, it would be possible to
predict the same prominence relations by a system of cyclic
application and stress lowering rules similar to the ones found
in SPE. The appeal of the system so far must come from its
simplicity and its contribution in general to phonological theory.
That is, without the use of the cycle or stress lowering rules,
it has been possible to capture generalizations about phrasal
stress in Spanish. The system further eliminates the need for
an *n*-valued feature of stress, possibly helping to eliminate the
use of such nonbinary features in universal grammar. The
difference in predictive power between the two systems comes
when we consider word stress, and in particular, examples of
stress shift.

2. **Spanish word stress.** In this section, I extend the
metrical analysis of Spanish stress to account for word stress.
Spanish words are generally stressed on the penultimate syllable, and are always stressed on one of the final three syllables.
Examples are *estúpido* 'stupid', *hablo* 'I speak', and *papél*
'paper'.[2] James Harris (1969, 1975) has proposed a series of
stress rules to capture these facts, the basic form of which is
given in (7).

(7) Spanish Stress Rule (SSR):

$$V \rightarrow [+\text{stress}] \; / \; \underline{\quad} \; C_0 V C_0 \#$$

This rule does, indeed, capture the generalization that Spanish
stress generally falls on the penultimate syllable. Furthermore,
Harris argues that if the rule applies at the correct level of
the phonological derivation, many of the apparent exceptions
turn out to be completely regular. I now deal with several of
these in turn.

2.1 Final stress. Infinitives, and nouns and adjectives ending in consonants, generally receive final stress: *felíz* 'happy',
abrír 'to open', *papél* 'paper'. Note that nouns and adjectives
not ending in consonants end in either the masculine ending
-o, the feminine *-a*, or the neutral *-e*, which is attached to
some masculine nouns and adjectives, and to some feminine
nouns and adjectives. Harris proposes that nouns, adjectives,
and infinitives (which behave like nouns in a number of respects) which end in consonants actually end underlyingly in
-e, which is truncated by a phonological rule.[3]
  The motivations for positing the final *-e* are threefold. First,
as will be seen, it allows stress to be generally regular.
Secondly, the final *e* on nouns and adjectives shows up phonetically in plurals (*felíces, papéles*). Finally, it is possible
to predict when the *e* will be deleted on the basis of what precedes it. The most general case is that final *e* is deleted
after single consonants other than *s*. Thus there are the
underlying forms /felis+e/, /abrir+e/, and /papel+e/. The
SSR must apply before the rule of final *e* deletion. The *e* is
not deleted in *triste* 'sad', since it follows a consonant cluster.

2.2 Antepenultimate stress in nouns and adjectives. Certain
nouns and adjectives are stressed on the antepenultimate syllable, although this cannot be readily explained from the synchronic facts about Spanish phonology--*cómodo* 'comfortable',
lágrima 'tear', *página* 'page', *próximo* 'next'--since differences
in vowel length are no longer represented underlyingly in
Spanish. Basically, antepenultimate stress occurs whenever
the penultimate syllable was light ($\breve{V}C$) at a certain point in
the history of Spanish. In addition, certain morphemes such

as -ic- never receive stress when in nouns and adjectives: *práctica* 'practice'. Harris (1975) suggests that the penultimate syllables for these words be marked with the feature X, and that the SSR be revised as shown in (8).

(8) Revised SSR:

$$V \rightarrow [+stress] \ / \ \underline{\hspace{1cm}} \ C_0 X C_0 V C_0 \#$$

The rule will skip over the penultimate syllable just in case it is marked with the feature X. For example, /practica/ will
$$X$$
receive stress on the antepenult, while /perro/ (dog) will be subject to the shorter version of the rule and receive stress on the penult.

2.3 Special verb forms. Forms such as the first person plural of the imperfect are stressed antepenultimately: *hablábamos* 'we were speaking', *comíamos* 'we were eating'. Also, past subjunctive first person plurals: *hablásemos*, *habláremos*; and the second person plural of the preterite: *hablásteis* bear antepenultimate stress.[4] Harris incorporates this into a more detailed version of the SSR, taking advantage of the fact that antepenultimate stress occurs only when there are two syllables following the theme vowel (the second *a* in *hablar*). Rule (9) apparently must precede Rule (8).

$$(9) \ V \rightarrow [+stress] \ / \underline{\hspace{2cm}}] \ stem \ C_0 V C_0 V C_0 \#]_{verb}$$
$$th \ vowel$$

Schane (1976) is able to do away with Rule (9) by marking certain verbal morphemes X, and generalizing these cases with Rule (8). Consider, for example, the imperfect forms of the verb *hablar* 'to talk'.

(10) Singular   Plural

	Singular	Plural
1.	hablába	hablábamos
2.	hablábas	hablábais
3.	hablába	hablában

All forms except for the first person plural and second person plural receive penultimate stress. By marking the syllable *ba* with X, and using Rule (8), Schane is able to handle these forms. The X-marked syllable only has an effect on the application of the rule when it occurs on the penultimate syllable. Rule (8), then, correctly predicts that only the first person plural and second person plural will receive antepenultimate stress.

A similar situation holds for the conditional forms, listed in (11).

(11) Singular   Plural

    1. hablaría   hablaríamos
    2. hablarías   hablaríais
    3. hablaría   hablarían

All of these words are stressed on i, regardless of where it occurs. Using the technology of X-marking, we can mark with the feature X the syllable with the vowel a, which occurs at the end of most of these forms. Rule (8) can now correctly apply, giving the right results. [5]

The generalization captured by Harris and Schane seems to me to be generally correct. That is, Spanish words are generally stressed on the penultimate syllable, and there exist certain lexical and morphological exceptions to this generalization, which must be mentioned separately. I am going to outline how the metrical theory of stress outlined in Liberman and Prince (1977) can do basically the same thing, while also bringing into focus certain facts about the rhythm of Spanish left unaccounted for thus far.

Let us first consider the simplest cases in which there is penultimate stress. I shall attempt to assign a metrical structure to Spanish words which automatically accounts for this. Looking at the word *abrígo* 'coat', let us group the last two syllables to form a metrical unit.

(12)

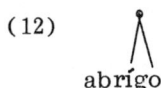

    abrígo

The remaining syllable, a, can be joined to the original structure, completing the metrical tree.

(13)

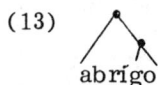

    abrígo

Of course, for words with only two syllables, this second step need not be taken, since the metrical tree will have been completed when all of the syllables are assigned to a structure in the tree, as in (14).

(14)

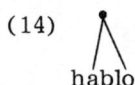

    hablo

Nodes on the tree are labeled with either S or W. Any branching metrical structure must immediately dominate one S and one W. We can extend the MNSR (3) to (15), which makes correct predictions for both phrasal and lexical stress.

(15) Metrical Spanish Stress Rule (MSSR):

In a configuration [A B]$_C$:

if C is a phrasal category, B is strong.
if C is a lexical category, B is strong iff it branches.

The MSSR handles both of the examples under discussion.

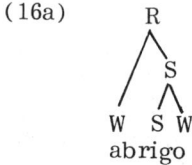

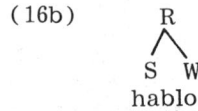

(16a)

```
        R
       /\
      /  S
     /  /\
    W  S W
    abrigo
```

(16b)

```
      R
     /\
    S  W
    hablo
```

Given the MSSR (15) and the LPPR (6), the main stress in words is assigned to the designated terminal element of the word or phrase.

The tree building convention can be extended by looking at some more complicated cases. Consider /aborrecer+e/ 'to hate'. Going through the word from right to left, we group the syllables pairwise. Each time we get two such pairs, we group them as well. Finally, if the word has an odd number of syllables, the first syllable is added to the structure.

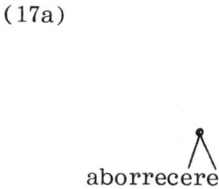

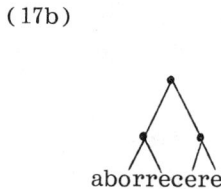

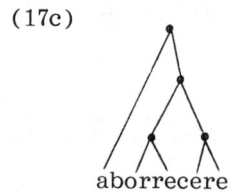

(17a)

```
       /\
  aborrecere
```

(17b)

```
     /\
    /\ /\
  aborrecere
```

(17c)

```
       /\
      /  \
     /\  /\
    /\/\ /\
  aborrecere
```

Assigning the proper labeling by the MSSR results in (18).

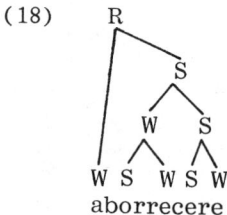

(18)

```
      R
     /\
    /   S
    |  /\
    | W   S
    |/\  /\
    W S W S W
    aborrecere
```

The final e is later deleted.

Now I turn to some of the exceptional cases discussed earlier. Words such as *práctica*, as has been seen, have underlying forms /practica/. In the Segmental Stress Rule (8), the

X

feature X indicates that the rule is to skip over a certain syllable. One can capture the same facts by amending the tree
building algorithm. The new version is stated in (19).

(19) Spanish Metrical Structure Assignment Rule (MSAR):

Apply from right to left the following metrical structure to the syllables in the word, connecting structures whenever possible. Attach an odd initial
syllable when necessary.

(X)

Structures such a *práctica* will take the 'long form' of the
metrical assignment rule, while forms such as *abrígo* will take
the 'short form', with an appended initial syllable. The X-
marked penultimate syllable of *práctica* signals the use of the
optional middle branch of the template in (19).
   To illustrate the application of the MSAR, let us consider
the imperfect forms of the verb *hablár* (10). In particular,
we will contrast *hablába* and *hablábamos*.

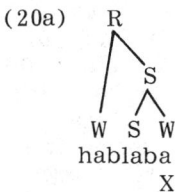

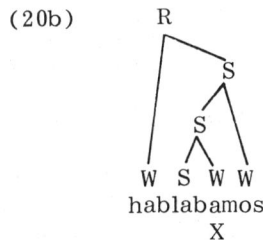

(20a)   R   (20b)   R

        S   S

    W S W   S
    hablaba   W S W W
        X   hablabamos
                                   X

Notice that even though both forms have an X-marked syllable,
only *hablábamos* meets the structural description of the long
form of the MSAR. Once the structures are assigned, the
MSSR automatically assigns the correct prominences, and the
LPPR interprets these prominences to assign the proper
stresses. In this theory, then, marking a syllable X indicates that it bears a different role in the metrical structure
of the word than it ordinarily would.
   So far, I have considered only final and penultimate syllables marked with the feature X. There are, however, other
cases. Harris (1975) gives the examples *teléfono* 'telephone'
and *telefónico* 'telephonic'. The antepenultimate stress in
teléfono indicates that the syllable *fon* is X-marked. But in
spite of this, it receives the word stress in the adjectival
form *telefónico*. This is no problem for the framework within

which I am working. The long form of the MSAR applies in both cases, since in each case the penultimate syllable is X-marked. The fact that in *telefónico* the antepenult is also X-marked is irrelevant. The MSSR is not sensitive to the feature X, and will assign *fon* the word stress independent of the presence of this feature.

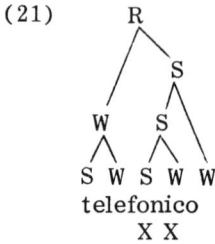

(21)

```
        R
       /\
      /  \ S
     /   /\
    W   S  \
   /\  /\   \
  S W S W    W
  telefonico
    X X
```

   Let us examine the tree-building algorithm a little more closely. First, the pairwise grouping is an iterative process. That is, it assigns prominence relations to the syllables throughout the word. This is significant, since the literature on Spanish stress, as far as I know, deals almost exclusively with the assignment of the main stress in the word. Given the LPPR, I predict that *aborrecér* 'to hate' not only is stressed on the last syllable, but that the o receives a greater degree of stress than the syllable to its right. This prediction is correct.
   Within a system which makes use of the cyclic application of rules, this generalization can also be captured. If Rule (8) were extended to apply iteratively from right to left, it would assign stress to every other syllable (ignoring X-marking for the moment). Using vacuous application of a rule with a stress lowering convention such as the one used in SPE, main stress would be assigned to the penultimate syllable, with the pre-antepenult receiving a lesser degree of stress. Thus, as in the case of the MNSR, the metrical theory does not account for phenomena which are not accountable by other theories, but it accounts for them without the addition of conventions such as the stress lowering convention and the cycle.
   That the preantepenult actually does receive some degree of metrical prominence can be demonstrated, using minimal pairs involving the diminutive suffix *(c)ito*.[6] This morpheme can be added to both nouns and adjectives. By adding it to three-syllable words ending in o or a, four-syllable words with different metrical prominence relations are created.

(22) Word   Diminutive

    paráguas   pàraguítas 'umbrella'
    obscúro   òbscuríto 'dark'
    abrígo   àbriguíto 'coat'

Considering, for example, *abrígo-àbriguíto* (the u is simply a spelling convention in this case), the following metrical structures are found.

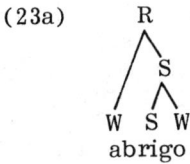

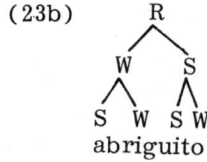

(23a)
```
        R
       / \
      /   S
     /   / \
    W   S   W
   abrigo
```

(23b)
```
        R
       / \
      W   S
     / \ / \
    S  W S  W
   abriguito
```

The primary syllable in the normal forms receives no stress, but in the diminutive forms, it does receive a greater degree of stress than the syllable to its right, which had previously borne the main stress of the word. It thus seems that the tree-building algorithm, combined with the LPPR and the MSSR, makes the correct predictions for these cases, and does so without recourse to additional mechanisms.

Before concluding the discussion of word stress, several short notes are in order. First, this theory says nothing about the stressing of monosyllabic words. Monosyllables cannot be assigned metrical structures by the MSAR, since no relative prominences are possible. The relative stress that a monosyllabic word receives in a sentence is determined by the MNSR (part 1 of the MSSR). Those monosyllables which never bear stress, such as certain pronouns and prepositions, are marked as such in the lexicon. This seems to be necessary in any theory.

Related to this issue is the fact that the iterations of the MSAR are sensitive to the word boundary #, but not to the boundary +.[7] We have already considered cases in which the + boundary is present (*hablar+e*). The claim is that prefixes which are attached by a # boundary are given prominence by part 2 of the MSSR. Let us consider a verb such as *reduplicár*, which, as I argue, has a # boundary between the prefix and the stem. In spite of the metrical structure of the verb stem, *re* can receive stress. That is, *re* is treated as a monosyllable, even though it is part of the entire verb. The only requirement is that the prefix receive less stress than the DTE of the verb because of the LPPR.

As evidence that *re* is indeed separated from the stem by a # boundary, let us consider the verb *reunír* 'to join'. Spanish has a rule of glide formation which changes a high vowel into a glide when it is adjacent to another vowel. According to Harris's (1969) version of the rule, it applies only to unstressed vowels, after the stress rules have applied, in words like *európa*. But even though the u in *reunír* is unstressed and adjacent to another vowel, the rule does not apply. By positing a word boundary between e and u, one can account for this and the stress facts at the same time. A similar example is /in#tolerancia/ 'intolerance' in which the *in* can receive more stress than the syllable to its right, in spite of the fact that the latter is dominated by S while the former is dominated by W. I assume the existence of this boundary for some prefixes, although in some cases I am able to provide independent phonological justification.

There exist cases for which allowing the MSAR to apply through a word without regard for # boundaries would prove to be disastrous. Consider *antepenúltimo* /ante#penultim+o/.

X

Only by making the MSAR sensitive to # boundaries, but not to + boundaries, does one get the right results. To do otherwise would cause the *e* of *ante* to receive prominence, while the *a* would be joined to the tree as a weak initial syllable. Note that a theory based on an iterative version of Rule (8) would also have to be sensitive to the same boundaries.

Finally, it should be noted that the metrical structures generated by the MSAR do not correspond to morphological structure. That is, the metrical trees are not constructed so that they reflect the grouping of syllables into stems, endings, suffixes, etc. Of course, this is true of other theories of stress as well, and reflects only that stress makes use of # boundaries and not + boundaries.

3. **The Rhythm Rule in Spanish.** Spanish has a rule which optionally shifts stress one, two, or three syllables to the left, under certain conditions. Nowhere have I seen this rule discussed in the literature. Compare the examples in (24).

(24) generál   gèneralménte 'generally'
     felíz   fèlizménte 'happily'
     actuál   àctualménte 'actually'
     naturál   nàturalménte 'naturally'
     fundamentál   fùndamentalménte 'fundamentally'

The shift in stress can be predicted from the metrical trees if a ban is imposed on certain sequences of more than one S in a row. Let us look more closely at *gèneralménte*.

(25)

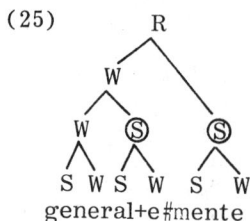

general+e#mente

This structure is posited by Suñer (1975) in response to Brame's (1974) analysis. The two circled S's are adjacent. As a first approximation, one can posit a rule which changes an S to a W when it is to the left of another S. This, incidentally, would have the effect of changing its sister node to an S, causing a reanalysis of the metrical prominences in the string.

(26) Rhythm Rule (first approximation):

$$S \rightarrow W/W \underline{\quad} S\#$$

At once it can be seen that this rule is too strong. The data which I have examined indicate that the Rhythm Rule does not apply in the cases given in (27).

(27) exácto   exàctaménte 'exactly'
     segúro   segùraménte 'surely'
     paradójico   paradòjicaménte 'paradoxically'
     precíso   precìsaménte 'precisely'

Metrically, *exàctaménte* is very similar to *gèneralménte*.

(28)

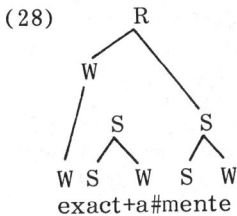

```
            R
           / \
        W /   \
         / S   S
        /  /\  /\
      W  S  W S  W
      exact+a#mente
```

That is, the two adjacent S's appear in exactly the same place. The difference is that *gèneralménte*, but not *exàctaménte* undergoes final e deletion. All of the forms in (24) surface as being consonant-final, whereas none of those in (27) do. We can take advantage of this difference by revising the Rhythm Rule to make it sensitive to it.

(29) Rhythm Rule (second approximation):

$$
\begin{array}{ccc}
S & W & S \\
| & | & | \\
V & \rightarrow V / & \underline{\quad} \ C_0 V
\end{array}
$$

Note now that the rule changes only terminal S's which are adjacent to other S's. This rules out all of the cases in (27), for which the rule should not apply. This rule must be ordered after the final e deletion rule in order to insure that the proper environment is met. [8]
    This version of the Rhythm Rule makes just the right predictions about the number of syllables that the secondary stress is moved. In all cases, the main stress falls on *mente*, as governed by the MSSR. But the secondary stress (the DTE of

the stem) shifts one syllable in words like *fèlizménte,* two syllables in *gèneralménte* , and three syllables in *fùndamentalménte.* The metrical trees for these examples at the time of the application of the Rhythm Rule are given in (30).

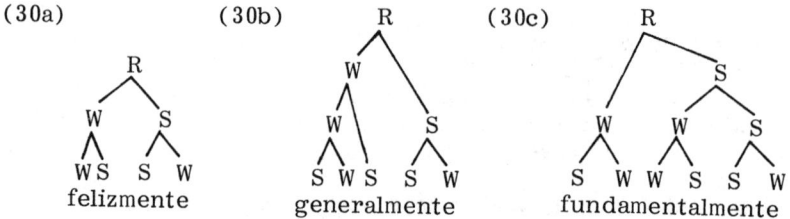

(30a)   (30b)   (30c)

felizmente   generalmente   fundamentalmente

Thus the sisterhood relations set up by the MSAR can also be sued to predict stress shift.

One further revision is needed. Notice that in all of the cases discussed so far, the two adjacent S's are separated by a single # boundary. As it turns out, this is significant. Because of the fact that the MSAR is sensitive to # boundaries, there is never a case in which two adjacent S's occur without any # boundary at all intervening. But there are a myriad of examples in which two such boundaries are present. For example, consider the NP, *el amór tríste* 'sad love'. Two # boundaries come between *amór* and *tríste* , and there is no shift in stress. The same holds true for any noun-adjective sequence. The Rhythm Rule can now be revised to its final version.

(31) Rhythm Rule:

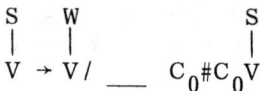

$$
\begin{array}{ccc}
S & W & S \\
| & | & | \\
V & \to V / & \underline{}\ C_0 \# C_0 V
\end{array}
$$

Additional examples of the operation of the Rhythm Rule occur in the language. Consider, for example, the utterance *Juan está aquí.* In rapid speech, the *a* in *aquí* is deleted as a form of contraction when it occurs after the same vowel. Since contraction has the effect of removing one of the word boundaries between the two words, one is left with a form such as (32), in which there are two adjacent S's across a single word boundary.

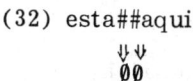

(32) esta##aqui

The Rhythm Rule applies, shifting the stress in *esta* from the *a* to the *e.*

(33) Juan##èsta#quí

It is interesting to note that the Rhythm Rule in Spanish is more restricted than the one for English, which is not sensitive to the number of word boundaries. The paradigm given by L&P is *thirteen men* in which the stress in *thirteen* has shifted. It is also worth noting that it would be very difficult to state these phenomena in an analysis which incorporates cyclic application and stress lowering rules. For one thing, stress shift involves more than adjacent stressed syllables. In a word such as *re#duplicar*, the rule does not operate, even though the *e* and *u* both receive some degree of elevated prominence. This is automatically accounted for by the Rhythm Rule, since *re* is not dominated by an S node. In addition, it would be somewhat tricky to make such a rule shift the stress the correct number of syllables to the left, since this number differs depending on the metrical structure of the word.

Finally, the Rhythm Rule in Spanish is optional, and is generally used only in rapid speech. For all of the examples of its application which I have cited, it is possible to find utterances in which the stress shift has not occurred. Harris (1969) makes some other, more general remarks about the role of the rapidity of speech in Spanish phonology.

4. **Conclusion.** A metrical analysis of stress in Spanish has been proposed here as an alternative to the segmental analyses in the literature. While both frameworks share many strengths and weaknesses, it has been argued that the metrical analysis is able to eliminate the need for certain conventions such as the cycle and the stress lowering device, while at the same time providing an account for alternating secondary stress and stress shift naturally. The metrical analysis, then, should be preferred. Evidence from many other languages, though, is needed in order to finally decide these questions about the primitives of phonological theory.

NOTES

I wish to thank Paloma Garcia-Bellido, James Harris, Jean Lowenstamm, Alan Prince, and Alberto Rivas for their comments and suggestions. While each of these individuals contributed to making this paper better than it would have been, none of them should be assumed to agree with everything that it contains, nor should they be held responsible for its shortcomings.

1. It should be noted, though, that all cases are not so clearcut. For cases in which the syntactic structure is either ambiguous or difficult to determine, stress rules based on syntactic structure are affected. This is true regardless of which framework is being used.

2. Spanish orthography utilizes an accent mark just when the stress does not fall on the penultimate syllable. In this

paper, whenever possible, I use standard Spanish orthography, with the exception of marking main stress wherever it occurs.

3. Saltarelli (1970) proposes an *e* epenthesis rule as an alternative to Harris's truncation rule (see also Foley 1967 for a truncation analysis). While Saltarelli claims that it is equally possible to capture the facts about Spanish stress given his analysis, his stress rules make crucial use of vowel length, a feature which does not seem to be part of the underlying phonology of present-day Spanish. Since stressed vowels are lengthened in Spanish, reference to length is also reference to stress. I therefore continue to use Harris's truncation analysis here.

4. Actually, the *i* in *hablásteis* is realized as a glide. However, if one accepts Harris's (1969) analysis that glide formation occurs after the stress rules have applied, then one must consider *eis* as consisting of two syllables. For the sake of discussion, I accept this analysis here, although no real theoretical issues depend on it. See also Brame and Bordelois (1973).

5. This discussion has omitted consideration of the future and conditional tenses. The first person singular of the future of *hablár* is *hablaré*, and the corresponding conditional form is *hablaría*. Harris claims that the endings are separated from the rest of the verb by a word boundary (*hablar#e, hablar#ia*). If this is the case, then the stress rules apply normally, yielding the correct results. The preterite has also been omitted from this discussion. Verbs in this tense are frequently end-stressed (*hablé*). This can be handled either phonologically, as attempted by Harris (1969), or simply marked in the lexicon.

6. The data to be reported on alternating stress patterns and on stress shift have all been confirmed by native speakers. It should be noted, however, that these phenomena are more pronounced for some speakers than for others, and depend further on rapidity of speech.

7. I have found no evidence for the = boundary in Spanish, and continue to discuss only the # and + boundaries.

8. Liberman and Prince (1977) state the conditions for the application of the Rhythm Rule in English in terms of a 'metrical clash'. That is, a S W sequence becomes a W S sequence when there are two syllables of a certain strength on a 'metrical grid', without an intervening syllable with less strength. The system proposed here can probably be translated into this type of framework, although it does not seem necessary to do so.

EXISTENTIAL PREDICATES: *HAY* vs. *ESTAR*

Margarita Suñer
Cornell University

The premise of this paper is that sentences like (1) and (2) are existential sentences (ES) which have the function of introducing the rheme.

(1) En la esquina *hay un policía.*
    'On the corner there is a policeman.'

(2) En la esquina *está un policía.*
    'On the corner is a policeman.'

The rheme of an affirmative ES is the part of the sentence which falls within the scope of assertion (Givón 1975, Babby 1978 and 1979). In (1) and (2), the italicized portion corresponds to the rheme. Notice also that while in (1) the rheme is the verb plus a direct object argument, in (2) the rheme encompasses the verb plus a subject argument.[1] This fact clearly indicates that the subject/predicate dichotomy is independent of that of theme/rheme. The purposes of this paper are threefold: (1) to demonstrate that indefinite arguments are compatible with both *hay* and *estar*; (2) to characterize the differences between the two verbs under discussion; and (3) to show that theme/rheme assignment belongs to sentence grammar.[2]

1. William E. Bull (1965:174) maintained that 'the difference between *haber* and *estar* for location is not a meaningful contrast. It is the product of useless specialization'. He purports that the choice between one or the other be made based on the concepts of definiteness and indefiniteness: *estar* is used to locate a definite entity, *haber* an indefinite one. Bull's main concern was to provide practical rules meant to guide students during the first steps of foreign language learning. Because

105

of previous research he had conducted on *haber* vs. *estar*, Bull was well aware that his pedagogical rules would only work in approximately 95 percent of the cases.[3] Here I account for the compatibility of *estar* with indefinite arguments in a principled way.

1.1 In the first place, it is necessary to define indefiniteness. 'Indefinite' is used here as an equivalent to 'nonidentifiable'. In other words, given the discourse, the speaker assumes that the hearer cannot properly identify or select the referent under consideration from among all other referents that might be denoted by the noun (cf. Chafe 1976 for a definition of definiteness).

1.1.1 Among the devices that Spanish uses to mark a given argument as indefinite, one finds the indefinite article, 'objective', numbers (*uno* 'one', *cuatro* 'four', *noventa y dos* 'ninety-two', etc.), 'subjective' numbers (expressions like *unos* 'some', *muchos* 'many', *varios* 'several', *pocos* 'a few', *tantos* 'so many', etc.), *otro/s* 'another', and bare plurality (*Hay sillas de paja* 'There are straw chairs'). As is evident, all of these devices are expressions of cardinality.

1.2 Before turning to the task of trying to discover the principles which prompt the selection of *estar* over *hay* (with indefinites), it is necessary to point out the functional differences between *hay* and *estar* sentences. *Hay* is essentially a one-place predicate that asserts the existence of the entity to which its NP refers. This existential assertion may be absolute (for example, (3a)) or relative, in which case the place and/or time are stated (3b).[4]

(3a) Hay una situación explosiva.
  'There-is an explosive situation.'
(3b) Hay una casa en ese barrio...
  'There-is a house in that neighborhood...'

In contrast to *hay, estar* is a two-place predicate. At the level of sentence grammar, *estar* requires both an NP and a locative.[5] To show this difference, compare the two messages in (4).

(4a) Hay un policía que quiere hablarle.
  'There-is a policeman who wants to-talk-to-you.'
(4b) ??Está un policía que quiere hablarle.
  'Is a policeman that wants to-talk-to-you.'

Example (4b) has an incomplete ring to it.
  Given that *estar* has two arguments, and given the relatively free word order of Spanish, at least two word order possibilities

come immediately to mind: NP-*estar*-Loc and Loc-*estar*-NP.[6]
It is to be expected that these two different word orders would
carry different informational potential, and indeed this is the
case. The structure NP-*estar*-Loc presupposes the existence
of the NP and asserts its location. Consider Example (5).

(5) El policía estaba en el bar.
'The policeman was in the bar.'

Example (5) takes for granted the existence of *el policía* and
asserts that he is in a particular place (*en el bar*) as opposed
to another place (his home, the police station, etc.). Under
noncontrastive intonation, the word order in (5) makes clear
that the Loc is the rheme. Now compare (5) to (6).

(6) En el bar estaba el policía.
'In the bar was the policeman.'

Sentence (6) is an example of the Loc-*estar*-NP word order.
This order has the effect of reversing the allocation of theme
and rheme.[7] In this instance the Loc constitutes the theme
and the NP the rheme. Example (6) states that in a given
location (*en el bar*), there was *el policía*, as opposed to any
other person. The contrast between (5) and (6) becomes
totally transparent when considering possible continuations for
these sentences. Observe (7) and (8).

(7a) ...y no en la esquina.
'...and not on the corner.'

...y no durmiendo en su casa.
'...and not sleeping at home.'

(7b) *...y no el capitán.
'...and not the captain.'

*...y no tu hermano.
'...and not your brother.'

(8a) ...y no el capitán.
'...and not the captain.'

...y no tu hermano.
'...and not your brother.'

(8b) *...y no en la esquina.
'...and not on the corner.'

...y no durmiendo en su casa.
'...and not sleeping at home.'

The appropriateness of (7a) as a possible continuation for (5) confirms the claim that the rheme in (5) is the Loc, while (8a) lends support to the contention that the rheme in (6) is the NP itself. Consequently, on the basis of these examples it is plausible to maintain that under noncontrastive intonation the rheme in *estar* sentences encompasses the argument that occurs in postverbal position. And furthermore, that the rheme and the scope of assertion coincide.[8]

So what is the interpretation of an *estar* sentence? Given its two-place predicate nature, its function consists of asserting either the location of an entity or the existence of the NP relative to a given location.[9] This difference correlates with the two word order possibilities explored earlier and depends crucially on the theme/rheme structure of the sentence.

1.3 Now I am ready to prove for the principles that determine the choice between *hay* and *estar* with indefinites.

I begin by pairing examples of *hay* (the (a)-sentences) with examples of *estar* (the (b)-sentences).

(9a) Hay un hombre en la puerta.
'There is a man at the door.'
(9b) Un hombre está en la puerta.
'A man is at the door.'

(10a) En la esquina hay un vigilante nuevo.
'On the corner there-is a new policeman.'
(10b) En la esquina está un vigilante nuevo.
'On the corner is a new policeman.'

(11a) Había una pecera de cristal sobre una mesita.
'There-was a glass fishbowl on-top-of a small-table.'
(11b) Una pecera de cristal estaba sobre una mesita.
'A glass fishbowl was on top of a small-table.'

Contrary to what Bull's pedagogical rules predict, the three (b) examples in (9)-(11) are grammatical. Some speakers hesitate at (9b) without additional context, some 'turn the sentence around' (type (10b)), that is to say, they apply subject inversion to make it sound more natural.

(9b') En la puerta está un hombre.
'At the door is a man.'

This interchange is not at all surprising since it makes the sentence conform to the intuitive principle that old information (i.e. common knowledge—observe the definite *la puerta* in (9b), and *la esquina* in (10b)) normally comes before new information. Because this dichotomy between old and new does not arise in (11b), the order of the elements does not cause any hesitation. This is not to say that sentences (11a) and (11b) are synonymous. In keeping with the meaning and function of *hay*, (11a) asserts the existence of the NP and goes on to locate it. On the other hand, (11b) presupposes the existence of *pecera de cristal* while asserting its location.

Another way to dispel any reluctance caused by (9b) is to bury it in context. Note example (12).

(12) Debido a los disturbios hay mucho control, un
      vigilante está en esta esquina, dos más están
      en la plaza y...
   'Due to the disturbances there-is a-lot-of control,
   a/one policeman is on this corner, two more are
   on the square and...'

Example (12) makes the cardinal value of *un* stand out by contrasting the location of one policeman to that of the others.[10] This same kind of contrast is implicit in *estar* sentences with other cardinal expressions. Observe that in these *estar* sentences the subject argument is outside the scope of assertion; therefore, the existence of the NP is presupposed. As expected, it is more difficult to presuppose the existence of something not easily identifiable (i.e. indefinite). The conflict is solved by interpreting the noun modifiers contrastively, that is, these cardinal modifiers set apart a certain number or group of the noun referents and contrast it to the whole set (cf. examples in (13)). No such contrast is detectable in the corresponding sentences with *hay* in (14). In this case the expressions of cardinality merely refer to an unspecified number of students.

(13) Algunos
     Unos
     Pocos
     Muchos
     Varios   } estudiantes estaban en la clase de biología.
     Cinco
     Más de diez
     Otros

     'Some
     'A few
     'Few
     'Many
     'Several   } students were in the biology class.'
     'Five
     'More than ten
     'Other

(14)

Había $\begin{Bmatrix} \text{algunos} \\ \text{unos} \\ \text{pocos} \\ \text{etc.} \end{Bmatrix}$ estudiantes en la clase de biología.

'There-were $\begin{Bmatrix} \text{some} \\ \text{a few} \\ \text{few} \\ \text{etc.} \end{Bmatrix}$ students in the biology class.'

In other words, in (13) the noun *estudiantes* is presupposed,
the 'weight' of the subject argument falls on the modifiers
which make explicit that only *a portion* of the possible total of
the set categorized by the noun was somewhere.[11] On the
contrary, (14) merely asserts that an undetermined number of
students was somewhere; no reference to a possible total is
implied. This difference in the reading of the modifiers correlates with the difference in the scope of assertion. The modifiers are inside the scope of assertion in (14), but outside it
in (13).[12]

Therefore, one of the reasons leading speakers to choose between *hay* and *estar* messages with indefinite subject in preverbal position seems to be the implicit contrast with the total
set carried by the construction in (13).

Still left to explain are the examples in (10). Could it be
the case that these sentences are synonymous? Notice that
both have *un vigilante nuevo* as part of the rheme. Nevertheless, there are some differences between the two, however
minute and subtle. First, recall that although the locative is
optional with *hay*, it is required with *estar*. This fact seems
to influence the impression caused by an *estar*-message of the
type found in (10b). This sentence does more than merely
assert the existence of the NP; it provides a description, almost a portrait, which is to say it produces the same effect as
that of looking at a photograph. Therefore, the *estar*-message
is more than merely presentational in character. The function
of it is to recreate the scene.

Atkinson (1973) refers to this impression as that of being
'on stage'. He describes Staged Activity thus (1973:59):

From the point of view of the reader, it is, when perfectly
realized, that part of the narrative that gives him the
illusion of direct participation in an objective world perceptible to his senses. From the point of view of the
writer, it is the result of a technique for re-creating an
objective world.[13]

This trait of the *estar*-message is very clearly exploited
(although unconsciously, I am sure) in (15).

(15) ...te acuerdas que, pasando por el Paseo Orinoco,
     están unas piedras enormes...[14]
     '...(you) remember that, going along the Paseo
     Orinoco, are some enormous rocks...'

Obviously, the speaker is trying to re-create an image, to
evoke in someone's mind the picture of something already seen
as if it were there, in front of them at the moment of speaking. This is, then, an excellent illustration of the 'on stage'
function of the *estar* sentence under consideration. And this
'pictorial' impression even affects *estar* sentences with other
word orders. In the following examples, although *hay* could
be used for *estar*, this replacement would cause the 'on stage'
quality to disappear.

(16a) Entonces sí la recuerdo, no verdaderamente a ella,
      no su pierna y su valija, sino a los hombres
      tambaleantes que salían, volviéndose uno tras
      otro, como si se hubieran pasado la palabra, como
      si se hubiera desvanecido el sexo de las mujeres
      que los acompañaban, para hacer preguntas e
      invitaciones insinceras a lo que *estaba* un poco
      más allá del borde de la pollera, de la valija y
      el zapato iluminado. (TE 40)
      'Then I do remember her, not really her, not her
      leg nor her suitcase, but the stumbling men who
      were leaving, turning one after the other, as if
      word had gotten out, as if the sex of the women
      that were with them had vanished, to ask questions
      and make insincere invitations to whatever *was* a
      little further up from the skirt's bottom edge, from
      the suitcase and the lighted shoe.'

(16b) --¿Cuántos soldados *están* aquí?--inquirió...(SXX 110)
      '--How many soldiers are here?--he inquired...'

(16c) --No *estaban* acquí más que doce;... (SXX 111)
      (lit: no were here more than twelve;...)
      'There weren't more than twelve here.'

(16d) El Flaco mira los zapatos. *Están* dos pares de zapatos
      en un rincón. (stage direction; TO 257)
      'The Flaco looks at the shoes. (There) are two pairs
      of shoes in a corner.'

No doubt the difference between *hay* and its colorless informational value, and *estar* and its vivid descriptive on stage
impact, constitutes a very subtle semantic contrast. If the
notion of markedness were duly exploited in syntax-semantics,
the *hay* sentences would represent the unmarked construction

whereas the *estar* sentences would be the marked member of the pair.

Consequently, two loosely interrelated factors determine the choice between *hay* and *estar* with indefinite subjects. The first is the different reading obtained from the indefinite modifiers which depends on whether these quantifiers fall inside or outside the scope of assertion. Thus, the NP-*estar*-Loc construction implies a contrast with the total set which is absent in the Loc-*estar*-NP type and in the *hay* sentences. The second factor centers around the obligatoriness of the Loc argument for *estar* sentences. These sentences provide us with a more pictorial description which produces an 'on stage' impact. I find support for this latter characterization by noticing that it accounts for other peculiarities related to these two existential constructions.

1.3.1 It has been noticed repeatedly for English that existential *there* is obligatory in certain contexts. For example, Kimball (1973) requires the *There*-Insertion rule to be obligatory for inalienable possession. His examples are given in (17) and (18).

(17) There is space in the manger.
*Space is in the manger.

(18) There is fire in his eye.
*Fire is in his eye.

Breivik (1975) accounts for the same facts by making *There*-Insertion obligatory whenever the subject is [+abstract].

(19) *No sign of life was in the house.
There was no sign of life in the house.
(Breivik 1975:63)

And Jenkins (1975), an advocate of the base generation of *there*, points out that many phrases with no grammatical paraphrases without the *there* occur. Some of his examples (1975: 49) are shown in (20).

(20a) There's an answer to the question.
*An answer is to the question.
(20b) There's a solution to the problem.
*A solution is to the problem.
(20c) There's a trick to it.
*A trick is to it.
(20d) There's no point to that.
*No point is to that.
(20e) There's nothing to it.
*Nothing is to it.

The same distribution of grammaticality and ungrammaticality holds true for Spanish if we generalize this observation to the dichotomy *haber/estar*. Only the *hay* version is possible in examples like those in (21).

(21a) Hay un mundo de diferencia entre los dos hermanos.
'There-is a world of difference between the two
    brothers.'
*Un mundo de diferencia está entre...

(21b) Ha habido mucho entusiasmo con el partido.
'There-has been a lot of enthusiasm for the game.'
*Mucho entusiasmo ha estado con el partido.

(21c) Hay un dejo de envidia en sus ojos.
'There-is a hint of envy in his eyes.'
*Un dejo de envidia está en sus ojos.

(21d) Había algo sospechoso en sus movimientos.
'There-was something suspicious in his movements.'
*Algo sospechoso estaba en sus movimientos.

Why is it that indefinite [+abstract] subjects are not allowed with *estar*-sentences?[15] Why are they permitted in *hay*-sentences? The reason for this apparent oddity is to be found in the meaning of the *estar* and *hay* constructions. Recall that one of the functions of an *estar*-message is to produce a descriptive impact, to re-create a scene vividly, to put something 'on stage'. Therefore, the more concrete this description is, the easier it becomes to give the hearer the feeling of being on stage. The prime candidates for *estar* subjects are, then, those things perceptible to the senses; this is why a native speaker verbalized her interpretation of the *estar* examples as 'it is like looking at a picture'. Consequently, [+abstract] subjects are not appropriate for *estar*-messages: they yield ungrammatical sentences because they are too weak to produce a descriptive impact. To exploit the metaphor, they cannot be easily captured in a photograph. In addition, notice that [+abstract] nouns do not lend themselves very readily to being quantified, that is, it is hard, if not impossible, to visualize a contrast between a subset of the whole and the whole; but this is precisely the requirement that *estar* sentences with indefinite subjects in preverbal position must fulfill. The sentences in (22) and (23) further confirm my hypothesis.

(22a) Había varias personas entre los dos hermanos.
'There-were several people between the two brothers.'
(22b) Varias personas estaban entre los dos hermanos.
'Several people were between the two brothers.'

(22c) Varias de las personas estaban entre los dos hermanos.
'Several of the people were between the two brothers.'

(23a) Había varias diferencias entre los dos hermanos.
'There-were several differences between the two brothers.'
(23b) *Varias diferencias estaban entre los dos hermanos.
'Several differences were between the two brothers.'
(23c) *Varias de las diferencias estaban entre los dos hermanos.
'Several of the differences were between the two brothers.'

The only difference between the examples in (22) and those in (23) is the [+Abstract] character of the relevant noun. Sentence (22b) implies that several, but not all, people were at a particular location; this reading is unequivocally transmitted in (22c). Instead, both (23b) and (23c) are uninterpretable. It is as if, with *estar*, the noun requires a concrete outline so that we can picture it in our minds.

Notice, furthermore, that it is possible to locate abstractions with *estar* provided that a definite determiner modifies the subject noun.

(24a) *La* idea ya estaba en su mente.
'The idea was already in his mind.'
(24b) *La* suerte de los acusados estaba en sus manos.
'The fate of the accused was in his/her/their hands.'
(24c) *La* autoridad de Dios está sobre nosotros.
Lit: 'The authority of God is over us.'
(24d) No había diferencias entre las mujeres. *Las* diferencias estaban entre los dos hermanos.
'There weren't any differences among the women. The differences were between the two brothers.'

The definite determiners do not imply a contrast between a subset of the whole and the whole; on the contrary, they make references to the whole set under consideration.

If one returns now to the examples in (21), abstraction like those found there—*un mundo de diferencia, un dejo de envidia, mucho entusiasmo*, and *algo sospechoso*—are perfectly matched to an *hay* sentence, because this latter type of construction has the sole function of asserting the existence of its NP; it is informational in nature, it reports a fact. Here no inconsistency arises between existence, factual information, and abstractions. Furthermore, since the pertinent noun does not receive a quantificational interpretation, no contrast is established.

In sum, my characterization of the differences between *hay* and *estar* sentences explains one of the facts that has been repeatedly noted in the literature.

1.4 To recapitulate the discussion up to this point, it has
been shown that both *hay* and *estar* are compatible with indefinite arguments. However, this does not imply that both predicates are used under the same circumstances. *Hay*, an essentially one-term predicate, has the primary function of introducing NPs into the discourse. The information it presents is
factual and to a certain degree colorless; in terms of markedness, it would represent the unmarked construction.

On the other hand, *estar* is a two-term predicate; within
sentence grammar it requires both an NP (the syntactic subject) and a locative. Its two-term predicate nature opens the
door to different word order possibilities. Thus, NP-*estar*-
Loc is primarily a locative construction which presupposes the
existence of whatever is being referred to by the NP. Whenever this NP is modified by means of an expression of cardinality, there arises an implied contrast with the total set.
This contrast is absent[16] when the NP argument is inside the
scope of assertion (in *hay* and Loc-*estar*-NP). Loc-*estar*-NP
is primarily an existential construction which asserts the existence of whatever is referred to by the NP. *Estar* sentences
with indefinite subjects re-create a scene and convey an 'on
stage' impact. Due to this vividness, they appeal to our
senses and to our imagination; in terms of markedness, they
represent the marked construction.

2. In this section, I show that theme/rheme assignment belongs to sentence grammar. In order to do this, it is first
necessary to demonstrate that the dichotomies theme/rheme and
given/new (information) cannot be equated with one another.
In the words of Halliday (1967:205):

> The functions 'given' and 'new' are however not the same
> as those of 'theme' and 'rheme'. The two are independently
> variable. But there is a relationship between them such
> that in the unmarked case the focus of information will fall
> on something other than the theme; it will fall at least within
> the rheme, though not necessarily extending over the whole
> of it.

In Spanish, it is also the case that there exists a high correlation between given and theme, and between new and rheme.
But again, this is a statistical fact, not a syntactic dictum. To
illustrate, I give some examples with existential verbs.

(25a) --En la reunión de anoche, ¿estaba Paco?
     In the gathering of last-night, was Paco?
     'Was Paco there at last night's gathering?'
(25b) --Sí, estaba Paco.
     Yes, was Paco.
     'Yes, Paco was there.'

(25c) --Sí, estaba Paco con su nueva mujer.
       Yes, was Paco with his new wife.
       'Yes, Paco was there with his new wife.'
(25d) --Sí, estaba el fulano ese.
       Yes, was the guy that.
       'Yes, that guy was there.'

Among the possible affirmative answers to a question like
(25a), I have listed three in which the rheme (or at least
part of the rheme, cf. (25c)), is restated, and thus constitutes given information. However, the point is that out of
context, there would not be any way of deciding whether *Paco*
or *el fulano ese* is given or new information. To decide, it is
necessary to resort to the larger context, to the situation or
the discourse. Consequently, there can be no doubt that the
parameters of given and new information belong to the larger
realm of the discourse and not to sentence grammar.
    To further confirm the hypothesis that new and rheme are
independent of each other, I give a slightly different type of
example with *haber*.

(26a) Era una muchacha como ya no *las* hay. (CT 155)
      She-was a young-woman like already no them there-are
      'She was a young woman the likes of whom no longer
        exist.'

(26b) Ha habido muchas dificultades y aún *las* hay.
      There-have been many difficulties and still them
        there-exist
      'There have been and still are many difficulties.'

(26c) ...En Mallorca...los turistas han ido allí desde hace
        mucho tiempo...o sea...el turista rico...típico inglés
        etc. Esto es del siglo pasado,...iban a Mallorca...
      --...con su...
      --*Los...los* había mucho tiempo antes. (VEA 59)
      '...In Mallorca...the tourists have gone there for a
        long time...that is...the rich tourist...typically
        English etc. This is from the last century...they
        went to Mallorca...
      --...with their...
      --They were there from a long time before.'
        (Lit: them...them there-were....)

The examples of (26) constitute instances in which existential
haber cooccurs with an anaphoric clitic. Anaphoric clitics[17]
are old information; their referents can only be identified taking into account the preceding context. Notice that while the
referents for the clitics in (26a,b) are to be found in the
immediately preceding sentence, the one for (26c), *los turistas*,
is to be found at a considerable distance. In spite of this,

all of these clitics are still part of the rheme, i.e. they are
within the scope of assertion of their respective sentences.
The speaker uses these anaphoric clitics to signal to the
addressee something like 'I haven't shifted my attention to
another matter, I'm still talking about the same situation'. The
clitics reintroduce (part of) the rheme into the discourse, and
this reintroduction is done anaphorically because this is one of
the ways in which recoverable information tends to be presented
in the discourse.[18]
The examples in (25) and (26) clearly show that rheme and
new information belong to different dimensions, since (at least)
part of the rheme may be given information. The determination
of what is new and what is old in a given sentence cannot always be done without resorting to the larger context of the discourse. On the other hand, to determine the rheme of an
existential sentence, it is only necessary to stay on the level
of sentence grammar. Allow me to quote once more from Halliday (1967:223):

> English is structured simultaneously on the dimensions of
> given-new and theme-rheme, the former determining its
> organization into discourse units and the status of each
> such unit as a component in the discourse, the latter
> starting from its organization in sentence structure and
> framing each clause into the form of a message about one
> of its constituents, with the further possibility of an
> optional 'key signature' in the form of a theme relating to
> discourse or speech function.[19]

And if this quote is true for English, it is even more true
for Spanish, since its relatively freer word order allows for
different orderings of the verb arguments.

2.1 Before bringing this section to a close, I would like to
hint at a theoretical corollary suggested by the facts discussed
here. Assuming the framework of the Extended Standard
Theory (especially as presented in Chomsky and Lasnik 1977)
as revised by Rochemont (1978), it is clear that the different
word orders that obtain with *estar* should not be arrived at by
means of a 'stylistic' rule. As defined by Rochemont, a 'stylistic' rule applies to surface structures, does not interact with
syntactic transformations, and is not relevant to the interpretive rules deriving logical forms. If our analysis of the existential predicates *hay* and *estar* is correct, different readings are
obtained from the expressions of cardinality, depending on
whether these quantifiers fall outside or inside the scope of
assertion (cf. examples (13), (14), and note 12). Williams
(1977:126) presents the following very general rule of Quantifier Interpretation, which assigns scope to quantifiers that
appear in surface structure by allowing the interpretation of
quantifiers at both VP and S level.

(27) $[\ldots Q \ldots]_{\{S \atop VP\}} \rightarrow [Q_i(\ldots x_i \ldots)]_{\{S \atop VP\}}$

By applying (27) to the sentences in (28), (29) is obtained.

(28a) Muchos estudiantes estaban en la biblioteca.
'Many students were in the library.'
(28b) En la biblioteca estaban muchos estudiantes.
'In the library were many students.'

(29a) $[\text{MUCHOS}_i \ (x_i \text{ estudiantes [estaban en la biblioteca]}_{Rh})]_S$

(29b) $[\text{En la biblioteca [MUCHOS}_i \text{ (estaban } x_i \text{ estudiantes)]}_{Rh}]_S$

Item (29) clearly captures the fact that MUCHOS is outside the rheme in (29a) but that it is part of the rheme in (29b).[20] This, in turn, implies that quantifier interpretation, one of the interpretive rules which derive LF, interacts with possible word-order arrangements.[21] This observation indicates that Subject Postposing[22] cannot be a stylistic rule in Spanish.[23]

3. **Summary.** Three major points have been tackled during the development of this paper on the existential predicates *hay* and *estar*. (1) It was shown that both predicates are compatible with expressions of cardinality. (2) The differences between these two verbs were characterized. (3) It was demonstrated that theme/rheme assignment is independent of the parameters of given/new; while the first dichotomy belongs to sentence grammar, the second pertains to the realm of discourse.

NOTES

I am grateful to L. Babby, E. J. Beukenkamp, A. Chacona, S. McConnell-Ginet, and M. L. Rivero for their comments on an earlier version of this article. The author accepts responsibility for any and all remaining errors.
1. This can be easily demonstrated. Pluralizing the subject of (2) produces a concomitant change in subject-verb agreement:

En la esquina están varios policías.
'On the corner are several policemen.'

2. These problems and many others pertaining to existential sentences in Spanish are dealt with in greater detail in my manuscript, 'Spanish existential sentences' (in preparation).
3. To quote W. E. Bull directly (1943:122):

This division of function is observed in 417, or 95.3 percent, of the 438 examples of the locative *estar* encountered in the present study. Twenty-one examples of *estar* were found in which the subject was indefinite. In contrast, the *haber* predicate is indefinite in 677, or 95 percent, of the 713 examples encountered.

4. To the best of my knowledge, Babby (1978) was the first to apply the notions of scope of assertion and scope of negation (Givón 1975) to existential sentences.
5. It is necessary to specify 'at the level of sentence grammar' because, given the discourse, the locative could be 'recovered' from context. For example:

A. - ¿Quién estaba contigo en el bar?
    'Who was with you in the bar?'
B. - (Estaba) Paco.
    '(Was) Paco.'

Given the question asked by (A), (B) does not need to reiterate the locative since it is transparent from the context.
6. There are other word order possibilities as well, but they are not crucial to the discussion.
7. The reader should resist the temptation of equating theme/rheme with given/new information.
8. This total overlap between rheme and scope of assertion is further confirmed by looking at what the negative particle *no* negates.

El policía *no* estaba en el bar (sino en su casa).
'The policeman was not in the bar (but at home).'

En el bar *no* estaba el policía (sino tu hermano).
'In the bar was not the policeman (but your brother).'

For more discussion on the scope of negation see Suñer (in preparation).
9. Or to put it differently, NP-*estar*-Loc is a locative sentence, while Loc-*estar*-NP is an existential sentence.
10. To a great degree, the Spanish facts correlate with those pointed out by Perlmutter (1970) for English. He claims that the indefinite article cannot occur with the subjects of certain stative predicates (*A boy is tall*); only the stressed numeral is acceptable in this environment. In Spanish, the so-called indefinite article and the numeral are the same morpheme. Nevertheless, some contexts--like our (12)--make this

numerical value more explicit and may, therefore, facilitate comprehension.

11. An appropriate context for structures of the type NP$_{indef}$-*estar*-Loc could be the following. Imagine an instructor who comes to teach a class only to find a nearly deserted building. This person asks:

> -- ¿Y dónde está la gente hoy?
> 'And where are the people today?'

A very plausible answer is:

> -- Hace media hora, algunos estudiantes estaban en la biblioteca pero me parece que la mayoría fue a una manifestación.
> 'Half an hour ago, some students were in the library but I have the impression that the majority went to a (protest) march.'

12. Thus, it should be anticipated that the modifiers in the word order Loc-*estar*-NP would not necessarily imply a contrast with the whole set, since they are inside the scope of assertion. This is exactly the case. Notice that (i) could be appropriately continued with (ib) but not with (ia).

> (i) En la clase estaba un policía.
> 'In the class was a policeman.'
> (ia) ...*y otro (estaba) en la cafetería
> '...and another one was in the cafeteria'
> (ib) ... y no un marino.
> '... and not a sailor.'

13. Atkinson uses Staged Activity to discuss the two forms of subject inversion in French:

> (i) arrive X
> (ii) il arrive X

Bolinger (1977:93-94) also resorts to this distinction in order to pinpoint the differences between

> (i) Across the street is a grocery.
> (ii) Across the street there's a grocery.

Sentence (i) presents something on stage while (ii) brings something into awareness, it presents something to our minds. In a note (1977:123), Bolinger claims that Spanish presentatives are essentially the same as those in English. His examples are:

En el patio está una mesa.
'On the patio is (stands) a table.'

En el patio hay una mesa.
'On the patio there is a table.'

The first is an instance of 'on stage', the second of 'bringing' something into 'awareness'. Although many of the native speakers I consulted have difficulties explaining the tenuous difference between *hay* and *estar* examples, once given, they agree with it. One native speaker expressed her feeling about the *estar* examples as 'It's like looking at a still picture, it is there in front of you'.

14. This example comes from the Norma Culta Project from Caracas, Venezuela. It is cited in Bentivoglio (1976:1-18).

15. Word order is immaterial in this case. The *estar*-sentences in (21) are just as bad when their subjects are postposed:

*Entre los dos hermanos está un mundo de diferencia.
*Ha estado mucho entusiasmo con el partido. etc.

16. More precisely, the contrast is absent under 'normal', noncontrastive intonation.

17. Spanish clitics are always unstressed (a fact which is implied in the label 'clitic'), so that they could not even be contrastive.

18. Other ways are by substitution or deletion. The reader should keep in mind that while the NP argument which appears with *hay* is the object argument, the one which co-occurs with *estar* is the subject argument. Clitic pronouns can only 'replace' object arguments in Spanish.

19. Halliday's 'key signature' appears to be related to William's notion of 'discourse conditioned' rules (cf. William 1977:102-103).

20. Observe that I have modified William's rule of semantic interpretation by substituting Rh(eme) for VP. What (29) fails to make explicit is that only in (29a) is MUCHOS acting as a restricted modifier, since the quantifier takes its value from the cardinality of a contextually determinate set of students representing a sizeable proportion but less than totality. Item (29) could be expressed more formally as in (ia,b).

(ia) (Muchos x, $x \varepsilon$ {x: estudiantes (x)}) (x estaban en la biblioteca)
(ib) En la biblioteca [(Muchos x) (estudiantes (x) and estaban LOC)]

These are sublogical forms which could be read in 'quasi-English' as in (iia,b).

(iia) Many among the students are such that they are in the library.
(iib) In the library, the students who are there are many.

21. As should be expected, negation also interacts with different word order possibilities (see Suñer in preparation).
22. Subject Postposing assumes that NP-*estar*-LOC is basic, and that the word order Loc-*estar*-NP is derived. These matters and many others are taken up in detail in Suñer (in preparation).
23. There is evidence from other languages that Subject Postposing also interacts with syntactic transformations. For example, in Zenéyse, under normal circumstances, the position of the subject with respect to the verb has an effect on Subject-Verb agreement. This concord is established with the NP subject when preverbal, but with the clitic *u* (3rd person masculine singular) when the subject follows the verb. In the latter case, the verb adopts the third person singular form regardless of the gender and number of the NP subject (cf. Browne and Vattuone 1975).

Russian offers a slightly different type of evidence. This language shows a correlation between case assignment and word order in existential sentences. Affirmative existential sentences have nominative subjects and 'fixed' verb-subject word order, while negated existential sentences have genitive subjects and either subject-verb or verb-subject word order (cf. Babby 1978 and 1979).

SOURCES OF DATA

SXX Anderson-Imbert, E., and L. B. Kiddle, eds. 1956. Veinte cuentos hispanoamericanos del siglo XX. New York: Appleton-Century-Crofts.
CT Arreola, J. J. 1961. Confabulario total [1941-1961]. México: Fondo de Cultura Económica.
VEA Ingamells, L., and P. Standish. 1975. Tapescript for Variedades del español actual. London: Longman.
TE Kadir, D., ed. 1976. Triple espera: Novelas cortas de hispanoamerica. New York: Harcourt, Brace, Jovanovich.
TO Tres obras de teatro. 1970. La Habana, Cuba: Casa de las Américas.

A SEMANTIC ANALYSIS
OF THE SPANISH COPULATIVE VERBS

Marta Luján
University of Texas at Austin

0. Introduction. The correct syntactic analysis of the distinction signalled by the two copulas, *ser* and *estar*, in Spanish is the one in terms of the aspectual distinction 'perfective/
imperfective'. This study attempts to define the content of
these terms and to elucidate the nature of the interpretation
and distribution of the predicates bearing these verbs.

I assume an analysis in terms of the features [STATIVE] and
[PERFECTIVE]. All adjectives and most past participles are
stative; the distinction determining their occurrence with one
or the other copula is represented by the opposing values for
[PERFECTIVE]; perfective states select *estar*, imperfective
states require *ser*. The readings assigned to the feature combinations defining perfective and imperfective states include a
temporal specification of a delimited and of an undelimited time
period, respectively. This characterization accounts for the
opposition of *ser/estar*, as well as for their partial synonymy.[1]

The analysis also accounts for various structural features of
the copulas such as their distribution with past participles,
locatives, frequency, and time adverbs. In addition, the proposed semantic readings are generalizable to the aspectual distinction of the same nature shown by the verbal predicates.
The present proposal thus brings the aspectual distinction
signalled by *ser/estar* in line with the overt distinction indicated by the two preterite forms, the simple past and the imperfect, and by the compound tenses.

1. Inadequacies of previous analyses. The analysis of *ser/*
estar in terms of the imperfective/perfective distinction is by
no means novel. Gili y Gaya (1961) cites Hanssen (1913) as
its originator, though when adopting it, he goes in fact well
beyond Hanssen's concise proposal. Gili y Gaya defines the

content of the aspectual distinction in relation to adjectives by resorting to the notion of 'modification'. While the characterization on the basis of this notion has gained popularity, this has not happened with the characterization in terms of the perfective/imperfective contrast.

The notion of modification has been used in recent years to discriminate what constitutes a state. It is claimed that attributive predicates with *estar*, but not with *ser*, denote states resulting from or capable of modifications. This characterization has superseded the more traditional one based on the Aristotelian dichotomy 'essential' vs. 'accidental' properties. Traditional grammar has usually attributed the use of the two copulas to the terms of that opposition (Keniston 1937, Bello 1958, Lenz 1925, Ramsey 1956). However, these broad notions can be shown to have little predictive value, while various counterexamples have been pointed out showing their insufficiency (Navas Ruiz 1963, Roca Pons 1958).

To overcome these problems, traditional grammarians have attempted to characterize the use of *estar* with an attribute as indicating a state or a condition (Keniston 1937, Ramsey 1956). But Keniston's criterion for identifying a state as 'that which results from an action' is too broad in one respect and too restricted in another. Many participles of active verbs cannot occur with *estar*, as shown in (1).

(1) La pared está
$$\begin{cases} \text{pintada} \\ \text{*tocada.} \\ \text{*mirada.} \\ \text{*señalada.} \end{cases}$$

'The wall is
$$\begin{cases} \text{painted.'} \\ \text{touched.'} \\ \text{looked at.'} \\ \text{pointed to.'} \end{cases}$$

Also, many participles of verbs referring not to actions but to mental or physical processes or states are excluded by Keniston's criterion. These are constructed with *estar*, but not with *ser*, as shown in (2).

(2) Sus padres
$$\begin{cases} \text{estaban} \\ \text{*eran} \end{cases}
\begin{cases} \text{angustiados.} \\ \text{cansados.} \\ \text{enojados.} \\ \text{satisfechos.} \end{cases}$$

'His parents were
$$\begin{cases} \text{anguished.'} \\ \text{tired.'} \\ \text{annoyed.'} \\ \text{satisfied.'} \end{cases}$$

The identification of a state has more recently been associated with the notion of change or modification. Gili y Gaya

(1961), Bull (1965), Roldán (1974), Querido (1976), among others, define a state as that which results from a change or is potentially modifiable. This definition seems to allow for the correct discrimination of the participles of active verbs that admit *estar*. For instance, a wall suffers a modification when it is painted, but not when it is merely touched, looked at, or pointed to. This would explain the examples in (1).

The definition also allows for the inclusion of the stative verbs illustrated in (2), for these verbs denote changes of state. *Angustiarse* 'to become anguished', *enojarse* 'to get angry', *cansarse* 'to get tired', etc., all refer to mental or physical changes that give rise to certain states that may be described by predicates with *estar*, e.g. *estar angustiado* 'to be anguished', *estar enojado* 'to be angry', *estar satisfecho* 'to be satisfied', *estar cansado* 'to be tired', *estar sorprendido* 'to be surprised', *estar roto* 'to be broken', etc.

With the notion of state it seems that the meaning and use of *ser/estar* may be defined in a simple and straightforward manner; namely, an attributive predicate describing a state takes *estar*, otherwise it takes *ser*. Now by replacing the term 'state' by the specification given for its recognition, the following version is obtained. An attributive predicate that describes the result of a modification or that which is modifiable takes *estar*, otherwise it takes *ser*. The seeming simplicity disappears in this version. For the expression 'that which is modifiable' itself expresses a generality of such extension that it invalidates the criterion for identifying a state. A similar difficulty arises in trying to identify states as results of modifications: the whole universe and every item in it must be conceived as resulting from modifications. Thus, every predicate attribute describing any existing item must be constructed with *estar*, and there would be no use for *ser*-predicates.

But even this broad definition is insufficient, for attributive predicates may be constructed with *estar* where no modification is implied, either as a cause or a future possibility, as (3) and (4) illustrate.

(3) Ana está siempre enojada.
   'Ann is always angry.'

(4) Su hermano está loco, internado en un asilo desde su temprana infancia.
   'His brother is crazy, shut up in an asylum since his early childhood.'

The interpretation of these examples does not suggest that there has been a modification causing the described states; neither does it imply a future modification of such states. In fact, these predicates seem to be describing rather intrinsic characteristics of the individuals concerned.

The elusiveness of the notion utilized to discriminate a state is made conspicuous by the need to widen the extension of the original criterion so that it may include the mere possibility of change, i.e. a potential modification. According to Roldán (1974), the possibility of a change in the future is not entertained in (5a), but it is in (5b).

(5a) Jacinta es soltera.
'Jacinta is single.'
(5b) Jacinta está soltera.
'Jacinta is single.'

Notice that another interpretation would be noticeably more natural for (5b) as that of a state resulting from not having followed an expected course of events in the past, namely, *Jacinta no se ha casado aún* 'Jacinta has not yet married'. However, this proposition would be compatible with (5a) as well.[2]

But Roldán's characterization also leads to incorrect predictions. If it were true that the predicates in (5) differ in that only the second one implies the possibility of a change, then it should not be possible to expand them as in (6).

(6a) Jacinta es soltera, pero no lo será por mucho tiempo.
'Jacinta is single, but she will not be so for long.'
(6b) Jacinta está soltera, y se quedará soltera toda su vida.
'Jacinta is single, and she will remain so all her life.'

The definition in terms of states related to given or potential modifications would also determine that examples (7) and (8) are unacceptable, which they are not.

(7) Ana es joven.
'Ann is young.'

(8) La gente vieja es canosa.
'Old people are gray-haired.'

Obviously, these predicates denote qualities or states which must be associated with a future and inevitable modification in the first example, and with a change in the past in the second one. However, they are constructed with *ser*.

From the data so far examined, two important conclusions may be drawn. First, *ser* is not incompatible with the notion of change. Second, *estar* need not always be related to a given or potential modification. It follows, in consequence, that the notion of modification and the characterization of state based on that notion are insufficient to describe adequately the distribution and meaning of the copulative verbs.

An alternative to defining states is given by Ramsey (1956), who characterizes the use of a *ser*-predicate as equivalent to

expressing 'is of such a class', while equating the use of an
estar-predicate with expressing 'is in such condition or state'.
However, Querido (1976) argues that by opposing 'states' to
'classes' it is arbitrarily decided that accidental properties are
uninteresting. He claims that since all predicates are potential
classifiers, Ramsey's characterization does not allow establish-
ing 'states' as a disjoint set with respect to the set of properly
classifying predicates.

However, what is needed is the specification of *estar*-predi-
cates not as a disjoint class, but rather as an inclusive class
with respect to the other attributive predicates. Querido
(1976) claims that it is always possible to find contexts where
the terms normally used with *ser*, illustrated in (9), are acceptable with *estar*, as shown in (10).

(9) *Ser*-adjectives:

cauto 'cautious', discreto 'discreet', inteligente 'intelligent', prudente 'prudent', sabio 'wise', cortés 'polite',
capaz 'able', justo 'just', leal 'loyal', etc.

(10) $\begin{Bmatrix} \text{Estuvo} \\ \text{Era} \end{Bmatrix}$ indiscreto. 'He was indiscreet.'

By contrast, the terms that are restricted to *estar*, illustrated in (11), are, without exception, unacceptable with *ser*,
as shown in (12).

(11) *Estar*-adjectives:

vacío 'empty', lleno 'full', contento 'content', satisfecho
'satisfied', harto 'fed-up', ausente 'absent', descalzo
'bare-footed', desnudo 'naked', distante 'distant', solo
'alone', próximo 'next', etc.

(12) $\begin{Bmatrix} \text{Estuvo} \\ \text{*Era} \end{Bmatrix}$ vacío. 'It was empty.'

These data indicate that *ser* and *estar* are partially synonymous. This is an important aspect of the predicates bearing
these copulas which has been overlooked so far.

The partial synonymy may be observed in the context of
adjectives and participles: a predicate with *ser* and one such
term always implies a similar predicate with *estar*, as shown in
(13).

(13) es elegante → está elegante 'is elegant'
     eran firmados → estaban firmados 'were signed'

But the inverse implication does not hold.

(14) está elegante →→es elegante
estaban firmados →→eran firmados

The validity of the implicational relationship is demonstrated by (15a) and (15b). Observe that while (15a) expresses a true proposition, (15b) represents a false statement.

(15a) Ana está hermosa porque es hermosa. (True)
  'Ann is (looks) beautiful because she is beautiful.'
(15b) Ana es hermosa porque está hermosa. (False)
  'Ann is beautiful because she is (looks) beautiful.'

It is also demonstrated by the fact that example (16a) is perfectly interpretable, but (16b) is contradictory.

(16a) Raúl está muy delgado, pero no es muy delgado.
  'Raúl's (looks) very thin, but he's not very thin.'
(16b) *Raúl es muy delgado, pero no está muy delgado.
  'Raúl's very thin, but he's not very thin.'

All of the data confirm that the copulas are partially synonymous. It may be seen that *ser* is sufficient for *estar*, while *estar* is not sufficient but necessary for *ser*. [3] An adequate analysis must characterize this hyponymous relation, in addition to the difference indicated by the two copulas. Hence, the definitions that are limited to characterizing only their opposition cannot give an adequate account of the predicates bearing distinct copulative verbs.

2. **Perfective and imperfective states.** The shortcomings of previous analyses may be overcome by adopting the premise that all adjectives are stative, i.e. describe mental or physical states (Querido 1976). The differentiation is introduced by distinguishing perfective states from imperfective states. [4] A syntactic analysis may formally express this characterization by assuming that the adjectives, and more generally, the predicates that may appear with one or the other copula, have the lexical feature composition, as shown in (17). [5]

(17) ser - obeso   estar - obeso

$$
\begin{bmatrix}
+ \text{ Adjective} \\
\vdots \\
+ \text{ STATIVE} \\
- \text{ PERFECTIVE}
\end{bmatrix}
\qquad
\begin{bmatrix}
+ \text{ Adjective} \\
\vdots \\
+ \text{ STATIVE} \\
+ \text{ PERFECTIVE}
\end{bmatrix}
$$

In this analysis, the semantic features that distinguish the two types of predicates have the syntactic function of determining the form of the copulative verb. Thus, when the

adjectives are used to refer to imperfective states, they select
the copula *ser*; when they are used to refer to perfective
states, they select the copula *estar*.[6]

Here I propose that the semantic rules assign two distinct
interpretations to the two combinations of features characterizing the two types of states.   The semantic interpretation
corresponding to 'perfective state' is as in (18).[7]

(18) PERFECTIVE STATE:

[+ Adj, + STATIVE, + PERFECTIVE]: $X \in A$ at time t_k

This formula indicates that to predicate *estar* A of an individual X is to say that X is in the class of individuals bearing
the property A at a delimited period of time whose beginning
and end are both known or assumed.

The interpretation corresponding to 'imperfective state' is
as in (19).

(19) IMPERFECTIVE STATE:

[+ Adj, + STATIVE, - PERFECTIVE]: $X \in A$ at time
$t_{j-1} \cdots t_{n+1}$

This says that to predicate *ser* A of an entity X is equivalent
to expressing that X is in the class of entities bearing the
property A in a period of time whose beginning or end is not
assumed and which stretches over a number of delimited time
periods.   A time period here designates a relative space of
time of some duration (e.g. a moment, an occasion, etc.),
such that any portion of the time axis consists of a succession
of such periods which are represented here by t_j, t_k, t_1, ...,
t_{n+1}, and which are assumed to be linearly ordered.[8]

One may proceed to express the readings of (18) and (19)
more generally in terms of the predicate calculus, as shown in
what follows, and one may also speak of perfective and imperfective predicates, and thus include verbal predicates (Gili y
Gaya 1961).   Consider (18') and (19'), for example.

(18') PERFECTIVE PREDICATE

$A(x)$ at time t_k

Predicates illustrating this denotation are: *estar obeso* 'to be
obese', *saltar* 'to jump, *escribir una carta* 'to write a letter',
among others.

130 / Marta Luján

(19') IMPERFECTIVE PREDICATE:

$A(x)$ at time $t_{j-1} \cdots t_{n+1}$

Predicates bearing this denotation are: *ser obeso* 'to be obese', *escribir* 'to write', *admirar* 'to admire', etc.

From the interpretations proposed a valid inference may be drawn which describes the partial synonymy of attributive predicates with *ser/estar*.

(20) $A(x)$ at $t_{j-1} \cdots t_{n+1} \supset A(x)$ at $t_{j-1} \overset{\vee}{t_j} \overset{\vee}{t_k} \overset{\vee}{t_1} \cdots \overset{\vee}{t_{n+1}}$

This says that if a predicate A is true of an individual X during a stretch of time covering a number of distinct time periods or occasions, such as $t_{j-1} \cdots t_{n+1}$, then it is also true of X at some time period properly included in that stretch of time, such as t_{j-1}, or t_j, to t_k, or $t_1,\ldots$, or t_{n+1}. This correctly describes the data previously cited. Recall example (15a), showing that a *ser*-predicate is sufficient for a synonymous *estar*-predicate to be true.

By contrast, the inverse relation between those predicates is appropriately excluded, as shown in (21).

(21) $A(x)$ at $t_k \not\supset A(x)$ at $t_{j-1} \cdots t_{n+1}$

This indicates that if a predicate A holds true of an individual X at a particular time period, such as t_k, it does not follow that it also holds true for any stretch of time extending over and above t_k. The invalidity of the inference is supported by example (15b), which shows that a predicate with *estar* is not sufficient to establish the truth of the corresponding version with *ser*.

The valid inference of the form $p \supset q$ given in (20), where p represents a statement with a *ser*-predicate and q one with an *estar*-predicate, is equivalent to the disjunction of the consequent and the negation of the antecedent, as shown in (22).

  (22a) Si es obeso, está obeso o ha estado obeso. ($p \supset q$)
        'If he's obese, he is or has been obese.'
  (22b) No es obeso, o está o ha estado obeso. ($-p \overset{\vee}{} q$)
        'He's not obese, or he is or has been obese.'

The inference in (20) is also equivalent to the negation of the conjunction of the antecedent and the negation of the consequent, as shown in (23).

(23) No se puede ser obeso y $\begin{cases} \text{nunca estar obeso.} \quad -(p \wedge q) \\ \text{no estar ni haber estado obeso.} \end{cases}$

'One cannot be obese and $\begin{cases}\text{never be obese.'}\\\text{neither be nor have been obese.'}\end{cases}$

These inferences are all valid, as attested by the truth of
the illustrative examples, and they accord with the facts
pointed out previously in (15) and (16). In addition, example (23) illustrates the fact that the implication holding between the p statement and the q statement in (20) is falsified
if p is true and q is false. Given that q represents a disjunction of predicates, then it is false in case the conjunction
of these predicates is false, that is, when A is not true of X
at time t_{j-1}, and at t_j, and at t_k, and at $t_1,\ldots$, and so on--
in short, when it is not true at any time period of the stretch
of time represented by $t_{j-1}\ldots t_{n+1}$.

(24) $-A(x)$ at $t_{j-1} \overset{\wedge}{t_j} \overset{\wedge}{t_k} \overset{\wedge}{t_1} \ldots \overset{\wedge}{t_{n+1}}$

Thus, while (23) is true, a statement such as (25) is false.

(25) *Es obeso, pero nunca está obeso.
'He's obese, but he's never obese.'

However, the implication given in (20) is not invalidated if
one (or more) of the disjoint predicates is false. Hence (20)
also accounts for the lack of contradiction in (26).

(26) Ana es hermosa, aunque hoy no está hermosa.
'Ann is beautiful, even though today she's not
beautiful.'

The validity of the implication represented in (20) is upheld
by an additional argument. Assuming the validity of $p \supset q$,
if q is false, as in (24), then by modus tollens p must be
false too. The argument is borne out by (27), which contains
a true statement.

(27) Su trabajo nunca está mediocre, por consiguiente su
trabajo no es mediocre.
'His work has never been mediocre, hence his work
is not mediocre.'

The inference in (20) finds support in other facts of the
language. Thus, it may be seen that while in general ser-
predicates imply the existence of corresponding estar-predicates, the latter do not imply the existence of corresponding
ser-predicates. There are many estar-predicates that cannot
be used with ser.

(28) estar lleno 'to be full'   *ser lleno
     estar vacío 'to be empty'   *ser vacío
     estar angustiado 'to be anguished'   *ser angustiado
     estar enojado 'to be angry'   *ser enojado
     estar muerto 'to be dead'   *ser muerto
     estar desmayado 'to be unconscious'   *ser desmayado
     estar desnudo 'to be naked'   *ser desnudo
     estar descalzo 'to be bare-footed'   *ser descalzo
     estar ausente 'to be absent'   *ser ausente
     estar presente 'to be present'   *ser presente
     estar contento 'to be merry'   *ser contento
     estar perplejo 'to be perplexed'   *ser perplejo
     estar solo 'to be alone'   *ser solo

This state of affairs is consistent with the semantic relation
assumed to hold between *ser*- and *estar*-predicates.

There is another semantic relationship that is considerably
clarified and more adequately understood within the present
framework.   That is the one holding between certain *estar*-
predicates and certain verbs denoting actions or changes of
state.   It was seen in the preceding section that it is usually
assumed that the *estar*-predicates imply a preceding necessary
change or modification.   For instance, *está abierta* 'is open'
would imply *ha sido abierta* 'has been opened'.   In the present
framework, however, the claim is that the relationship holds in
the opposite direction rather, as (29) shows.

(29) ha sido abierta 'has been opened' → está abierta 'is open'
     se alegró 'became merry' → estuvo alegre 'was merry'

This direction of the implication is deducible from the present analysis, for every state resulting from the change of
state or the action denoted by one such verb necessarily presupposes a beginning, and must be conceived, consequently,
as a perfective state.   Thus, with respect to such verbs there
must be expressions in terms of perfective states that are
lexically related.   But the inverse relation, as assumed so far
in the literature, does not and need not hold.   That is, perfective states are not necessarily associated with changes of
states or actions.

(30) está abierta 'is open' ↛ ha sido abierta 'has been opened'
     estuvo alegre 'was merry' ↛ se alegró 'became merry'

All the arguments developed earlier are compatible with this
view, while it was also shown that the insufficiency of the
definitions on the basis of modification for *ser/estar* may be
traced to assuming precisely the opposite premise.

As predicted by the analysis, for every active verb produc-
ing a resulting state and for every stative verb denoting a

change of state there is an *estar*-predicate describing the resulting state by means of a lexically related adjective or past
participle. Examples are given in (31).

(31) Verbs: estar + Adjectives

    abrir 'to open'   estar abierto 'to be open'
    pintar 'to paint'   estar pintado 'to be painted'
    cortar 'to cut'   estar cortado 'to be cut'
    cansarse 'to get tired'   estar cansado 'to be tired'
    alegrar 'to make merry'   estar alegre 'to be merry'
    engordar 'to get fat'   estar gordo 'to be fat'
    ausentarse 'to leave'   estar ausente 'to be absent'

But the language has numerous *estar*-predicates with adjectives
describing perfective states for which there are no lexically
related (active or stative) verbs, as shown in (32).

(32) estar + Adjectives: Verbs:

    estar perplejo 'to be perplexed'   *perplejizarse
    estar solo 'to be alone'   *solitariarse
    estar delicioso 'to be delicious'   *adeliciarse
    estar listo 'to be ready'   *alistarse [9]
    estar obeso 'to be obese'   *obesidarse
    estar obsceno 'to be obscene'   *obscenizarse
    estar bonita 'to be pretty'   *bonitizarse
    estar soltera 'to be single'   *asolterarse
    estar sabroso 'to be savory'   *saborizarse
    estar feliz 'to be happy'   *afelizarse
    estar vivo 'to be alive'   *avivarse [9]
    estar maltrecho 'to be battered'   *maltrecharse
    estar contento 'to be merry'   *contentarse [9]

Demonte (1978) points out this lack of correspondence with
the adjectives *perplejo* 'perplexed' and *solo* 'alone', and describes it as a lacuna in the lexicon to be attributed to its
'typically idiosyncratic nature'. But such an interpretation of
the data follows from assuming that every state must be resultative, i.e. must result from a preceding action or modification. Since this is not assumed in the present analysis, the
absence of lexically related verbs for the adjectives of (32) is
a normal state of affairs, which is consistent with the assumption that perfective states do not imply preceding actions or
changes.

Moreover, that the verbs imply resulting states, and not
inversely, is demonstrated by an example such as (33); (33a)
is true while (33b) is false.

(33a) Había adelgazado haciendo dieta, por lo tanto estaba
      delgado. (True)
     'He had become thin dieting, hence he was thin.'

(33b) Estaba delgado, por lo tanto había adelgazado
haciendo dieta. (False)
'He was thin, hence he had become thin dieting.'

Notice that the falsity of (33b) is corroborated by the fact
that the *estar*-predicate may be overtly disassociated from the
related verb, as (34) illustrates.

(34) Estaba delgado, no porque hubiera adelgazado, sino
porque era delgado.
'He was thin, not because he had become thin, but
because he was (had always been) thin.'

In short, the semantic analysis here proposed accounts for
the partial synonymy of *ser*- and *estar*-predicates, while
effectively characterizing their truth conditions and their lexical relationship to other verbs in the language. The analysis
is also applicable to the lexical distinction between lexically
imperfective and perfective verbs (Gili y Gaya 1961). Moreover, it is basically the analysis that must be assumed for the
distinction falling under grammatical ASPECT, although this
study does not explore what the specifications must be of the
meanings of lexically perfective and imperfective predicates
when used with perfect and imperfect grammatical aspects.

3. **Additional arguments.** The proposed semantic analysis
throws light on several features of copulative predicates which
have until now remained unexplained. For instance, it is frequently noticed, as (35) shows, that *estar* is normally used
with locative predicates, while a class of examples like (36)
has become notorious for accepting either copula.

(35) Mi hermano $\begin{Bmatrix} está \\ *es \end{Bmatrix}$ en Buenos Aires.
'My brother is in Buenos Aires.'

(36) El baño $\begin{Bmatrix} está \\ es \end{Bmatrix}$ allí. 'The bathroom is there.'

In the present framework, this distribution of the copulas is
explained by the kind of entity with respect to which these
predicates are applied. Animate entities are not normally conceived as fixed in a spatial point. Consequently, a reference
in that sense requires presupposing a delimited time period.
Hence, the perfective copula is indicated for these predicates
when their subjects are animate, as in (35). Motionless inanimate entities, instead, may be viewed as fixed in a point
in space; in their case the reference need not be restricted
to a definite time period. Thus, the locative phrases may be
predicated of them with one or the other copula, as in (36).

The analysis also accounts for an observed feature concerning the meaning of a class of nouns, such as *discurso* 'speech', *conferencia* 'lecture', *concierto* 'concert', *sinfonía* 'symphony', and others. These terms are ambiguous and may denote either events or concrete objects. However, when they are constructed with a locative predicate, they refer to an event if the copula is *ser*, and they denote a concrete object if the copula is *estar*, as (37) shows.

(37) El discurso $\begin{Bmatrix} \text{era} \\ \text{estaba} \end{Bmatrix}$ allí.   'The speech was there.'

It was previously seen how concrete entities that are mobile and not characterized by a fixed position in space require the perfective copula to describe their location in space. Hence, this type of predicate must be compatible with those nouns in their reading as concrete objects. The imperfective predicate, by contrast, must be incompatible with such reading, according to this analysis. Such a predicate can only be compatible with their interpretation as events, for only in that meaning may they be characterized as occurring in a fixed spatial point.

The present analysis also accounts for the ability of *ser*- and *estar*-predicates to combine with different types of time adverbials. For instance, frequency adverbs and time adverbials which select definite or delimited periods in the time continuum, require a perfective predication and are incompatible with *ser*. Thus the adjectives *callada* 'quiet/silent' and *tímida* 'shy', which may be used with both copulas, are unacceptable with *ser* if constructed with frequency adverbs.

(38) $\begin{Bmatrix} \text{Estuvo} \\ \text{*Fue} \end{Bmatrix}$ callada tres veces.
'She was silent three times.'

(39) $\begin{Bmatrix} \text{Estuvo} \\ \text{*Fue} \end{Bmatrix}$ tímida varias veces.
'She was shy several times.'

In the present analysis this distribution follows from the interpretation of the frequency adverbs. They denote sets of occasions, i.e. delimited time periods; thus, they require the perfective copula.

Imperfective predicates are compatible with time adverbs that do not pick out a delimited time period, as shown in (40) and (41).

(40) Era callada antes.
'She was quiet before.'

(41) Era tímida cuando la conocimos.
'She was shy when we first met her.'

However, most time adverbs may denote a time period in its duration, as stretching indefinitely over numerous occasions, or they may refer, alternatively, to a delimited period in the time axis. Thus, the time adverbs of (40) and (41) are also compatible with the perfective copula, as in (42) and (43).

(42) Estuvo callada antes.
'She was quiet before.'

(43) Estuvo tímida cuando la conocimos.
'She was shy when we first met her.'

There is, however, a very noticeable meaning difference between the two sets of predicates. Their truth conditions are quite different. Notice that only one of them may be followed by the statement shown in (44).

(44a) Era callada antes. *No había dicho una sola palabra.
'She used to be quiet before. *She had not said one word.'
(44b) Estuvo callada antes. No había dicho una sola palabra.
'She was silent before. She had not said one word.'

The distribution of frequency adverbs and the two distinct interpretations of predicates bearing other time adverbs find a satisfactory explanation in the proposed analysis, thereby providing a strong supporting argument.

The analysis also predicts that the area of overlap of *ser* and *estar* must be larger than is generally supposed, so it cannot be true that 'except in two respects, they are in perfect complementary distribution' (Stockwell et al. 1965:170). For instance, it is commonly assumed that predicate sentences with sentential subjects are restricted to copula *ser* (Stockwell et al. 1965:257). However, *estar*-predicates should be acceptable with sentential subjects, since these, as other entities, may be conceived in terms of states specifiable in relation to a delimited time period. Example (45) bears out the prediction.

(45) $\begin{Bmatrix} \text{Está} \\ \text{*Es} \end{Bmatrix}$ bien claro que tú no sabes nada.
'It's quite clear that you know nothing.'

Again, it is also claimed that phrases denoting origin, ownership, material, or purpose of an entity must take *ser* but not *estar* in a predicate sentence. Observationally, this is generally true, but it is not always so, as shown by (46), where both copulas are acceptable.

(46) Esta toalla $\begin{Bmatrix} es \\ está \end{Bmatrix}$ para secar platos.
'This towel is for drying dishes.'

Besides adequately accounting for the distribution and interpretation of copulative predicates, the proposed analysis reflects the distinction between essential vs. accidental properties. The former correspond to those characteristics that individuals have over stretches of time covering a number of distinct occasions, while the latter correspond to those properties
that individuals may have at delimited time periods, i.e.
occasionally. Thus, rather than superseding the traditional
distinction, the analysis succeeds in incorporating it by giving
an explicit definition of the terms of the distinction. Likewise, it defines what the relationship is between perfective
predicates and those denoting actions or modifications. But
notice that these consequences are by-products of the analysis, since it does not require that perfective predicates be
resultative, nor does it prohibit imperfective predicates to
refer to resultant states.

That attributive predicates must be distinguished aspectually
is further corroborated by the existence of two types of
inchoative verbs. On the one hand, there are inchoative reflexive verbs that must be perfective, such as *ponerse* 'to
put', and *quedarse* 'to remain', for they are compatible with
perfective attributes, as in (47) and (48).

(47) Se puso contento al vernos.
'He became happy upon seeing us.'

(48) Nos quedamos solos todo el día.
'We remained alone all day.'

On the other hand, there are inchoative verbs that must be
imperfective, such as *volverse* 'to turn into' and *hacerse* 'to
be made into', for they must be combined with predicates displaying the same interpretation they have when they occur with
ser, as in (49) and (50).

(49) Se volvió muy pesimista.
'He turned into a great pessimist.'

(50) Nos hicimos ricos en poco tiempo.
'We were made rich in a short time.'

Thus, the existence of inchoative verbs denoting changes of
states for the imperfective predicates as well as for the perfective ones raises no problems. The definition of imperfective predicates as denoting properties characterizing individuals
over indefinite stretches of time also throws light on the semantic difference between the two types of inchoatives. It

seems clear that examples (49) and (50) denote a more radical kind of change undergone by the individuals concerned. That is, the inchoative verbs there denote a change of state with respect to the essential properties of the Aristotelian distinction. But the inchoatives in (47) and (48) must refer to changes of state with respect to accidental properties; thus, they are understood as involving superficial changes.

The semantic interpretation of the aspectual distinction imperfective/perfective finds an independent justification in the verb forms, which show two distinct endings for the past tense, e.g. *cantó/cantaba* 'sang'. The interpretation of these two forms of preterite requires a specification with respect to time period as proposed here for the attributive predicates. A rough approximation would be as in (51), where C stands for the predicate *cantar* 'to sing', t_0 represents the present time or time of utterance, and > indicates a precedence relation.

(51a) $C(x)$ at $t_k > t_0$

(51b) $C(x)$ at $t_{j-1} \ldots t_{n+1} > t_0$

It may be seen that (51a) corresponds to the interpretation of *cantó* as predicated of an individual X, while (51b) describes the interpretation of *cantaba*, the latter being ambiguous between the reading of a habitual action (equivalent to *solía cantar* 'used to sing') and that of an action in progress (equivalent to *estaba cantando* 'was singing').

The validity of these interpretations is corroborated by the fact that the inferences are parallel to the one described in relation to the copulas. The simple (perfective) and the imperfective preterites are also partially synonymous. The latter implies the former, but the inverse relation is not valid.

(52) IMPERF. S. PRET.   S. PRET. IMPERF.

cantaba	→ cantó	cantó	↛	cantaba	'sang'
hacía	→ hizo	hizo	↛	hacía	'made/did'
corría	→ corrió	corrió	↛	corría[10]	'ran'

Similarly, the distribution of some frequency adverbs is parallel, i.e. the perfective, but not the imperfective past readily combines with them.[11]

(53) $\begin{Bmatrix} \text{Cantó} \\ \text{*Cantaba} \end{Bmatrix}$ varias veces. 'She sang several times.'

Again, there are time adverbs that are compatible with both forms, although the resulting combinations are not semantically equivalent, as in (54).

(54a) Lo hacía cuando era pequeña.
     'She used to do it when she was small.'
(54b) Lo hizo cuando era pequeña.
     'She did it when she was small.'

The semantic difference in the sentences of (54) resides in the relative time periods denoted by the preterite forms. The imperfect refers to an undelimited (indefinite) period stretching over a number of different occasions, while the simple preterite denotes one particular occasion or delimited period. These data, then, show that the interpretation and the consequences of the proposed analysis are generalizable to other verbal forms, providing an account for the interpretation of time adverbs with perfect and imperfect tenses.

    4. **Adjectival participles.** Past participles may be constructed with both copulas. The participle combined with *ser* differs from that combined with *estar* in that the latter does not admit an agentive phrase.

(55a) La carta fue escrita por ella.
     'The letter was written by her.'
(55b) *La carta estuvo escrita por ella.
     'The letter was written by her.'

Bello has called these participles 'adjectival' to distinguish them from verbal participles occurring in perfect tenses with *haber* 'have'. Adjectival participles must agree in gender and number with the subject of which they are predicates, thus being characterized by their gender and number endings. The verbal participle, instead, always presents the invariable participial ending *-do/-to*. Moreover, the adjectival participles behave like adjectives in another respect; they may be modified by adverbs of degree or quantity (e.g. *muy* 'very'), which are clearly incompatible with a verbal participle.

    However, not all participles that may be constructed with a copula should be considered adjectives. To my mind, two classes of adjectival participles must be distinguished. One class includes participles like *escrit-* 'written'; the other consists of participles like *enojad-* 'annoyed'. Only the latter may be considered true adjectives, and are henceforth referred to as participial adjectives. The two types of participles behave differently in two important respects. First, while the participles like *escrit-* 'written' do not admit all types of adverbial modifiers, the participial adjectives like *enojad-* 'annoyed' may be modified by any kind of adverbs. Second, like true adjectives, the participles like *enojad-* 'annoyed' may occur as attributive modifiers in pre- and postnominal position. But the participles like *escrit-* 'written' are restricted to postnominal position and cannot occur prenominally.[12]

The participial adjectives are related to a class of reflexive inchoative verbs which denote changes of physical or mental states, and are restricted to *estar*.

(56) *Son angustiados por su culpa.
'They are anguished on his account.'
*Fue enojada por su hijo.
'She was annoyed by her son.'

The adjectival participles, for their part, may be constructed with either copula.

(57) La puerta está/fue abierta.
'The door is/was open(ed).'
La comida está/ha sido preparada.
'The meal is/has been prepared.'

However, not every participle may be included in the same class with *escrit-* 'written', for not every participle may function as an *estar*-predicate, as (58) shows.

(58) *El auto está manejado.
'The car is driven.'
*La sopa está tomada.
'The soup is eaten.'
*La pared está tocada.
'The wall is touched.'
*Sus valijas estuvieron traídas.
'His suitcases were brought.'
*Su cabeza estaba movida.
'His head was moved.'
*Las manos estuvieron dadas.
'Hands were shaken.'

Thus, two questions arise in connection with adjectival participles: why are participial adjectives like *enojad-* 'annoyed' restricted to *estar*? and which participles are in the same class as the adjectival participle *escrit-* 'written'? The answers to these questions require a close scrutiny of the semantic nature of the verbs involved.

The participial adjectives are related to verbs denoting changes of state, and like the verbs they are stative. But the reason why these participles and those like *escrit-* 'written' may combine with *estar* is that they must occur in perfective predicates. The verbs from which these two types of participles derive fall within the categories postulated by Vendler (1967) as 'accomplishments' (see (59)) and 'achievements' (see (60)).

(59) Accomplishments:

> escribir una carta 'to write a letter', preparar la cena 'to prepare dinner', abrir la puerta 'to open the door', correr una milla 'to run a mile', morirse 'to die', enojarse 'to get annoyed', prender la luz 'to turn on the light', etc.

(60) Achievements:

> ganar una carrera 'to win a race', detectar un error 'to detect a mistake', descubrir un tesoro 'to discover a treasure', sorprenderse 'to be surprised', alegrarse 'to be glad', asustarse 'to be frightened', etc.

Vendler (1967) contrasts these categories with 'activities' and 'states' by examining the time schemata required by the different types of predicates. He defines accomplishments and achievements as requiring or implying unique and definite time periods, while activities and states would involve periods of time that are nonunique and indefinite. The main criteria for determining the required time schemata lie in the types of time adverbs and questions involving temporal reference that make sense or are appropriate with the different predicates.

Vendler's classification is specially useful here because of the distinction he draws between accomplishments/achievements and activities such as *manejar el auto* 'to drive the car', *empujar la carreta* 'to push the cart', etc., whose past participles cannot occur with *estar*, as seen previously in (58). The unacceptable constructions of (58) would correspond to the activity predicates in (61).

(61) Majena el auto.   'He drives the car.'
     Tomó la sopa.   'She ate the soup.'
     Tocaron la pared.   'They touched the wall.'
     Trajeron sus valijas.   'They brought their suitcases.'
     Movía la cabeza.   'He was moving his head.'
     Se dieron la mano.   'They shook hands.'

The predicates in (61), unlike accomplishments and achievements, cannot be modified by a time adverbial indicating a unique or definite time period, such as the phrases introduced by *en* 'in'.

(62) *Maneja el auto en media hora.
     'He's driving the car in half an hour.'
     *Tocaron la pared en un instante.
     'They touched the wall in an instant.'
     *Movió la cabeza en toda la entrevista.
     'He moved his head in the whole interview.'

Nor does it make any sense to ask of the activities in (61) a question such as ¿*Cuánto tiempo le lleva/llevó, etc. ... hacer ...?* 'How long does/did it take ... to do so and so?', as shown in (63).

(63) *¿Cuánto tiempo les llevó tocar la pared?
'How long did it take them to touch the wall?'
*¿Cuánto tiempo le llevaba mover la cabeza?
'How long did it take him to move his head?'
*¿Cuánto tiempo les llevó darse la mano?
'How long did it take them to shake hands?'

By contrast, a question of that sort is appropriate about accomplishments or achievements, as shown in (64), just as it is appropriate to qualify them by means of a time adverb indicating a unique or definite time period, as in (65).

(64) ¿Cuánto tiempo le llevó escribir la carta? (Accomplishment)
'How long did it take her to write the letter?'
¿Cuánto tiempo te llevaba detectar un error?
(Achievement)
'How long did it take you to detect a mistake?'

(65) Escribió la carta en una hora.
'She wrote the letter in an hour.'
Detectabas un error en menos de un segundo.
'You detected a mistake in less than a second.'

It is precisely with the past participles corresponding to accomplishment and achievement predicates that the copula *estar* may be used.

The distribution of past participles with *estar* is explained by the aspectual nature of the predicates involved. Accomplishments and achievements, unlike activities, are perfective, denoting modifications or the coming about of states. They denote an activity or a process with a terminal phase. When the activity or process takes place, the direct object (in the case of a transitive verb like *escribir* 'to write') or the subject (in the case of an intransitive verb like *morir* 'to die') suffers a modification or comes into being--that is, it is found in a different state or condition. The related participial constructions require *estar* because they describe states whose beginning must be assumed.

By contrast, *manejar el auto* 'to drive the car', *empujar la carreta* 'to push the cart', *darse la mano* 'to shake hands', *traer cosas* 'to bring things', and so forth, generally denote activities with no terminus. Unlike accomplishments and achievements, these predicates hold true for any subinterval of the interval during which the activity they describe takes place: if it is true that 'Ann drove the car', then it is also true that she drove the car as soon as she started doing so. With a perfective predicate, instead, it does not follow that, for instance, if 'Mary wrote a letter', it is also true that 'Mary wrote the letter' as soon as she started doing it; the predicate is true only if it is completed. Hence, predicates like *manejar el auto* 'to drive the car' are imperfective and their participial constructions are incompatible with *estar*.

By adopting Vendler's semantic characterization, one may derive the required specifications for the perfective copula in the past participles of verbs such as *escribir* 'to write', *preparar* 'to prepare', *abrir* 'to open', and many others. Thus, the characterization as stative and perfective for their participles is predictable from the specifications characterizing accomplishments and achievements, in particular [+PERFEC-TIVE].[13] Given this specification in the complex symbol of the verb in a phrase marker, one only needs to postulate a lexical rule to replace in that complex symbol the feature [+ACTIVE] for [+STATIVE], when the verb is combined with the ending *-do* to form the past participle.

$$(66) \qquad [\text{+ACTIVE}] \rightarrow [\text{+STATIVE}] \; / \; \begin{bmatrix} \text{+V} \\ \text{+PERFECTIVE} \\ \underline{\hspace{3cm}} \end{bmatrix} \text{-do}$$

The participial adjectives like *enojad-* 'annoyed', *angustiad-* 'anguished', *satisfech-* 'satisfied' do not undergo this rule, since, besides being adjectives, they are also stative.[14] But their specification as [+PERFECTIVE] may be derived from the inchoative verbs to which they are lexically related.[15]

5. Conclusions. It has been shown here that traditional definitions in terms of undefined notions such as essential vs. accidental properties, modification and state, are insufficient to describe the use of the Spanish copulas. The choice of copula in a predicate sentence entails an aspectual distinction which is formally defined in the grammar by means of the feature [PERFECTIVE] and two distinct semantic interpretations assigned to the opposing values of the feature. *Estar*-predicates are perfective and must be interpreted as inherently referring to a delimited time period, i.e. a period of time whose beginning or end is assumed. *Ser*-predicates are imperfective in that their temporal reference involves an undelimited period of time covering a number of distinct occasions, i.e. a stretch of time with indefinite beginning and end. The formal definition of these two types of temporal reference was shown to characterize correctly the partial synonymy of the copulas, as well as the traditional dichotomy (essential vs. accidental) they are said to express. They also throw light into an apparent lexical gap and the relationship holding between

certain inchoative verbs and certain perfective predicates
bearing related participles or adjectives. In addition, the
analysis provides an account of previously unaccounted
structural and semantical features such as the distribution of
the copulas with past participles, locatives, frequency adverbs,
and time adverbials. It has also been seen that the semantic
definitions here proposed are applicable to the aspectual distinction observed in other verbal forms, such as the two
preterite tenses. Their distribution and interpretation, and
their combination with time adverbs, are consistent with the
analysis. What needs to be further investigated is the exact
nature of the combinations of perfect/imperfect grammatical
aspects with perfective/imperfective types of predicates.

NOTES

1. An earlier and slightly different version of this analysis
is presented in Chapter 1 of *Sintaxis y Semántica del Adjetivo*
(Luján 1979).
2. Roldán's choice of examples here is hardly felicitous, as
the predicate *estar soltera*, used nonfiguratively, pragmatically
implies *ser soltera* (see Note 3). And, given that the latter
always implies the former, the copulas in this context are
equivalent.
3. With some predicates *estar* is sufficient for *ser*.

```
está loco          → es loco 'is crazy'
está casado        → es casado 'is married'
está soltero       → es soltero 'is single'
está divorciado    → es divorciado 'is divorced'
```

4. In reviewing the Spanish attributive predicates with
distinct copulas, Comrie (1976) draws a distinction between
'contingent' and 'absolute' states corresponding to the use of
estar and *ser*, respectively. Thus, for Comrie all adjectives
refer to states.
5. My classification in terms of the features 'perfective'
and 'stative' is quite different from the one proposed by G.
Lakoff (1966). For a discussion of this point, see Luján
(1979).
6. For a discussion of the syntactic analysis, see Chapter 1
in Luján (1979).
7. In these, as in definitions (18') and (19'), I follow Gili y
Gaya's use of the terms 'perfective' and 'imperfective', which
does not conform to the general use. His distinction would
correspond very roughly to the 'durative' vs. 'punctual'
differentiation of traditional English grammar (see Comrie
1976). Since I agree with Gili y Gaya in equating this aspect
of the inherent meaning of lexical items with the meaning of
the grammatical distinction signalled by perfect and imperfect

tenses in Spanish, it is only appropriate to use the terminology reflecting this view. However, no confusion should arise since throughout the paper 'perfective/imperfective' are used to refer to the lexical content of the predicates, while 'perfect/imperfect' are used when referring to grammatical aspect.

8. As used here, the notion is different from the one standard in tense logic. In the latter, it refers to instants or moments in an absolute sense and obeying the axioms of density and continuity.

9. These verbs are in the language but not with the meaning related to the corresponding adjectival predicates of (32).

10. Since activities such as *cantar* 'to sing', *hacer* 'to do', and so on, have duration, their simple past implies the imperfect in its sense of action in progress. However, it does not imply the habitual action sense of the imperfect.

11. This restriction is not absolute. For instance, notice that *cantaba varias veces* could be rendered acceptable in the following context.

(i) Cantaba varias veces cuando se lo pedían.
   'She used to sing several times when she was asked.'

However, the interpretation of *varias veces* 'several times' in (i) differs quite sharply from the one in (53). In the context of perfect/imperfect preterites, the frequency adverbs behave like the rest of the time adverbs; their interpretation is determined by the tense of the verb with which they occur. Thus, in (i) the adverb refers to an indefinite number of occasions (open-end type of reading), while in (53) it refers to a definite number of occasions (close-end type of reading).

12. Morphologically, they are also like adjectives: they admit the superlative suffix -*ísimo* and they may serve as base for the formation of adverbs in -*mente* '-ly'. The modifiers that are exclusively postnominal do not share these morphological properties (Luján 1979).

13. The verbs themselves cannot be marked in the lexicon with this specification, for the same verb may be used to describe an accomplishment or an activity (e.g. *escribir* 'to write' with/without a direct object). However, the feature specification is predictable from the contextual features of the verb in a phrase marker, in particular, the occurrence of a direct object and the aspect in AUX.

14. In the case of the participial adjectives, their related verbs must be lexically marked as [+PERFECTIVE]. These change-of-state verbs are inchoative, and as such, they denote the initiation of a mental or physical state, and are incompatible with the sense of duration or incompletion (Luján 1977).

15. G. Lakoff (1965) has proposed a transformational derivation of inchoative verbs from structures containing predicate adjectives. Roldán (1970, 1971) has developed such an

analysis for Spanish reflexive verbs. However, it can be demonstrated that the analysis is untenable (Luján 1977). A transformational derivation of the *estar* + past participle constructions from structures with the reflexive verbs is also untenable (Luján 1979).

THE CASE FOR BASE-GENERATED ATTRIBUTIVE ADJECTIVES IN SPANISH

Heles Contreras
University of Washington

Chomsky's (1957:72) original hypothesis that English attributive adjectives derive from predicative adjectives through a Relative Clause Reduction transformation went unchallenged for several years. Although no arguments were given by him in favor of this derivation, other than the statement that 'it is not difficult to show that this transformation simplifies the grammar considerably', its correctness was deemed to be so obvious that Smith (1964), in her analysis of determiners and relative clauses in English, did not see any need to provide further justification and limited herself to the explicit formulation of the relevant rules; later, Bach (1968), in his paper on nouns and noun phrases, simply stated that 'there are numerous reasons for deriving most attributive adjectives from underlying relative clauses (93)', without further elaboration.

Nontransformationalists, of course, disagreed. Winter (1965),[1] for instance, questioned the validity of Chomsky's proposal on the basis of the fact that many Adj+N phrases have no corresponding sentences and vice versa, e.g. *a criminal court/*the court is criminal; the boy is ill/*the ill boy*; but his criticism was summarily dismissed (see Bach 1968:102n) as nothing more than an enumeration of exceptions which did not invalidate the rule. True enough, Winter did not propose an alternative theory, but in retrospect his listing of exceptions was far more damaging to the transformational theory than transformationalists were willing to accept.

It is not until the publication of Chomsky's (1970) seminal paper on nominalizations that an alternative explanation is given serious consideration in transformational circles. Thus, Jackendoff (1972:59-62), on the basis of the distributional parallelism between adjectives and adverbs, suggests that at least some attributive adjectives are base-generated in English.

In his view, however, the Relative Clause Reduction rule is still needed to derive phrases like *the sleeping child*. Basically the same position is presented in Emonds (1976:169ff.).

Given the wide acceptance of the transformational analysis of attributive adjectives in English, it should come as no surprise that a similar analysis for Spanish has gone practically unquestioned among transformationalists, although other explanations do exist. Typically, these alternative explanations, e.g. Bull (1954) and Ringo (1954), tend to be dismissed by transformationalists either as simple taxonomies or as lacking in explicitness.

The case for the transformational derivation of Spanish attributive adjectives has been made by Cressey (1966) and Luján (1972). The latter in particular has the great merit of containing a number of explicit arguments in support of the analysis proposed. [2]

In this paper, I intend to show that the transformational analysis is incorrect for all attributive adjectives, which must instead be base-generated.

I first argue against the specific claims made in Luján (1972), and then against the transformational derivation of attributive adjectives in general.

Finally, I suggest an alternative analysis where attributive adjectives are base-generated as constituents of the Noun Phrase.

Luján's analysis of Spanish attributive adjectives, with roots in Bello (1847) and even the Port Royal grammarians (see A. Arnaud and P. Nicole 1662), claims that N+Adj and Adj+N phrases derive from restrictive and appositive clauses, respectively. She goes beyond the classical theory, however, by claiming that, in addition, there are N+Adj phrases, with an intonational break between the two constituents, which derive from appositive clauses, and Adj+N phrases, with contrastive stress on the adjective, which derive from restrictive clauses. Thus, under this analysis, sentences (1) and (2) derive from restrictive clauses, and (3) and (4) derive from appositive clauses.

(1) Tengo un libro interesantísimo.

(2) Tengo un interesantísimo libro.
   'I have a most interesting book.'

(3) Las mansas ovejas dormían plácidamente.
   'The meek sheep slept placidly.'

(4) Las ovejas, mansas por naturaleza, dormían plácidamente.
   'The sheep, meek by nature, slept placidly.'

The basic argument offered in support of this analysis rests on the correspondence between postnominal adjectives and restrictive clauses, on the one hand, and prenominal adjectives and appositive clauses, on the other. This correspondence is illustrated by examples (5)-(7), which are grammatical with restrictive clauses and postnominal adjectives, but ungrammatical with appositive clauses and prenominal adjectives.

(5a) Conozco a alguien feliz.
     'I know someone happy.'
(5b) Conozco a alguien que es feliz.
     'I know someone who is happy.'
(5c) *Conozco a feliz alguien.
(5d) *Conozco a alguien, que es feliz.

(6a) ¿Qué mujer hermosa no es vanidosa?
     'What beautiful woman is not vain?'
(6b) ¿Qué mujer que es hermosa no es vanidosa?
     'What woman who is beautiful is not vain?'
(6c) *¿Qué hermosa mujer no es vanidosa?
(6d) *¿Qué mujer, que es hermosa, no es vanidosa?

(7a) Carecemos de una solución apropiada.
     'We lack an appropriate solution.'
(7b) Carecemos de una solución que sea apropiada.
     'We lack a solution which is appropriate.'
(7c) *Carecemos de una apropiada solución.
(7d) *Carecemos de una solución, que sea apropiada.

First, it is noticed that the argument does not in fact support the theory proposed, where both appositive and restrictive adjectives may surface either pre- or postnominally, but rather the original proposal implicit in Bello's analysis, where restrictive adjectives are always postnominal and appositive adjectives always prenominal. Since Luján has rejected this simple correspondence, the relevance of the argument to her analysis is not clear.

Second, the argument fails to support Bello's theory in any event, because the correspondences on which it is based are considerably less than perfect. Thus, classificatory adjectives like *nacional* 'national', *francés* 'French', *socialista* 'socialist', etc. occur freely in appositive clauses but not in prenominal attributive position, as shown in (8).

(8a) Este producto, que es nacional, es de muy buena calidad.
     'This product, which is national, is of high quality.'
(8b) *Este nacional producto es de muy buena calidad.

On the other hand, adjectives like *pobre* 'pitiful' occur only
prenominally and not in appositive clauses, nor in the predicate position of any clause.

(9a) El pobre hombre no sabía qué hacer.
'The poor man didn't know what to do.'
(9b) *El hombre, que era pobre, no sabía qué hacer.[3]

Third, some noun phrases containing a noun and a prepositional phrase which are incompatible with restrictive clauses
accept attributive adjectives quite readily, as shown in (10)
and (11).

(10a) ...en la mano derecha del anillo presidencial
(García Márquez 1975:77)
'...on the right hand with the presidential ring'
(10b) *...en la mano que era derecha del anillo presidencial

(11a) (fue servido en mesa de gala) el cadáver exquisito
del general Rodrigo de Aguilar (García Márquez
1975:134)
'the exquisite corpse of general Rodrigo de Aguilar
(was served on a banquet table)'
(11b) *...el cadáver que era exquisito del general...

In these noun phrases, the noun plus the prepositional
phrase identify an object uniquely. Consequently, no restrictive clause is allowed, for the same reason that restrictive
clauses do not follow proper names. However, an attributive
adjective is perfectly acceptable. It could be argued that the
adjective in these sentences derives from an appositive clause.
Such a derivation would have some plausibility for (11a), but
none for (10a), given the ungrammaticality of the putative
source (12).

(12) *la mano del anillo presidencial, que era derecha...
'the hand with the presidential ring, which was right...'

Under this assumption, (10a) would have to derive from (13),
with a richer transformational apparatus than would be necessary if a source like (12) were available, and, most significantly, with the adjective *derecha* in attributive position within
the appositive clause.

(13) la mano del anillo presidencial, que era la mano derecha

Finally, one notices that this theory makes the wrong predictions. If the restrictive vs. appositive interpretation of
attributive adjectives depended on their position with respect
to the noun, one would expect this difference to be reflected
somehow in those pairs of adjectives which have different

meanings associated with pre- and postnominal position, e.g. *antiguo* 'former' and 'old', *nuevo* 'new' and 'young', *pobre* 'unfortunate' and 'indigent'. In none of these cases does the semantic difference have anything to do with the contrast appositive vs. restrictive. It is true that for those adjectives that do not change meaning and which can occur both before and after the noun, the postnominal position is often associated with a restrictive meaning. But this is only so because postnominal adjectives often occupy the focus position, that is, the position reserved for new information, as in (14).

(14) Quiero una casa grande (no una pequeña).
'I want a big house (not a small one).'

If the focus is shifted to another constituent, say a prepositional phrase, the adjective no longer has a restrictive interpretation, and it can be shifted to prenominal position with no appreciable change in meaning. Thus, (11a) is interchangeable with (15), and the adjective *exquisito* in no way 'restricts' the meaning of the noun.

(15) ...el exquisito cadáver del general Rodrigo de Aguilar

The problems associated with the analysis under consideration can best be appreciated by considering the actual transformations posited and the exception mechanisms which must be invoked when the correspondence between clauses and attributive adjectives fails. The relevant rules are the following.

(A) Appositive Clause Formation

This rule, which we need not state formally, converts a conjoined sentence into a structure like (16).

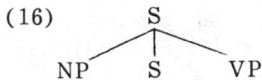

(16)

```
              S
          /  |  \
       NP   S   VP
```

(B) Relative Clause Formation

An updated version of this rule along the lines suggested by Chomsky (1977) would move a WH-phrase into the COMP position of the embedded sentence both in a structure like (16) and in a restrictive clause.

(C) Relative Clause Reduction

Luján formulates this rule as follows:

X - +REL - Y - AP - Z

1   2   3   4   5 ===> 1 ∅ ∅ 4 5

where 1 is not an S,
2-3-4 is an S with an empty
V node, and 3 contains
no Negative, Modal, or Past[4]

Finally, there are two Adjective Preposing rules, both optional: one that preposes simple adjectives, and one that preposes adjective phrases containing a contrastively stressed element, given here as (D) and (E).

(D) Simple Adjective Preposing

W - X - N - Y - A - Z

1   2   3   4   5   6 ===> 1 2 5+3 4 ∅ 6

where 2-3-4 is an NP of
which 3 is the head and
where 5 is an AP, and 5-6
do not form a constituent.

(E) Contrastive Adjective Phrase Preposing

W - X - N - Y - AP - Z

1   2   3   4   5   6 ===> 1 2 5+3 4 ∅ 6

where 2-3-4-5 is an NP of
which 3 is the head, 5 is
[+CONTRASTIVE], and the head
of 5 is rightmost in 5.

It is apparent that these rules are fairly complex and greatly exceed the restrictions imposed by Chomsky (1976) on transformations. This fact in itself should cast some doubt on the validity of the analysis proposed. But the complexity does not stop here. Various additional mechanisms are needed to account for the lack of correspondence between clauses and attributive adjectives. Thus, classificatory adjectives like *nacional* 'national', *francés* 'French', etc., which occur freely in clauses and in postnominal attributive position but are never prenominal, must be marked as negative exceptions (in the sense defined in Lakoff 1970) to both rules (D) and (E).

It is not clear how adjectives like *pobre* 'unfortunate' would be treated under this analysis, but if *pobre* is allowed to occur in predicative position, it has to be marked as a positive exception to both rules (D) and (E). Some items, then, are negative exceptions, and some are positive exceptions to rules (D) and (E). If these are two independent rules, as Luján argues, one would expect to find exceptions to one of them, not the other. This is not the case, however, and one is led to suspect that there is only one Adjective Preposing rule, if any. But, of course, such a conclusion would be damaging to an analysis which is predicated on the correspondence between restrictive clauses and postnominal adjectives, and between appositive clauses and prenominal adjectives.

Next, consider how the analysis in question would deal with items like (10) and (11). Example (10a) could be generated by marking the adjective *derecha* 'right' as a positive exception to Relative Clause Reduction. It would also have to be marked as a negative exception to Adjective Preposing to block ungrammatical strings like *la derecha mano*. This, of course, does not involve anything new. If there are going to be exception features, one more or less makes no big difference. However, the case of (11) is different. Notice that (11b) is ungrammatical only because the NP *el cadáver del general Rodrigo de Aguilar* 'the corpse of general Rodrigo de Aguilar' identifies a unique object. The difference between (11a) and (11b) cannot be accounted for simply by putting a feature on the adjective *exquisito* 'exquisite', since if the noun plus the prepositional phrase fail to identify an object uniquely, a restrictive clause including *exquisito* is perfectly acceptable.

(17a) Comí un pastel exquisito de almendras.
'I ate a delicious almond pastry.'
(17b) Comí un pastel de almendras que era exquisito.
'I ate an almond pastry which was delicious.'[5]

Consequently, the mechanism that would block (11b) while allowing (11a) would have to make the application of Relative Clause Reduction contingent upon uniqueness versus nonuniqueness of reference, a state of affairs which must certainly be made impossible under any reasonably restrictive theory of transformational grammar.

Finally, consider the problem posed by sentences like (18), which Luján (1974) derives from (19).

(18) Es un estupendo estudiante.
'He is a magnificent student.'

(19) Es estupendo siendo estudiante.
'He is magnificent being a student.'

Regardless of the plausibility of this analysis,[6] unless it is assumed that (18) is ambiguous--a claim which would be hard to defend--we must prevent it from deriving from an appositive or a restrictive clause. But how is this to be done? Certainly we do not want to ban *estupendo* from

restrictive clauses in general, nor do we want it to be an
exception to Relative Clause Reduction and Adjective Preposing, since under this analysis sentences (20a-c) should certainly come from the same source.

(20a) Tengo un estudiante que es estupendo.
　　　 'I have a student who is magnificent.'
(20b) Tengo un estudiante estupendo.
　　　 'I have a magnificent student.'
(20c) Tengo un estupendo estudiante.
　　　 (same as (20b))

Nor do we want to ban *estupendo* from the restrictive clause
of a predicate nominal--which would allow (20a) while banning
a similar source for (18)--since this would block perfectly
good sentences like those in (21).

(21a) Es una casa que es estupenda.
　　　 'It is a house which is magnificent.'
(21b) Es una casa estupenda.
　　　 'It is a magnificent house.'

It appears, then, that Luján's grammar has to generate
(18) from a relative clause regardless of whether it is also
generated from a different source. Since (18) is not ambiguous, this is an unfortunate consequence.

In conclusion, once this analysis is made explicit it is not
clear how it solves the problems it purports to solve. It is
also clear that it entails considerable complexity in the lexicon,
and an extension of the power of transformations far beyond
the limits which are considered tolerable.

Even admitting the inadequacy of Luján's analysis, one could
still argue in favor of a different transformational analysis of
attributive adjectives. I maintain that any such analysis is
bound to be inadequate. This claim is based on the following
arguments.

1. The crucial argument in favor of the transformational
analysis, based on the identical selectional restrictions of
attributive and predicative adjectives, and illustrated in (22),
is far less persuasive now that we have an enriched conception of the lexicon, as suggested by Chomsky (1970) and
elaborated by Hust (1976), among others.

(22a) *Es un problema que es rojo.
　　　 'It is a problem which is red.'
(22b) *Es un problema rojo.
　　　 'It is a red problem.'
(22c) Es un problema que es difícil.
　　　 'It is a problem which is difficult.'

(22d) Es un problema difícil.
'It is a difficult problem.'

2. The transformation essentially responsible for the
derivation in question, Relative Clause Reduction, should
probably be considered ill formed, since it deletes an arbitrary string, not a constituent.

3. There are attributive adjectives for which no reasonable
predicative source exists. If they are to be base-generated,
semantic interpretation rules will be needed anyhow, which
could apply to the rest of the adjectives without much additional complexity. Some representative examples are found in
(23).

(23a) el presunto asesino
      'the alleged murderer'
(23b) el futuro rey de España
      'the future king of Spain'
(23c) el probable origen del lenguaje
      'the probable origin of language'
(23d) un obrero metalúrgico
      'a metallurgical worker'
(23e) un visitante ocasional
      'an occasional visitor'
(23f) un constructor civil
      'a civil engineer'
(23g) una feliz coincidencia
      'a happy coincidence'
(23h) el pensamiento gramatical de Bello
      'the grammatical thought of Bello'

4. Any transformational analysis will involve the kinds of
complicated exception features discussed in connection with
Luján's analysis.

5. Finally, there is some evidence based on language acquisition suggesting that it is unlikely that children learn a rule
which derives attributive adjectives from relative clauses.
They use attributive adjectives before they are able to embed
sentences, and there is no evidence that their derivation of
attributive adjectives changes when they learn to form relative clauses (see Maratsos 1978). The studies in question are
based on English speakers, but it is reasonable to assume that
the same is true of Spanish-speaking children.
In summary, the transformational derivation of attributive
adjectives must be rejected for the following reasons: (a) it
involves a theoretically objectionable rule, Relative Clause
Reduction; (b) it requires extremely powerful exception devices; (c) it cannot account for attributive adjectives

uniformly, since for some of them there is no reasonable
transformational source; (d) it is not supported by language
acquisition data.

I now propose an alternative analysis of attributive adjectives. The first question to be answered refers to the form
of the Phrase Structure rule responsible for the introduction
of attributive adjectives. I propose Rule (24).

(24) NP → (DET) (AP) N (AP) (PP)

Given this rule, adjectives may be subclassified according
to whether they can occur before or after the noun or in both
positions. We thus have the representative subcategorizations
in (25).

(25a) pobre 'unfortunate'   +[___N]
(25b) nacional 'national'   +[N___]
(25c) magnífico 'magnificent' +[N___], +[___N]

For adjectives like *antiguo, nuevo*, etc., which have a
different interpretation depending on their position, each subcategorization feature is associated with a different set of
semantic features.

In addition to the positions specified by Rule (24), Adjective Phrases may follow the Prepositional Phrase, as in (26).

(26a) ...un inválido de palacio incapaz de concebir una
      orden (García Márquez 1975:101)
      '...a palace invalid incapable of conceiving of an
      order'
(26b) su mano de sirena endurecida de rabia (García Márquez
      1975:73)
      'her mermaid hand hardened with rage'

Since any postnominal adjective may also occur in this position, and since the Adjective Phrases which are found here
are normally 'heavy', one may assume that a transformational
rule which moves heavy constituents to the right is responsible
for phrases like (26).[7] Consequently, Rule (24) need not be
modified to accommodate phrases of this sort.

The next question is how to express similarity of selectional
restrictions between attributive and predicative adjectives in
this model. The conception of the lexicon developed in Hust
(1976) makes it possible to express this kind of relationship in
a straightforward way. Under this theory, lexical entries are
in the form of branching diagrams, where the top node contains all features common to all the different meanings of the
word, and every other node is associated with sets of features
which characterize a particular reading of the word. By way
of illustration, I show what the entry for *antiguo* would look

like. As is known, this adjective means 'former' in prenominal position, and 'old' in postnominal position. Furthermore,
when it is used in the predicate it means 'old'. With the meaning 'former', it can be associated with animate or inanimate
nouns, but with the meaning 'old', it only combines with inanimate nouns. These facts are illustrated in (27).

(27a) Vi a mi antiguo maestro.
     'I saw my former teacher.'
(27b) Este es un edificio antiguo.
     'This is an old building.'
(27c) Este edificio es antiguo.
     'This building is old.'
(27d) Esa es mi antigua casa.
     'That is my former house.'
(27e) *Mi maestro es antiguo.
     'My teacher is old.'
(27f) *Ese es mi maestro antiguo.
     'That is my old teacher.'

These facts can be accounted for by assuming a lexical
entry like (28).

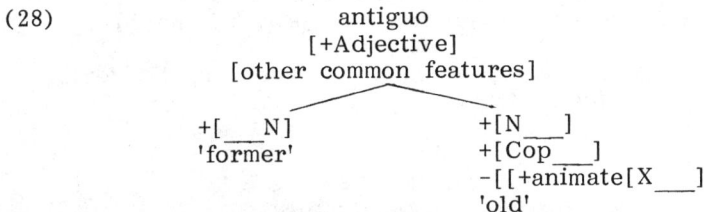

(28)
$$
\begin{array}{c}
\text{antiguo} \\
\text{[+Adjective]} \\
\text{[other common features]}
\end{array}
$$

+[___N]	+[N___]
'former'	+[Cop___]
	-[[+animate[X___]
	'old'

The leftmost node contains the subcategorization feature
+[___N] and the semantic features which give the adjective
the meaning 'former'. It has no selectional features, so it
can occur with an animate or an inanimate noun, as in (27a)
and (27d), respectively. The rightmost node allows the adjective to occur either postnominally or in the predicate. Its
semantic features give it the reading 'old', and the selectional
feature -[[+animate]X___] prevents it from occurring in structures like (27e) or (27f).

Let us consider one more example. The adjective *aburrido*
may mean either 'boring' or 'bored'. Let us call these meanings 'active' and 'passive', respectively. The active meaning
is compatible with both pre- and postnominal position and with
both copulas, *ser* and *estar*. It may be associated with either
an animate or an inanimate noun. It is incompatible, however,
with the copula *estar* when it is followed by a prepositional
phrase. These facts are illustrated in (29).

(29a) mi aburrido amigo
'my boring friend'
(29b) mi amigo aburrido
'my boring (or bored) friend'
(29c) mi amigo es/está aburrido
'my friend is boring'
(29d) la película es/está aburrida
'the movie is boring'
(29e) mi amigo está aburrido de estudiar ≠ my friend is
boring of studying

On the other hand, the passive meaning is compatible with
a preceding but not with a following noun, with the copula
estar but not with *ser*, and with a following prepositional
phrase, and it can only be associated with an animate noun.
These facts are illustrated in (30).

(30a) mi amigo aburrido
'my bored (or boring) friend'
(30b) mi aburrido amigo ≠ my bored friend
(30c) mi amigo está aburrido de estudiar
'my friend is bored with studying'
(30d) la película aburrida ≠ the bored movie
(30e) la película está aburrida ≠ the movie is bored

These facts can be accounted for by assuming the lexical
entry for *aburrido* in (31).

(31)   aburrido [8]
                          [+Adjective]
                     [other common features]

+[___N]   +[N___]
+[N___]   +[estar___]
+[Cop___]   +[___PP]
'active'   −[[−animate]X___]
                                 'passive'

It should be clear, on the basis of these examples, that
Hust's conception of the lexicon makes it unnecessary to relate
predicative and attributive adjectives by means of transformations. In fact, the lexical entries of the type illustrated
here account for everything the transformational approach
accounts for and more, and does so without recourse to powerful exception features or complex conditions on transformations.
But there is more to the analysis of adjectives than the
assignment of the correct subcategorization and selectional
features. The grammar must include a number of semantic
interpretation rules to account for the different ways in which
adjectives relate to nouns. Limitations of space prevent me

from dealing with more than one of these aspects.[9] I discuss the semantic rules which assign constituency to noun phrases which, in addition to the noun and the determiner, include an adjective phrase and a prepositional phrase. I assume, following Chomsky and Lasnik (1977:431), that these semantic rules apply to surface structures, as defined by them, that is, structures prior to deletion.

The need for semantic rules assigning constituency--one may call them semantic bracketing rules--is demonstrated by examples like (32).

> (32a) los concursos anuales de reinas de la belleza
> (García Márquez 1975:40)
> 'the annual beauty queen contests'
> (32b) los juegos florales de marzo (García Márquez 1975:40)
> 'the March flower festivities'

There is no motivation for assigning to these two phrases a different syntactic constituent structure. Yet semantically, (32a) requires an interpretation where *anuales* is a more peripheral modifier than the prepositional phrase *de reinas de la belleza*, whereas (32b) must be interpreted as having the prepositional phrase *de marzo* as a more peripheral modifier than the adjective *florales*. The semantic component must then provide two different bracketings for noun phrases of this type, namely (33a) and (33b).

> (33a) ((N PP) AP)
> (33b) ((N AP) PP)

In addition to (32a), the phrases in (34) would seem to require bracketing (33a).

> (34a) el escrutinio meticuloso de la casa (García Márquez
> 1975:48)
> 'the careful search of the house'
> (34b) la complacencia callada de la guardia (ibid.:32)
> 'the silent complacency of the guard'
> (34c) la mirada escuálida de los sietemesinos (ibid.:12)
> 'the lean look of the premature children'

In addition to (32b), the phrases in (35) would seem to require bracketing (33b).

> (35a) las campanas maestras de la catedral (ibid.:31)
> 'the main bells of the cathedral'
> (35b) un hombre medio de nuestro tiempo (ibid.:49)
> 'an average man of our time'
> (35c) la razón última de su ansiedad (ibid.:23)
> 'the ultimate reason for his anxiety'

There also seem to be some phrases that require the bracketing indicated in (36).

(36) N((AP) (PP))

This is illustrated in (37).

(37a) paredes descascaradas de color amarillo (ibid.:76)
      'pealing yellow walls'
(37b) unos hombres pálidos de levitas grises (ibid.:94)
      'some pale men with grey tuxedos'

These phrases, unlike the ones in (34) and (35), allow the
conjunction y 'and' between the adjective phrase and the prepositional phrase, which indicates that neither is subordinate to
the other.

It is an open question whether these semantic bracketing
rules operate freely or whether they are sensitive to semantic
information. Under the first alternative, many phrases would
be assigned the wrong bracketing, and the grammar would
have to be supplemented with some kind of filter to weed them
out. Under the second alternative, no wrong bracketing would
be assigned. Whether the relevant information is available to
the semantic bracketing rules or is built into the filters, it is
clear that it must be highly specific and that its function is to
determine degrees of semantic closeness between constituents.
Much more must be learned about semantics and the structure
of the grammar before we can make more precise claims about
these matters.

It appears that some noun phrases must be assigned more
than one semantic bracketing. Thus, phrase (38) is treated
as a case of (33a) in sentence (39), and as a case of (33b)
in sentence (40).

(38) el pensamiento gramatical de Bello
     'Bello's grammatical thought'

(39) El pensamiento gramatical de Bello es más interesante
     que su pensamiento político.
     'Bello's grammatical thought is more interesting than
     his political thought.'

(40) El pensamiento gramatical de Bello es más interesante
     que el de Cuervo.
     'Bello's grammatical thought is more interesting than
     Cuervo's.'

In contrast with N AP PP sequences, which admit more than
one semantic bracketing, it appears that AP N PP phrases
allow only the bracketing shown in (33a). Evidence for this
claim comes from sentences like those in (41).

(41a) Un buen trago de cognac es mejor que uno malo.
(deleted trago de cognac, not buen trago)[10]
'A good shot of cognac is better than a bad one.'
(41b) Un buen trago de cognac es mejor que uno de pisco.
(deleted trago, not buen trago)
'A good shot of cognac is better than one of pisco.'

An N AP PP sequence with heavy stress on the AP must also be bracketed as in (33a), as shown in (42).

(42a) los tiempos heróicos de la casa
'the heroic times of the house'
(42b) los lugares solitarios de la casa
'the empty areas of the house'

Finally, a superlative, whether pre- or postnominal, always requires the bracketing in (43).

(43) N (AP PP)

Examples are those in (44).

(44a) el mejor calígrafo de la nación
'the best calligrapher in the nation'
(44b) el hombre más viejo de la tierra
'the oldest man on earth'

The preceding remarks are a very rough attempt to characterize one type of semantic interpretation rule affecting attributive adjectives. I hope, however, that these highly tentative remarks prove useful in identifying an area of significant research.

In conclusion, I have shown that the transformational derivation of attributive adjectives is inadequate for a variety of reasons. I have also indicated how a base-generated analysis can account for their syntactic and semantic behavior. Crucial to this analysis are an enriched view of the lexicon modeled after Hust (1976) and some rules of semantic interpretation which specify how the adjective relates to its sister constituents.

NOTES

1. See also Bolinger (1967) for a strong case against the transformational derivation of attributive adjectives.
2. In this respect, Luján's work offers a refreshing contrast to the English references I have cited as well as to works like Hadlich (1971), which assume the correctness of the transformational derivation without supporting arguments.
3. This sentence is grammatical, of course, but with a different meaning for *pobre* than the one intended.

4. The requirement that the V node be empty is meant to prevent excessive ambiguity in the grammar, since if an actual verb were deleted, it could be either *ser* or *estar*.

5. Notice, indicentally, that this pair of sentences suggests the need of yet another rule which would move the adjective from its underlying position in (17b) to that in (17a).

6. There are, in fact, serious objections to this analysis. First, it requires two transformations which are theoretically objectionable: one that deletes the gerund formative plus *ser*, that is, a nonconstituent, and one that inserts the indefinite article, thereby creating new structure. Second, it must assume some ungrammatical sources; for example, *Es una feliz coincidencia* must come from **Es feliz siendo coincidencia*. Finally, it assigns incorrect derived structures. For instance, structure (i) becomes (ii) after the application of the relevant transformations, and the phrase *un estupendo estudiante* ends up being a nonconstituent.

(i)
```
                    S
          _____/ _____
        NP                   VP
        |           _____/ _____
       Juan        V    Adj          Manner
                   |     |          __/ \__
                   es estupendo   -ndo  V      NP
                                        |       |
                                       ser   estudiante
```

(ii)
```
                    S
          _____/ _____
        NP                   VP
        |         ___/  |  |  \___
       Juan      V    ?   Adj    Manner
                 |    |    |        |
                 es  un estupendo  NP
                                    |
                               estudiante
```

7. I suspect that a nonlinear structure of the type proposed by daughter-dependency grammarians (see Hudson 1976) is more adequate than a PS rule like (24), and that matters of linear order must be treated independently from matters of constituency. I keep the PS formulation, however, because it makes comparison with the transformational analysis easier.

8. This is simplified for the purpose of exposition. Actually, it is a subentry which in a real lexicon would be combined with the entry for the verb *aburrir* 'to bore'.

9. Other semantic interpretation rules deal with various matters which have been discussed in the literature. One of them is the question of reference. Under what conditions does

the adjective refer to a proper subset of the class designated by the noun? The relevant rules are probably very complex, and involve notions like specificity and definiteness. For some relevant observations, see Bull (1954).

A second problem refers to what Vendler (1968) has called 'transferable' vs. 'nontransferable' adjectives. Thus, *a good thief* is probably a bad citizen, but *a white house* is a white object. For different approaches to this problem, see Bolinger (1967), Luján (1974), and Waugh (1976c).

10. See Sag (1977) for an argument that deletion rules are sensitive to semantic structure.

NEUTERALITY, OR THE SEMANTICS
OF GENDER IN A DIALECT OF CASTILLA

Flora Klein
Georgetown University

1.   I propose to address the question of the analysis of
gender by considering its actual use in a dialect of Spanish.
Preliminary evidence from an on-going investigation of spoken
usage indicates that gender is used communicatively, in ways
that are closely allied to the communicative function of the
particular linguistic elements with which gender occurs.   In
this instance I examine, specifically, the occurrence of gender
in the third person oblique clitics--*le, la,* and *lo*--in a Castilian dialect in which these elements are used without regard
to case.

The vernacular of a fairly large part of northwestern and
central Spain (apparently comprising, roughly, most of Castilla la Vieja and adjacent areas to the south, including Madrid)
differs from most varieties of Spanish in that its use of the
clitics *le, la,* and *lo* does not reflect considerations of case.
Accordingly, in this area, utterances such as those listed
(1b-8b) occur as the counterparts of the 'Standard Spanish'
utterances (1a-8a) in conveying the messages given in the
English glosses.

(1a) Lo conocí en la mili.
(1b) Le conocí en la mili.
     'I met him in the army.'
(2a) Le dieron un cargo oficial.
(2b) Le dieron un cargo oficial.
     'They gave him an official post.'
(3a) La conocí en una fiesta.
(3b) La conocí en una fiesta.
     'I met her at a party.'
(4a) Su novio le dió una sortija.
(4b) Su novio la dió una sortija.
     'Her fiancee gave her a ring.'

(5a) Lo compramos de segunda mano.
(5b) Le compramos de segunda mano.
 'We bought it second-hand (e.g. the car = masc.).'
(6a) Le cambiamos la tapicería.
(6b) Le cambiamos la tapicería.
 'We changed the upholstery on it (e.g. the car =
 masc.).'
(7a) Lo tomamos con las comidas.
(7b) Lo tomamos con las comidas.
 'We take it with our meals (e.g. wine = masc.).'
(8a) Hoy día le añaden de todo.
(8b) Hoy día lo añaden do todo.
 'Nowadays they add all kinds of things to it (e.g.
 to wine = masc.).'

Of the two ways of using the clitics, the usage in (1a-8a)
is the more conservative and the usage in (1b-8b) is the more
innovative. For as Figure 1 shows, the clitics can be traced
to the corresponding forms of the Latin demonstrative ILLE
as differentiated for gender and as declined for case.

Figure 1. Origin of Spanish 3p oblique clitics.

Dative	Accusative		
	fem.	ILLAM >	la
ILLI > le	masc.	ILLUM	> lo
	neuter	ILLUD	

Because the etymological usage in (a) is currently accepted
as 'standard', it is common for modern treatments of clitic
use in Spain to concentrate attention on those individual uses
which constitute overt departures from etymology--that is, on
uses such as those illustrated in (b) which differ from their
counterparts in (a). To the extent that traditional grammars
take a more holistic view of the differences, the usage in (b)
is generally regarded as 'extending distinction of gender at
the expense of distinction of case' (Lapesa 1959:260). Presumably, the various innovations are viewed as departing from
a system such as that outlined in (a) of Figure 2 and leading
to one such as that outlined in (b) of Figure 2. Whereas in
(a) of Figure 2 the difference between le, on the one hand,
and lo and la on the other reflects the antecedent's case role
in the utterance, in (b) the same formal elements are differently opposed, so as to maintain constant the distinction between different antecedents--in particular, between antecedents
of different gender.
 Now this interpretation presents some problems, both diachronic and synchronic. The difficulties with the process of

change it implies are treated in Klein (1979). Here I would like to note some of the synchronic problems, specifically as regards the analysis of the caseless usage (b).

Figure 2. Present-day systems of clitic use.

Case-distinguishing (a)		Caseless (referential) (b)
Dative	Accusative	
le	feminine *la* nonfeminine *lo* (i.e. masc. or neuter)	feminine *la* masculine *le* neuter *lo*

Looking back on Examples (1)-(8), it is seen that the (b) usage does not, in fact, distinguish case: thus the same clitic form is found to occur in both members of the pairs (1) and (2), (3) and (4), (5) and (6), and (7) and (8), which (a) distinguishes as contexts for Accusatives vs. Datives, respectively. It is less obvious, however, that abandonment of case distinction has favored distinction of gender. For, as is illustrated by Example (7b), and by its Dative-context counterpart (8b), masculine antecedents are not cliticized consistently as *le*, but in fact quite frequently as *lo*. And to further complicate matters, precisely in caseless speech one also finds *lo* referring to feminine antecedents. This is illustrated in Examples (9) through (12), taken from my recorded data.

(9) Speaking of glorias, a kind of horizontal, under-the-floor chimney found in this area:

(Antes) s'encendían con paja, pero duraba mucho la paja. Pero ahora, esta paja larga lo metes y a la media hora no hay nada.
'(Formerly) they burned straw, but the straw lasted a long time. But now, this long straw (fem.) you put it (lo) in and a half-hour later there's nothing left.'

(10) Por ejemplo, hiervo el agua, lo tengo hervido en una botella, toos los días lo hiervo. Y luego na más es templarlo.
'For instance, I boil the water (fem.), I keep it (lo) boiled (nonfem.) in a bottle, every day I boil it (lo). And then I just have to warm it (lo).'

(11) El orégano lo pasaba luego... ¿Qué más había d'especies? Pimienta, pimienta molida, que también si no estaba molida pues lo molíamos.
'The oregano (masc.), we ground it (lo) next... What

other spices were there? Pepper, ground pepper
(fem.), which again if it wasn't ground (fem.), well,
we ground it (lo).'

(12) A fuego muy lento tiene que sacarse para que salga la
manteca como agua de clara... Salía como agua la
manteca, sabiéndolo sacar, porque hay quien lo
requemaba a lo mejor.
'Rendering had to be done on a very low flame so that
the lard would come out clear as water... It came out
like water, the lard (fem.), knowing how to render
it (lo), because some people maybe burned it (lo).'

It is therefore not at all apparent how caseless usage can
be viewed as based on gender, unless gender is somehow
drastically redefined. At all events the following seems clear:
just as arriving at an analysis of the case-distinguishing usage (a) depends on determining the conditions for the use *le*,
as opposed to *lo* and *la*, so an analysis of the caseless usage
(b) must depend on understanding the conditions for the
occurrence of *lo*, as opposed to *le* and *la*.

2. As a first approximation to this problem I cite a small
sample of caseless speech: about four hours recorded by
two middle-aged rural informants--a man and a woman--in the
province of Valladolid. Since single-object utterances are the
most frequent contexts for cliticization, to begin with I am
going to consider only clitics occurring as unique objects--
irrespective of whether case-distinguishing usage would have
treated them as Accusative or as Dative. I am concerned
with the distribution of *lo*, as opposed to *le* or *la*, as a function of the clitic's reference as determined by redundancy in
the immediate context--usually provided by an overt antecedent, among other things. Accordingly, instances in which
the clitic's reference is not altogether clear from context are
left out of consideration.

Figure 3a shows the distribution of *le*, *la*, and *lo* in single-
object utterances, and Figure 3b gives the percentage of *lo*
as a function of whether the antecedent is masculine or feminine, and of whether its referent is animate or inanimate. It
is seen that masculine antecedents are cliticized by *lo* somewhat more often than feminine ones, though the percentage of
lo is also quite high for feminine singular inanimates (57%).
However, the most striking differences are associated with the
other two factors considered: animateness and number. Thus
one finds that, of the 132 instances of *lo* in this sample, 130
(or 98.5%) refer to inanimate entities, and 128 (or 97%) refer
to a singular antecedent.

Now, the finding that the occurrence of *lo* in caseless usage
is so strongly influenced by singularity, as well as by in-
animateness, suggests that it may be favored by reference to

Figure 3. Frequency of *lo/s* as a function of the antecedent's gender and number and of its referent's animateness.

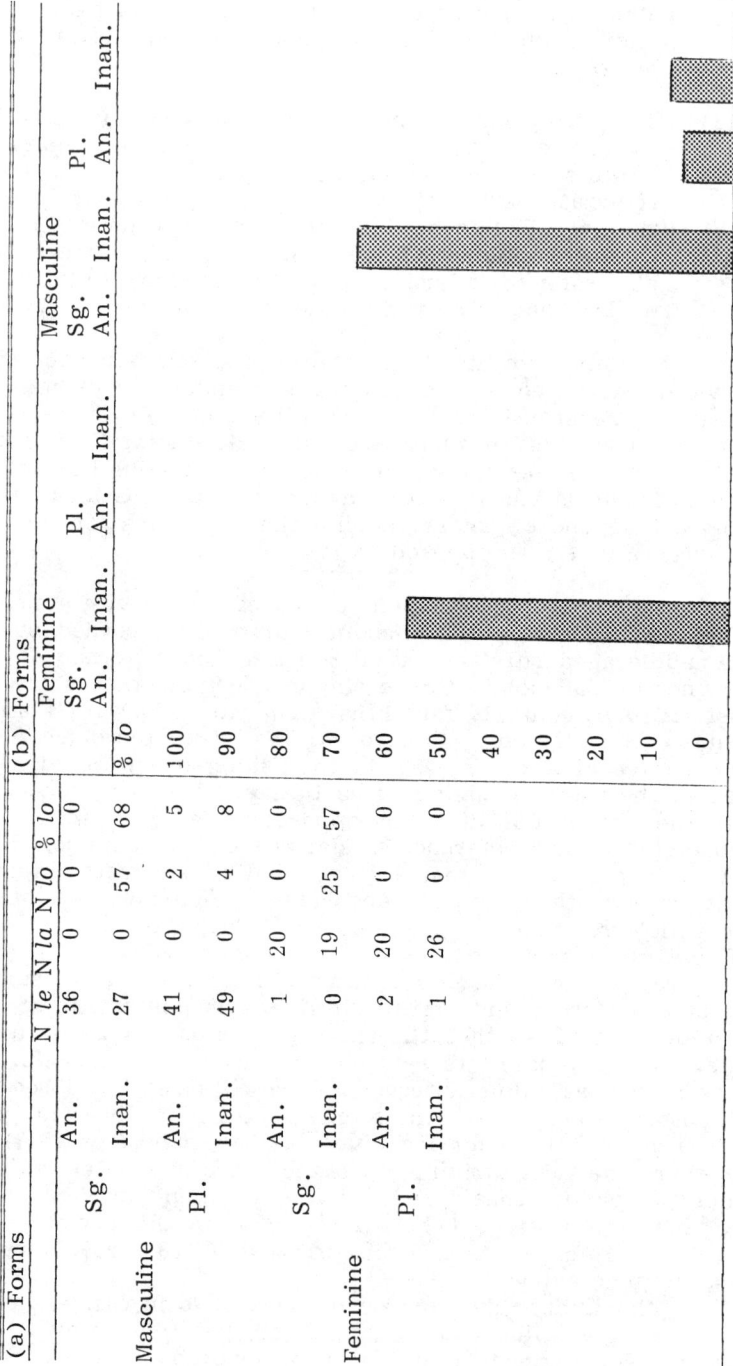

(a) Forms

			N le	N la	N lo	% lo
Masculine	Sg.	An.	36	0	0	0
		Inan.	27	0	57	68
	Pl.	An.	41	0	2	5
		Inan.	49	0	4	8
Feminine	Sg.	An.	1	20	0	0
		Inan.	0	19	25	57
	Pl.	An.	2	20	0	0
		Inan.	1	26	0	0

(b) Forms

Feminine — Sg. An. Inan. — Pl. An. Inan.
Masculine — Sg. An. Inan. — Pl. An. Inan.

% *lo*: 100 90 80 70 60 50 40 30 20 10 0

entities as nondelimited or nondiscrete--or in other words, to what traditionally have been called 'masses'--as opposed to discrete individuals. To test this hypothesis, the singular inanimates cliticized in the sample were further broken down according to whether the context indicates that reference is to a substance or abstraction as such, or to an individual entity. Again, those instances were disregarded whose classification in this respect is not altogether clear, owing to insufficient contextual redundancy.

The results, shown in Figure 4, strongly support the hypothesis. As (4b) shows, the percentage of cliticization by *lo* is indeed much higher for nondelimited referents than it is for discrete ones. It thus appears that at least the caseless vernacular of Valladolid makes a distinction in clitic choice, based on the relative discreteness of the referent.

As it turns out, a distinction of discreteness is also plausible historically in this particular geographic area. For monographic descriptions of neighboring non-Castilian dialects--the currently isolated renmants of Astur-Leones--nearly always note the occurrence of a so-called *neutro de materia* 'neuter of substance' (for example, Penny 1970; see also Hall 1972). By this is meant that, where reference is to nondelimited entities (i.e. substances, abstractions), in these dialects one finds clitics, other pronouns, and seemingly adjectives as well, in a form that is different from the form which would correspond to the linguistic gender of the antecedent: masculine or feminine.

3. At this point, then, there is evidence that in at least one caseless Castilian dialect the occurrence of *lo*, as opposed to *le* or *la*, depends to a great extent on the nature of the clitic's referent. Further, there is evidence that both the particular referential distinction involved (roughly similar to the 'count' vs. 'mass' distinction in English) and the formal means by which it is made ('agreement' vs. 'nonagreement' of clitics with the linguistic gender of their antecedents) are plausible in the particular geographic area in which they are found.

There remains the more interesting theoretical question of just how this distinction should be analyzed. Are these occurrences of *lo* to be considered 'neuters'? I suggest that they are. But then, what is a neuter, anyway, and what is it doing in places like this--the particular discourse contexts in which it is found? This leads to the more general question of what is linguistic gender--in the first place as it occurs in Spanish clitics, and specifically in their caseless use.

It would seem that any answer to this traditionally vexing question must necessarily be tied to a particular theoretical view of the linguistic elements with which gender occurs--in this instance, the Spanish third person oblique clitics *le*, *la*,

Figure 4. Frequency of *lo/s* for inanimates as a function of the referent's discreteness and linguistic gender.

(a)

| | | Total | | | %lo |
		N	N lo	% lo	% lo
Masculine	Discrete	28	6	21	100
	Nondiscrete	56	50	91	90
Feminine	Discrete	14	3	21	80
	Nondiscrete	26	21	81	70

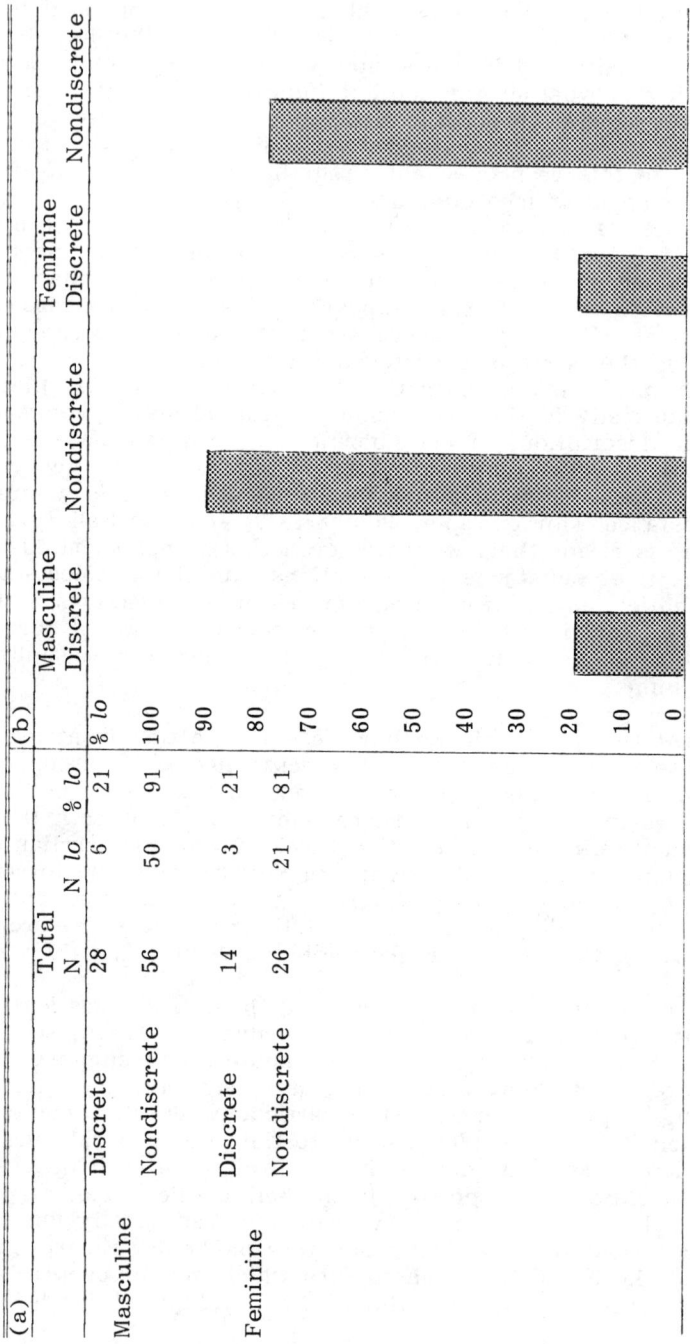

(b)

and *lo*. I therefore take as a point of departure the analysis
of these clitics proposed by Erica Garcia. According to Garcia,
they are 'deictic forms, with "deixis" defined as "an instruction to the hearer" to identify the (clitic's) referent' (Garcia
1975: 65).

It seems to me that by viewing the clitics as deictic forms,
and with this particular definition of deixis, one can account
for the actual distribution of neuters in Spanish, in general,
as well as for the caseless system of Castilla and, in particular, its use of *lo*. To see why, consider first just what is so
unusual about the occurrences of *lo* illustrated earlier in (9)
through (12).

Two circumstances stand out: (1) there is a noun as antecedent; and (2) it occurs in the immediate context of the
clitic. Now these two points seem to capture an essential
discourse difference between these uses of *lo* and traditional
neuters, as illustrated in (13) through (15).

(13) Lo dicen pero no lo creo.
     'They say so, but I don't believe it.'

(14) Es inteligente pero no lo parece.
     'He/she is intelligent but he/she doesn't seem so.'

(15) Todo nos lo quitaron.
     'They took everything away' (lit.: 'Everything they
     took it away from us')

Paradoxically, just these contextual conditions also bring to
the fore the formal nature of neuters in general: since Spanish nouns are either masculine or feminine, it is precisely in
the immediate vicinity of a nominal antecedent that disagreement with its linguistic gender is flagrant and unmistakable.
Yet this is, in fact, the formal character of all neuters in
Spanish: namely, that they do not refer to the linguistic
gender of any noun.

Now, what is the communicative consequence of this, and
how might it be exploited? If the clitics, in fact, 'instruct
the hearer to identify the referent', it seems reasonable to
assume that any additional information they convey--such as
gender or number--will be taken, among other things, as a
clue to the referent's identity. With masculines and feminines
the hearer can be referred to a specific lexical item--the
antecedent--which in turn is construable as a plausible designation for a contextually probable referent. With neuters,
on the other hand, this strategy is truncated. Insofar as
neuters in Spanish do not refer to specific terms for entities,
in effect they convey the 'instruction to find the referent'
with a minimum of clues. The net result is that neuters
differ from masculines and feminines in relative precision of

reference: whereas masculines and feminines are relatively precise, the reference effected by neuters is necessarily vague.

Where traditional neuters are concerned, the pragmatic exploitation of 'vague reference' seems straightforward: apparently, it is negative in character, in effect an avoidance of precise reference (Mariner 1973). Accordingly, the antecedents of traditional neuters are either nonsubstantive (Examples (13) and (14)), semantically vague in themselves (15), or at least not present in the immediate context. The Castilian 'neuters of substance', however, appear to extend 'vague reference' in a positive sense, to suggest particular kinds of entities otherwise described contextually as being relatively 'vague' in themselves, inasmuch as their boundaries are vague. These entities, therefore, can be specifically identified in the immediate context, without contradiction.

The referential plausibility of the strategy involved is especially apparent when it is viewed the other way round: that is, in terms of the relative likelihood which different kinds of referents have of being referred to precisely, by their linguistic gender. The percentages for my sample are given in Figure 5.

Figure 5. Percentage of clitics in lexical gender of antecedent (masc. = le(s), fem. = la(s)) as a function of referents.

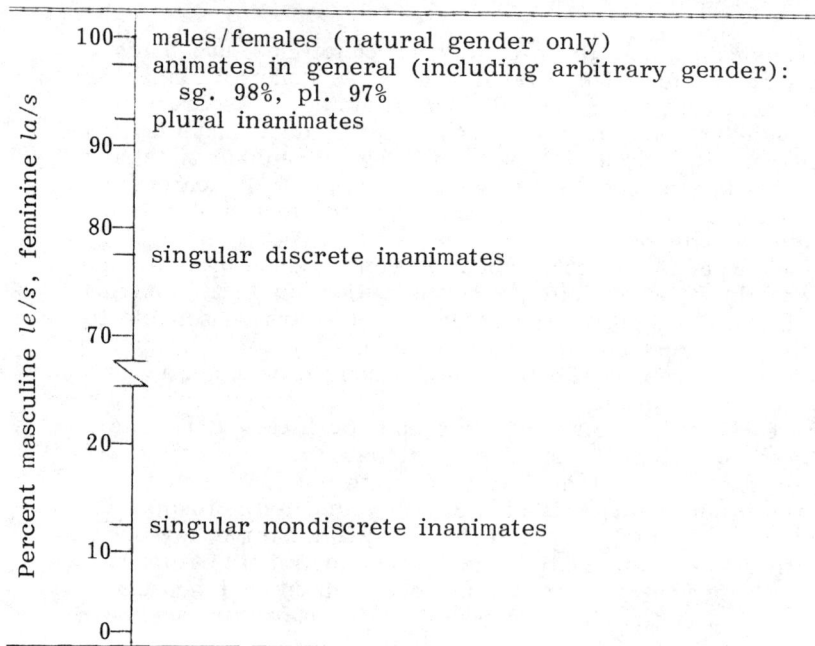

4. The peculiar theoretical interest of the Castilian 'neuter of substance' resides in the fact that its occurrence is so strongly and obviously influenced by the character of the referent itself, rather than by aspects of its lexical designation--specifically, its gender. Thus this dialect makes it especially clear that the occurrence of the neuter--and consequently, the occurrence of nonneuter forms as well--is not determined by automatic 'rules of agreement', but in the first place by a communicatively motivated decision as to whether the clitic will 'agree' or not.

This is, of course, in keeping with a communicative view of language, given the deictic analysis of the clitics. For if they convey an 'instruction to the hearer to identify the referent', then there is no reason why other information the clitics provide should not be utilized toward this end in any way possible. For this approach, then, it is no problem if it turns out that the clitic's gender is associated with referents directly, rather than indirectly, through their lexical designation.

But how, then, should one analyze the feminine and the masculine? The problem here is, of course, that their obvious reference--female vs. nonfemale sex--is simply inapplicable to the vast majority of entities which the language designates as feminine or as masculine. Yet even here, notwithstanding that in so many cases what the feminine and the masculine convey is simply the referent's arbitrary linguistic designation, a communicative account appears preferable to an appeal to automatic agreement. For it seems that only a communicative analysis can explain distinctions which speakers make in their actual use of gender, depending precisely on whether it can be understood as having real-world reference or not. Such distinctions seem to be especially typical of the Castilian caseless use of clitics. This would seem to follow, first, from the clitic's deictic nature, on the further assumption that, where case is lacking, deixis will be based more closely on characteristics of the referent itself.

Returning once more to the Valladolid sample, consider how animates are cliticized. Figure (6a) shows the distribution of le, la, and lo, and Figure 6b the percentage of le, as a function of the antecedent's gender and number. It is seen that, without exception for singulars, and with only two exceptions for plurals, masculine animates are cliticized as le. Similarly, feminine animates are cliticized as la with only three exceptions, one singular and two plurals. Now the nature of these exceptions is revealing in itself, for in each case they involve instances of arbitrary gender, which does not correspond to real-world sex. Thus, of the three instances of le(s) for feminines, one refers to gente 'people' and two to gentes 'persons'; similarly, the two instances of los for masculines do not refer to males, but--as is often true of plural masculines-- to groups whose sex is indeterminate (irrelevant) or mixed (lechacines 'little lambs' and mis hijos 'my children', in fact, a

Figure 6. Frequency of *le/s* for animates as a function of linguistic gender.

(a)

		N le	N la	N lo	% le
Masculine	Singular	36	0	0	100
	Plural	41	0	2	91
Feminine	Singular	1	20	0	5
	Plural	2	20	0	9

(b)

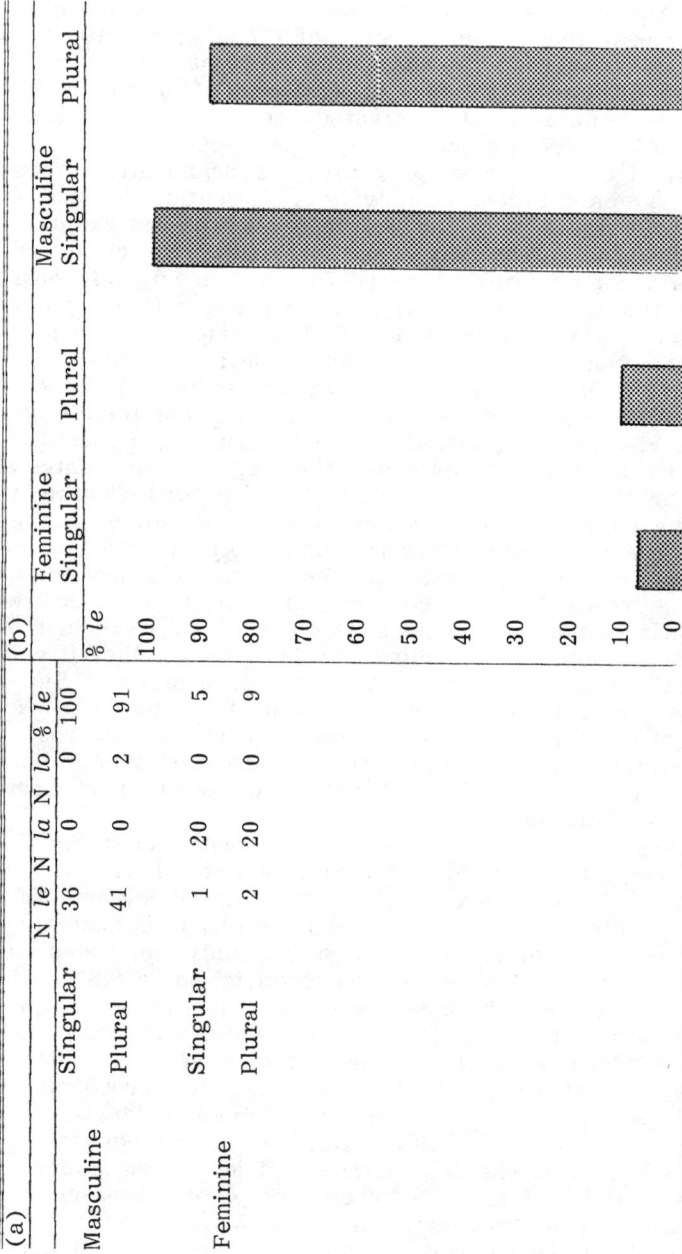

son and daughter). It appears, then, that in this sample
males are referred to without exception by *le*, and females
without exception by *la*. This situation should be contrasted
with the treatment given inanimate, and therefore sexless,
entities. As was seen in Figure 5, inanimates are less likely
to be cliticized in the form appropriate to their linguistic
gender--especially if they are nondelimited as well.

Other indications that caseless Castilian speakers have an
especially strong tendency toward 'natural' interpretation of
gender are more fragmentary, but worth noting nonetheless--
especially given their consonance with the data from actual
speech. I should mention, first, some 'intuitions' volunteered
by caseless informants. To my surprise, I found negative
reactions to the spoken use of *le* in reference to women. Now
this finding was quite unexpected, given that the 'standard'
usage employed in the written language, radio, TV, etc.
distinguishes case, at least with feminine antecedents and with
all inanimates. Accordingly, since the Dative is *le* regardless
of gender, it is difficult to imagine anyone who is not accus-
tomed at least to hearing *le* refer to women--if not to actually
using this form in the appropriate situations.

Conversely, because the use of *la* in Dative contexts is currently prescriptively condemned, it is virtually nonexistent in
formal written language. It is therefore remarkable that the
very few examples of *la* in Dative context which I have man-
aged to find in journalistic writing (only three last year) occur
precisely in contexts where the referent not only is a woman,
but where female sex is essential to the sense of the utterance,
as in Examples (16) and (17).

(16) Los Marx llevan la conducta del hombre a un terreno
     inesperado, como pasa cuando Harpo ataca a las
     señoras y las echa la pierna encima (Cambio 16 No.
     356: 71).
     'The Marx Brothers carry man's behavior to unexpected
     extremes, as for instance when Harpo attacks women
     and throws his leg around them.'

(17) Una mujer... entró a la consulta y salió con la cara
     más relajada. Cuando estaba a punto de abandonar
     el local contestó a esta revista que la acababan de
     colocar un dispositivo intrauterino.
     'A woman... entered the doctor's office and came out
     looking more relaxed. When she was about to leave
     she told our reporter that they had just prescribed
     (lit.: inserted) her an IUD.' (Cambio 16 No. 340:
     55)

5. To conclude, the analysis proposed also raises important questions--among them, the status of the plural *los*, which it seems may turn out to be different in different caseless dialects. Yet despite its preliminary character, it brings to light evidence of different kinds suggesting that a communicative approach--which has provided revealing accounts of other seemingly intractable phenomena--might likewise be applied with profit in attempting to explain gender, as it is actually used and understood.

NOTES

1. The special aversion to using the form interpreted as 'masculine' (*le*) for women is evident in the earliest normative recommendations which reflect caseless usage (see, for example, Cuervo 1895:Part II). Not surprisingly, human females seem to be taken as the prototypal referents of the feminine.
2. As my data show (Figure 6), at least in the caseless dialect of rural Valladolid the plural of *le* is *les*--not *los*, as traditional treatments suggest (for example, Lapesa 1968).

WH-MOVEMENT IN COMPARATIVES IN SPANISH

María-Luisa Rivero
University of Ottawa

0. **Introduction.** In this paper, I study the syntactic properties of comparative sentences that involve WH-movement in Spanish. One example is shown in (1), which I label a 'comparative relative'.

(1) Esta niña no es lo inteligente que era su madre.
    This girl not is the intelligent that was her mother
    'This girl is not as intelligent as her mother was.'

I propose that a movement rule which applies in direct and indirect questions, and relatives, transports an X̄-phrase modified by a degree or measure phrase into COMP position. X ranges over nouns, quantifiers, adjectives, and adverbs. The movement obeys the Relativized A-over-A principle (Bresnan 1976a). In certain cases, the degree or measure phrase may be moved in isolation into COMP, in accordance with this principle. In the case of relative clauses, including comparative relatives of the type of (1), a further rule raises a nominal, adjectival, or adverbial structure into the lexically empty antecedent position of the relative clause. The movement can be considered structure-preserving, if the notion of nondistinctness is defined in terms of specified features, but not if defined in terms of unspecified ones.

Once the analysis for comparative relatives is presented, I discuss the consequences of my proposal for comparative constructions that have been treated within the context of Bresnan's Comparative Subdeletion (Bresnan 1973, 1975, 1976a, 1976b, 1977). In Spanish, sentences that could be analyzed as cases of Subdeletion are of the type shown in (2).

(2) Este niño tiene tanto miedo como nervios (tiene) su madre.
    'This child has as much fear as his mother (has) nervousness.'

177

I propose that the analysis postulated for interrogative and relative constructions accounts for the properties of comparatives lacking a measure phrase in the compared constituent. WH-movement places a maximal phrase of type $\bar{\bar{X}}$ in COMP. In certain dialects, movement of the measure phrase in isolation occurs in, accordance with the Relativized A-over-A principle.

1. **Syntactic properties of measure phrases in questions and relatives.** Before discussing comparatives, I am going to turn to certain interrogative and relative constructions, in order to present in a general way the characteristics of the analysis that I use later on for comparatives as well.

In Spanish, left-branch modifiers belonging to the general class of degree/quantity/measure/quality phrases can be moved in isolation from the constituent they modify by WH-movement, as in the direct questions in (3). Indirect questions exhibit similar properties but are not discussed here.

(3a) ¿Cómo dices que llegaron de cartas?
How (you) say that arrived of letters?
'How many letters do you say arrived?'
(3b) ¿Cómo dices que es de inteligente?
'How intelligent do you say he is?'
(3c) ¿Cómo dices que corre de rápidamente?
'How fast do you say he runs?'
(3d) ¿Cómo dices que hay de pocos libros?
'How few books do you say there are?'

In (3a), the degree modifier *cómo* 'how' within the NP *cómo de cartas* 'how (many) of letters' is moved into COMP. In (3b), the degree modifier moves out of an AP; in (3c) the movement is out of an AdvP, and in (3d) it is out of a QP. In Rivero (1978b), I propose that the *cómo* modifier is the specifier of an $\bar{X}$ category (where X ranges over N, A, Adv, and Q). The preposition *de* is inserted by transformation. Thus, the element in initial position in the examples in (3) originates in a structure of the type of (4). DE-Insertion has already applied.

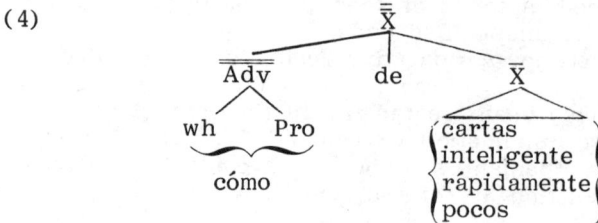

(4)

$$\bar{\bar{X}}$$

$$\overline{\overline{\text{Adv}}} \qquad de \qquad \bar{X}$$

wh   Pro   cartas
                    inteligente
cómo   rápidamente
                    pocos

The WH-morpheme is placed (in the base, or by transformation) within $\bar{X}$ categories. The rule of WH-movement is as in (5). The preposition *de* is a context predicate in the sense of

Bresnan (1976a). The target predicate is the $\overline{\overline{X}}$-phrase that
contains the WH-morpheme, that is, elements 3, 4, and 5 of
the structural condition.

(5) WH-movement:

$$\text{COMP} - W_1 - \overline{\overline{X}}[W_2 - \text{WH} - W_3] - (\text{de}) - W_4$$

1	2	3	4	5	6	7
3 4 5	2	Ø	Ø	Ø	6	7

In accordance with the Relativized A-over-A principle, WH-
movement applies under a proper analysis in which an $\overline{\overline{X}}$-phrase
which is maximal in relation to the value assigned to the con-
text predicate *de* is selected; *cómo* is the maximal phrase when
term 6 of the structural description is satisfied by *de* in (4),
and the examples in (3) can be generated.

The element *de* of the structural description in (5) is
optional. It can be satisfied by *e* (empty) as well. Thus, the
dominating $\overline{\overline{X}}$-catetory in (4) can be moved, as seen in the
examples in (6).[1]

(6a) ¿Cómo de cartas dices que llegaron?
     How of letters (you) say that arrived? (gloss as in
     (3a))
(6b) ¿Cómo de inteligente dices que es? (gloss as in (3b))
(6c) ¿Cómo de rapidamente dices que corre? (3c)
(6d) ¿Cómo de pocos libros dices que hay? (3d)

In (6a), $\overline{N}$ moves; in (6b), $\overline{\overline{A}}$ moves; in (6c), $\overline{\overline{Adv}}$; and in
(6d), the $\overline{N}$ that contains the $\overline{\overline{Q}}$ category moves.

I cite one instance of derivation in more detail. The structure of the embedded clause in (4b) and (6b), once DE-
Insertion has applied, is represented in (7). There are two
proper analyses which are in accordance with the Relativized
A-over-A principle, in view of the structural description provided for WH-movement in (5). Analysis A has term 6 of the
structural description satisfied by *de*; analysis B has term 6
satisfied by *e*. Under proper analysis A, the $\overline{\overline{Adv}}$-phrase
moves. Under proper analysis B, the $\overline{\overline{A}}$-phrase moves.

Left-branch modifiers in relative constructions exhibit the
formal properties seen earlier in interrogative sentences. It
is possible to relativize APs and AdvPs that include in their
semantic interpretation a degree or quantity modification, as
in (8). I call the relatives in (8) 'degree relatives'.

(8a) Se asusta de lo inteligentes que dicen que son.
     Himself frightens of the intelligent that (they) say
        that (they) are
     'He is frightened by how intelligent they say they are.'

(7)

```
                        S̄
        ┌───────────────┴────────────┐
      COMP                            S
        │                    ┌────────┴────────┐
        △                   NP                 VP
                             │          ┌───────┴───────┐
                            él          V              Ā̄
                             │      ┌────┴──────────────┴───┐
                            es      │                 Ā
                                    │            ┌────┴────┐
                                  Adv̄  de        Ā
                                ┌──┴──┐       ┌───┴────┐
                               WH    Pro    inteligente
                                φ                        φ
```

A	1		2	3	4	5	6	7	
B	1		2	3	4		5		6 7

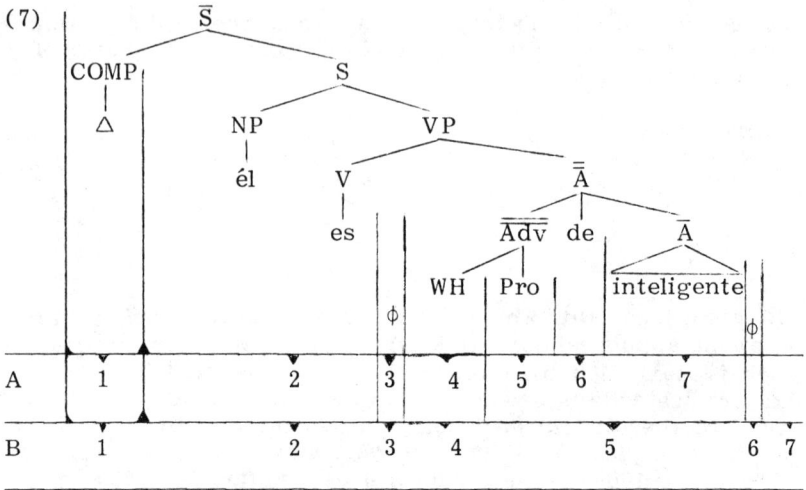

(8b) No puedo creer lo rápido que corren.
  'I cannot believe how fast they run.'

In Rivero (1978b), I assumed the basic structure in (9) for
the relative clause *lo rápido que corren* in (8b).   Example (8a)
can be analyzed along similar lines.

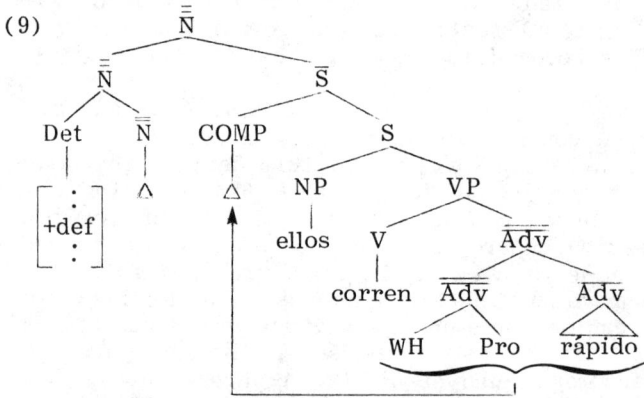

(9)

```
                          N̄̄
              ┌───────────┴────────────┐
            N̄̄                          S̄
        ┌────┴────┐            ┌────────┴────────┐
      Det         N̄̄          COMP               S
        │         │           │          ┌───────┴───────┐
     ┌─────┐      △           △          NP              VP
     │  :  │                            │         ┌──────┴──────┐
     │+def │                           ellos     V            Adv̄̄̄
     │  :  │                                      │       ┌─────┴─────┐
     └─────┘                                    corren  Adv̄̄        Adv̄̄
                                                      ┌──┴──┐     ┌───┴───┐
                                                     WH    Pro    rápido
```

I have selected Ross' analysis for relative clauses because it
simplifies the discussion.   My proposal could be reformulated
easily if relatives are treated as complements of N̄ (Schachter
1973, Jackendoff 1977).
    In (9), the antecedent of the relative is lexically empty.
WH-movement places the dominating Adv̄ in COMP, in accordance with the Relativized A-over-A principle (i.e. the transformation moves the maximal Adv̄, not the dominated Adv̄ that

contains the WH-morpheme). The rule is formulated as in (5). X ranges over the same categories in interrogative and relative constructions: N, Q, A, and Adv. The examples in (8) are standard sentences in all varieties of Spanish.

If DE-Insertion applies, it is possible to relativize the degree adverbial in isolation, leaving the head Adv of the construction in its basic position, as seen in (10)--a more marginal sentence than (8b) that many speakers find grammatical, nevertheless. DE-Insertion does not apply in relative clauses for some speakers. Those speakers have (8) as the only possibility. The same situation is found in relation to comparative relatives.

(10) No puedo creer lo que corren de rápido.
  Not (I) can believe the that (they) run of fast
  (see (8b) for gloss).

After DE-Insertion, the adverbial in (10) has the structure in (11). De can be considered the element that satisfied term 6 of the structural description in (5). The maximal phrase in relation to the context predicate is then moved; that is, the dominated and not the dominating Adv moves into COMP. For those speakers who find (10) ungrammatical, DE-Insertion does not apply in relative clauses, but the rest of the analysis remains unchanged.

(11)

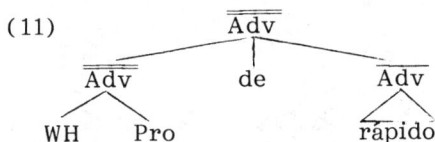

In view of the parallel nature of degree relatives and degree interrogatives, I conclude (Rivero 1978b) that these two types of structures are derived by the same transformation, namely, WH-movement.

In the case of relative clauses, I proposed that a raising transformation places the phrase in COMP position into the antecedent position; the WH-phrase in COMP is erased, along the lines proposed by Vergnaud (1974). The raising transformation is structure-preserving, as will be seen. In Section 2 I generalize this analysis to comparative structures.

2. **Measure phrases in comparative relatives.** The analysis proposed for degree relative clauses of the type of (8a-b) can be generalized to a class of comparative structures that involve WH-movement. Consider the examples in (12), standard sentences in all varieties of Spanish.

(12a) Juan no es lo guapo que era su hermano.
  John not is the handsome that was his brother
  'John is not as handsome as his brother was.'

(12b) Juan no corre lo rápidamente que corría su hermano.
　　　 John not runs the fast that ran his brother
　　　 'John does not run as fast as his brother did.'

　　The comparative relatives in (12) are parallel in structure to
the degree relatives in (8). In surface structure, the antecedent position begins with the definite article in the so-called
neuter form. In the case of (8a) and (12a), there is no gender
and number agreement between the definite article and the adjective that immediately follows. The head of the antecedent
position is occupied by an adjective in (8a) and (12a), and by
an adverb in (8b) and (12b). The complementizer *que* appears
in initial position in the embedded clause, which has a gap in
the location in which the constituent that moves originated.
The analysis proposed for degree relatives is therefore applicable to comparative relatives. The relative clauses *lo guapo que
era su hermano* in (12a) and *lo rápidamente que corría su
hermano* in (12b) have the basic structure presented in (13a)
and (13b), respectively.

(13a)

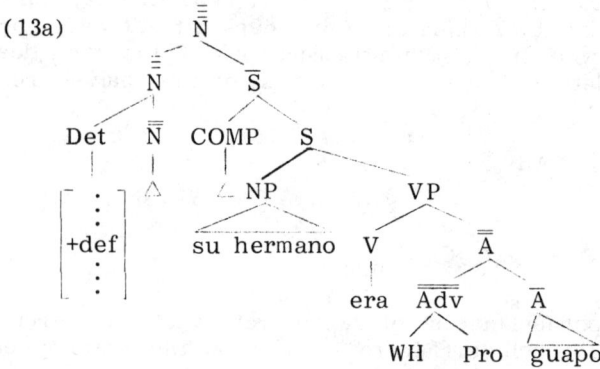

(13b)

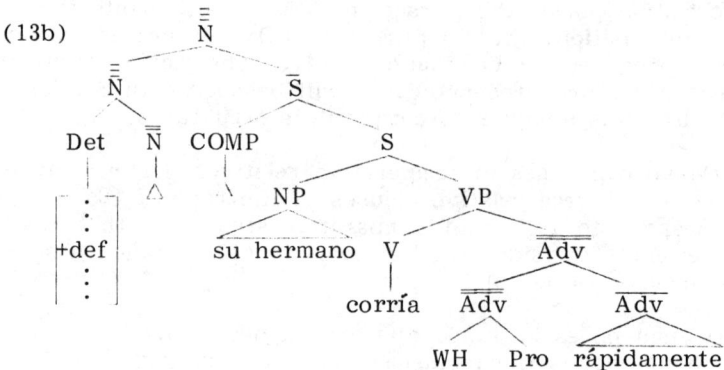

In (13a-b), the antecedent of the relative is lexically empty. The relative contains an $\bar{\bar{X}}$-phrase that has a left-branch modifier of the $\overline{Adv}$ class. That Adv contains the WH-morpheme. According to the structural description of WH-movement in (5), the phrase to be moved into COMP position must be the maximal $\bar{\bar{X}}$-phrase: the $\bar{\bar{A}}$ in (13a), and the dominating $\overline{Adv}$ in (13b). After WH-movement applies, the intermediate structures for (12a) and (12b) should be (14a) and (14b), respectively.

(14a)

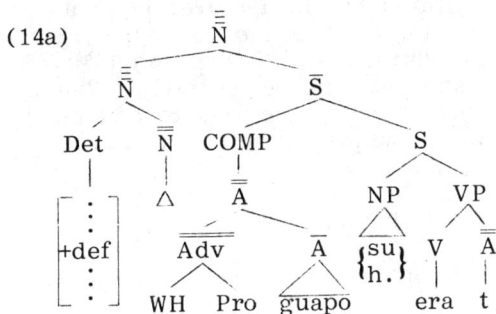

(14b)

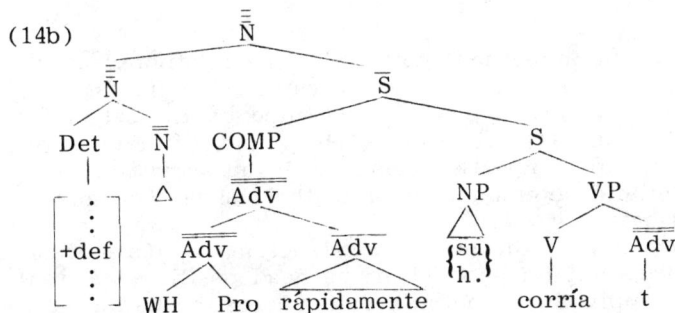

When in COMP position, the WH-element--or perhaps the WH-Pro sequence--is erased in the case of relative clauses. The remaining portion of the moved phrase is then raised to the antecedent position within the matrix clause. The rule that moves a constituent from the COMP position into the head was presented as a structure-preserving transformation in Schachter (1973), Vergnaud (1974): a nominal structure moves into an empty nominal node. The degree relatives discussed in Rivero (1978b) and the comparative relatives considered here are an exception to the normal hierarchical arrangement of syntactic categories predicated by the $\bar{X}$-convention: they are dominated by NP, as indicated by (15), and contain no head N, but an A or Adv as head.

(15a) Lo rápidamente que contestaron nos tranquilizó.
'How fast they answered relaxed us.'

(15b) Fuimos tranquilizados por lo rápidamente que
      contestaron.
      'We were relaxed by how fast they answered.'

As is well known, the distinction between features and categories is eliminated within the $\overline{X}$-convention. All the symbols
in the grammar are regarded as sets of features. Features
can be marked plus or minus, or left unspecified. In Spanish,
nominal categories are constituted by the features [+N] and
[-V], together with features for number and gender: [+Sgl]
and [-Sgl] for Singular and Plural respectively, and [+Masc]
and [-Masc] for Masculine and Feminine respectively. When a
nominal category is not lexically filled, the number and gender
features can be marked plus or minus, or left unspecified.

(16a) El que es bueno
      'The one (masc., sg.) that is good'
(16b) La que es buena
      'The one (fem. sg.) that is good'
(16c) Lo que es bueno
      'That (neuter) which is good'

I assume that the antecedent position of the relative clauses in
(16) is formed by a determiner and a category N filled by a
dummy node. In (16a) the N is constituted by the set of features indicated in (17). Example (16b) would differ in having
the feature for gender marked minus. By an agreement process, the definite determiner acquires the number and gender
of the head category.
    Let us turn now to the neuter construction in (16c). Number
and gender are left unspecified in the head position. Agreement cannot apply to the definite determiner; the definite form
with no number and gender surfaces: *lo*.

(17)

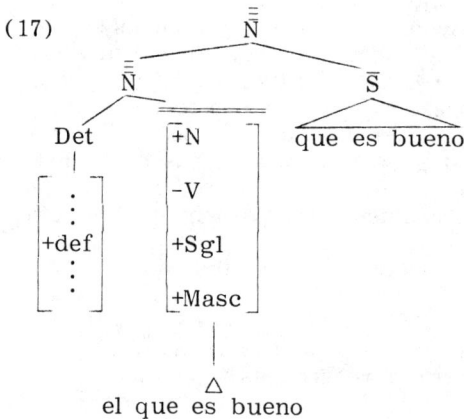

        el que es bueno

If one assumes as well that the [V] feature is left unspecified, one would have a nominal category that can appear with the feature [N] marked plus, and all other features left unspecified, when it dominates Δ in the base, as in (18). The fact that the feature is unspecified is indicated by 0.[2]

I assume that the dummy node in which the constituent from COMP position is moved in degree and comparative relatives is as in (18) for the rule to have a well-formed output.

(18)

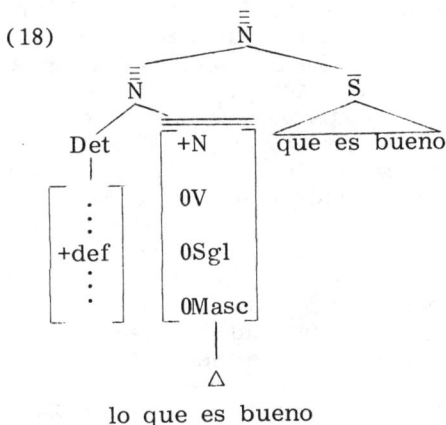

lo que es bueno

The raising rule is structure-preserving if the notion of non-distinctness is defined as in (19).

(19) Let Y and Z and their primes (i.e. $\bar{Y}$, $\bar{\bar{Y}}$, etc., $\bar{Z}$, $\bar{\bar{Z}}$, etc.) represent categories (that is, sets of features). Y is nondistinct from Z if: (a) for every feature F marked plus or minus in Y, it is not the case that F is marked with the opposite value in Z; and (b) for every feature F left unspecified in Y, F is left unspecified in Z, marked plus or minus, or absent.

We can postulate that a category Z can be moved, inserted, or copied into a category Y, if Y is nondistinct from Z, in accordance with the structure-preserving hypothesis.

I now return to the comparative relatives in (12). The antecedent $\bar{\bar{N}}$ represented in (13a) and (13b) will have the feature composition in (18). WH-movement applies to the maximal $\bar{X}$-phrase in the embedded clause in accordance with the Relativized A-over-A principle. The $\bar{A}$-phrase moves into COMP in (12a), as diagrammed in (14a); it is later moved to the antecedent position. Given that the category that dominates the dummy symbol is specified [+N], but has no specification for the other features, it will be nondistinct from $\bar{A}$, the moved category, that is specified [+N,-V] (plus number and gender). There are no features which are specified with opposite values in $\bar{\bar{N}}$ and $\bar{\bar{A}}$; the only feature which is specified in $\bar{\bar{N}}$ matches the specification in $\bar{A}$. The raising can occur within the limits of structure-preservation, because $\bar{\bar{N}}$ is nondistinct from $\bar{A}$. Example (12b) has the same characteristics.

Agreement between the Determiner in the antecedent position and the $\bar{A}$ in (13a) does not occur because the process depends on the presence of the features [+N] and [-V] in the head category. This proposal does not let 0 count as a third feature value, distinct from plus and minus. Only plus and minus values are counted when nondistinctness is defined. This use of unspecified features in the categorial component is consistent with the view that feature values are binary.

Together with the comparative relatives in which the dominating $\bar{A}$ or $\bar{Adv}$ moves, there are structures in which the degree phrase moves in isolation, as in (20). This example is more marginal than (12a-b), and is judged ill formed by the speakers who reject (10). Remember that this distinction depends on the application of DE-Insertion in relatives.

(20) Juan no corre lo que corría de rápido su hermano.
    John not runs the that run of fast his brother
    'John does not run as fast as his brother did.'

In (20), DE-Insertion has applied, as indicated in (21). Using *de* as a context predicate, it is possible to transport the $\bar{Adv}$ that immediately dominates the WH-morpheme, and not the dominating category.

(21)

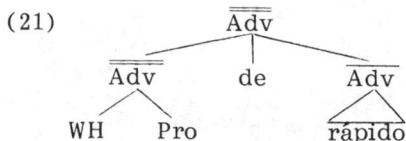

I now turn to two arguments that lead to the proposal that the phrase in COMP, after WH-movement, is raised into the head position of the antecedent within the matrix. Rivero (1978b) points out that one of the reasons to propose a rule that raises a phrase into antecedent position is that the AP thus raised must agree in number and gender with the subject of the embedded clause, as in (22a).

(22a) Se dio cuenta de lo guapos que eran los niños.
    (He) realized of the handsome (masc. pl.) that were the children
    'He realized how handsome the children were.'

(22b) Se dio cuenta de lo {*guapo (masc. sg.) / *guapa (fem. sg.) / *guapas (fem. pl.)} que eran los niños.

The examples in (22b) are ungrammatical because the agreement condition is not met, given that *los niños* is a masculine plural noun phrase. The proposal that the AP originates in the embedded position, and that agreement applies to it before it is moved to the matrix, accounts easily for this situation.

A somewhat different argument can be provided in the case of comparative relatives. It is parallel to the one presented by Vergnaud (1974) for sentences containing predicative nominals in French, as in *Il n'est pas le comédien que son père était* 'He is not the comedian that his father was'.

(23) Estos niños no son lo guapos que fueron sus abuelos.
'These children (masc. pl.) are not as handsome (masc. pl.) as their grandparents (masc. pl.) were.'

(24) Estas niñas no son lo {*guapas / *guapos} que fueron sus abuelos.
'These girls are not as handsome {(fem. pl.) (masc. pl.)} as their grandparents (masc. pl.) were.'

The basic structure of (23) is presented in (25), with irrelevant details simplified.

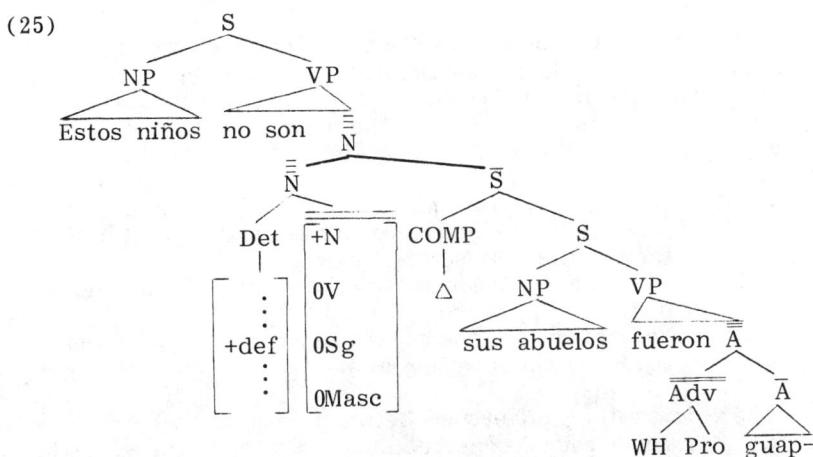

(25)

```
                          S
              ┌───────────┴───────────┐
             NP                       VP
           ┌──┴──┐              ┌──────┴──────┐
        Estos niños          no son          N̿
                                    ┌──────────┴──────────┐
                                   N̄                       S̄
                              ┌─────┴─────┐          ┌──────┴──────┐
                            Det   ⌈ +N ⌉          COMP            S
                             │    │ 0V │           │         ┌─────┴─────┐
                          ⌈  .  ⌉│ 0Sg│           Δ         NP          VP
                          │  .  ││0Masc⌋               ┌─────┴──┐    ┌───┴───┐
                          │ +def│                   sus abuelos  fueron    A
                          │  .  │                                     ┌────┴────┐
                          ⌊  .  ⌋                                    Adv        Ā
                                                                  ┌──┴──┐
                                                                 WH    Pro   guap-
```

The adjective originates in the embedded clause only. It is marked with the number and gender of the embedded subject *sus abuelos* in the relative clause cycle. The output is the masculine plural form *guapos*. The Ā-phrase is moved into COMP by WH-movement, given that it is the maximal X̄-phrase that satisfies the structural description of the rule; it is later promoted to the matrix. In the matrix cycle, the A is marked again with the features of the matrix subject *los niños*. The features of the matrix and embedded subjects are identical, and no conflict arises. In (24) the situation is different. The

A originates in the embedded clause, and is marked for masculine and plural in that cycle. The phrase is then raised to the matrix, where it is marked as feminine and plural. Given that the adjective is now marked [+masc] and [-masc], the output is ungrammatical. Notice that in (23), the adjective must agree with the subject of the matrix clause, but the determiner which precedes the raised adjective does not agree with it in number or gender (and does not agree with the subject of the matrix either). As already mentioned, agreement between the determiner and the head occurs when the head has the features [+N, -V]; the adjective is marked [+N, -V]. I am assuming that agreement between an adjective and an NP is a cyclic process (Fauconnier 1973, Quicoli 1976, Luján 1974).

Comparative constructions that do not have the surface form of relative clauses do not require the type of double agreement just discussed.

(26a) Esta niña es tan guapa como sus abuelos.
'This girl is as handsome (fem. sg.) as her grandparents (masc. pl.).'
(26b) No son más guapos que su padre.
'They are not more handsome (masc. pl.) than their
father (masc. sg.).'

Irrespective of the details of their derivational history, the sentences in (26) do not involve raising into the matrix. Compare in this respect (27a) and (27b). Sentence (27a) had an adjective which is generated in the matrix. Sentence (27b) has an adjective which has its origin in the embedded clause.

(27a) Estas niñas no son más guapas que (fue) su padre.
'These girls are not more handsome (fem. pl.) than
their father (masc. sg.) (was).'
(27b) *Estas niñas no son lo {guapas, guapo} que fue su
padre.
'These girls are not as handsome {(fem. pl.) (masc.
sg.)} as their father was.'

There is another difference between comparative relatives and other comparative constructions. Compare the examples in (28) and (29). As seen in (29a), it is not the case that comparative relatives can have resumptive pronouns.

(28a) Juan no es tan ágil como lo era en el pasado.
'John is not as nimble as he was it in the past.'
(28b) Juan no es tan ágil como era en el pasado.
'John is not as nimble as he was in the past.'

(29a) *Juan no es lo ágil que lo era en el pasado.
John not is the nimble that it (he) was in the past
(gloss as in (28a))
(29b) Juan no es lo ágil que era en el pasado
(gloss as in (28b))

In my view, the lack of resumptive pronouns in comparative
relatives motivates a movement analysis for such structures.
Consider (28a). If it is assumed that pronouns are generated
in the base, no transformational process would be required in
the compared clause, other than placing the clitic in preverbal
position (under the hypothesis that it is generated postverbally). Deletion or movement would be required for (28b),
but I am not going to discuss this aspect now. In comparative relatives, it is impossible to have a structure with a pro-
form instead of a gap, as seen by the deviance of (29a).
Under the movement analysis, this is to be expected; let us
see why. The AP that contains *ágil* in (29) originates in the
embedded clause, and it occupies the position that the clitic
must occupy in the base in (29a). In other words, no proform
can occupy the AP position in the embedded clause in the base
because that position is filled by the AP that dominates *ágil*.
The AP moves by transformation and must necessarily leave a
gap, as in (29b), the grammatical structure. The movement
analysis accounts for the obligatory absence of a clitic in (29).
Consider a sentence such as (30). In view of the proposals
in this paper, the (simplified) basic structure of (30) should
be (31).

(30) Elena es lo que era el año pasado.
'Helen is what she was last year.'

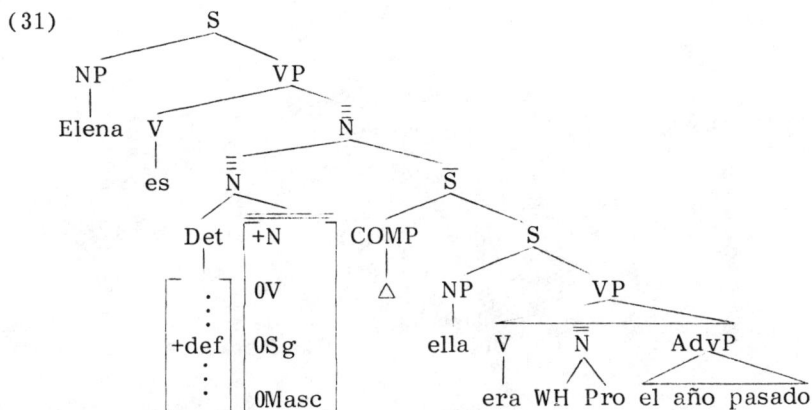

(31)

```
                    S
          ┌─────────┴─────────┐
         NP                   VP
          |          ┌────────┴────────┐
        Elena        V                 N̿
                     |        ┌─────────┴─────────┐
                     es       N̿                   S̄
                           ┌──┴──┐        ┌────────┴────────┐
                          Det  ┌+N ┐    COMP               S
                           |   │   │      |          ┌──────┴──────┐
                          ┌─┐  │0V │      △         NP            VP
                          │.│  │   │               |       ┌──────┼──────┐
                          │:│  │0Sg│              ella      V    N̿     AdvP
                          │+def│   │                        |   ╱╲    ╱────╲
                          │:│  │   │                       era WH Pro  el año pasado
                          │.│  │0Masc│
                          └─┘  └───┘
```

There is no overt indication of movement in a surface structure such as (30). However, the gap in the embedded clause
is also obligatory, as seen in (32).

(32) *Elena es lo que lo era el año pasado.
'Helen is what she was it last year.'

The same analysis proposed before can be used for (30). The WH-proform moves into COMP. Depending on the details of the rule that deletes the WH-element in COMP, there could be raising to the antecedent position as well. This is a question that I have not studied.

Example (33) is similar in basic structure to (30), except that the lexically empty antecedent position must be specified for number and gender (and must be marked [-V] if agreement between determiner and head is to apply).

(33) Elena es la que era el año pasado.
'Helen is the (one) (fem. sg.) that (she) was last year.'

A sentence such as (34) involves WH-movement in relation to the comparative relative. The basic structure of the relative is presented in (35). The derivation proceeds as for (30).

(34) Elena no está más delgada de lo que estaba el año pasado.
Helen not is more thin of the that (she) was last year
'Helen is not thinner than (what) she was last year.'

The $\overline{\overline{A}}$-phrase moves into COMP by WH-movement. The WH-element is deleted in COMP. The adjective is raised into the antecedent position, and deleted under identity with the previous *delgada* in the matrix. [3] This analysis seems to be required for sentences of the type of (36), in which the two APs are not totally identical, and the second AP is emphatic.

(35)

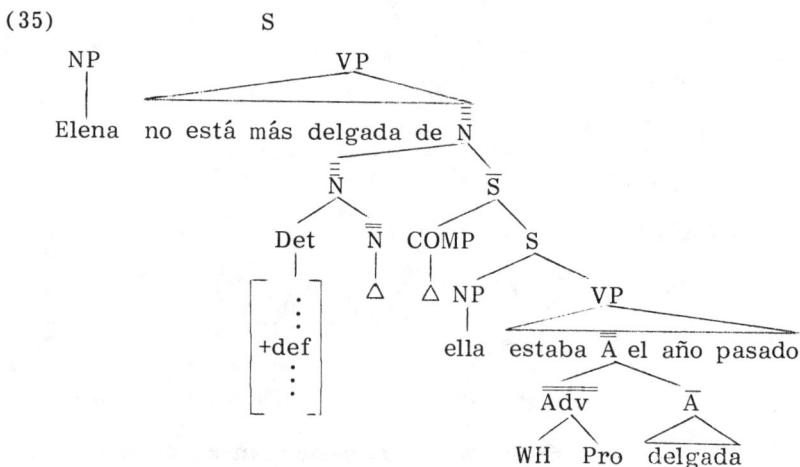

(36) Elena no puede estar más delgada de lo increíblemente
   delgada que estaba ya el año pasado.
   'Helen cannot be thinner than she was incredibly thin
   already last year.'

In this section I have proposed that comparative relatives are
generated by WH-movement, and a raising process that pro-
motes a phrase in COMP position to the antecedent position in
a relative construction. WH-movement selects the maximal $\bar{\bar{X}}$-
phrase, in accordance with the Relativized A-over-A principle.
In those dialects of Spanish that allow DE-Insertion in relative
clauses, degree and measure modifiers may move in isolation in
accordance with the principle. The raising-into-antecedent process is a structure-preserving rule, under the view that only
specified features are computed to define distinctness. Thus,
it is possible to 'relativize' APs and AdvPs within this interpretation of structure preservation. The movement-into-COMP
analysis for comparative relatives receives confirmation from
the impossibility of having resumptive pronouns in the embedded clause. The raising-into-antecedent rule is motivated
by agreement phenomena involving displaced adjectives.

   3. Comparative Subdeletion. I now turn to the consequences
that the proposals in Sections 1 and 2 have for a class of sentences that have proven controversial in the literature, namely,
those that Bresnan has discussed under her rule of Comparative Subdeletion (C-Sub). Let me summarize the controversy
in a few lines.
   Bresnan (1975, 1977 for a summary of her position) has
argued that English comparative sentences of the type of (37a)
involve a rule of deletion under identity that uses an essential
variable in its structural description (that is, unbounded deletion), and is sensitive to island constraints. A special case of
comparative deletion, C-Sub, deletes only a measure phrase,
as in (37b).

(37a) John is taller than Bill is ---
(37b) They have more enemies that we have --- friends

Chomsky (e.g. 1977) does not accept unbounded rules in sentence grammar, nor rules of identity deletion, which are considered part of discourse grammar. He argues that comparative sentences of the type of (37a) involve WH-movement and
the deletion of a designated terminal *what* in COMP position.
As a possible analysis for (37b), he proposes WH-movement
of a bare WH, not subject to the Relativized A-over-A principle, with the subsequent deletion of WH when in COMP.
   In this paper, I do not discuss comparatives that have not
been associated with C-Sub. However, I would like to point
out that general comparatives of the type of (28a) seem to require an analysis that does not involve movement or deletion.

If pronouns are generated in the base, all that is required is the rule that interprets the clitic in the embedded structure.

I now turn to Subdeletion-type structures. Consider the sentences in (38).

(38a) Aqui hay tantos libros como -- revistas espero que
      prometas que comprarás tú.
      'Here there are as many books as I hope you will
      promise to buy journals.'
(38b) *Aqui hay tantos libros como -- revistas espero tu
      promesa de que comprarás tú.

Sentence (38a) has two different gaps. On the one hand, it lacks a measure phrase preceding the compared constituent *revistas* 'journals'; the measure phrase gap is indicated by --. On the other hand, it has a gap in the object position of the mostly embedded clause, the basic location of the compared constituent -- *revistas*. A similar analysis to the one proposed for interrogative, degree relative, and comparative relative constructions can be hypothesized for (38a). The basic structure of the compared clause in (38a) is (39).

(39)
$$\bar{\bar{S}}$$
COMP   S

Δ espero que prometas que tú comprarás $\bar{\bar{N}}$

$\bar{\bar{Q}}$ $\bar{\bar{N}}$

WH Pro revistas

The maximal X-phrase moves into COMP, that is, $\bar{\bar{N}}$ must move. The WH-element is deleted in COMP. *Revistas* appears in COMP position, and it cannot be raised into the antecedent position (there is no antecedent). If we assume that *como* in (38a) is a complementizer, then -- *revistas* comes to occupy a position after the complementizer, which is also the case for WH-phrases in indirect questions, as in *Dime que para qué quieres el dinero* 'Tell me that for what you want the money' (Rivero 1978a, 1978b).

In brief, structures in which the compared clause has an unmodified compared constituent in surface structure can be analyzed as cases in which a maximal $\bar{\bar{X}}$-phrase moves into COMP, with the deletion of the WH-element. As (38b) indicates, the movement is subject to the CNPC (in Chomsky's terms, to Subjacency).

Speakers who allow DE-Insertion in relative clauses may allow the rule to apply in nonrelative comparatives as well. In addition to (40a), they find sentences of the type of (40b) well formed.

(40a) Mi hermana se siente tan tranquila como intranquila me cuentan que se se sintió la semana pasada.
'My sister feels as relaxed as they tell that she felt tense last week.'
(40b) Mi hermana se siente tan tranquila como me cuentan que se sintió de intranquila la semana pasada.

Sentence (40a) is parallel to (38a). In (40b), DE-Insertion has applied in the $\overline{\overline{A}}$-phrase that contains the measure proform; the output is presented in (41).

(41)

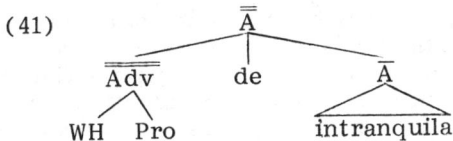

WH-movement selects the maximal $\overline{\overline{X}}$-phrase in view of the context predicate *de*, and moves it into COMP; that is, it moves the $\overline{Adv}$ in isolation. The sequence *de intranquila* remains unaffected in basic position. The sequence WH-Pro is deleted in COMP.[4]

If it were proposed that there is no measure phrase in the compared $\overline{\overline{A}}$-phrase in (40b), there would be no explanation for the presence of the preposition *de*, which depends on measure modification, as in *así de libros* 'so of books, these many books' and *una barbaridad de libros* 'a large quantity of books'. Therefore, I do not entertain the possibility that *intranquila* is an unmodified head in (40a). Even if the adjective were unmodified, a movement analysis would still be required, but the rule would not be WH-movement. It could perhaps be connected with Topicalization, along the lines of the analysis proposed in Rivero (1978a).

4. **Conclusion.** In this paper, I have dealt with two types of comparative structures: comparative relatives, and sentences that have been discussed under C-Sub in the literature. I have shown that, in Spanish, WH-movement operates in comparative, relative, and interrogative constructions. WH-movement obeys the Relativized A-over-A principle in all its applications; it selects the maximal $\overline{\overline{X}}$-phrase that satisfies its structural condition, and moves it into COMP position. Under certain situations, a measure phrase may be moved in isolation, but within the limits set by the RAOA principle. In questions, where a rule of DE-Insertion locates a preposition between a measure phrase and the head of the construction, WH-movement can affect the measure phrase in isolation by defining the

inserted preposition as a context predicate. Under such circumstances, the measure phrase can be considered the maximal $\overline{\overline{X}}$-phrase. This situation obtains in all varieties of Spanish. Dialects that allow DE-Insertion in relatives and comparatives exhibit WH-movement of the measure phrase alone, using *de* as a context predicate in these constructions too.

In degree and comparative relatives, the phrase that has been placed in COMP position by WH-movement is raised into a lexically empty antecedent. This process--which allows adjectives and adverbs to be 'relativized'--can be considered structure-preserving if the dummy node in the antecedent position is dominated by a category marked [+N], and all other features (namely [V], gender, and number) are left unspecified.

Comparative sentences that do not have the structure of relative clauses, and, in particular, comparative structures that could be analyzed as the result of C-Sub (that is, the unbounded deletion of a measure phrase under conditions of nondistinctness) have the same formal properties as comparative relatives. Thus, they can be analyzed as involving WH-movement of the maximal $\overline{\overline{X}}$-phrase into COMP. In dialects in which DE-Insertion is possible in comparatives, the measure phrase may move in isolation in accordance with the Relativized A-over-A principle. Comparatives that contain a clitic in the compared clause instead of a gap do not seem to require the application of any transformation (other than the unrelated clitic movement rule in certain analyses), but a semantic interpretation rule to associate the clitic with the antecedent of the compared clause.

In conclusion, it is not necessary to postulate rules of unbounded deletion for comparatives in Spanish. The rule of WH-movement can reflect the parallelism between questions, relatives, and comparatives. When hypothesizing that comparatives involve WH-movement, it is not necessary to assume that the rule does not obey the Relativized A-over-A principle (as proposed by Chomsky 1977 in connection with mixed terms (Woisetschlaeger 1976). As has been seen, in sentences with a gap in the measure phrase position, the maximal $\overline{\overline{X}}$-phrase moves into COMP, as required by the principle: the phrase that contains the head of the construction in all dialects, or the measure phrase in isolation in those dialects with DE-Insertion. The elimination of an unbounded rule of deletion does not imply the postulation of an exceptional behavior in relation to an otherwise general principle.

NOTES

Work for this paper was completed under Research Grant 410-77-0417 of the former Canada Council.

1. This type of structural description has been rejected for French by Obenauer (1978). See Rivero (1978b) for its advantages in Spanish. Baltin (1978a, 1978b) has also discussed the French constructions.

Notice that even though this formulation of the rule allows specifiers (that is, elements to the left of the head (Chomsky 1970)) to move in isolation, no distinction is needed between specifiers and other syntactic categories.

2. For discussions of *lo*-constructions within a transformational approach, see Contreras (1973), Luján (1972). Here, I follow more closely the analysis proposed by Contreras. Since Luján did not consider empty nodes (Δ) in her treatment, it is unclear to me whether the two analyses are not in fact equivalent.

3. It would also be possible to propose an analysis with an embedded $\overline{\overline{A}}$-phrase that dominates the sequence WH-Pro exclusively. This type of configuration seems to be required on independent grounds as well.

4. Ivonne Bordelois has pointed out to me that in sentences in which the compared constituent is an NP that appears in its basic position, the measure phrase may be absent even though the preposition *de* is not present.

(i) Tengo tantos libros como tú (tienes) revistas.
   'I have as many books as you (have) journals.'

In my dialect, sentence (i) could perhaps be analyzed as a case of bounded deletion. I find (iia) ungrammatical. Sentence (iib) is well formed and covered by my analysis.

(iia) *Le hablaron tantos alumnos como parece que le
      hablarán -- profesores.
(iib) Le hablaron tantos alumnos como parece que le hablarán
      de profesores.
      'As many students spoke to him as it seems professors
      will.'

If (iia) is judged grammatical in certain dialects, WH-movement could have a subcase formulated as in (iii).

(iii) COMP $-$ W$_1$ $-$ $_{\overline{\overline{X}}}$[$_{\overline{\overline{X}}}$[W$_2$ $-$ WH $-$ W$_3$] $-$ W$_4$] $-$ W$_5$

The outer $\overline{\overline{X}}$-brackets would constitute a context predicate. X would range over N and Q, excluding adjectives and adverbs to eliminate the possibility of generating (iv), examples which are deviant in all dialects, as far as I can ascertain. The values for W$_4$ could be $\overline{\overline{N}}$ or $\emptyset$.

(iva) *María es tan inteligente como parece que dicen que
      es -- tonto su hermano.

'Mary is as intelligent as it seems that they say that
her brother is silly.'
(ivb) *María corre tan rápidamente como parece que dicen
que corre -- lentamente su hermano.
'Mary runs as quickly as it seems that they say that
her brother runs slowly.'

The movement analysis is independently needed for the structures discussed in this paper, and it can be modified to accommodate other cases, as indicated in this note.

DISCOURSE CONDITIONS
AND GENDER SMEARING IN FRENCH

Martine Dorel and Engin Sezer
Harvard University

0. **Introduction.** Gender agreement cannot be said to have received the attention it deserves. In French, for example, it is generally assumed that the process may be handled by gender copying rules which copy the syntactic feature of a noun [+feminine] to the determiner and adjective(s) that modify it. A set of morphophonemic rules then applies to yield the correct surface forms. For example, the two words *rime* 'rhyme' and *crime* 'crime' carry the inherent [+feminine] and [-feminine] syntactic features, respectively. Then, the feature copying and relevant morphophonemic rules derive the correct surface forms (1) and (2).

(1) Cette rime était ingénieuse.
    'This rhyme was ingenious [+feminine].'

(2) Ce crime était ingénieux.
    'This crime was ingenious [-feminine].'

In this type of approach to French gender agreement, it is tacitly assumed that only syntactic features are relevant in determining the correct surface forms, and that semantic features like [+female] are not. It should be mentioned in this context that traditional grammarians knew better. Under the general term 'natural gender,' they acknowledged the crucial role of the semantic properties of nouns in gender agreement. We show in this paper how the semantic features of gender triggering NPs are important for gender agreement. The examples here involve [+human] nouns which contain a single syntactic feature, i.e. [+feminine], which can be paired with either one of two semantic features, i.e. [+female] and [-female].

The term 'clash' is used just in case the semantic feature of a noun is the opposite of its syntactic feature (α vs. $-\alpha$). For instance, sentences (3a) and (3b) illustrate a clash, while (4a) and (4b) illustrate a perfect matching of the syntactic and the semantic features.

(3a) Ce professeur est ma cousine.
'This teacher $\begin{bmatrix} -\text{feminine} \\ +\text{female} \end{bmatrix}$ is my cousin.'

(3b) Cette victime était mon père.
'This victim $\begin{bmatrix} +\text{feminine} \\ -\text{female} \end{bmatrix}$ was my father.'

(4a) Ce professeur est mon père.
'This teacher is my father.'

(4b) Cette victime était ma cousine.
'This victim $\begin{bmatrix} +\text{feminine} \\ +\text{female} \end{bmatrix}$ was my cousin.'

Other [-feminine] nouns include *médecin* 'doctor', *censeur* 'vice-principal', *pharmacien* 'pharmacist' (we are not considering those dialects in which the [+female] term for 'pharmacist' is *pharmacienne*, but, rather, those dialects in which *pharmacienne* means 'pharmacist's wife'), *orateur* 'speaker'; other [+feminine] nouns include *vedette* 'star', *célébrité* 'celebrity', and *brute* 'brute'.

Lyons (1968) observes that while (5) is ambiguous, (6) is not.

(5) Le nouveau professeur.
'The new teacher $\begin{bmatrix} -\text{feminine} \\ +/-\text{female} \end{bmatrix}$,'

(6) Le nouveau professeur est beau.
'The new teacher $\begin{bmatrix} -\text{feminine} \\ -\text{female}/*+\text{female} \end{bmatrix}$ is handsome [-feminine].'

The grammar of French must somehow be able to block (6) in its [+female] reading. Comparing the ambiguity of (5) with the unambiguity of (6), Lyons (1968) conjectures that, within NP, agreement is triggered strictly by the relevant syntactic feature of the noun, whereas for predicate adjectives the semantic feature (natural gender in his terms) is relevant. We show that semantic gender features are crucially important for gender agreement even within an NP. In addition, evidence is presented that certain semantic properties of the adjectives which undergo gender agreement determine the correctness of certain surface forms. Finally, we challenge the assumption that gender agreement is solely a part of sentence grammar.

It is generally believed that within an S, the surface form of a predicate adjective can show agreement only with the syntactic feature of the noun it modifies. For instance, (7a) and (8a) are grammatical, while (7b) and (8b) are not.

(7a) La victime est très belle.
(7b) *La victime est très beau.

'The victim $\begin{vmatrix} +\text{feminine} \\ +/-\text{female} \end{vmatrix}$ is very handsome [+f/*-feminine].'

(8a) Le professeur est très beau.
(8b) *Le professeur est très belle.

'The teacher is very handsome [*+feminine/-feminine].'

Not all sentences like (7b) and (8b) are ungrammatical. In fact, under strong discourse conditions, a sentence such as (8b) would be the only possible sentence, if the N had been previously established as having a +female feature. The term 'gender smearing' is used if, in a grammatical sentence, the surface form of an adjective, a determiner, or a pronoun does not agree with the syntactic feature of the N it modifies.

1. **Clash and the nature of the adjective.** As was mentioned in the introduction, Lyons (1968) argues that agreement within NP follows the syntactic feature of the clash noun, without the inherent semantic ambiguity of the noun being altered. Thus, in (9), the subject NP *le nouveau professeur* can be understood as referring to a man or a woman.

(9) Le nouveau professeur (vient d'arriver).
'The new teacher (has arrived).'

This would indicate that a clash between the syntactic and the semantic features is allowed within NP. Here we present evidence that this is far from being a general rule, but that, rather, adjectives must be divided into different types, according to whether or not they allow the existence of a clash.

1.1 **Physical scale adjectives.** Adjectives referring to the physical qualities of the referent of the noun, such as *vieux/vieille* 'old', *gros/grosse* 'fat', *beau/belle* 'handsome', or *grand/grande* 'tall' always block an interpretation where the syntactic feature of the NP clashes with its semantic feature. Thus, in (10) and (11), [-feminine] (henceforth [-f]) implies [-Female] (henceforth [-F]), while [+f] implies [+F].

(10a) Nous allons avoir un vieux professeur cette année.

'We are going to have an old $\begin{bmatrix} -f \\ -F \end{bmatrix}$ teacher this year.'

(10b) Ils avaient une vieille vedette hier à Saturday Night Live.

'They had an old star $\begin{bmatrix} +f \\ +F \end{bmatrix}$ yesterday on Saturday Night Live.'

(11a) On a rencontré le vieux pharmacien à la boulangerie.

'We met the old pharmacist $\begin{bmatrix} -f \\ -F \end{bmatrix}$ at the bakery.'

(11b) La grosse victime a eu du mal à se relever.

'The fat victim $\begin{bmatrix} +f \\ +F \end{bmatrix}$ had a hard time getting back on her feet.'

(12a) Le beau censeur du Lycée Honoré de Balzac va être renvoyé.

'The handsome vice-principal $\begin{bmatrix} -f \\ -F \end{bmatrix}$ of H. de B. is going to be sacked.'

(12b) La belle vedette du Festival est désormais célèbre.

'The handsome star $\begin{bmatrix} +f \\ +F \end{bmatrix}$ of the Festival is now famous.'

Note that (10a) and (10b) could be interpreted as referring to a woman or a man, respectively, if *vieux/vieille* had a temporal reading, i.e. 'old' in the sense that he/she has been a teacher/a star for a long period of time. In addition, it must be mentioned that the interpretation of NPs containing a physical scale adjective is always unambiguous, whether or not the NP has a specific (anaphoric) or a nonspecific reading, which, as will be argued later in this paper, is not the case with other types of adjectives. The only time when there may be a clash between features is, as is the case with all adjectives, when the NP has a generic reading, as in (13).

(13a) Un vieux professeur a toujours des chances d'être renvoyé.

'An old teacher $\begin{bmatrix} -f \\ +F \end{bmatrix}$ / $\begin{bmatrix} -f \\ -F \end{bmatrix}$ is always likely to be sacked.'

(13b) Une vieille célébrité a toujours des rides extra-ordinaires.

'An old star $\begin{bmatrix} +f \\ +F \end{bmatrix}$ / $\begin{bmatrix} +f \\ -F \end{bmatrix}$ always has formidable wrinkles.'

We return to this problem of specificity/nonspecificity and genericness in Section 3.2 of this paper.

It is now clear that Lyons' analysis was but an assumption, and that the choice of adjective is a determining factor in the interpretation of sentences containing [+F] nouns. In the same way that clash is not allowed in attributive position with physical scale adjectives, it is also not allowed in predicative position.

(14a) Ce professeur est vraiment trop vieux pour enseigner.

'This teacher is really too old $\begin{bmatrix} -f \\ -F/*+F \end{bmatrix}$ to be teaching.'

(14b) La vedette était trop vieille pour le rôle.

'The star $\begin{bmatrix} +f \\ +F/*-F \end{bmatrix}$ was too old for the part.'

(15a) Tu aurais dû voir comme le censeur de leur lycée
était gros!
'You should have seen how fat the vice-principal of
their grammar school was / $\begin{bmatrix} -f \\ -F/*+F \end{bmatrix}$!"

(15b) Tu aurais dû voir comme la vedette d'hier soir était
grosse!
'You should have seen fat last night's star $\begin{bmatrix} +f \\ +F/*-F \end{bmatrix}$
was!'

Thus, in the case of physical scale adjectives, grammatical
gender agreement implies a match between the syntactic and
the semantic features.

1.2 Ordinal adjectives. The reason why Lyons' example
(cf. (9)) was ambiguous is that *nouveau* belongs to the class
of what we call 'ordinal adjectives', which includes adjectives
such as *ancien/ancienne* 'former', *premier/première* 'first', and
all the ordinal numbers, and *vieux/vieille* in the temporal
sense mentioned earlier. These adjectives always allow a clash
between the semantic and the syntactic features of the NP.

(16a) L'ancien médecin est venu soigner ma mère.

'The former doctor $\begin{bmatrix} -f \\ +F/-F \end{bmatrix}$ came to take care of my
mother.'

(16b) L'ancienne vedette des Jeux Olympiques est arrivée
hier.

'The former star $\begin{bmatrix} +f \\ +F/-F \end{bmatrix}$ of the Olympic Games
arrived yesterday.'

(17a) Le dernier ingénieur a quitté l'usine en 1970.

'The last engineer $\begin{bmatrix} -f \\ -F/+F \end{bmatrix}$ left the factory in 1970.'

(17b) La dernière idole du moment me déplaît profondément.'

'I really dislike the last idol of the day $\begin{bmatrix} +f \\ +F/-F \end{bmatrix}$.'

Here again, the interpretation seems to be the same in
predicate position.

(18a) Cette année, le professeur de biologie est nouveau.

'This year, the biology teacher $\begin{bmatrix} -f \\ -F/+F \end{bmatrix}$ is new.'

(18b) Hier soir, la vedette était nouvelle.

'Last night, the star $\begin{bmatrix} +f \\ +F/-F \end{bmatrix}$ was new.'

Contrary to what happens with physical scale adjectives, syntactic gender agreement for ordinal adjectives does not force an interpretation where the semantic feature matches the syntactic one. The semantic component of the grammar must look at the quality of the adjective for the final interpretation to be assigned to sentences containing [+F] nouns.

1.3 Neutral adjectives. In the case of all the other adjectives, it seems that the first available reading is the one in which there is no clash, but the other reading is also available. We therefore refer to such adjectives as 'neutral adjectives'.

(19a) Un professeur très sérieux est arrivé hier.

'A very reliable teacher $\begin{bmatrix} -f \\ -F/+F \end{bmatrix}$ arrived yesterday.'

(19b) Une célébrité très sérieuse nous affirme que la terre est carrée.

'A very reliable celebrity asserts that the earth is square.'

(20a) Au Lycée Honoré de Balzac, ils ont un censeur intelligent.

'At H.de.B. grammar school, they have a smart vice-principal.'

(20b) Pour une fois, ils avaient une vedette intelligente.

'For once, they had an intelligent star $\begin{bmatrix} +f \\ +F/-F \end{bmatrix}$.'

(21a) Ils ont donné le Prix Goncourt à un auteur inintéressant.

'They gave the Goncourt Prize to an uninteresting author $\begin{bmatrix} -f \\ -F/+F \end{bmatrix}$.'

(21b) Ils avaient une vedette inintéressante hier.

'They had an uninteresting star yesterday $\begin{bmatrix} +f \\ +F/-F \end{bmatrix}$.'

In examples (19)-(21) the (a)-cases are less ambiguous than the (b)-cases. This might be due to the fact that the [-f] nouns have typical [-f] endings.

The crucial fact about this class of neutral adjectives is that they produce much less ambiguity (if any) in VP position than in NP position, as illustrated by examples (22)-(24).

(22a) Le professeur de français n'est pas très sérieux.

'The French teacher $\begin{bmatrix} -f \\ -F/??+F \end{bmatrix}$ is not very reliable.'

(22b) La célébrité qui dit que la terre est carrée n'est pas très sérieuse.'

'The celebrity who says that the earth is square is

not very reliable $\begin{bmatrix} +f \\ +F/?-F \end{bmatrix}$.'

(23a) Cet auteur est vraiment inintéressant.

'This author $\begin{bmatrix} -f \\ -F/?+F \end{bmatrix}$ is really uninteresting.'

(23b) La vedette du film est vraiment inintéressante.

'The star $\begin{bmatrix} +f \\ +F/?-F \end{bmatrix}$ in this film is really uninteresting.'

(24a) Le professeur de biologie est complètement idiot.

'The biology teacher $\begin{bmatrix} -f \\ -F/??+F \end{bmatrix}$ is really stupid.'

(24b) La vedette de ce film est complètement idiote.

'The star $\begin{bmatrix} +f \\ +F/?-F \end{bmatrix}$ in this film is really stupid.'

It can be seen, from these examples that sentences containing [-f] nouns are much less ambiguous than those containing [+f] nouns. This, as argued in Section 2, is due to the fact that it is extremely difficult to smear agreement for adjectives referring to feminine nouns. The availability of counterparts with feminine agreement on the adjective in the case of (22a), (23a), and (24a) is responsible for their lesser degree of ambiguity.

We would now like to present evidence for smearing of the syntactic feature outside strong discourse contexts, and to argue that NP-bound adjectives behave differently from VP-bound adjectives.

2. Smearing outside strong discourse contexts

2.1 Within NP. First, the syntax and the semantics of [+F] nouns are very delicate areas of French grammar. Judgments are therefore bound to be fuzzier and more inconsistent than anywhere else. However, it is quite possible to reach a number of generalizations, the first one being that the syntactic features of the determiner and the adjective within NP need to agree with that of the noun, unless the determiner is covert or neutral with respect to gender.

2.1.1 The determiner. As exemplified in (25) through (28), the determiner must agree syntactically with the noun if it is overt.

204 / Martine Dorel and Engin Sezer

(25) *La professeur de français est malade.

'The [+f] French teacher $\begin{bmatrix} -f \\ +F \end{bmatrix}$ is sick.'

(26) *La censeur de leur lycée n'est pas très agréable.

'The [+f] vice-principal $\begin{bmatrix} -f \\ +F \end{bmatrix}$ of their grammar school is not very pleasant.'

(27) *Le victime était un homme.

'The [-f] victim $\begin{bmatrix} +f \\ -F \end{bmatrix}$ was a man.'

(28) *Ce vedette ne me plaît pas du tout.

'I don't like this [-f] star $\begin{bmatrix} +f \\ -F \end{bmatrix}$ at all.

If the determiner were unspecified with respect to gender, or if its gender could not be identified because of contraction, the resulting sentences would be grammatical, but there would be no way to check whether the determiner comes from the [-f] or from the [+f] alternative.

(29) Cette ingénieur ne me plaît pas du tout.

'I don't like this [+f] engineer $\begin{bmatrix} -f \\ +F \end{bmatrix}$ at all.'

(30) L'ingénieur qui vient d'arriver ne travaille pas assez.
    'The (+ or -f?) engineer who has just arrived doesn't work enough.'

In (29), *cette* is marked [+f], but actually would sound the same as *cet* [-f]. Since such sentences would not come up in writing, it is safer to say that the determiner cannot be smeared.

2.1.2 **The adjective.** It seems that the only adjectives which can be smeared are ordinal adjectives, although, even in that case, the resulting sentences are not very good. In all the cases, the outcome is much better if the determiner is contracted or unspecified for gender. This, however, only holds for [-f] nouns. Under no circumstances is it possible to smear an adjective within an NP containing a [+f] noun.

(31a) ?La nouvelle professeur de maths vient d'arriver.

'The new (+f) maths teacher $\begin{bmatrix} -f \\ +F \end{bmatrix}$ has just arrived.'

(31b) Leur nouvelle professeur de maths vient d'arriver.
    'Their (UNSP) new maths teacher has just arrived.'

(32) L'ancienne censeur était bien plus sympathique.

'The former [+f] vice-principal $\begin{bmatrix} -f \\ +F \end{bmatrix}$ was much more sympathetic.'

(33a) *Le nouveau victime des terroristes a été emmené à l'hôpital.

'The new (-f) victim $\begin{bmatrix} +f \\ -F \end{bmatrix}$ of the terrorists was taken to the hospital.'

(33b) *Leur nouveau victime a été emmené à l'hôpital.

'Their (UNSP) new [-f] victim...'

(34a) *Le premier célébrité des américains était John Wayne.

'The first (-f) celebrity of the Americans was John Wayne.'

(34b) *Leur premier célébrité était John Wayne.

'Their (UNSP) first [-f] celebrity was John Wayne.'

The case is the same for neutral adjectives as for physical scale adjectives: in neither case can the syntactic feature of the adjective clash with that of the N.

(35a) ?*La grosse professeur fait un régime.

?'The fat (+f) teacher $\begin{bmatrix} -f \\ +F \end{bmatrix}$ is on a diet.'

(35b) ?*Leur grosse professeur fait un régime.

'Their (UNSP) fat [+f] teacher is on a diet.'

(36a) ?*La belle censeur fait du charme à tous les hommes.

(36b) ?*Notre belle censeur fait du charme à tous les hommes.

'The [+f]/our (UNSP) handsome [+f] vice-principal $\begin{bmatrix} -f \\ +F \end{bmatrix}$ flirts with all the men.'

(37a) *Le gros vedette m'a dégoûté.

'The fat (-f) star $\begin{bmatrix} +f \\ -F \end{bmatrix}$ repulsed me.'

(37b) *Leur gros vedette m'a dégoûté.

'Their (UNSP) fat [-f] star $\begin{bmatrix} +f \\ -F \end{bmatrix}$ repulsed me.'

(38a) *Ce vieux victime me fait pitié.

'I feel sorry for this old (-f) victim $\begin{bmatrix} +f \\ -F \end{bmatrix}$.'

(38b) *Leur vieux victime me fait pitié.

'I feel sorry for their (UNSP) old (-f) victim $\begin{bmatrix} +f \\ -F \end{bmatrix}$.'

(39a) *La professeur italienne repart demain.

'The [+f] Italian [+f] teacher is leaving tomorrow.'

(39b) ?*Notre professeur italienne repart demain.

(40) ???L'ingénieur italienne repart demain.

'The (UNSP) Italian [+f] engineer $\begin{bmatrix} -f \\ +F \end{bmatrix}$ is leaving tomorrow.'

(41) ???L'auteur intéressante doit passer tout à l'heure.

'The (UNSP) interesting [+f] author $\begin{bmatrix} -f \\ +F \end{bmatrix}$ is going to come by later on.'

Compare with: *Le professeur intéressante doit passer tout à l'heure.

(42a) *Le victime italien a eu le bras cassé.
'The [-f] Italian [-f] victim had his arm broken.'
(42b) ??Notre victime italien a eu le bras cassé.

Examples such as (40) through (42) illustrate the fact that sentences are always better if the article is covert (contracted), for nouns having a [-f] syntactic feature. With the [+f] nouns, it seems that postnominal [-f] adjectives are more acceptable than prenominal ones, if the determiner is unspecified with respect to gender, as shown in (42b).

From the foregoing examples, we can draw the generalizations: (1) that smearing within NP is possible; (2) that it is possible if the adjective belongs to the class of ordinal adjectives and if the syntactic feature of the determiner is unspecified; (3) that (1) and (2) hold for [-f] nouns, but not for [+f] ones; and (4) that smearing with other types of adjectives than ordinal adjectives is always better for [-f] nouns.

Thus, although it is difficult to smear syntactic agreement within NP, we cannot maintain that it is impossible, following Lyons. The nature of the determiner and of the adjective, and the syntactic feature of the noun should all be taken into consideration when studying gender agreement.

Another conclusion that we may (tentatively, for the moment) draw from this section is that, in case a sentence is unambiguous, we cannot smear the syntactic feature of the NP-bound determiner or adjective. This directly follows from the fact that no smearing can take place if the (prenominal) adjective is a physical scale adjective (cf. (35)-(38)). Section 1 illustrated the fact that all physical scale adjectives led to an unambiguous reading of the NP, where the syntactic feature matched the semantic one. That ordinal adjectives be the most available to smearing is equally related to the fact that they are the most ambiguous of all adjectives. The case of neutral adjectives is not as clear, but we show later on in this paper that these adjectives lead to an unambiguous interpretation of the NP when the NP is marked specific-discourse anaphoric. This might be the reason why they behave similarly to physical scale adjectives in (39)-(42). Note that we could not attempt to check the grammaticality of (39)-(42) in a nonspecific context, since *un/une*, the French indeterminate article, never contracts. Since smearing is only available to cases where the determiner is covert, nonspecific examples would not tell us anything.

2.2 Within VP. Gender agreement within VP is more easily available to smearing than within NP. It seems, as Lyons pointed out, that it is more likely to follow the rules of natural gender agreement than those of syntax. In this section, we show (1) that the same adjectives that could not be smeared within NP (i.e. the physical scale adjectives) cannot be smeared in predicative position, (2) that ordinal adjectives are easily available to smearing, here again, in the case of [-f] nouns, and (3) that the third type of adjectives (i.e. neutral adjectives) are much better candidates for smearing here than within NP. In addition, we demonstrate that participial predicative adjectives are extremely easy to smear, and that they must, therefore, be compared to predicate nouns, which follow the rules of natural gender agreement, rather than to other adjectives. As a general rule, smearing is shown to apply much more widely in predicative position than within NP. This section emphasizes the need for two gender agreement rules, i.e. one for NP-bound elements and one for VP-bound elements, as well as the relevance of the semantic component in gender agreement.

2.2.1 The adjective. The examples in (43)-(46) illustrate the fact that the syntactic feature of a physical scale adjective must match that of the noun, unless the determiner is covert.

(43a) *Ce professeur est vraiment trop vieille pour enseigner.
'This [-f] teacher $\begin{bmatrix} -f \\ +F \end{bmatrix}$ is really too old [+f] to be teaching.'

(43b) ?Leur professeur de maths est vraiment trop vieille pour enseigner.
'Their maths teacher ...'

(44a) *Le censeur est vraiment trop grosse.
'The [-f] vice-principal $\begin{bmatrix} -f \\ +F \end{bmatrix}$ is really too fat [+f].'

(44b) ?Notre censeur est vraiment trop grosse.
'Our (UNSP) vice-principal ...'

(45a) *Cette vedette est vraiment trop vieux pour un rôle comme ça.
'This star $\begin{bmatrix} +f \\ -F \end{bmatrix}$ is really too old [-f] for such a part.'

(45b) ??Leur vedette est vraiment trop vieux pour un rôle comme ça.
'Their (UNSP) star is really too old for such a role.'

(46a) *La victime était trop grand pour rentrer dans
l'ambulance.

'The victim $\begin{bmatrix} +f \\ -F \end{bmatrix}$ was too tall [-f] to fit in the ambulance.'

(46b) ?Leur victime était trop grand pour rentrer dans
l'ambulance.
'Their (UNSP) victim ...'

It appears from these examples that, although physical scale
adjectives had to agree syntactically with the N in NP position,
they may be smeared in case the determiner is covert, when
they belong to the VP. It is crucial that this be the case for
[+f] nouns as well as for [-f] ones. It indicates that the process of GA is more semantically governed within VP than within
NP.

Ordinal adjectives, however, do not seem to be available to
smearing in case they refer to [+f] nouns. They may still be
smeared if the noun is marked [-f].

(47a) ?Le professeur de maths est nouvelle, cette année.

'The maths teacher $\begin{bmatrix} -f \\ +F \end{bmatrix}$ is new [+f] this year.'

(47b) Notre professeur de maths est nouvelle cette année.
'Our (UNSP) ...'

(48a) *La vedette d'hier soir était nouveau.

'Last night's star $\begin{bmatrix} +f \\ -F \end{bmatrix}$ was new [-f].'

(48b) *Leur vedette d'hier soir était nouveau.
'Their (UNSP) ...'

(49a) ??Le pharmacien du Boulevard Raspail était première.

'The pharmacist $\begin{bmatrix} -f \\ +F \end{bmatrix}$ of the Boulevard R. was first
[+f].'

(49b) Notre pharmacien était dernière, bien sûr.

'Our pharmacist $\begin{bmatrix} -f \\ +F \end{bmatrix}$ was last [+f], of course.'

Comparing the degree of grammaticality of sentences such as
(47a) and (49a) with that of (43a) and (44a), we may advance
that ordinal adjectives are far more available to smearing than
physical scale adjectives, as could be expected.

As far as neutral adjectives are concerned, it is clear that
they are the easiest to smear, whether they refer to [-f] or
to [+f] nouns.

(50) L'auteur de ce livre est furieuse de ne pas avoir été
payée.

'The author $\begin{bmatrix} -f \\ +F \end{bmatrix}$ of this book is furious [+f] not to have been paid.'

(51) Ce professeur de maths n'est bonne à rien.

'This maths teacher $\begin{bmatrix} -f \\ +F \end{bmatrix}$ is good [+f] for nothing.'

(52) Le pharmacien du Boulevard Raspail est allemande.

'The pharmacist $\begin{bmatrix} -f \\ +F \end{bmatrix}$ of the Boulevard R. is German [+f].'

(53) ?La victime de l'accident était furieux contre le conducteur.

'The victim $\begin{bmatrix} +f \\ -F \end{bmatrix}$ of the accident was furious [-f] at the driver.'

(54) ?La vedette d'hier soir(n)'était bon à rien.

'Last night's star $\begin{bmatrix} +f \\ -F \end{bmatrix}$ was good [-f] for nothing.'

(55a) ??La vedette du dernier film est allemand.
(55b) ??Leur vedette est allemand.

Examples (55a) and (55b) are extremely strange. In such cases, it seems that it would be more natural to have recourse to a noun, as in (56).

(56) La vedette du dernier film est un allemand.
'The star of the last film is a German.'

It is worth pointing out that one [+f] noun accepts smearing on the adjective. That noun, i.e. *brute* 'brute', however, has a direct [-f] connotation (!), which probably explains the facts.

(57) Cette brute est pourtant très gentil quand on ne l'embête pas.

'This brute $\begin{bmatrix} +f \\ -F \end{bmatrix}$ is very nice [-f], though, when you don't bother him.'

On the other hand, there is another [+f] noun which can never accept a [-f] adjective, and that is the noun *personne* 'a person'.

(58) *Cette personne était furieux/*allemand/*vraiment très gentil, etc.

'This person $\begin{bmatrix} +f \\ -F \end{bmatrix}$ was furious /German/ really very nice [-f].'

2.2.2 **Past participles.** As was mentioned earlier, past participles in predicative position are much easier to smear than regular adjectives.

(59) Le professeur de maths était surprise de nous voir tous là.

'The maths teacher $\begin{bmatrix} -f \\ +F \end{bmatrix}$ was surprised [+f] to see us all there.'

(60) L'auteur de ce livre n'a pas été comprise.
'The author of this book was not understood [+f].'

(61) La victime de l'accident s'est vite remis sur pied.

'The victim $\begin{bmatrix} +f \\ -F \end{bmatrix}$ of the accident recuperated [-f] very fast.'

(62) La vedette d'hier soir a été pris en photo au moins 200 fois.
'Last night's star $\begin{bmatrix} +f \\ -F \end{bmatrix}$ was taken [-f] in photo at least 200 times.'

It is true that agreement has become laxer in the case of participial adjectives, and that may well be one reason why (59)-(62) are acceptable.

2.2.3 **Predicate nouns.** The agreement of predicate nouns has nothing to do with syntax. In all the following cases, the syntactic feature of the predicate noun clashes with that of the subject NP, and yet the results are perfectly grammatical.

(63) Le médecin était une femme.
'The doctor [-f] was a woman [+f].

(64) Cet ingénieur est une imbécile.

'This engineer $\begin{bmatrix} -f \\ +F \end{bmatrix}$ is an idiot [+f].'

(65) La vedette est un idiot fini.

'The star $\begin{bmatrix} +f \\ -F \end{bmatrix}$ is a complete idiot [-f].'

(66) La victime était un puceau.

'The victim $\begin{bmatrix} +f \\ -F \end{bmatrix}$ was a virgin [-f].'

This section shows that gender agreement in VP follows a different pattern from gender agreement within NP. We need two processes of gender agreement, in order to account for the difference between ???*L'auteur intéressante doit passer tout à l'heure* (cf. (41)) and *L'auteur de ce livre est très intéressante.* We can now say that agreement is more likely to follow the rules of natural gender in predicative position than within NP. This section has also emphasized the relevance of the semantics of the adjective, the contrast between [-f] and [+f] nouns, and the special behavior of participial adjectives and predicate nouns, whose syntactic feature may clash with that of the N to which they refer.

2.3 **Smearing of appositive adjectives and pronouns.** It is quite clear that both appositive adjectives and pronouns may be smeared when the speaker wants to force an interpretation where the semantic and syntactic features of the noun clash with one another. Section 3 shows that there exist discourse limitations on this apparently free process, however. Sentences (67)-(70) illustrate the availability of smearing for appositive adjectives.

(67) Pris de panique, la victime s'enfuit à toutes jambes.
'Panick-striken [-f], the victim $\begin{bmatrix} +f \\ -F \end{bmatrix}$ took to his heels.'

(68) Furieux contre lui-même, la vedette décida de partir.
'Furious [-f] with himself [-f], the star decided to leave.'

(69) Prise de court, le médecin ne savait que faire.
'Taken [+f] at short notice, the doctor $\begin{bmatrix} -f \\ +F \end{bmatrix}$ did not know what to do.'

(70) Furieuse, le professeur de français quitta la salle.
'Furious [+f], the French teacher $\begin{bmatrix} -f \\ +F \end{bmatrix}$ left the room.'

Examples (67)-(70) show that there is no contrast between regular adjectives and participial adjectives in apposition. Note also that, here, all three types of adjectives behave similarly.

(71) Vieux comme il l'était, la vedette d'hier soir m'a fait pitié.
'Old [-f] as he was, last night's star [+f/-F] made me feel sorry (for him).'

(72) Vieille comme elle l'est, le pharmacien ne tiendra pas longtemps.
'Old [+f] as she is, the pharmacist $\begin{bmatrix} -f \\ +F \end{bmatrix}$ will not last very long.'

Sentences (68), (71), and (72) already illustrate the smearing of pronouns, which is emphasized further by examples such as (73) and (74).

(73) Si tu avais vu la victime, tu aurais eu pitié de lui.
    'If you had seen the victim $\begin{bmatrix} +f \\ -F \end{bmatrix}$, you would have felt sorry for him.'

(74) Si tu avais vu le travail que ce médecin avait, tu aurais eu pitié d'elle.
    'If you had seen the work that this doctor $\begin{bmatrix} -f \\ +F \end{bmatrix}$ had, you would have felt sorry for her.'

It appears, therefore, that smearing outside S is quite easy to achieve.

3. **Prohibited smearing.** In certain cases, the smearing of a predicative adjective, an appositive adjective, or a pronoun, which would otherwise be available to smearing, is prohibited. The first case occurs when the N is modified by a prenominal physical scale adjective, which conveys an unambiguous reading to the NP.

3.1 **The N is modified by a prenominal physical scale adjective.** Sentences (75)-(76) illustrate the prohibition of smearing in predicative position.

(75) *Le vieux professeur de maths est nouvelle.
    'The old maths teacher $\begin{bmatrix} -f \\ *+F \end{bmatrix}$ is new [+f].'

(76) *La grosse victime était furieux contre le conducteur.
    'The fat victim $\begin{bmatrix} +f \\ *-F \end{bmatrix}$ was furious [-f] at the driver.'

The same holds for appositive adjectives and pronouns.

(77) *Prise de court, le beau professeur ne savait que faire.
    'Taken at short notice [+f], the handsome teacher $\begin{bmatrix} -f \\ *+F \end{bmatrix}$ did not know what to do.'

(78) *Pris de panique, la belle victime s'enfuit à toutes jambes.
    'Panick-striken [-f], the handsome victim $\begin{bmatrix} +f \\ *-F \end{bmatrix}$ took to his/her heels.'

(79) *Si tu avais vu le vieux ingénieur, tu aurais eu pitié d'elle.

'If you had seen the old engineer $\begin{bmatrix} -f \\ *+F \end{bmatrix}$, you would have felt sorry for her.'

(80) *Si tu avais vu la grosse vedette, tu aurais eu pitié de lui.

'If you had seen the fat star $\begin{bmatrix} +f \\ *-F \end{bmatrix}$, you would have felt sorry for him.'

All these sentences would be fine if the syntactic feature on the adjective or the pronoun were reversed.

3.2 **Specificity vs. nonspecificity.** This section concerns the third class of adjectives, i.e. the neutral class. We mentioned in Section 2.1.2 that neutral adjectives could lead to an unambiguous reading of the noun they modify in case the NP is discourse anaphoric. Thus, sentences (81a) and (82a) are unambiguous, as opposed to (81b) and (82b), which can have +F or -F referents.

(81a) J'ai rencontré un célèbre professeur américain hier.
   'I met a famous American professor -[*+F] yesterday.'
(81b) Je vais chercher un professeur américain pour le cours de syntaxe.
   'I am going to look for an American professor $\begin{bmatrix} -f \\ -F/+F \end{bmatrix}$ for the syntax class.'

(82a) J'ai parlé avec une vedette italienne hier.
   'I talked with an Italian star $\begin{bmatrix} +f \\ +F/?*-F \end{bmatrix}$ yesterday.'
(82b) Chabrol cherche une vedette italienne pour son prochain film.
   'Chabrol is looking for an Italian $\begin{bmatrix} +f \\ +F/-F \end{bmatrix}$ for his next film.'

It is impossible to continue the discourse containing (81a) or (82a) in the way of (83) and (84), respectively.

(83) *Tu la connais peut-être, d'ailleurs.
   'Maybe you know her, actually.'

(84) *Tu le connais peut-être, d'ailleurs.
   'Maybe you know him, actually.'

Rather, (84) would be the correct continuation of (81a), while (83) would be the correct continuation of (82a).
   In the case of (81b) and (82b), however, both a [+f] and a [-f] pronoun could be used to refer to the NP in a following discourse.

(85) Tu en connais peut-être un, ou une?
     'Maybe you know one [-f] or one [+f]?'

Sentence (85) could continue either (81b) or (82b). Clearly, what is going on here has nothing to do with sentence grammar, but belongs, rather, to the area of discourse grammar.

It is hoped that this section has demonstrated the usefulness of an analysis of gender agreement which takes both sentence and discourse grammars into account. We intend to pursue our research in this domain, and to add to the present facts.

4. **Obligatoriness of smearing.** We here present further evidence in favor of an analysis of gender agreement which combines sentence and discourse grammars. In cases where the previous discourse has established the semantic feature of a [-f] noun as being [+F], the adjective in predicative position must be smeared.

(86) Toutes ces dames étaient très élégantes. Même le
      pharmacien était élégante/*élégant.
     'All the ladies were quite elegant. Even the pharmacist $\begin{bmatrix} -f \\ +F \end{bmatrix}$ was elegant [+f/*-f].'

(87) Toutes ces dames sont beaucoup trop grosses. Même
      le professeur de français est trop grosse/*gros.
     'All these ladies are much too fat. Even the French teacher $\begin{bmatrix} -f \\ +F \end{bmatrix}$ is too fat [+f/*-f].'

Judgments are much more delicate concerning [+f] nouns. Some informants rejected the sentences containing a smeared adjective, others rejected those that contained a nonsmeared adjective.

(88) ?Tous les hommes qui jouent dans le film sont furieux.
      Même la vedette est furieux/furieuse.
     'All the men who act in the film are furious. Even the star $\begin{bmatrix} +f \\ -F \end{bmatrix}$ is furious [-f/+f].'

More research needs to be done concerning [+f] nouns. For the moment, we only say that the case for [-f] nouns is very clear. Crucially, but not surprisingly, once the adjective has been smeared, one may not refer to the N with a pronoun that contradicts the syntactic feature of the adjective and the semantic feature of the N.

(89a) *Il avait mis son plus beau pantalon.
(89b) Elle avait mis son plus beau pantalon.

Only (89b) can serve as a continuation of (86).

5. **Conclusion.** This paper has shown (1) that gender agreement for [+human] nouns is not as straightforward as is usually believed; (2) that we cannot take agreement to apply across the board, from NP-bound adjectives to VP-bound ones, to elements that are outside the S that contains the noun, following the syntactic feature of that very noun; but rather (3) that agreement within NP differs from agreement outside NP; and (4) that such factors as the quality of the adjective, the overtness of the determiner, and a context of specificity or nonspecificity have to be taken into account. We also hope that it is now clear that gender agreement is as much part of discourse grammar as of sentence grammar. Many areas are still unexplored, and the analysis here needs to be developed further, but we intend to work on this area of grammar until we come to clearer conclusions.

AN ALTERNATIVE TO WH-MOVEMENT IN FRENCH RELATIVE CLAUSES

Denis Bouchard
University of Montreal

0. Introduction. I present here two problems for a trans-formational approach to WH-interrogatives and restrictive rela-tive clauses (RRC) in advanced dialects of French. The first problem is that RRCs allow some form of stranding, whereas WH-interrogatives do not. The second problem has to do with a similar behavior of these constructions relative to preposition deletion. Instead of adding new constraints to the grammar, I look at the possibility of explaining the facts without the use of WH-movement, and sketch an approach where these con-structions are base generated.

1. Stranding in restrictive relative clauses. If (1c) is derived by a rule of WH-movement as in (2), one could expect an intermediate form such as (3), which would correspond to the intermediate form of (1a) given in (1b), where Free Dele-tion in COMP has not applied.

(1a) La fille avec qui tu parles est correcte.
　　'The girl with whom you are talking is OK.'
(1b) La fille avec qui que tu parles est correcte.
　　'The girl with whom that you are talking is OK.'
(1c) La fille que tu parles avec est correcte.

(2) La fille [$_{\bar{S}}$[$_{COMP_\uparrow}$ que][$_S$ tu parles avec qui]]

(3a) *La fille qui que tu parles avec
(3b) *La fille qui tu parles avec

But although (1b) does show up in some dialects of French, the sentences in (3) never do. There could be some reason to exclude (3a) since the sequence QU-QU does not appear in RRCs anyhow, unless it is oblique, as shown in (4).

(4a) *La fille qui que tu as vue
'The girl who that you saw'
(4b) *La fille qui que est venue
'The girl who that came'

But (3b) cannot follow from such an explanation. I have no evidence therefore that WH-movement has applied to derive (1c) since there are no intermediate forms with an overt WH-word. As the sentences in (5) show, QU-QU sequences are possible in interrogatives in some dialects of French.

(5a) Qui qui est venu?
'Who that came?'
(5b) Qui que tu as vu?
'Who that you saw?'

Whatever constraint blocked the surfacing of an overt WH-word in stranded RRCs does not seem to be operative here. One could then expect to find some evidence for WH-movement in interrogatives with overt WH-words and stranded prepositions. But as the sentences in (6) show, stranding is not possible in interrogatives.

(6a) *Qui (que) tu parles avec?
'Who (that) you are talking with?'
(6b) *Qui (que) tu es pour?
'Who (that) you are for?'

Free relatives do not allow stranding either. The matching effect as advocated in Grimshaw (1977) is also operative in French, as shown in (7a-b).

(7a) [$_{NP}$ Qui a bu] boira
'Who drank will drink'
(7b) *[$_{PP}$Avec qui je suis sorti hier] m'a dit... (Hirsch-bühler 1976)
'With who I went out yesterday told me...'
(7c) Whoever you spoke to is probably a joker.
(7d) *Qui (que) Jean est pour, je suis contre.
'Whoever John is for, I am against.'
(7e) Qui que ce soit que Jean est pour, je suis contre.
'Whoever it is that John is for, I am against.'

The matching effect problem is solved in English by stranding the preposition as shown in (7c). But French does not have stranding in free relatives (7d) and must use a cleft sentence to get around that problem (7e). It seems then that stranding is not generalized to all WH-constructions in French, but only to those which have no overt WH-word and which have an antecedent.

2. **Prepositions that delete.** According to Chomsky and Lasnik (1977), WH-words in RRCs are semantically empty, and therefore they may delete freely in COMP. If the WH-phrase is a PP, no deletion is possible because deletion of the preposition would not be recoverable. This would explain why (8a) is ruled out.

(8a) *La fille que je sors est correcte.
'The girl that I go out is OK.'
(8b) *La fille [$_{COMP}$avec que] je sors est correcte.
'The girl with that I go out is OK.'

But there is no principled reason to rule out (8b) since everything is recoverable. Chomsky-Lasnik designed their deletion rule and filter so that the whole WH-phrase is deleted, a sort of modified A over A (A/A). But it is only an artifact of the theory since there is no such A/A for stranding.

A problem for this theory is that some prepositions do delete, as in (9) and (10).

(9a) La maison dans laquelle j'habite
'The house in which I live'
(9b) La maison où j'habite
'The house where I live'

(10a) La tablette sur laquelle est le dictionnaire
'The shelf on which is the dictionary'
(10b) La tablette où est le dictionnaire
'The shelf where is the dictionary'

In (9b) and (10b), prepositions *dans* and *sur* are lost. But the WH-word *où* retains the information that the argument is a LOCATIVE. If we have functional structures similar to those proposed by Bresnan (1978), then the sentences may be interpreted without these prepositions, and therefore the sentences are accepted. There are other examples of this type in advanced French, as shown in (11).

(11a) Je pense à Pierre.
'I am thinking about Pierre.'
(11b) Je parle de Pierre à Jean.
'I am talking about Pierre to Jean.'
(11c) Si c'est le gars que je pense, il est ben correct.
(à → ∅)
'If it's the guy I think, he is OK.'

(11d) Le gars que je te parle, il est correct. (de → ∅)
'The guy that I talk to you, he is OK.'
(11e) *La cuillère que je mange est trop grosse.
'The spoon that I eat is too big.'
(11f) La cuillère que je mange avec est trop grosse.
'The spoon that I eat with is too big.'

It seems that if the preposition is strictly subcategorized, it can delete because it is easily recoverable in the lexicon.[1] If one tries to explain these facts in the spirit of Chomsky-Lasnik (1977), one could say that these prepositions have no semantic content and are only place holders like WH-words in RRCs, and that they delete because they are fully recoverable. But this would create problems elsewhere. If one looks at Chomsky (1978) and his approach to infinitival relative clauses, one would then be drawn to delete all strictly subcategorized prepositions in the COMP of these structures.

Deletion in COMP is obligatory in the context (61).
(61) ___infinitive complement
We now understand 'obligatory deletion' to mean: delete wherever possible, i.e. except where deletion is unrecoverable (Chomsky 1978:28).

Example (12) could therefore not be generated.

(12) A man to whom to give the book

There is a bigger problem: some nonstrictly subcategorized prepositions delete as shown in (13).

(13a) Je coupe le fromage avec le couteau.
'I cut the cheese with the knife.'
(13b) Je coupe le fromage.
'I cut the cheese.'
(13c) Le couteau que je coupe (Remacle 1960)
'The knife that I cut (with)'

It seems that, in order to stick to the [-semantic] feature, one has to say that *avec* is the instrumental preposition and that *couper* is strictly subcategorized for INSTRUMENTAL, so that the deleted preposition in (13c) is recoverable by the functional structures. *Couper* would then have three entries in the lexicon.

(14) couper: V, ___ NP PP NP_1 COUPER NP_2 INSTR.

V, ___ NP   (x) NP_1 COUPER NP_2 $x_{instr.}$

V, ___ NP   (x) NP_1 COUPER x INSTR.

Thus (15a) would be amgibuous between (15b) and (15c).

(15a) Le fil que je coupe
'The wire that I cut'
(15b) Le fil que je coupe [e] (direct object)
'The wire that I cut'
(15c) Le fil que je coupe avec [e] (PP instrument)
'The wire that I cut with'

But (15a) is not ambiguous: it only has the direct object reading and thus COUPER does not seem to be strictly sub-categorized for INSTR. Why then is (13c) accepted? It seems that although nonstrictly subcategorized prepositions are not recoverable like strictly subcategorized prepositions by the lexicon, they may be deleted and are recoverable if they have a close semantic relation to the verb. COUTEAU and COUPER are related in this way because COUTEAU is an expected in-strumental for COUPER. If one goes back to (15a), it can have the instrumental reading even if it does not have the preposition *avec* when it has a direct object, as in (16).

(16) Le fil que je coupe le fromage
'The wire that I cut the cheese'

In (16), *fil* is unambiguously read as the instrumental of *coupe* because the strictly subcategorized direct object or argument is lexically filled, and so *fil* is not taken for the direct object.

It must be noted that there is, however, a major difference between relatives and interrogatives here: interrogatives are not possible without the preposition, as illustrated in (17).

(17a) *Qu'est-ce que tu coupes le fromage?
'What do you cut the cheese?'
(17b) Avec quoi est-ce que tu coupes le fromage?
'With what do you cut the cheese?'
(17c) *Qu'est-ce que tu coupes le fromage avec?
'What do you cut the cheese with?'

Sentence (17c) is blocked too because, as seen earlier, there is no stranding in French interrogatives. It is not as bad as (17a) because, although it is syntactically deviant, it can get an interpretation where *qu'est-ce que* is the INSTR argument bound to *avec*, whereas (17a) is absolutely uninterpretable.

Summarizing, in some French dialects RRCs have stranding and preposition deletion, whereas interrogatives never allow stranding or preposition deletion. If a transformational ap-proach is taken, one has to postulate different constraints on the rule of WH-movement when it applies in RRCs and in interrogatives, and the problem of preposition deletion would require additional theoretical mechanisms.

I now sketch an approach where these constructions are
base generated: it seems to be a simple and natural solution
to these and other problems.

3. **A possible solution: POD.** I propose that (18) be the
base rule for S.

(18) S → POD V'''

I ignore for now the exact nature of V'''. POD is the node
PODIUM: it is the old COMP, but without the complementizer,
which I now take to be an affix similar to that of Jackendoff
(1977). The POD in (18) 'commands' the elements in V'''
according to the usual definition.

(19) Command:

An element A commands an element B if B is part
of a structure dominated by the first S above A
(Langacker 1969).

The lexical insertion under POD is somewhat similar to that of
clitics in the base, as illustrated in (20).

(20a) Paul donne le cadeau à Marie.
'Paul gives the gift to Marie.'
(20b) Paul le donne à Marie.
'Paul it gives to Marie.'
(20c) *Paul le donne le cadeau à Marie.
'Paul it gives the gift to Marie.'

There are two syntactic positions for the direct object in the
base: one clitic and one nonclitic. If both positions are filled
as in (20c), the sentence is uninterpretable. A principle of
functional interpretation accounts for this. [2]

(21) Principal of Functional Interpretation (PFI):

An S will be functionally interpreted if all the
strictly subcategorized arguments of the verb are
identified and if all the arguments are related to a
verb.

When I say that an argument is 'related' to a verb, I mean
that the argument is incorporated in the functional structures
of the verb.
Coming back to (20c), it must be said that some dialects
accept it as grammatical. But the clitic and the full NP have
to be the same argument, and a sentence like (22) is never
accepted, as predicated by PFI.

(22) Paul la donne le cadeau à Marie.

The insertion under POD is done in the same way as in (23).

(23a) Tu as donné le cadeau à qui?
      'You gave the gift to who?'
(23b) [$_{POD}$ A qui]as-tu donné le cadeau?
      'To who did you give the gift?'
(23c) *A qui as-tu donné le cadeau à Marie?
      'To who did you give the gift to Marie?'

In (23a), the WH-phrase is inserted in its indirect object position according to the lexical subcategorization of the verb. In (23b), it is under POD, which is the other possible position for an argument. In (23c), both positions are filled, and the sentence is deviant by PFI since one of the arguments is not related to any verb.
   But there is a major difference between POD and clitics: insertion under POD is not clause bound, as shown in (24).

(24) [$_{POD}$ Qui] Marie a-t-elle dit que Jean connaît bien[e]?
     'Who did Marie say that Jean knows well?'

I account for this by the rule of control by POD.

(25) Control by POD:

     An argument under POD is related to a verb in its
     domain.

The domain of POD is the structure which the POD commands. The control by POD and PFI assures us that in (24), qui will be related to connaît and not to dit, since qui must be related to a verb and connaît must have an object argument.
   Turning to RRCs, for ease of exposition, I adopt the structure given in (26) for RRCs.

(26) [$_{N''}$ N' S]

The rule of control in RRCs is as in (27).

(27) Control in RRCs:

     In the context [$_{N''}$ N' S], N' is related to a verb
     in S.

This rule accounts for RRCs without WH-phrases such as (1c). In this type of RRC, it is the structure of the clause which makes the relation between the antecedent and the verb in the relative clause.

In RRCs with a WH-phrase, it is the nature of the WH itself which allows the relation between antecedent and verb. For Chomsky, the WH-word is a quantifier, but as Brame (1978) points out, the WH-word does not quantify, but binds. The WH-word, then, is a 'matchmaker', an operator that puts elements in relation.

Bonnard (1961) shows that the distribution of QU-words in French falls into two systems: system A, where there is no antecedent; and system B, with antecedents.

Figure 1. QU-word distribution, system A.

qui			PERSONS	Class
∅	que	quoi	THINGS	
SUBJECT	NONACCENT	ACCENT		
	ATTRIBUTES AND COMPLEMENTS			
	Function			

Figure 2. QU-word distribution, system B.

		qui	PERSONS		Antecedent
qui	que	∅	Masc. or Fem.	THINGS	
		quoi	Neutral		
SUBJECT	NONACCENT ACCENT				
	ATTRIBUTES AND COMPLEMENTS				
	Function				

Bonnard summarizes the use of the two systems as in (28).

(28)

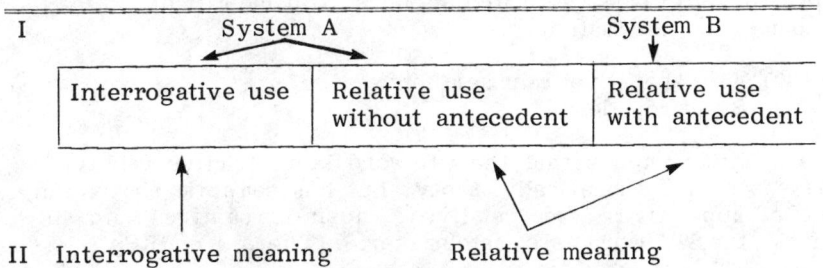

I	System A		System B
	Interrogative use	Relative use without antecedent	Relative use with antecedent

| II | Interrogative meaning | Relative meaning |

Bonnard comments (1961:172):

> The partition *I* rests on a morphological discrimination:
> the belonging to system A or to system B. Now to find
> out to what system belongs a pronoun in its use, one
> must look at its syntactic context, essentially *the absence
> or presence of an antecedent.*

The WH-matchmaker then has two possible ways of operating:
(a) if the WH-word has an antecedent, it relates this antecedent to a verb in its domain; (b) if the WH-word does not
have an antecedent, it relates an element outside of the sentence to a verb in its domain. Case (a) is straightforward:
it is the case of RRCs and appositives. Case (b) has two
possibilities: free relatives and interrogatives. In free relatives, as in (29), the WH-word relates an element which is
specified in the discourse or which is left unspecified.

(29a) Quoi qu'a fait Jean, je m'en fous.
      'Whatever did Jean, I don't care.'
(29b) Qui a bu boira.
      'Who drank will drink.'

Interrogatives such as (30) ask for a matching element to be
related to a verb in the sentence.

(30a) Où vas-tu?
      'Where go you?'
(30b) Qui as-tu vu?
      'Who have you seen?'
(30c) Que fais-tu?
      'What do you?'

The intention of the speaker could be to ask for a specific
matching in the discourse, as in (31).

(31) A: Ali is the greatest. Who is the greatest?
     B: Marciano is the greatest.
     A: (Bang!)

Speaker B refused the matching here. Speaker B of (32)
also refused the matching. [3]

(32) A: What's your name, honey?
     B: Drop dead.

All of this implies that the WH-word in restrictive relative
clauses is not semantically empty, but has semantic content in
RRCs, appositives, free relatives, and interrogatives: in all
cases, the WH-word is a matchmaker. [4] There are RRCs

without WH-words because the structure of these clauses allows the antecedent to be related to a verb in the embedded sentence, as in (27). The tendency not to have WH-words in RRCs in advanced dialects of French comes from the fact that the WH-word is redundant, not that it is semantically empty.

Our attention can turn now to the two problems presented in the previous sections: the difference in stranding and preposition deletion between RRCs and interrogatives.

3.1 Stranding. If there is no WH-movement, then a sentence such as (33a) is accounted for by the control in RRCs stated in (27) in conjunction with PFI. By (27), *fille* is related to *sors*; it has two possibilities: object argument or prepositional argument; by PFI, object argument is rules out because the prepositional argument *avec x* would then be uninterpreted.

(33a) La fille que je sors avec est correcte.
      'The girl that I go out with is OK.'
(33b) La fille avec qui que je sors est correcte.
      'The girl with who that I go out is OK.'
(33c) *La fille qui que je sors avec est correcte.
      'The girl who that I go out with is OK.'

In (33b), the WH-word plays its role of matchmaker. Sentence (33c) is excluded by a constraint in French which prohibits discontinuous insertion of arguments unless this argument is under POD and is referential, as in (34).

(34) Trudeau, je suis contre, mais Lévesque, je suis pour.
     'Trudeau, I am against, but Lévesque, I am for.'

This constraint would also explain the agrammaticality of the sentences in (35).

(35a) *Qui (que) tu sors avec?
      'Who (that) you go out with?'
(35b) *Qui (que) tu es pour?
      'Who (that) you are for?'

3.2 Deletion. In a sentence such as (36a), the preposition is deletable because it is recoverable, and it is recoverable because the antecedent has semantic content which specifies it as a possible INSTRUMENTAL.

(36a) Le couteau que je coupe est pas coupant.
      'The knife that I cut is not sharp.'
(36b) Le fil que je coupe avec...
      'The wire that I cut with...'
(36c) Qu'est-ce que tu coupes?
      'What do you cut?'

In (36b), unless the context is very special, *fil* is most likely to be related to *coupe* as an object argument. In (36c), *qu'est-ce* is never a possible INSTRUMENTAL because it has no referential content, and therefore cannot be an INSTRU-MENTAL for *coupe*; a nonreferential element without a preposition identifying it as such cannot be related to a verb as an INSTRUMENTAL.

In conclusion, the difference in stranding and preposition deletion seems to depend on whether the controller has referential content or not. This is easier to explain by a dominance type grammar than by a transformational one.

NOTES

1. Other examples of this type can be found in Bauche (1920), Frei (1929), Remacle (1960), for European dialects.

2. It is very close to Brame's Principle of Functional Deviance, except that it is positive and goes beyond strict subcategorization.

3. I owe this example to Susanne Carroll.

4. To hold such a position (i.e. that the WH-word is empty in RRCs), one would also have to explain why WH-words are not semantically empty in appositive RCs, since they are not deletable.

THE FRENCH INTERROGATIVE PRONOUN *QUE*

Paul Hirschbühler
Université d'Ottawa

0. Introduction. Kayne (1974) has offered several arguments supporting the view that *que* and *qui* in (1a) and (1b) are complementizers and not relative pronouns. They are thus assigned to the same category as *que* and *qui* in (2a) and (2b), respectively. The claim that *qui* in (2b) is a complementizer was first made by Gross (1968).[1]

(1a) La table que tu vois est belle.
     'The table that you see is pretty.'
(1b) La table qui se trouve ici est belle.
     'The table that is here is pretty.'

(2a) Tu veux que Pierre vienne.
     'You want Peter to come.'
(2b) Quel artiste veux-tu qui vienne?
     'Which artist do you want to come?'

Under this view, French is simply like many other languages which can construct some or all of their restrictive relative clauses without a relative pronoun at the surface level. Yiddish is of the first type, as Lowenstamm (1977) has shown, and English is of the second type, as argued by, among others, Stahlke (1976) and Chomsky and Lasnik (1977).
   Similarly, Obenauer (1976, 1977) and Tranel (1977b) claim that the *que* found in direct questions like (3a-c) is the complementizer, and not an interrogative pronoun for inanimates, as has always been assumed.

(3a) Que veux-tu?
     'What do you want?'
(3b) Que va-t-il devenir?
     'What will he become?'

(3c) Que crains-tu qui se passe?
'What are you afraid will happen?'

If the claim that there is no pronoun at the surface level in
(1a) and (1b) does not come as a surprise, given comparative
evidence, the claim that there is no pronoun in the examples
of (3) at the surface is more surprising: as far as I know,
French is the first case for which it is claimed that some constituent questions lack a question phrase at the surface (omitting concealed questions (Baker 1970)). In this paper I argue
that French is not so different from what has usually been
taken for granted and that *que* in (3) is an interrogative pronoun.

The discussion is organized as follows. In Section 1 I present the essentials of Obenauer's analysis of direct questions.
In Section 2 I list the facts to be accounted for. In Section 3
I propose an analysis for these facts, defending the position
that interrogative *que* is a pronoun.

1. **Obenauer's analysis.** In this section, only that part of
Obenauer's analysis that accounts for the facts given in (4)
and (5) is presented. Other aspects of his analysis are introduced in subsequent sections.

(4a) Tu fais quoi?
(4b) *Quoi fais-tu?
(4c) Que fais-tu?
(4d) Quoi que tu fais?
'What are you doing?'

(5a) Tu penses à quoi?
(5b) A quoi penses-tu?
(5c) A quoi que tu penses?
'What are you thinking about?'

Item (6) is the structure underlying all the examples in (4) at
some point in the derivation;[2] *que* is the complementizer
(Kayne 1974:277, Obenauer 1976:124).

(6) $_{\bar{S}}[_{COMP}[que]_{S}[tu\ fais\ quoi]]_{\bar{S}}$

If WH-movement does not apply, the complementizer *que* is
obligatorily deleted (Obenauer 1976:125) and (4) is generated.
If WH-movement applies, *quoi* is moved to the left of *que*, giving (4d), which is found in popular varieties of French; to
account for Standard French (4c), Rule (7) is postulated
(Obenauer 1976:119, 1977:321) and Subject-Clitic inversion
must take place.

(7) Pas-de-QUOI

$$[\underbrace{\text{quoi X}}_{1} \underbrace{\text{que}}_{2}] \rightarrow \emptyset\ 2$$
COMP

This rule applies before *que*-Dalle (Obenauer 1977:321), Kayne's (1974:276) *que*-Deletion. The first factor in the rule must be nonnull.

(8) *que*-Dalle[3]

$$[\text{A que}] \rightarrow 1\ \emptyset$$
COMP 1 2

Obenauer (1977:324) adds that (7) and (8) are obligatory in Standard French only. In addition, (8) should be prevented from applying in nonstandard varieties of French, so that (4b) is not generated.

Let us consider the examples in (5). The underlying structure for all these examples is assumed to be as in (9) at some point in the derivation.

(9) $[_{\bar{S}}$ COMP [que] [tu penses à quoi]]$_{S}$

If WH-movement does not apply, *que* is deleted and (5a) is generated. Non-Standard French (5c) results from the sole application of WH-movement. At the output of the application of WH-movement, the structural description of (7) is not met, but the structural description of (8) is, and its obligatory application in Standard French gives (5b).

Obenauer's analysis thus allows for an elegant account of the facts considered until now. The analysis against which he argues is, however, as elegant, I would submit, when the same facts are taken into consideration. A preliminary form of such an analysis could be stated as follows: there is no such rule as (7), but a rule like (10) which is ordered after (8) and states that the allomorph of *quoi* is /kə/ when it is alone in COMP.

(10) $[\text{QUOI}]_{\text{COMP}} \rightarrow [/\text{kə}/]_{\text{COMP}}$

Let us consider now all the facts that have to be accounted for before evaluating the respective merits of each approach.

2. Relevant facts

2.1 In addition to the alternation between *que* and *quoi* in tensed direct questions, one must account for the fact that *que* behaves to a certain extent as a clitic with respect to the adjacent verb complex (i.e. the verb and other clitics attached to it) in that generally it may not be separated from it; interrogative *que* is the only *que* to have this property and *quel* is the only other WH-phrase to have the same behavior. [4]

(11a) Que fait Paul?
(11b) *Que Paul fait-il?
       'What is Paul doing?'
(11c) Qui Paul a-t-il rencontré?
       'Who did Paul meet?'

(12a) *Que, d'après toi, fait Paul?
       'What, according to you, is Paul doing?'
(12b) Qui, d'après toi, a rassemblé Paul?
       'Who, according to you, did Paul bring together?'

(13) Quel (*, d'après toi,) est le métier de mon père?
      'What (, according to you,) is my father's job?'

2.2 If, however, *que* is followed by *diable* 'the hell', it loses its clitic-like property.

(14a) Que diable Marie faisait-elle là?
       'What the hell was Mary doing there?'
(14b) Que diable, me dit-il, alliez-vous faire là?
       'What the hell, he asked me, were you going to do there?'

2.3 In a direct question, only an embedded subject can be questioned by *que*; said in another way, if interrogative *que* is adjacent to the questioned position, the result is ungrammatical; *qui* can no longer be used in that case, although it was possible to do so until the seventeenth century; (16c) is correct in non-Standard French.

(15) Que crains-tu qui se passe?
      'What are you afraid will happen?'

(16a) *Que se passe?
(16b) *Qui se passe?
(16c) Quoi qui se passe?
       'What is happening?'

2.4 *Que* alone may not introduce an embedded question, or (as pointed out by Obenauer) a free relative or an exclamative clause.

(17) *Je me demande que tu fais.
      'I wonder what you are doing.'

(18) *J'ai acheté que tu as acheté.
'I bought what you bought.'

(19) *C'est fou que tu as invité de gens!
'It's crazy how many people you invited!'

In addition, an embedded exclamative introduced by a fronted
phrase whose first element is *que* is also excluded.

(20) *C'est fou que de gens tu as invités!

2.5 In infinitival questions, the facts in main and embedded
clauses vary. In main clauses, *que* is said to be preferred to
quoi, although *quoi* is not excluded. In embedded clauses,
quoi seems to be the only possibility in most cases, although I
know of people who still systematically use sentences like (22a).
The grammaticality judgments here reflect my own speech.

(21a) Que faire?
(21b) Quoi faire?
      'What shall we do?'

(22a) *Je ne sais pas que faire?
(22b) Je ne sais pas quoi faire?
      'I don't know what to do.'

This (allowing for some variation in the judgments) represents
the minimal set of facts that any analysis of *que* found in WH-
constructions should account for. Additional facts are introduced in the following discussion.

3. The pronoun *que*

3.1 In this section I sketch an analysis for the facts mentioned in Sections 2.1 and 2.2, i.e. for the *quoi-que* alternation and the clitic-like properties of *que*, as well as for the
fact that *que* loses its clitic properties when it is followed by
diable.
   The idea has often been entertained that the alternation
quoi-que is to be treated along similar lines to that of *moi-me*,
toi-te, *soi-se* (see Moignet 1974:170 and Goldsmith 1978):   the
/wa/ form is the strong form, while the /ə/ form is the weak
one. These interrogative and noninterrogative forms have a
certain number of other properties that tend to support the
parallelism, even if they differ in other respects. *Moi, toi,*
and the other noninterrogative direct object pronouns are
obligatorily replaced by their weak counterparts and cliticized,
unless separated from the verb by restrictive *que.*

(23a) *J'aime toi.
(23b) Je t'aime.
'I love you.'

(24) Je n'aime que toi.
'I love only you.'

As has been seen, bare interrogative *quoi* is allowed postverbally, but when fronted, the weak clitic form is required,
unless complementizer *que* shows up.[5]
  Moi, toi (and *soi*, as may be expected from the fact that it
is a reflexive), but not the other strong pronouns are also excluded from subject position, unless they are modified or coordinated. Modified and coordinated fronted *quoi* is also
allowed, as shown in (26) from Obenauer (1977, note 32).
There is not, however, a total parallelism, since in the case
of noninterrogative pronouns, coordinated or modified, direct
objects are clearly less acceptable than subjects.

(25a) Moi étais présent.
       'I was present.'
(25b) Moi seul étais présent.
       'Only I was present.'
(25c) Pierre et moi avons décidé de partir.
       'Peter and I have decided to leave.'
(25d) ?J'ai intivé Marie et toi.
       'I invited Mary and you.'

(26a) Qui ou quoi vous a donné cette idée?
       'Who or what gave you this idea?'
(26b) Quoi de plus intelligent veux-tu qu'il dise?
       'What that would be more intelligent do you want him
         to say?'
(26c) Quoi d'autre pourrait m'amener chez toi?
       'What else could bring me to your place?'

From a look at the behavior of the noninterrogative pronouns,
it is clear that the rules accounting for the distribution of the
weak and strong forms are fairly specific, taking into account
at least such matters as subject vs. direct object (or preverbal
vs. postverbal), whether the strong form is a /wa/ form or
not, whether it is modified or coordinated, or not. In the
case of *quoi/que*, I suggest that the morpheme QUOI is marked
[-strong] by some syntactic rule when it occurs alone in COMP
and that the [-strong] allomorph is /kə/.

(27)   [QUOI]   1
     COMP   1   [-strong]

I assume that unless there is a specification to the contrary, weak forms are clitics, and--following Perlmutter (1971), Selkirk (1972), and Goldsmith (1978)--that preverbal clitics must form a string of contiguous morphemes. [6]

I can now turn to the case of examples like (14a) and (14b). Let me first observe that *diable* follows the WH-word itself rather than the whole moved phrase. [7]

(28a) Combien diable de gens veux-tu que j'invite?
'How the devil many people do you want me to invite?'
(28b) Qui diable d'autre as-tu en tête?
'Who the hell else do you have in mind?'

I assume that *diable* and the preceding WH-word form a constituent at some point in the derivation. Exactly how the distribution of *diable* should be accounted for is unclear to me. One could adopt Obenauer's suggestion that *diable* is introduced very late in its surface position (but what is its source then?), or one may suggest that *diable* is added to WH-words by a compounding rule in the morphological component, and that the appearance of the resulting phrase is limited to COMP.

Whatever the analysis, the presence of *diable* should not affect the choice between *que* and *quoi*. Let us assume that somehow *que diable* is a compound word. This means that one now has a bisyllabic word. Can the distinction between monosyllabic and polysyllabic play some role? Selkirk (1972) claimed that in French, monosyllabic and polysyllabic prepositions behaved differently with respect to liaison, liaison being obligatory with monosyllabic, while it would not be so with polysyllabic prepositions. Her account at the time was that polysyllabic prepositions were flanked by word boundaries introduced transformationally, while monosyllabic prepositions were not surrounded by word boundaries. Kaye and Morin (1979) have shown that some of the facts about liaison as stated by Selkirk are incorrect, but that the distinction between monosyllabic and polysyllabic prepositions is necessary.

If we turn to prepositions, we observe that in French some of them may be clitic (i.e. belong to the same phonological word as the following lexical word) while others are not. As shown in Selkirk (1972) monosyllabic prepositions are clitic when they are followed by an NP, and non-clitic when they are either polysyllabic or used alone. This is evidenced by the possibility of pause after non-clitic prepositions, and again by the distinctive intonation contours (Kaye and Morin 1979, Section 3.3).

Their account, like Selkirk's, is in terms of the number of word boundaries that separate each preposition from the following word. I propose then that similarly the polysyllabic nature

of *que diable* is what sets it apart from *que* as far as cliticization is concerned. Formally, one may simply have a rule adding a feature [-clitic] to *que diable* or propose to erase word
boundaries around the pronoun *que* but not around *que diable*.
There is still one point that has to be dealt with: a subject
clitic may not follow interrogative *que* (it must be moved by
subject clitic inversion) while it may follow other WH-phrases
in colloquial French.

(29a) *Que tu cherches?
(29b) Que cherches-tu?
       'What are you looking for?'

(30a) Où tu vas?
       'Where are you going?'
(30b) Qui tu vois?
       'Who do you see?'

One way to account for this would simply be to say that there
is a surface filter excluding the cooccurrence of *que* and subject clitic. However, Goldsmith (1978) suggests a much more
illuminating account, based in part on facts pointed out by
Dubuisson. Although *que diable* is not a clitic, since an NP
may follow it, the subject clitic must appear and has to follow
the verb, whether the subject NP is there or not, in direct
questions, unless the subject NP is itself moved by stylistic
inversion.

(31a) Que diable Jean a-t-il fait?
       'What the hell John has done?'
(31b) *Que diable Jean a fait?
(31c) Que diable a fait Jean?
(31d) *Que diable il a fait?
       'What the hell he has done?'
(31e) Que diable a-t-il fait?

I adopt Goldsmith's proposal that interrogative *que* (and thus
que diable) be marked as requiring obligatorily subject clitic
inversion, when its structural description is met, as it is with
toujours in examples like (32).

(32a) Toujours est-il qu'il a tort!
(32b) *Toujours il est qu'il a tort!
       'Still is it that he is wrong.'

Moreover, other WH-phrases modified by *diable* do not require subject clitic inversion, so that in cases like (33) the
inversion of the clitic subject is not a consequence of the
presence of *diable*.

(33a) Que diable tu m'amènes là?
  'Who the hell you're bringing?'
(33b) Qui diable Paul nous amène là?
  'Who the hell Paul is bringing us?'

Let us turn to the next point, that of the impossibility of questioning some subjects.

3.2 As mentioned in 2.3, while sentences like (34a) are perfect, (34b) is impossible.

(34a) Que crains-tu qui se passe?
(34b) *Que se passe?

As things stand at the moment, my analysis generates both of them: the interrogative for nonanimate is moved to the front, where it shows up as *que*. The ungrammaticality of (34b) is, however, not surprising when other facts of French are taken into account. Each time a subject is removed by a transformation which in Bresnan's (1977) framework is seen as unbounded and in Chomsky's (1977) as involving a bounded WH-movement rule, so that a *que* would come in contact with the removal site, the result is ungrammatical. Replacing *que* by *qui* results in grammatical sentences except in the case of comparative and interrogative *que*.[8]

(35a) Que crains-tu $\begin{Bmatrix} *que \\ qui \end{Bmatrix}$ se passe?
  'What are you afraid will happen?'
(35b) Le garçon $\begin{Bmatrix} *que \\ qui \end{Bmatrix}$ va venir.
  'The boy that will come.'
(35c) Plus de français sont venus que tu ne voulais $\begin{Bmatrix} *que \\ qui \end{Bmatrix}$ viennent.
  'More French people came than you wanted to come.'
(35d) Plus de français sont venus $\begin{Bmatrix} *que \\ *qui \end{Bmatrix}$ sont partis.
  'More French people came than left.'
(35e) C'est Pierre $\begin{Bmatrix} *que \\ qui \end{Bmatrix}$ va venir.
  'It's Peter who will come.'
(35f) *Qui se passe?
  'What's happening?'

Notice that all the grammatical *qui* correspond to cases where in English either a *that* shows up (in clefts) or a *that* (or a *for*) complementizer is deleted: comparative *than* and *as* are not deleted, and interrogative *what* is not, either. One can account for the ungrammaticality of all the examples with *que* by a filter like (36).

236 / Paul Hirschbühler

(36) $*$ [que [[e] ...]]
$\overline{S}$ S NP$_i$

     when NP$_i$ is free in S (i.e. when it is not controlled within S).

The condition on the filter is necessary so that examples like (37), with stylistic inversion, where the trace of the subject is controlled within the S by the moved subject, will not be excluded.

     (37) Le garçon que va rencontrer Jacques est ici.
         'The boy that Jacques will meet is here.'

Let us assume, moreover, that there is some rule realizing the complementizer as *qui* in some environments. In the case of comparative *que*, two possibilities come immediately to mind then. It is possible that the comparative clause introducer is not the complementizer. This possibility was first discussed by Kayne (1974:176–177 and note 30); see also Kayne and Pollock (1979:Section 4); Hirschbühler (1976); and Chomsky and Lasnik (1977) for English *than*. Or it is possible that it is the complementizer, as might be suggested by examples of comparatives with the appearance of a *comme* in front of the subordinate clause introducer in Canadian French.

     (38) Marie a une robe pareille comme que celle que
         Francine a.
         'Mary has a dress like the one Francine has.'

If the first hypothesis is correct, *que* would not be affected, and (36) would exclude sentences like (35d) with *que*. If the second approach is correct, then it is quite possible that the interpretive rule for comparative simply requires a *que*, just as that for English requires *as* or *than*. Turning then to interrogative *que*, if it is not a complementizer, it will not be replaced by *qui*, so that (35f) will never be generated. And (34b) will be excluded by (36). Even if the rule introducing complementizer *qui* is written in such a general way that complementizer *qui* is substituted for interrogative *que*, one would have a violation of recoverability of deletion. In short, under the hypothesis that interrogative *que* is a pronoun, and that there is a constraint of the type of (36), the contrast between (34a) and (34b) is explained. The last thing that one has to specify is that the pronoun *qui* is [+human] only.[9]

     3.3 I now consider the ungrammaticality of Examples (17) to (20). Some comments on exclamatives are necessary first.
     Once the position is adopted that *que* in direct questions is an NP, an allomorph of *quoi*, one is naturally led to expect

this *que* to show up in indirect questions, since the paradigm of the other WH-words is not different in direct and indirect questions in French; it would also not be surprising if *que* appeared in free relatives, given that *qui* and *quoi* both appear in questions and free relatives.[10]

There is, however, no reason to believe that the *que* found in exclamative clauses is an allomorph of an NP *quoi*. One reason is that it occurs in environments where interrogative *que* is excluded, i.e. as part of a larger NP.

(39a) Que de gens il a invités!
    'How many people he invited!'
(39b) Que d'eau!
    'What a large quantity of water!'

In these examples, *que*, within the NP, seems to be in the same position as quantifiers like *beaucoup*, *peu*, *tant*, etc. I thus adopt the hypothesis that *que* in (30a-b) is a quantifier, and I tentatively assume that it has the same status in examples like (40a-b), though this is more controversial.

(40a) Qu'elle est belle!
    'How pretty she is!'
(40b) Que vous avez de poils sur la poitrine!
    'How much hair you have on your chest!'

The ungrammaticality of examples (17) to (20) can then be accounted for by a constraint like (41).

(41) * [... [que ...]]
    $\overline{S}$ $\overline{S}$ [+WH]

This constraint states that embedded clauses introduced by a WH-word whose realization is *que*--as opposed to the complementizer *que*--are ungrammatical. Examples like (42), where *que* is analyzed as the complementizer (Kayne 1974) are thus not excluded.

(42) Le garçon que tu vois est malade.
    'The boy that you see is ill.'

Interestingly, Obenauer (1977:Section 3.4) argues that the facts given in (17) to (19) provide support for an analysis that considers all these *que* to be the complementizer, since such an analysis is able to trace the ungrammaticality of all these examples to a syntactic feature shared by all of them. An analysis which treats some *que* as pronouns and others as quantifiers, he claims, cannot account in a unified way for (17) to (18) and (19). Although Obenauer does not consider examples like (39a) in the discussion of ungrammatical embedded

clauses introduced by *que*, his position is exactly the same
with respect to them since he analyzes the *que* in such examples as a complementizer, too.

Consider now the constraint he proposes.

(43) In a structure

$$[\ _{\bar{S}} \ldots \ [\ _{\bar{S}} que \ldots \ ]]$$

where there exists no possible antecedent of *que*,
the interpretation can only be that of neutral
embedding.

Notice that although it was supposed to be crucial for all
the *que*'s in (17) to (19), and also (20), to be the same complementizer, there is no reference to the categorial status of
que in (43), so that it correctly marks as ungrammatical
Examples (18) to (20), whatever the category of *que* in each
of them. There are thus at least two analyses of the facts
not based on Obenauer's assumption about *que*!

I suppose that Obenauer's intuition probably was that if in
the relevant constructions the *que* is a complementizer, rather
than a WH-word, then it is not surprising that the embedded
clauses are interpretable only as complement clauses. Let us
see then what sort of analysis is offered for (39a), where the
null hypothesis is clearly the one that I have defended, i.e.
que is a WH-quantifier. The sort of underlying structure
adopted by Obenauer is as in (44a), where the NP to be moved
contains an abstract WH-quantifier; (44b) results from the
application of WH-movement. At this point a new transformation, COMP-Attraction, given in (45), substitutes the complementizer *que* for the WH-quantifier; (44c) is the result.

(44a) $[que]$ vous avez $[_{WH}^{\Delta}$ de poils] sur la poitrine
     COMP

(44b) $[[_{WH}^{\Delta}$ de poils]que] vous avez sur la poitrine

(44c) [que de poils] vous avez sur la poitrine
    WH

(45) COMP-Attraction

      $[WH \ X \ que] \rightarrow [que \ X \ \emptyset]$
  COMP   WH

This transformation is very peculiar, and rather suspect,
since it inserts a complementizer under a quantifier node, so
that, on the surface, *que* apparently is a quantifier.

Obviously, then, the most natural way to account for the surface quantifier status of *que* is to recognize that it was a quantifier all along. Elliptical exclamatives such as (39b) could, in fact, be used to support this, if they are not derived as reduced sentences, i.e. if they are generated as direct expansions of NP. This is the position adopted by Gérard (1977), but I believe the question is still an open one.

Until new and strong evidence is provided, I see no reason to treat the *que* of examples like (39a-b) as anything else but quantifiers.[11] Given that (20) is ungrammatical, I do not think then that the ungrammaticality of (17) to (19) provides evidence in favor of one or the other analysis discussed as far as the categorial status of interrogative *que* in direct questions is concerned.

3.4 Let us end this tour by considering *que* and *quoi* in infinitival questions.

It has been noticed that *que* usually occurs in direct questions, while *quoi* is required for most speakers in indirect questions, except for a few cases. The following judgments, for example, are reported by Obenauer (1976: 112-113).

(46a) ??Quoi lui offrir pour sa fête?
(46b) Que lui offrir pour sa fête?
  'What to give him/her for his/her birthday?'

(47a) Je me demande quoi lui offrir pour sa fête.
(47b) *?Je me demande que lui offrir pour sa fête.
  'I wonder what to give him/her for his/her birthday.'

All the examples of the type of (46a) given by Obenauer are always better than those of the (47b) type. This seems to be correct. The facts are, I believe, somewhat more complex (see Gougenheim 1970; and Hirschbühler 1978 for some observations which need to be confirmed), but they are enough for now. The question is: how they can be integrated into our analysis?

Consider main clauses first. Kayne (1974) has claimed that the complementizer *que* is present in the COMP of all tensed clauses at some point in a derivation, while this is not true for infinitival clauses. The hypothesis that *que* is a pronoun in (46b) rather than a complementizer is thus the natural hypothesis. Since *quoi* is not totally excluded, I tentatively assume that the rule assigning the feature [-strong] to *quoi* when it is alone in COMP is optional in infinitival clauses. One may wonder why the fact that the verb is in a finite tense or in the infinitive would make a difference. This distinction does not play a role today in the case of other pronouns, for example, in the case of *me-moi*. But a look at earlier stages of the language shows that the distinction was necessary then. Initially, only strong forms of personal

pronouns could precede the infinitive and it is only progres-
sively that weak forms have been allowed in this position.
What is found in the case of *que-quoi* should be seen as a
remnant of an earlier regular distinction.

Consider embedded infinitival clauses now. Limiting the dis-
cussion to the data given here, I have to say that embedded
QUOI never becomes [-strong] in front of an infinitive.[12]
All the facts can then be captured by Rules (48a) and (48b).

(48a) $\text{QUOI} \xrightarrow{\text{oblig}} [\text{-strong}] / \underset{\text{COMP}}{[\underline{\quad}]} [\dots V_{\text{tense}} \dots]$

(48b) (root): $\text{QUOI} \to [\text{-strong}] / \underset{\text{COMP}}{[\underline{\quad}]} [\dots V_{\text{inf}} \dots]$

I assume that general conventions ensure that only the verb
in the same $\bar{\text{S}}$ cycle as the relevant COMP-node is accessible
in the factorization.

I now consider Obenauer's analysis. Pointing out first
Kayne's observations about the incompatibility between complementizer *que* and infinitival clauses, the appearance of *quoi* in
embedded clauses is easily accounted for: since there is no
que, QUOI-deletion cannot apply, because the structural
description of the rule mentions *que*. *Que*, however, appears
in direct infinitival questions, and there, too, it is analyzed
as the complementizer by Obenauer. The analysis goes as
follows. *Que* is introduced as a complementizer for all clauses
at some point in a derivation, whether in a finite tense or not,
and a special rule, *Que-Non*, deletes *que* from embedded infinitival clauses before *Pas-de-Quoi* removes *quoi*. The complementary distribution of *que* and *quoi* is thus accounted for.

Clearly, the crucial step in this analysis is the assumption
that *que* is a complementizer for infinitival clauses. In fact,
there are constructions where *que* is found in front of an infinitival clause.

(49a) J'aime mieux partir en France que vivre sur Mars.
    'I'd rather go to France than live on Mars.'
(49b) Elle n'est pas si naïve que de croire cela. (Kayne
    1974: 277)
    'She isn't so naïve as to believe that.'
(49c) A moins que changer de sexe, elle ne saurait
    empêcher qu'on la haïsse. (G. de Balzac, in
    Haase 1969: 204)
    'Unless she would change her sex, she couldn't
    prevent people from hating her.'
(49d) Je les tenais là en vue, afin que me souvenir toujours
    de les vous envoyer. (Malherbe, in Haase 1969: 205)
    'I had them there in sight, so as to always remember
    to send them to you.'

The first example can be seen as a reduction of (50), so that *que* is, in fact, not associated to the infinitive clause.

(50) J'aime mieux partir en France que j'aime vivre sur Mars.

Examples like (49a-d) were found in a few constructions involving expressions like: *devant que(de), avant que(de), à moins que (de), plutôt que(de), plus que(de), moins que(de), mieux que(de)*.

Such archaic examples do not justify the introduction of the complementizer *que* with all infinitival clauses. Introducing the complementizer *que* here just to explain the appearance of a *que* in direct infinitival questions goes against an otherwise well-supported generalization: that the complementizers for tensed clauses are different from those for infinitival clauses. Direct infinitival questions thus support the allomorphic approach. Note also that in Obenauer's analysis it would not be surprising to find examples like (51a) in those varieties of French that allow questions like (51b); such examples, however, are never found.

(51a) *Quoi que faire?
(51b) Quoi que tu fais?

Finally, the sort of approach I propose is implicitly accepted by Obenauer for the seventeenth century (and earlier periods), since he considers that interrogative *que* was a pronoun at that time (Obenauer 1977: 329, note 25). Just as today, interrogative *que* was found only in fronted position (i.e. alone in COMP) and unmodified (except by *diable, diantre*), so that a rule like (10) or (27) was necessary. One of the differences today is that sentences like (17) were grammatical, but free relatives like (18) no longer were (they were grammatical earlier; see Moignet 1976: 159). This can be explained if a filter similar to (41) existed for free relatives in the seventeenth century and if later on it was generalized to indirect questions.

4. Conclusion. In the previous sections, I have developed an analysis of interrogative *que* supporting the tradition that sess this *que* as an allomorph of *quoi*, just as *me* is an allomorph of *moi*. As a weak pronoun, the clitic properties of *que* are not surprising, and the absence of clitic properties of *que diable* can be attributed to the fact that it is polysyllabic. In addition, the assumption that interrogative *que* (and *que* in *que diable*) is not a complementizer seems to fit very well with the observation that its presence obligatorily triggers the inversion of the subject clitic when it shows up, since the complementizer does not otherwise trigger such an inversion, while a few designated lexical items like *toujours* and *quel* do. It has also been seen that the assumption that

que was a pronoun for inanimates, and that *qui* did not belong to the paradigm of inanimates, allows an explanation for the distribution of grammaticality judgments for sentences like (15), (16a), (16b), given the general prohibition of *que* being adjacent to a subject trace not controlled within its S. The analysis of interrogative *que* as a pronoun is furthermore re-inforced by its use in infinitival direct questions. It has also been seen that the ungrammaticality of (17) to (20) does not support any claim about the categorial status of *que* in these constructions. Finally, the impossibility of *que* in (the majority of) infinitival embedded questions may be a conse-quence of the mechanism already necessary to account for (17) to (20).

NOTES

1. The complementizer status of *que* and *qui* in (1a) and (2b) is not accepted by everybody; for different views, see Huot (1974) and Milner (1977). Tranel (1977a) offers nice phonological evidence in favor of Kayne's analysis.
2. Obenauer (1976:124) introduces *que* in complementizer position in all clauses before WH-movement.
3. Rule (8) will have to be modified in order to account for sentences such as (i), where *peut-être* is probably in COMP position.

   (i) Peut-être qu'il est malade.
      'Maybe he is sick.'

For a discussion of this construction, see Dubuisson and Goldsmith (1976), and Goldsmith (1977, 1978).
4. Among the restricted usages of interrogative *que* we count (i) and (ii).

   (i) Que sert-il de s'emporter?
      'What good is it to get angry?'
  (ii) Que ne le disait-il pas?
      'Why didn't he say it?'

I think that these *que* may not be modified by *est-ce que*. I have no explanation for this.

  (iii) ?*Qu'est-ce qu'il sert de s'emporter?
  (iv) ?*Qu'est-ce qu'il ne le disait pas?

5. *Quoi* is found in direct questions, in examples like (i) and (ii), from Moignet (1974:175).

   (i) Quelque chose m'a étonné. -- Quoi t'a étonné?
      'Something surprised me. -- What surprised you?'

As pointed out by Obenauer (1976:93, note 18), in such
examples *quoi* is stressed and the interpretation is that of
an echo-question. One could suggest that in such cases,
quoi is unmoved, i.e. it is treated on a par with cases like
(ii).

(ii) Tu fais quoi?
'You're doing what?'

This would be supported by the fact that a bare fronted
is always much worse than *quoi* in (i).

(iii) *Quoi tu as fait?
(iv) Qui tu as vu?

Against this view one can, however, point out that when embedded, a question as in (i) is not totally out (contrary to
what I erroneously said in Hirschbühler 1978:129), although
WH-movement is normally obligatory in embedded clauses.

(v) ?Je me demande quoi a pu t'étonner!

6.   This must be qualified in several ways. First of all,
as noted by Kayne (1978:79, note 7), *pas, rien, plus, trop,
jamais* may separate *ne* from the other clitics, or *y* and *en* from
the verb, when they precede a verb in the infinitive.
Secondly, although it is always stated that the subject clitic
may no longer be separated from the other clitics, I have come
across many speakers who allow a parenthetical clause to follow
the pronominal subject, i.e. for which examples like the following one are good, in the right discourse.

(i) Je, si vous me permettez, voudrais vous répondre ceci...
(ii) Tu, me dit-il, vas t'en aller à Paris et voir ce qui se
     trame là-bas.

That the subject clitic is less closely dependent on the verb
than the object clitics may also be supported by the fact that
the nonrepetition of the subject clitic is much better than the
nonrepetition of the object clitics.

(iii) Je viendrai et lui montrerai comment faire.
(iv) *Je lui parlerai et donnerai un peu d'argent.

As far as the clitic character of interrogative *que* is concerned, it is clear that *que* is nearly always adjacent to the
verbal complex, but everybody also knows of counterexamples:
Obenauer (1976:86, note 7) mentions three examples; Renchon
(1967:55) gives several others. I take this as an indication
that interrogative *que*, although a weak form, is not morphologically part of the verb as the object clitics and *ne* are.

7. This is the case in other languages as well--for example, in English and in German (Obenauer 1978:note 76).

(ia) What the hell else did you buy?
(ib) How the hell many times will I have to tell you that!
(ii) Was zum Teufel will er nun für eine Schallplatte?
     'What the devil does he finally want for a record?'

The positioning of *diable* may suggest that *que* in (14a) and (14b) is a WH-word and not the complementizer. The validity of this hangs, however, on the quality of examples like (iiia) and (iiib) which are usually analyzed as concealed questions with a relative clause structure and where, consequently, *diable* would follow complementizers. These examples are not as good as examples like (iva) and (ivb), but they are not ungrammatical.

(iiia) ?Je me demande ce qui diable a bien pu arriver.
       'I wonder what the hell could have happened.'
(iiib) ?Je me demande ce que diable il a fait de mon argent.
       'I wonder what the hell he did with my money.'

(iva) Je me demande à qui diable il a bien pu s'adresser.
      'I wonder to who the hell he spoke.'
(ivb) Je me demande comment diable il a fait cela.
      'I wonder how the hell he did that.'

8. It is quite possible that constructions as in (i) involve a very local rule of control rather than WH-movement, and *qui* is necessary.

(i) Je le vois $\begin{Bmatrix} \text{*que} \\ \text{qui} \end{Bmatrix}$ vient.
    'I see him coming.'

9. I mention that questions like (35a) used to be found in the sixteenth and seventeenth centuries, but that *qui* was also found to a limited extent in questions in other positions at the same time and more frequently (as can be seen in Huguet, under *qui*, p. 286) in restrictive relatives with a nonhuman antecedent.

(a) 1. *Qui* faict les coquins mendier? C'est qu ilz n'ont en leurs maisons dequoy leur sac emplir. (Rabelais, III, 14, in Huguet, *qui*, 289)
    2. *De qui* me dois-je (helas) plustost douloir...? Ou de l'ardeur qui mon désir transporte, Ou du désir qui force mon vouloir? (Tyard, Erreurs am, sonn. 6, ibid.)
    3. Un poignard *de qui* le pommeau est d'un diamant. (Aubigné, Faeneste III, 17, ibid.)

Similar examples from the seventeenth century can be found in Haase. In addition, *qui* was not necessary in all cases in front of a subject gap, as shown by (b), representing different constructions.

(b) 1. ...Je advertiray le roy des enormes abus *que* sont forgez ceans. (Rabelais, I, 20, in Huguet, *que*, 169)
   2. ...*ce que* delecte est brief et transitoire, mais ce que crucie et tourmente est éternel. (Changy, tr. Instit., I, 15, in Huguet, *que*, p. 270)
   3. Nous tirasmes tous a ung coup, *que* fust cause que cinq ou six hommes tumbarent mortz par terre. (Monluc, I, I (I, 95), ibid.)

And as might then be expected, there seem to be examples of inanimate interrogative subject *que*.

(c) *Que* pouvoit estre impossible a celuy duquel le froc estoit si miraclifique qu'il donna la veue a trois aveugles? (Estienne, Apol. Herod., ch. 39 (II, 408), in Huguet, *que*, p. 271)

At first sight then, the surface differences between sixteenth century and twentieth century French would be due to the nonexistence of a constraint like (36) in the sixteenth century, and from the fact that *qui* could represent nonanimates. The facts are more complex, however, and a detailed study of the distribution of *qui* and *que* in various constructions in the sixteenth century (and other periods) is still to be done.

Let me quickly mention another argument put forward by Obenauer in favor of the hypothesis that *que* in examples such as (a) is not a WH-phrase. He observes that stylistic inversion applies with *combien* but not with *que*, in (b) and (c).

(b) i. Combien de chevelus sont arrivés!
   ii. Combien sont arrivés de chevelus!
(c) i. Que de chevelus sont arrivés!
   ii. *Que sont arrivés de chevelus!

This would be explained, according to Obenauer, if stylistic inversion was triggered by the presence of a lexical item in COMP. In the case of (b) ii., an intermediate step would be (d) i., while it would be (d) ii. in the case of (c) ii., with only an abstract WH-quantifier word (Obenauer 1976:125).

(d) i. [[combien (que)][-de chevelus sont arrivés]]
      S̄ COMP   S

ii. [[WH (que)] [-de chevelus sont arrivés]]
$\overline{S}$ COMP   S

In the case of interrogative *que*, an intermediate step would
be (iii).

iii. [[quoi (que)][Pierre fait]]
$\overline{S}$ COMP   S

If stylistic inversion is ordered before *pas de quoi*, then
stylistic inversion will not apply in the case of (d) ii.
  Consider, however, the case of comparatives like the following.

(e)   i. Plus de français sont venus que d'anglais ne sont
          restés.
      ii. Plus de français sont venus que ne sont restés
          d'allemands.

Chomsky (1976) proposes that WH-comparatives are formed by
WH-movement. In this case, what would be moved would be
an abstract WH-quantifier. Kayne and Pollock (1978) have
suggested that the inversion in (e) ii. is evidence in favor of
the idea that WH-movement is involved. How can one reconcile the facts of (e) ii. with (c) ii.? In the first case, the
abstract quantifier is enough, while in the second it is not.
This is not the time to try to answer everything concerning
comparatives and exclamatives and I leave it to another
occasion. Let me add, however, that is is not clear to me
that (c) ii. is ungrammatical. If this is correct, then
Obenauer's tentative argument disappears.
  10. *Quoi* appears in free relatives like (i), which I assume
are derived from something like (ii). For details, see Hirschbühler (1978: Chapter VII).

(i) Je me suis assis sur quoi tu t'es assis.
    'I sat on what you sat on.'
(ii) Je me suis assis sur [Δ [[sur quoi] [tu t'es assis]]]
     NP $\overline{S}$ COMP   S

  11. This is not enough. The distribution of NPs containing
exclamative *que* is restricted: they may not, generally, be
part of a prepositional phrase. Let us now examine a possible
argument against our analysis of quantifier *que*. Consider the
following examples.

(i) Que de gens il a invité!
(ii) ?*A que de gens il a parlé!
(iii) ?*Avec que d'entrain il s'est précipité chez nous!

Let us assume that the judgments are as indicated, although I
do not find (iii) really bad. To account for the ungrammaticality of such examples, it is necessary to assume that there
is a minimal role of case in French, i.e. that quantifier *que*
is [-oblique]. In fact, this extends to interrogative and relative *que*.

12. Wondering why (48b) would be a root transformation,
one may consider the following hypothesis: suppose that in
the sixteenth century both *que* and *quoi* were possible in front
of infinitives, root and embedded ones. The generalization of
the choice of *que* in COMP creates no problem in root sentences.
But the generalization of *que* in embedded clauses would, in
fact, create a gap if (41), or (43), or any principle used to
exclude (17) to (20), also applies to embedded infinitival
clauses (I ignore here the rather idiomatic 'Je ne sais que
faire'). The only way not to have a gap then is to allow *quoi*
in embedded infinitival questions, by restricting (48b) to root
sentences. As a matter of fact, (48b) could be optional in
both root and embedded clauses, and filter the result of its
application in embedded clauses by a constraint like (41).
For those speakers for whom *quoi* is rather bad in main
clauses, the text formulation, with the transformation being
obligatory, is preferable.

HEADLESS RELATIVES AND REDUCED RELATIVES
IN QUEBEC FRENCH, RUMANIAN, AND SPANISH

William Kemp
Université du Québec à Montreal

0. Introduction. Our knowledge of free relatives has recently been greatly enhanced by the work of Bresnan and
Grimshaw (1978), Woolford (1978), Hirschbühler (1978), and
van Riemsdijk and Groos (1978). In addition to discussion
concerning the structural position of the WH-phrase, Bresnan
and Grimshaw have made an interesting attempt to distinguish
cross-linguistically those free relatives originating through
WH-movement and those like English that they claim are base
generated in the NP position.

Contrary to this work, however, I argue that the existence
of semantic and surface differences makes it necessary to distinguish between WH-*ever* clauses, which are semantically conditional, and free relatives in the narrow sense I use here,
which are not semantically conditional. In this paper, I deal
only with semantically nonconditional free relatives.

The main body of this paper consists of a study of two
types of free relatives, reduced relatives *(that which)* and
headless relative *(what)*, as they appear in Quebec French,
Spanish, and Rumanian. Most of the aforementioned work has
centered on headless relatives. Since, cross-linguistically,
reduced relatives appear to be more common than headless
relatives, I believe that a comparison of these two free relative marking strategies will further our understanding of nonconditional free relatives in general.

Romance languages are a particularly pregnant domain for
a further investigation of such matters since some of them
(Quebec French and Rumanian) mark nonconditional free relatives with lexically interrogative items, while others (Spanish
and Standard French) use reduced relatives. A study of free
relatives in certain Romance languages is all the more interesting in that, as opposed to Germanic languages, such languages generally do not permit preposition stranding.

In Section 1, I indicate that I am treating only semantically nonconditional free relatives, and that I distinguish two types of free relatives: reduced relatives and headless relatives. In Section 2, I present the various surface forms that occur as free relatives in Quebec French, after which I compare headless relatives and reduced relatives in that dialect. Section 3 contains a brief logical analysis of reduced relatives and headless relatives. Based on the foregoing, I then look at free relatives as they appear in Rumanian and Spanish (Section 4). Finally, in Section 5, I try to account for the fact that, cross-linguistically, headless relatives tend to be marked by lexically interrogative items.

1. **Free relatives, conditional relatives, and question word clauses.** Notwithstanding Jespersen's strictures (1927-1953) and the practice of recent studies, for the purposes of this paper I wish to distinguish between free relatives and conditional relatives. Consider the typical sentences (1)-(2) from Montreal French.

(1) Mange qu'est-ce qui est devant toi. (free relative)
'Eat what is in front you.'
(2) Tu mangeras qu'osque tu voudras. (conditional relative)
'Eat whatever you want.'

As logicians since Frege have pointed out, the best translation of (2) involves a universal quantifier and a conditional clause (thus the term 'conditional relative').

(2a) For all x (if you want to eat x, eat x).

Sentence (1), on the other hand, has nothing conditional about it. On the contrary, such a phrase is normally used only when there is a plate of food in front of the addressee. Sentence (1) is to be analyzed as is any other nonconditional relative.

This semantic distinction can be very well reflected in surface structure. In pre-seventeenth century English, *what* did not appear in free relative contexts. A sentence like (3) could only be interpreted as a conditional relative.

(3) Do what I tell you.

If one were to overlook the difference between conditional and nonconditional relatives, it would be impossible to describe accurately the change in nonconditional free relative marking from *that which* to *what* that occurred in seventeenth century prose (Kemp 1979).

Similarly, in Old French, *que* appears not only in interrogative and embedded interrogative clauses but also in at least some conditional relative contexts, as in the still current expressions: *advienne que pourra* 'come what may', *coûte que coûte* 'cost what it will', etc. On the other hand, I know of no instance of nonconditional relative *que*.

This paper is concerned only with nonconditional free relatives. It should be noted that recent discussion of free relatives has been more concerned with conditional relatives than with what I call free relatives.

Needless to say, both of these clause types are to be distinguished from embedded interrogative clauses, which are sentential in nature. Thus, as originally pointed out by Hintikka (1962), Sentence (4) is best analyzed semantically as (4a).

(4) Jean sait ce que Paul a fait.
    'John knows what Paul did.'
(4a) For at least one x (Jean knows that Paul did x)

(For this clause type, see the recent analyses of Hausser and Zaefferer 1978, and Boër 1978).

Finally, I deal only with 'nonhuman' free relatives. In Quebec French, *qui* may mark 'human' conditional relatives, but not free relatives in the sense I have just given to this term. (Kuroda 1968:note 8 has made the same observation about English.)

I want also to distinguish between two types of free relatives. (1) Structurally, reduced relatives resemble full NP relatives. A generally determiner-like element which appears to occupy the determiner position is followed by the usual relative pronoun.[1] Examples include Fr. *ce que*, Sp. *lo que*, Eng. *that which* (and *that that* before the seventeenth century). For French, see Gross (1968:103-104). (2) The other, perhaps slightly less common strategy I want to focus on, consists in using an item lexically identical to the nonhuman interrogative word. This is the case in English and, in Romance languages, in Quebec French, Rumanian, and certain Gallo-Roman dialects such as Jersiais.[2]

Excluding conditional relatives, there are then two types of free relatives: reduced relatives and headless relatives. I argue among other things in the following sections that there are good reasons for keeping the two separate.

2. **Free relatives clauses in Quebec French.** Quebec French is a propitious domain for a study of free relatives because of the impressive array of free relative markers to be found, including both headless and reduced relative forms. Note that nonconditional free relatives appear in pseudo-clefts, proxy clauses (*what is called* ...), comparatives, and equationals, in addition to straightforward relatives.

2.1 **Basic free relative forms.** In Quebec French, free relatives may be marked by any of the forms in (5).

(5) Mange
$\begin{cases} \text{ce qu'} \\ \text{qu'est-ce qu'} \\ \text{qu'osqu'} \\ \text{de qu'asqu'} \\ \text{ce que c'est qu'} \end{cases}$
$\begin{cases} [\text{sk}]\text{ou}[\text{sək}] \\ [\text{kəsk}] \\ [\text{kɔsk}] \\ [\text{dəkwask}] \\ [\text{skəsek}] \end{cases}$
$\begin{cases} \text{il y a sur ton} \\ \text{assiette.} \end{cases}$

    'Eat what is on your plate.'

Of course, *c'que* is the standard form, of which *ce que c'est que* is a nonstandard complex form.[3] The other three represent distinct though not unrelated forms, each of which also serves as a question word.[4] (1) The form *qu'osque* is a complex form which serves both as a question word and as a headless relative marker made up of *quoi + est-ce que* or *c'est que*. To the extent that there exists what appears to be a noninverted form [kɔsekɔ], it is best seen as a semilexicalized or semifossilized form (see Langacker 1972 and Casagrande 1975 for discussion of these terms). The form [wa] has gone to [ɔ] through semiproductive rules of backing and raising. A parallel instance is that of *poigner* [pɔɲe]. Possible forms are: [kɔskə], [kɔs], [kɔsekə], [kɔse], [kɔskəsekə], [kɔskəse]. (2) The form *qu'est-ce que* is another complex form serving as question word and headless relative marker, composed of *que + est-ce que* or *c'est que*. It appears in exactly the same forms as *qu'osque*. (3) The form *de qu'asque* is another semilexicalized complex form, composed of *de + quoi + est-ce que* or *c'est que*. Note that the *de* is lexicalized and does not signify that it is oblique (see (5)). Forms: [dəkwaskə], [dəkɔskə], [dəkɔsekə], etc.

All such forms may also appear as the object of a preposition occurring within the matrix VP.[5]

(6) Je l'ai fabriqué avec
$\begin{cases} \text{ce que} \\ \text{qu'est-ce que} \\ \text{etc.} \end{cases}$
vous m'avez donné.

    'I made it with what you gave me.'

Note that interrogative *que*, which is not common in Quebec French, cannot appear either in embedded interrogations or in headless relatives. This means that in Quebec French (including Acadian) not just one but all the common nonhuman interrogative words may also be used as headless relative markers.

From a dialectical point of view, the evidence I possess at this moment shows that the basic forms in rural Quebec around and to the south and southwest of Quebec City, on both sides of the St. Lawrence River, are *qu'osque,* and *de qu'asque*. The same is also the case in Acadian. In these dialects, *ce que*, and even *qu'est-ce que*, appear only in the speech of people showing strong normalizing tendencies. In Montreal, the variants are *qu'est-ce que, qu'osque*, and *ce que*; *de qu'asque* is rare.

It is noteworthy that of the Romance languages that have complex interrogative words of the *qu'est-ce que* variety (i.e. Spanish, Portuguese, and French), Quebec French and a few French 'patois' seem to be the only languages or dialects that permit complex question words, not only in embedded interrogatives but also in conditional relatives and headless relatives.

2.2 Properties of free relatives in Quebec French.

In order to get a better view of free relatives in general, I examine in detail free relatives as they appear in Quebec French. I discuss in order: (1) headlessness, (2) gender and number, (3) case marking, (4) subject-verb inversion, (5) a relative infinitive construction, and (6) universal quantifier combinations.

In this section, I highlight ways in which free relatives are different from headed relatives. I use general terms such as neutralization, nondiscreteness, and restrictedness to describe these properties. In particular, it is seen that reduced relatives are more neutralized and restricted in their surface forms than headed relatives, and that lexically interrogative free relatives are generally more restricted than reduced relatives.

2.2.1 'Headlessness'.

Free relatives are very much like true relatives to the extent that they obey all the various NP constraints that apply to the headed variety. In fact, violation of the complex NP constraint (Ross 1967) gives an output that is considerably more incomprehensible than is the case with relatives, since, to take one instance, the displaced constituent also serves as a clause boundary marker.

(7a) John ate what Mary had given to Paul.
(7b) *What did John eat Mary had given to Paul?

Not surprisingly, whatever the correct structural description of free relatives may be, there are a number of facts that indicate that free relative 'heads' are not true heads.

1. Rather obviously, they cannot appear individually in other NP slots.

(8) *J'ai vu ce.

2. Genitives are only possible in instances where there is a lexical noun or demonstrative pronoun (*celui*, etc.) in the head NP slot. Thus (9) is ungrammatical.

(9) *C'est ce dont la patte est cassée. (*ce* = une table)

3. No parenthetical material can intervene between the free relative head and the relative pronoun.

(10) J'ai pas trouvé les coupes, tu sais, que tu voulais.
(11) *J'ai pas trouvé ce, tu sais, que tu voulais.

A closer look at free relatives and headed relatives reveals an important syntactic and semantic difference between the two. Headed relatives represent the intersection of two sets--the larger domain, established by the head, and the restricting sentence, or relative clause itself (Keenan 1972:169). But, as Tobler noted (1886:97), free relatives 'make use of the relative clause proper without indicating the wider circle within which the particular individuals are determined'. Since there is no real head, *qu'est-ce que Marie veut* 'what Mary wants' may refer to butterflies, a ride, some friends, or a nice theory.

2.2.2 Gender, number, and discreteness. In comparison with relatives per se, free relatives in general tend to mark fewer distinctions: certain traits present in headed relatives are neutralized in free relatives. [6]
With respect to gender, singular relatives in French must be marked for gender (*le/la*), while free relatives are not so marked. With respect to number, relatives are marked for number, i.e. either singular (*le/la*) or plural (*les*). Even though free relatives may refer specifically to singular or plural objects, they may not be so marked.
Note that the apparently related forms *celui que, celles que*, etc. are instances of pronoun headed relatives and not of free relatives, as can be seen in Table 1.

Table 1.

	Masculine	Feminine	Neuter
Singular	celui	celle	--
Plural	ceux	celles	--
Neuter	--	--	ce

As Otheguy (1978) has shown for Spanish, the neutral form not only shows a lower degree of deixis, but is semantically distinct from the demonstrative forms: the demonstrative forms are generally discrete, whereas the 'neuter' form is nondiscrete in the sense that it 'conveys the meaning of unclear, diffuse, and not well-delineated boundaries' (Otheguy 1978:243). That is all the more evident in Quebec French, given that the lexically interrogative forms show no morphological relation to demonstratives, and yet are semantically equivalent to the reduced relative *ce que* forms.
It should be noted that with respect to both number and gender, free relatives are more neutral than an analysis in

terms of *thing(s) that,* or *le/la/les chose(s) que.* Note also that, as concerns both gender and number, free relatives can only be coreferenced by *le,* even though the object in question may be feminine or plural.

2.2.3 Case-marking. In Quebec French, there is one important difference between the forms cited in (5): *ce que* alone may appear in the oblique case.

(12a) J'ai brûlé ce dans quoi les insectes s'étaient installés.
'I burned what the insects were installed on.'

(12b) *J'ai brûlé $\begin{cases} \text{qu'est-ce que} \\ \text{qu'est-ce que sur quoi} \\ \text{sur qu'est-ce que} \end{cases}$ les insectes étaient installés.

Although, as Keenan and Comrie (1977) have stated, French permits relativizing on all positions on the hierarchy of accessibility except that of object of comparatives, the possibilities in the case of nonhuman free relatives are more limited. The indirect object position would be possible only in such instances as when *ce à quoi* refers to an animal.

(13) Ce à quoi j'ai donné le reste de mon lait, c'est
      mon chat.
      'What I gave the rest of my milk to is my cat.'

And, as mentioned, genitives are not possible.
About all that remains of the three positions lower on the hierarchy than object is the oblique. But even this position is largely circumvented in Quebec French, as mentioned by Bouchard (this volume) (for French 'patois', see Bruneau 1926:220). Underlying oblique forms based on *de* appear almost always as surface objects.

(14) Ce que j'ai besoin, c'est ... (avoir besoin de)
      Qu'osque j'ai peur, c'est ... (avoir peur de)

The preposition *à* may also be deleted.

(15) Ce que ça sert, c'est ... (servir a)

As Lefebvre and Fournier (1978) have pointed out, there also exists a stranding strategy in the case of prepositions such as *sur, sous,* and *dans,* which appear postverbally as *dessus, dessous,* and *dedans.*

(16) Ce que je comptais dessus, c'est ...
      'That which I was counting on, is ...'

Thus, in the case of spoken Quebec French, prepositional case marking is reduced to a minimum. To cite facts, in the Montreal French corpus, out of 17 cases of underlying *de* or *à*, only two appear as surface obliques.

On the other hand, standard *ce que* provides a prime example of a reduced relative. Not only does it admit prepositional case marking after the determiner 'head' *ce*, but it easily accommodates contexts in which there are two back-to-back prepositions: the first, part of the matrix VP; the second, in connection with the embedded VP.

(17) On placera une commande pour ce dont on a besoin.
'We'll place an order for what we are in need of.'

I am going to show that in some other languages reduced relatives are not so versatile.

It should be noted that while *ce que*, as opposed to the lexically interrogative forms, admits prepositional case marking, in point of fact this difference is of minimal importance in free relatives, and such forms tend to be exploited only by the most educated segment of the population.

2.2.4 Subject-verb inversion. Similar to relatives, the *ce que* type of free relative admits subject-verb inversion in Standard French (see Kayne and Pollock 1978, and Dubuisson 1979).

(18) Jean a mangé ce que voulait Marie.
'John ate what Mary wanted.'

In Quebec French, such inversion is not used in normal conversation, though it may occur in more formal contexts. In the case of lexically interrogative free relatives, however, such inversion does not occur.

(19) *Jean a mangé qu'est-ce que voulait Marie.

Whether this is a result of the fact that *qu'est-ce que* as an interrogative form is never followed by inversion, or some other reason, what is important to note is that, once again, the lexically interrogative form is more restricted than the *ce que* form.

2.2.5 Nonfinite free relatives: *de quoi*. In spite of the neutralization and nondiscreteness of free relatives, there exists in Quebec French (and French in general) a very specialized headless relative construction involving infinitives.

Relatives of quantity such as (20) can be analyzed logically roughly as (20a).

$$(20)\ J'ai \begin{cases} \text{les ingrédients qu'il faut} \\ \text{la quantité d'ingrédients qu'il faut} \\ \text{assez d'ingrédients} \end{cases} \text{pour que}$$

tu puisses faire à manger.
'I have the ingredients that are necessary so that
you can cook.'

(20a) (QUANT x) ((if you want to cook, it is necessary
that you have x ingredients) AND (I have x ingredients)).

There are free relatives on the same model.

$$(21)\ J'ai \begin{cases} \text{ce qu'} \\ \text{qu'est-ce qu'} \\ \text{etc.} \end{cases} \text{il faut pour que tu puisses faire}$$

à manger.
'I have what is necessary in order that you may cook.'

But there is also a special modal infinitive construction (mentioned in Hirschbühler 1978) that occurs only when infinitivi-
zation has applied under identity of subject.

(22) J'ai de quoi (pour) faire à manger.
'I have what it takes to make dinner.'

In this case, the free relative marker is *de quoi* and the
modal predicate is obligatorily deleted.[7] Since *de quoi* has the
same distribution as *ce qu'il faut*, it must be considered a nonfinite free relative marker. This construction is, in fact,
parallel to question-word modal infinitives as shown in (23).

(23) Je sais pas quoi lui dire.
'I don't know what to say to him.' (= 'what I should
say to him')

Like them, it applies only to nonsubject positions (i.e. object
and oblique).
Thus, the *de quoi* construction is at once very specialized
and at the same time restricted in its distribution.

2.2.6 Universal quantifier combinations. Finally, let us
examine combinations of free relative markers with the universal quantifier *tout*.
Here are the most important clause types involving universal quantifier free relative combinations (see Andersson
1954:166ff.). They appear in French, as in English, in both
relative (24) and conditional relative (25) contexts.

(24) J'ai mangé tout ce que tu as laissé.
'I ate all you left.'

(25) Tu fera tout qu'osque tu voudras.
'Do anything you want.'

Depending on the matrix predicate and its mood, the conditional relative may also take on a quantitative sense.

(26) Tu mangeras tout qu'est-ce que tu voudras.
'Eat as much as you want.'

Finally, they appear with a restrictive sense in sentences like (27).[8]

(27) Tout ce que je veux, c'est que tu te taises.
'All I want is for you to shut up.'

In English there is an interesting restriction with respect to universal quantifier combinations. Though *all* may combine with any definite NP, *all what* is ungrammatical.[9] Whatever the reason for this gap in at least one language, it represents another instance of a special restriction applying to free relatives.

In Quebec French, as in Rumanian, German, and other languages, universal quantifiers combine freely with lexically interrogative free relative markers. Quebec French is interesting because of the large number of forms one finds (omitting phonetic brackets).

tuskə	tutskə	tus
tuskəsekə	tuskəse	
tutkɛskə	tutkɛs	
tutkɔskə	tutkɔs	
tutdəkwaskə	tutdəkwas	
tutdəkɔskə		

Though these are the main forms, speakers do not reject other combinations such as [tutkɛsekə], etc.

So it is seen that in Quebec French *tout* combines not only with the *ce que* forms but also with all of the lexically interrogative free relative markers.

The foregoing study of free relatives in Quebec French has served to show the degree to which free relatives are at once neutralized with respect to traits such as gender and number and in certain cases restricted, for instance, with respect to case marking or subject-verb inversion. In particular, it has been seen that in Quebec French, though semantically equivalent, reduced relatives are hardly restricted at all, whereas headless relatives are restricted in many different ways. Interestingly, in Quebec French, given the existence of preposition deletion and preposition stranding, whatever forms reduced relatives can take, can also generally appear in headless clauses.

I conclude that free relatives are more neutral and nondiscrete, and more restricted than headed relatives, and that headless relatives tend to be more so than reduced relatives, though the latter two are equally neutral and nondiscrete. Note that despite such characteristics, free relatives can still serve very specific functions, as in the case of the *de quoi* infinitive clause type. Though I do not examine other languages in such detail, what I say about Rumanian and Spanish supports the preceding description.

3. **The logical structure of headless relatives.** From a logical point of view, headless relatives can be analyzed in terms of a WH operator (with a noninterrogative semantics) which forms complex names from sentences with empty argument slots (developed from Harman 1975). The variable which such an operator binds is class marked (in this case nonhuman) and is, of course, neutral with respect to gender and number. Thus, *what Mary wants* would have the logical structure in (29).

(29) WHx (Mary wants x $\begin{bmatrix} \text{nonhuman} \\ \emptyset \text{ gender} \\ \emptyset \text{ number} \end{bmatrix}$)

On the other hand, there are headed relatives, whose heads can be seen logically (Keenan 1972:454) as one-place predicates which combine with coindexed sentences to form complex names.

Reduced relatives are somewhere in between. On the one hand, syntactically, oblique *ce avec quoi* resembles a surface relative. On the other hand, *ce* is not a name; it is a proname which could combine with coindexed Ss to form complex names. Such complex names would be very similar to those formed by the WH operator, since there is no intersection of sets.

It is these logical and semantic properties that make the two forms equivalent, as is the case in Montreal French (see (5)), and as was the case in seventeenth century English prose, in which *that which* and *what* were variants (Kemp 1979).

The closest approximation to the WH operator system referred to earlier is that of modern English, in which relative *what*, due to preposition stranding, is always and uniquely the 'head' of its clause.[10] On the other hand, as I am going to show, in languages without preposition stranding, prepositionally marked oblique forms frequently represent the limit of the WH operator strategy.

4. **Free relatives in Rumanian and Spanish.** In this section, I cite facts from Rumanian, indicating a not insignificant limitation on headless relative clauses, and from Spanish,

showing that the distinction between reduced relative and headless relative may in some cases function in very similar ways.

4.1 Headless relatives as objects of prepositions in Rumanian.

In Rumanian (see Manoliu-Manea 1978), the question word *ce* 'what' is the usual free relative marker (*ceeace* 'that-what' is also possible, but much less common). There is no preposition stranding in Rumanian. It turns out that Rumanian not only admits *ce* clauses as objects of matrix clause prepositions (30), but also as objects of clause-initial prepositions in the dependent clause (31).

(30) Am lucrat cu ce mi-ai dat.
    I-PAST worked with what me-you PAST gave
    'I worked with what you gave me.'

(31) Am folosit de ce ai avut nevoie.
    I-PAST used of what you-PAST had need
    'I used what you were in need of.'

But what happens if both clauses are oblique? In Rumanian, or any other language that makes use of such a headless relative strategy, a sequence of two consecutive prepositions, each depending on a different clause, is perfectly conceivable. In Rumanian, such sentences are ungrammatical, as in (32).

(32) *M-am folosit de cu ce l-ai fabricat
    me-I-PAST made use of with what it-you-PAST made
    'I made use of what you made it with.'

But in the case of *de*, if both prepositions are *de*, the first may be deleted and the sentence is then acceptable.

(33) M-am folosit de ce ai avut nevoie.
    me-I-PAST made-use of what you-PAST had need
    'I made use (of) what you had need of.'

(See Bresnan and Grimshaw 1978:373 for similar considerations pertaining to Finnish). In order to render such sentences, Rumanian speakers are obliged to switch from headless to headed relatives, especially with demonstrative pronoun heads. One might say that at least in Rumanian such back-to-back prepositional sequences represent the limit of the fully consistent WH operator strategy (for another context that prohibits headless relatives per se, see notes 1 and 5). As has been seen, in Quebec French, such an output does not occur as a result of preposition deletion in the matrix or embedded clause, or both. In modern English, it is, of course, preposition stranding in the embedded clause that makes a totally consistent WH operator strategy possible.

4.2 Apparent reduced relatives in Spanish. In Spanish, free relatives are marked exclusively by the reduced relative form *lo que*. No nonhuman question word may be so used in any Spanish dialect that I know of. Second, Spanish does not permit preposition stranding. However, instead of the relative-like *ce dont* and *ce avec quoi* of Standard French, the oblique occurs with the preposition dominating *lo que* as a whole.

(34) Esto es con lo que lo hice.
    'This is what I made it with.'

While its surface form and morphology lead us to believe that *lo que* is a reduced relative, the fact that, contrary to headed relatives in Spanish, the preposition does not occur between *lo* and *que*, but in front of *lo*, indicates that *lo que* should be analyzed as a bimorphemic unit. Thus, in spite of its surface form, *lo que* resembles in this respect a WH operator, which in the other languages considered has taken the form of the nonhuman question word.

However, the same restriction on back-to-back prepositional sequences presented for Rumanian occurs also in Spanish in free relatives. But interestingly, such a construction is possible in Spanish in embedded interrogatives.

(35) Eso depende de con qué lo hiciste.
    'That depends on what you made it with.'

Such a sequence in at least one clause type indicates that any filter concerning double preposition sequences must be language (and construction) specific and not universal.

If I have chosen to discuss Rumanian and Spanish, it is because they represent opposite but complementary tendencies which show up at precisely that point where headed clauses become headless clauses and vice versa.

5. Lexically interrogative free relative markers. In addition to the previously noted instances of English and other Germanic languages cited in the literature, I have examined two Romance languages (Quebec French and Rumanian) that use lexically interrogative free relative markers. The same pattern exists in other languages from diverse language families--for instance, Hebrew and classical Arabic, Polish and Bulgarian, Modern Greek, Fula, and Ojibwa.

Such facts give rise to the following question, posed clearly by Kuroda (1968) with respect to English: how can one account for the fact that all the SVO languages that I know of that do not mark free relatives with reduced relatives, mark them with the nonhuman interrogative word?

5.1 Competing grammatical regularities. I believe that this situation results from a competing grammatical regularity. On the one hand, free relatives are still relatives: they are NPs and they are frequently used to form definite descriptions. On the other hand, the parallel marking of free relatives and question word clauses results from the existence of another regularity, according to which all grammatically headless constructions tend to be marked the same way, whatever their syntactic category or discourse function: i.e. questions, embedded questions, and all the headless relative contexts: pseudo-clefts, equationals, comparatives, conditional relatives and free relatives.

There are, then, two organizing principles that may affect the surface form and in some cases even the structure of free relatives: (1) relativeness, which accentuates vertical, intra-clause-type similarities; and (2) headlessness, which represents the development of horizontal, cross-construction similarities.

Given the degree of neutralization and restrictedness of free relatives which I have presented, such Janus-like behavior is in the end not so surprising. In particular, the headlessness principle affords some reason to believe that the lexically interrogative marking of free relatives is not the result of pure chance or of some vague 'analogy'.

In Section 3, I proposed the use of a WH operator as the best translation of headless relatives. I now go one step further and claim that the same or a similar operator could be used to generate embedded question word clauses (excluding *whether* clauses) and what Jespersen (1924:303) called 'x-question' (in the latter case, in conjunction with the appropriate modal operator). The use of such an operator in interrogative clauses is nothing new: similar propositions can be found in Ajdukiewicz (1928) and Carnap (1934). Its extension to include headless relatives would require some adjustment from a semantic viewpoint. Since this would lead to a reconsideration of all three clause types, a more specific presentation must be left for another occasion.

That this is not the minor question it might at first appear to be can be seen from the fact that the distribution of such structures varies cross-linguistically. In some languages, headless clauses are limited to direct questions (for instance, Niger-Congo languages); in others, they occur in both direct questions and embedded questions but not headless relatives (as in Italian); and finally, there are languages which show headless clauses in questions, embedded questions and free relatives, i.e. not only as Ss but also as NPs (Quebec French, Rumanian, English).

5.2 Word order. There is one further prerequisite to the appearance of lexically interrogative markers in free relatives which can be formulated negatively as follows. This sort of free relative marking strategy is most unlikely in languages

where: (1) marking strategies in embedded interrogatives
and free relatives are very distinct; (2) word order in embedded interrogatives and free relatives is distinct. I examine
each of these aspects briefly without going into a myriad of
cross-linguistic details.

First, though in embedded interrogatives most SOV languages use question words either in clause-initial or in their
base assigned position, they tend to mark relatives and free
relatives morphologically with heads appearing to the right.
In addition, as Kuno has pointed out (1974:126-127), in many
SOV languages sentential complements, including embedded
interrogatives, appear postverbally. Such structural differences between relatives and embedded interrogative make it
improbable that such SOV languages would use an interrogative lexeme to mark free relatives.

A similar situation prevails in SVO and VSO languages
which do not mark interrogative clauses initially (see Kemp
1977) for a description of a number of such languages).
Thus, for Tok Pisin (Woolford 1978) there are structures like
that in (37).

(37a) EI: SV   [SV 0_{wh}]

(37b) FR: SV   [0_{rel} SV]

(EI = Embedded interrogative, FR = free relative.)

In all the foregoing cases, the use of lexically interrogative
free relative marking would introduce a major breach in existing marking and word order patterns. Languages in which
the two clauses are identically marked show a lexical item
marking free relatives clause initially, as in embedded interrogatives, and the word order must be parallel. These conditions are met by many SVO and VSO languages.

(38a) EI: SV   [0_{wh}SV]

(38b) FR: SV   [0_{rel}SV]

Such structural similarities can be seen as a condition for
lexically interrogative free relative marking, but, of course,
they in no way dictate such a policy.

Conclusion. The real question is: to what extent should
surface structure be taken literally? It is, of course, possible
in the case at hand to derive *what* from *that which*, as Kuroda
(1968) does. But I believe that to do so is to miss a not
insignificant surface generalization. Another way to respect
the surface structure of headless clauses in languages like
Quebec French, etc. involves adopting a system similar to the

one I have sketched. It is perfectly consistent to proceed as if such regularities are only of secondary importance in comparison, for instance, to the opposition between WH-complementizers and non-WH-complementizers (Chomsky 1973). I have presented a number of reasons for adopting an analysis which can account for certain cross-construction surface similarities, though I suspect that, as with most systems, if fully developed, the benefits that accrue from it may turn out to have hidden costs.

NOTES

I wish to thank Pierrette Thibault for insightful comments on this paper. I am also beholden to the following linguists for information on: Acadian (Marie-Marthe Roy), Italian (Anne-Marie di Sciullo), Rumanian (Sorin Georgescu), and Spanish (Henrietta Cedergren). They are hereby absolved from any horrors that may occur in this paper.

1. Certain languages, such as German and Polish, may simply place a determiner in front of the lexically interrogative marker (thus, not the normal relative marker). The determiner is obligatory if there is case marking resulting from either clause (see note 5(i)). Since this type of marker is not central to a discussion of Romance languages, I do not deal with it here.

2. I have not made a close study of Gallo-Roman dialects (called 'patois') but complex question words are found in conditional relatives in Jersiais (Le Maistre 1966) and in the Gondecourt dialect (Cochet 1933:201).

3. Standard French is most unusual in that, while permitting all other question words as embedded interrogative markers, in cases marked 'nonhuman', it permits only the noninterrogative form *ce que*, and not *qu'est-ce que, que,* etc.

4. In opposition of Obenauer's claim (1977) that interrogative *que* is, in fact, the basic complementizer *que*, Goldsmith (1978) has recently proposed that *que* be analyzed as an allomorph of *quoi* resulting from a rule of cliticization. Parallel to *moi/me, quoi* is the strong and *que* the weak form. See also Hirschbühler (this volume).

5. In German, when the matrix VP requires a dative, *was* 'what', which may occur either as subject or object but not as oblique, is not a possible form unless preceded by the dative marked determiner *dem* (Rolf Max Kully, personal communication).

(i) Der Zweifel beruth nur auf $\begin{Bmatrix} \text{*was} \\ \text{dem was} \end{Bmatrix}$ ausser Zweifel ist.

'Doubt rests only on $\begin{Bmatrix} \text{what} \\ \text{that which} \end{Bmatrix}$ beyond doubt is.'

6. Here is Trubetzkoy's well-known definition: 'In those positions in which a neutralizable opposition is actually neutralized, the specific marks of an opposition member lose their distinctive force. Only those features which are common to both opposition members [...] remain relevant' (1939:70, tr. Baltaxe 1969:78-79).

7. It appears that *de quoi* holds the middle ground between *assez pour*, which may have the sense of 'barely enough', and *tout pour*, which suggests an abundance. Note that of the latter two, only *tout* is syntactically a free relative. Like *de quoi*, it appears with infinitives.

(i) J'ai tout pour faire a manger.
    'I have all it takes to make dinner.'

Once again, with an infinitive, the modal predicate must be deleted.

8. Contrary to Andersson's statement for Standard French, L-*tous* (Kayne 1975) may apply in free relative combinations.

(i) J'ai tout fait ce que tu voulais.
    'I did everything you wanted.'

However, in the Montreal French corpus, while L-*tous* applies about 50 percent of the time in the case of plural NPs, it applies only about 15 percent of the time in free relative combinations (3/20). For a discussion of *tout* in Montreal French, see Daoust-Blais and Lemieux-Niéger (1979).

9. As Jespersen points out (1927:129), there are recorded occurrences of *all what*. The OED (*what*: C.7) has quotations from 1597, 1718, 1740, and 1919. Nevertheless, the combination is highly unusual.

10. In short sequences, it is possible not to mark the dependent clause on the surface. At about three years of age, my daughter went through a brief period in which sentences like (i) occurred in relation to a specific thing such as a coat.

(i) Comment appelle, Papa a?
    'What do you call, what Dad has?'

SUBJECTLESS TENSED CLAUSES: BIUNIQUENESS AND LOCALITY

Jean-Yves Morin
Université de Montréal

Eric Wehrli
McGill University

1. **A generalization.** There is a correlation, in French, between the presence of a (morphological) tense marker and the (obligatory) appearance of a lexical subject. This is true of subordinates as well as of main clauses, as shown in (1)-(4).

(1) (Max pense que) ∗ ($\left\{\begin{array}{l}\text{j'}\\\text{tu}\\\text{il, elle, on}\\\text{nous}\\\text{vous}\\\text{ils, elles}\end{array}\right\}$) $\left\{\begin{array}{l}\text{avertis}\\\text{avertis}\\\text{avertit}\\\text{avertissons}\\\text{avertissez}\\\text{avertissent}\end{array}\right\}$ Luc.

(2a) Max avertit Luc.
(2b) *___ avertit Luc.

(3) Max pense avertir Luc.

(4) *Max pense $\left\{\begin{array}{l}\text{Anne}\\\text{il}\end{array}\right\}$ avertir Luc.[1]

1.1 Exceptions. This generalization admits a restricted and well defined class of exceptions.

1.1.1 Imperatives. In nonsubordinate clauses, there is the case of imperatives, which cannot have a lexical subject.

(5a) Avertis Luc!
(5b) Avertissons Luc!
(5c) Avertissez Luc!

265

1.1.2 **WH-movement in relatives.** In subordinate clauses, there is the case of WH-movement, especially in relatives, when it is the subject itself that is relativized.

(6) Le gars $[_{S'}[_{COMP}$ qui][$_S$ a averti Luc est arrivé.]]

1.1.3 **Stylistic inversion.** A third class of exceptions consists of clauses, main or subordinate, where the so-called rule of stylistic inversion has applied (cf. Kayne and Pollock 1978 for a detailed treatment of this rule).

(7a) Où va la linguistique?
(7b) Je me demande où va la linguistique.

2. **Filters.** These facts have been handled, within the framework of transformational generative grammar, by postulating surface structure filters.

2.1 **Perlmutter (1971).** For instance, Perlmutter (1971:100) proposes the filter shown in (8).

(8) Any sentence other than an imperative in which there is an S that does not contain a subject in surface structure is ungrammatical.

As he notes, this filter does not appear to be universal. Certain languages, like Italian and Spanish, do not follow it.

(9) Finisco il lavoro. (Italian)
(10) Acabo la obra. (Spanish)

It is obvious that such a filter has no explanatory value. First, the fact that it does not apply to imperatives does not follow from any independent property of imperatives. Second, the fact that some languages do not obey the filter does not follow either from independent properties of the grammar of these languages. Third, it does not take into account the case of WH-movement in relatives and of stylistic inversion. [2]
Within the framework of a highly restrictive theory of grammar (outlined in more detail elsewhere: cf. Morin and Wehrli 1978, Wehrli 1978 and in preparation, Morin 1979) we are going to propose a global solution to this problem. But, before we do that, we must examine a filter postulated by Chomsky and Lasnik (1977) (henceforth CL) which overlaps with Perlmutter's.

2.2 **Chomsky and Lasnik (1977).** Noting that sentences such as those in (11) are ungrammatical, CL propose the universal filter given in (12).

(11a) *Who do you think that saw Bill?
(11b) *Qui crois-tu que viendra.

(12) *$[_{S'} \underline{+}WH \; [_{NP} e] \; ... \;]$, unless S' or its trace is in the context $[_{NP} NP\underline{} \; ...]$

This filter covers only part of the phenomena in which we are interested. It does not take into consideration the case of nonembedded Ss. Moreover, the case of WH-movement in relatives remains an unexplained exception which must be stated as such (i.e. the 'unless' condition of the filter). Notice that sentences such as (13), which are allowed by the filter, are grammatical in English but not in French.

(13a) $[_{NP}$ The man $[_{S'} [_{COMP}$ that] $\underline{}$ works here]$_{S'}$ NP] is a blackmailer.
(13b) *$[_{NP}$ L'homme $[_{S'} [_{COMP}$ que] $\underline{}$ travaille ici]$_{S'}$ NP] est un maître-chanteur.

As a consequence, CL would have to interpret the 'unless' condition of (12) not as part of the (universal) filter itself but as a language (i.e. English)-specific parameter narrowing its scope down to nonrelatives.

Furthermore, filter (12), which is assumed to be universal, contains another parameter restricting its application to languages that do not have a rule of subject pronoun deletion (cf. (14)).

(14a) Creo que partio.
(14b) Je crois qu'il est parti. (*Crois qu'est parti.)
(14c) I think that he left. (*Think that left.)

CL show that this parameter does not have to be included explicitly in the conditions of the filter, provided the deletion of a subject trace is permitted as a special case of subject pronoun deletion.

Nevertheless, the fundamental problem remains unsolved: why should certain languages (and not others) allow subject pronoun deletion?

2.3 **NIC.** Chomsky (1978), in the context of a redefinition of constraints on binding, proposes a constraint, which seems to come closer to expressing directly the generalization that tensed Ss must have lexical subjects. This result appears to be attainable only through the introduction of a complex Case assignment system (assigning Cases to NPs in different structural positions) coupled with a reformulation of the Tensed S (or Propositional Island) Constraint (TSC or PIC) as a

Nominative Island Constraint (NIC).[3] We give the relevant
part of Case assignment in (15) and NIC in (16).

(15) The subject of a tensed clause receives nominative
Case.

(16) A nominative anaphor cannot be free in S'.[4]

For Chomsky, only nonlexical NPs (i.e. trace and PRO) are
anaphors. Consequently, any tensed S containing a nonlexical NP in subject position is ruled out by NIC, unless the NP
in question is not free in S'.

(17a) *PRO vient.
(17b) *Tu dis$[_{S'}$ $[_{COMP}$ que] PRO vient.]
(17c) Je me demande $[_{S'}$ $[_{COMP}$ quand]t_i arrivera Jean$_i$]

In (17a) and (17b), PRO is completely free, so that both
sentences are ruled out by NIC. In (17c), the trace in subject position is not free in S', making the sentence grammatical.[5]
 However, NIC cannot rule out sentences like (11a) since,
for Chomsky, such sentences have the structure given in (18),
where the t_i in subject position is not free in S' because it is
bound by the t_i in COMP, which is itself bound by 'who$_i$'.

(18) *Who$_i$ do you think $[_{S'}$ $[_{COMP}$ t_i that] $[_S$ t_i left]]

NIC incorrectly predicts that such sentences are grammatical.
Filter (12) would thus be needed anyway. But it is redundant
with NIC and, moreover, it incorrectly rules out sentences
like (19), where stylistic inversion has taken place.

(19) $[_{NP}$Le fait $[_{S'}$ $[_{COMP}$ que]$[_S$ t_i t'a communiqué
 [cette fille]$_i$ $_S]_{S'}]_{NP}]$ ne nous intéresse pas.

One might then be tempted to say that sentence (11a) is
actually ruled out by NIC, i.e. the subject anaphor being in
fact free in S', as in (20), without a t_i in COMP position of
S'.

(20) Who$_i$ do you think $[_{S'}$ $[_{COMP}$ that] $[_S$ t_i left]]

It might be thought that the trace in COMP position in (18)
has to be deleted by the rule of free deletion in COMP (giving (20) as the output) and that this would be guaranteed by
filter (21), provided WH-phrase in (21) may also be interpreted
as the trace of a WH-phrase.

(21) *[$_{COMP}$ WH-phrase, ϕ] $\phi \neq$ e (= CL (53))

But such a solution cannot work for two independent reasons.
First, if WH-phrase in filter (21) can be interpreted as
trace of WH-phrase,[6] then filter (21) would force the deletion
of t_i in (22) (where it is not the subject but the object that
is moved), resulting in (23).

(22) Who$_i$ do you think [$_{S'}$[$_{COMP}$ t_i that][$_S$Bill saw t_i]]

(23) Who$_i$ do you think [$_{S'}$[$_{COMP}$ that][$_S$ Bill saw t_i]]

Structure (23) is then incorrectly rejected, not by NIC, but
by Opacity this time.

(24) Opacity

> If α (t_i in (23)) is an anaphor in the domain of the
> subject of β (Bill in (23)), then α cannot be free in
> β (β = S'). (cf. Chomsky 1978:17)

Therefore, if conditions (i.e. NIC and Opacity) apply to the
output of deletion rules and filters, (11a) is (correctly) ruled
out by NIC but (23) is also ruled out (incorrectly).
Second, if, as Chomsky (1978) (and CL) propose, rules of
construal and conditions (i.e. NIC and Opacity) apply independently of deletion rules and filters (cf. schema (25)),
Opacity does not block (23) but neither is NIC able to block
(11a).

(25) 1 Base rules
     2 Transformational rules

3a Deletion rules	3b Construal rules
4a Filters	4b Interpretive rules
5a Phonology and stylistic rules	5b Conditions on binding

(cf. Chomsky 1978:4)

Therefore, filter (12) with all the problems it creates (i.e.
redundancy with NIC and difficulties with stylistic inversion,
which, by the way, is not a stylistic rule) cannot be done
away with within Chomsky's framework.
Later on, we propose a constraint, the locality constraint,
which incorporates the interesting aspects of NIC without having its undesired consequences, and we show that such a constraint can be formulated only within our more restrictive
framework.

3. Inflection and recoverability

3.1 Traditional grammarians. Interestingly enough, the existence of a correlation between the richness of the verbal inflection paradigm in a language and the optionality of the subject in tensed sentences had been noticed by traditional grammarians. Grevisse, for instance, observes:

> Ces pronoms ont essentiellement pour fonction d'indiquer une forme particulière de conjugaison aux modes personnels et ils ne possèdent d'autre valeur que celle d'une désinence. Ainsi le pronom personnel sujet permet, dans la langue orale, de distinguer l'une de l'autre certaines formes verbales homonymes: (Je) parle, (tu) parles, (il) parle. -- (Je) parlais, (tu) parlais, (il) parlait. -- (Tu) iras, (il) ira. -- (Nous) serons blessés, (ils) seront blessés.
>   Les formes atones du pronom personnel sujet sont *proclitiques* ou *enclitiques*; elles font, pour ainsi dire, partie intégrante des formes verbales qu'elles accompagnent....
>   Au moyen âge, le pronom sujet faisait ordinairement défaut, parce que les terminaisons verbales, étant encore sonores, indiquaient suffisamment les personnes grammaticles: *Adam, où es?* (*Adam*, 386.) -- *Que ferai-je donc?* (*Eneas*, 8729.) -- *Ma chiere amie que avez?* (BEROUL, *Le Roman de Tristan*, 3175.) -- *Où est?* (*Floire et Blancheflor*, 676.) -- *Feras?* (*Pathelin*, 1390.) -- Peu à peu le pronom sujet s'est imposé dans la conjugaison (Grevisse 1964: 410).

However, the formalism these grammarians had at their disposal did not allow them to express that relationship in a precise and systematic way. The lack of an adequate formalism prevented them from capturing the phenomenon in its full generality. In particular, it prevented them from seeing that the case of imperatives in languages such as English or French follows the same principle: subject NPs are (or can be) missing in surface structure only if, for every element of a given verbal paradigm, they are recoverable from the morphological form of the verbal element; in other words, if there is a bi-unique relationship between the set of morphological forms of a verbal paradigm and the set of possible interpretations (in person and number in this case) of the subject. Figure 1 illustrates that relationship.

The traditional grammarians' hypothesis of a correlation between the richness of a verbal paradigm and the lack of a subject in tensed sentences is rejected by Perlmutter on the basis of the example of French. As a matter of fact, although the verb morphology is richer in French than in English, this language does not allow the absence of subjects (except in imperatives, of course). However, if it is true that verb morphology is richer in French than in English, the crucial observation is that verb paradigms in most cases are not bi-unique, as shown in Figure 2. The only biunique paradigm in French is precisely the imperative, as shown in Figure 3. Since this paradigm has fewer elements than the other para-digms, it needs fewer morphological distinctions to be bi-unique. [7]

Figure 1. Paradigm of the present indicative in Spanish (first conjugation).

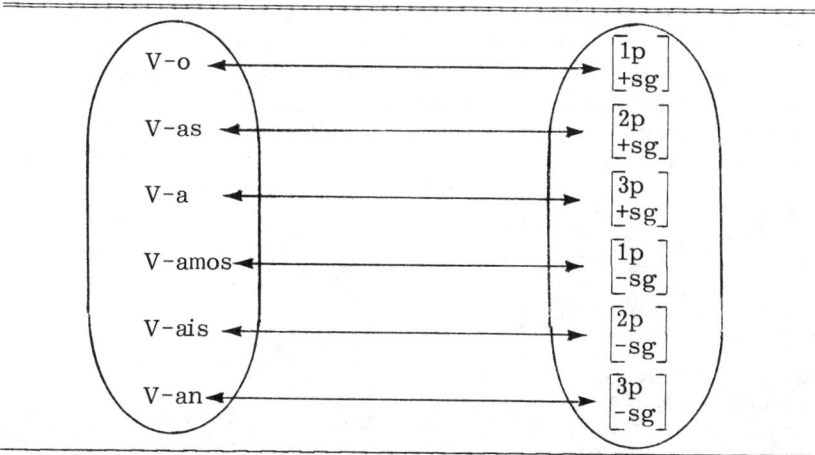

Figure 2. Paradigm of the present indicative in French (first conjugation).

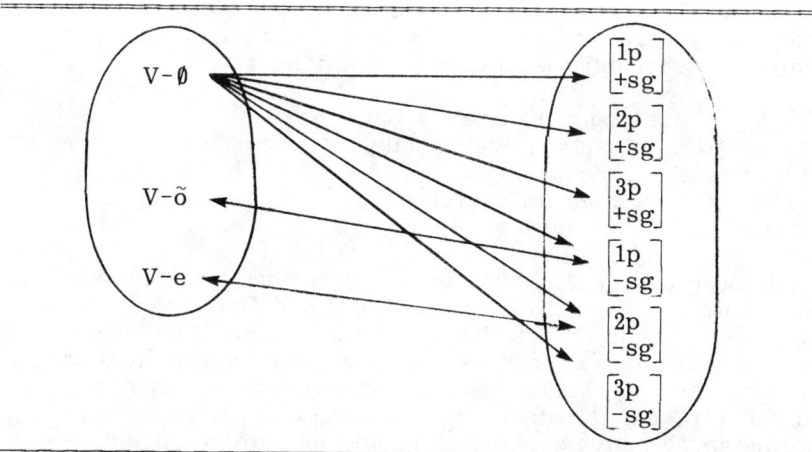

Figure 3. Paradigm of the imperative in French (first conjugation).

$$
\begin{array}{ccc}
\text{V-}\emptyset & \longrightarrow & \begin{bmatrix} 2p \\ +sg \end{bmatrix} \\
\text{V-}\tilde{o} & \longleftarrow \; \longrightarrow & \begin{bmatrix} 1p \\ -sg \end{bmatrix} \\
\text{V-e} & \longrightarrow & \begin{bmatrix} 2p \\ -sg \end{bmatrix}
\end{array}
$$

3.2 Biuniqueness. Within a standard transformational framework, this important generalization cannot be captured in a straightforward way. The formalism of transformations does not allow any reference to the richness of a morphological paradigm with respect to a semantic paradigm. Thus, it is not possible to integrate this condition directly in a subject deletion rule such as (26).

(26) NP → $\emptyset$ / ___ V
        +tense

Rule (26), constrained by the condition of recoverability of deletions, seems to be adequate to account for the Italian or Spanish data. In those languages, where most paradigms are biunique, the condition of recoverability of deletions is sufficient to restrict the application of a rule such as (26) to those NPs whose content is recoverable from the morphological form of the verb, i.e. to pronouns that carry only person and number.

On the other hand, in languages such as English or French, which, in general, do not have biunique paradigms, the condition of recoverability is obviously insufficient.

(27a) *(Nous) pouvons avertir Luc.
(27b) *(Vous) pouvez avertir Luc.
(27c) *(Je) serai absent.
(27d) *(J') ai reçu du courrier.
(27e) *(Ils) vont arriver.

In all these cases, the deletion of the subject pronoun would not violate the recoverability condition since each verb form allows only one interpretation in person and number. However, deletion is not possible. Notice, incidentally, that if the verb forms in (27) satisfy the recoverability condition individually, the paradigm they belong to is not biunique. For instance, *pouvons* allows only one interpretation for its first argument, but in the same paradigm, there are other forms such as *peux* for which more than one interpretation is possible.

The description of this phenomenon has to integrate the Biuniqueness Condition (28).

(28) Biuniqueness Condition (BC):

The subject of a tensed verb can be deleted only if the verb belongs to a biunique paradigm.

A verb paradigm is said to be biunique if and only if for each of its morphological forms there is one and only one interpretation in person and number.

BC strengthens the recoverability condition to the extent that the former is defined with respect to sets of morphological forms and semantic interpretations, whereas the latter is defined only with respect to single pairs of morphological forms and semantic interpretations.

BC governs the interpretation of RC with respect to subjects of tensed clauses.

In languages where most verb paradigms satisfy BC, Rule (26) applies in a uniform way: that is the case of Italian and Spanish. The case of French is a little more complex: several morphological distinctions have been neutralized by blind phonetic changes, making most paradigms nonbiunique. A given morphological form in a given paradigm can be related to several configurations of morphological features, e.g. aim-∅.

(29a) aim-∅   (29b) aim-∅   (29c) aim-∅   (29d) aim-∅

$$\begin{bmatrix} 1p \\ +sg \\ +pres \end{bmatrix} \quad \begin{bmatrix} 2p \\ +sg \\ +pres \end{bmatrix} \quad \begin{bmatrix} 3p \\ +sg \\ +pres \end{bmatrix} \quad \begin{bmatrix} 3p \\ -sg \\ +pres \end{bmatrix}$$

In this case, Rule (26) cannot apply. However, the same form allows (or rather requires, as we show directly) the application of (26) in the imperative paradigm which is biunique. If, following Chomsky (1978), we assume that deletion rules are obligatory, notwithstanding the recoverability condition, constrained by the Biuniqueness Condition in cases of subject deletion, we can account for the fact that biunique paradigms (i.e. imperative in French and English, most paradigms in Spanish and Italian) have a lexical subject only if it bears more features than person and number.

4. Consequences for the theory of grammar

4.1 Biuniqueness and markedness. The Biuniqueness Condition has interesting implications for the theory of markedness. Suppose we state the hypothesis given in (30).

(30) The Subject Deletion Rule (26) is universally
constrained by the Biuniqueness Condition on
recoverability.

Clearly, this is the strongest hypothesis we can make about
the role of the Biuniqueness Condition in the theory of grammar. It would imply, that, for all languages, subjects are
deletable only in biunique paradigms; in other words, that a
subject pronoun is optional in a tensed clause: (a) everywhere in languages having only biunique paradigms; (b) only
in the biunique paradigm(s) in languages having some biunique
paradigm(s); (c) nowhere in languages having no biunique
paradigm.
If this hypothesis were combined with Chomsky's suggestion
that deletion rules are obligatory (notwithstanding recoverability), we would predict that anywhere a subject pronoun is
deletable, it must actually get deleted, something which remains
to be tested.
Following the logic of the theory of markedness, we propose
that (30) does not constitute an absolute prohibition against
subject pronoun deletion in nonbiunique paradigms, but rather
that such a deletion, where it is possible, is highly marked
and falls outside the domain of sentence grammar proper. The
case of the present subjunctive in Italian is very interesting
in that respect. In Italian, the three persons in the singular
of the present subjunctive are identical in all conjugations.

(31) essere: *sia, sia, sia,* siamo, siàte, siano
     avere: *abbia, abbia, abbia,* abbiamo, abbiate, abbiano
     amare: *ami, ami, ami,* amiamo, amiate, amino
     credere: *creda, creda, creda,* crediamo, crediate,
     credano
     partire: *parta, parta, parta,* partiamo, partiate,
     partano
     finire: *finisca, finisca, finisca,* finiamo, finiate,
     finiscano

Nevertheless, the subject is always deletable in these cases
as well as in other paradigms which are biunique.
Notice that such a deletion is not even recoverable stricto
sensu, since it destroys the distinction between the first three
persons. We expect this to result in intolerable ambiguity.
As a matter of fact, speakers tend to use subject pronouns in
this context whenever the discourse context is not sufficient
to disambiguate them. This is entirely consistent with our
approach. Most paradigms in Italian are biunique; the only
exceptions are the subjunctive present and imperfect (where
the first two persons are identical). As a consequence, nonbiunique paradigms have been regularized and they allow subject pronoun deletion under a discourse recoverability condition, which makes them highly marked. It must be noted that

the subjunctive is a marked mood anyway, not only in Italian but in Romance languages in general. Interestingly enough, Bourciez (1967:508) notes that the subjunctive has disappeared almost completely from the dialects of the south of Italy. When the distinctions in -im, -is, -it (< -em, -es, -et) and -am, -as, -at (the endings of the present subjunctive in Proto-Italian) were lost, after the final consonant had fallen, it seems that two choices were open, both of them being marked: (a) to have subject deletion in regular (i.e. biunique) paradigms but not in the (irregular) subjunctive; (b) to have subject deletion everywhere with a discourse recoverability condition for the (nonbiunique) subjunctive present (and imperfect). [8]

In any case, these facts are entirely consistent with the view that the unmarked case for subject deletion is the one which is constrained by the Biuniqueness Condition, and that this condition can only be violated at a cost.

5. Consequences for syntactic change

5.1 Old French. Notice that the Biuniqueness Condition also makes interesting predictions concerning diachrony and that it is completely supported by the history of French. As soon as neutralizations appear in a paradigm, subject deletion becomes the marked case. The more nonbiunique paradigms a language has, the more marked subject deletion will be.

In Old French, the subject is always deletable (except when it is stressed, but it is well known that stressed elements are usually not deletable). This is an aspect of recoverability (cf. Chomsky 1955). Verbal paradigms in Old French were biunique as in Modern Spanish and Italian. For instance, the paradigm of the present indicative is as shown in (32).

(32) chant - Ø
     chant - es
     chant - e(t)
     chant - ons
     chant - ez
     chant - ent

However, following an independent phonetic change, a schwa appeared in the first person, while the third person /-t/ had disappeared previously. This change seems to have occurred at the end of the twelfth century (cf. Fouché 1928). It is precisely at that time that stressed pronouns started to appear in subject position, especially, as noted by Foulet (1928:326-327), in texts very close to the spoken language. There is evidently a difficult problem in interpreting the relation between literary language and spoken language, but the coincidence of the loss of the distinction between the first and third persons and the emergence of unstressed subject pronouns seems to confirm our hypothesis.

One can expect, then, that being no longer functional, the inflections of a nonbiunique paradigm tend to disappear. This is exactly what happened in French: *chant-ez* and *chant-ent* have both lost their final consonant; the first person plural has merged with the indefinite *on*, e.g. *nous on a couru* (except in the imperative, a biunique paradigm); final schwa has disappeared in all forms.

Therefore, the only remaining distinction in the present indicative of the first (most productive) conjugation is that between second person plural /-e/ and all other persons /-Ø/.

BC is also compatible with a proposal already made by some traditional grammarians, which is to consider the subject pronouns of Modern French as prefixes, i.e. as verbal inflections themselves.

En moyen français, à mesure que les diverses personnes du verbe se confondaient davantage entre elles... les pronoms sujets se sont immobilisés devant le verbe en qualité d'affixes (Bourciez 1967:614).

Par suite de l'effacement progressif des désinences verbales, l'emploi d'un pronom sujet devient peu à peu nécessaire, même en dehors des cas cités. L'usage primitif représenté par *chant, chantes, chante, chantons, chantez, chantent* est remplacé par *je chante, tu chantes, il chante, nous chantons, vous chantez, il(s) chantent*. Ici, il faut bien remarquer qu'au moment où la présence d'un pronom sujet est devenue obligatoire, le pronom a perdu de sa force et est devenu atone; ainsi l'équivalent moderne de l'ancien *chant* (lat. canto) est *je chante*, tandis que l'ancien *je chant* se rendrait dans la langue moderne par *moi, je chante* ou *je chante, moi*. Le pronom sujet a tendu de plus en plus à se souder à son verbe; on peut même dire qu'aujourd'hui il fait partie intégrante de la forme verbale, et peut être considéré comme une sorte de flexion préposée. Ce dernier fait contribue à expliquer son emploi pléonastique dans *mon père il vient*. On dit *j'viens* pour *venio* et de même *i'vient* pour *venit*; la combinaison *mon père i'vient* était donc inévitable (Nyrop 1925:212).

En français moderne les personnels se sont substitués aux flexions. Ils ne forment avec le verbe qu'un mot phonétique, qu'on prononce: *je chante* ou bien: *ch'chante*. De même ils ne font avec lui qu'une forme (Brunot 1965:259).

This phenomenon could be seen as the expression of a normal tendency to recreate biunique paradigms.[9] We are only noting that possibility here.

6. **The Locality Condition.** We return to the facts which have motivated the introduction by Chomsky and Lasnik (1977) of filter (12).

(12) $*[_{S'} \pm$ WH $[_{NP}$ e$] \dots]$, unless S' or its trace is in the context $[_{NP}$ NP $\underline{\quad} \dots]$

We are now in a position to propose a fairly general hypothesis about the subject of tensed Ss.

(33) Locality Condition (LC):

> The subject of a tensed sentence must be interpreted *locally*.

This constraint, which, we assume, is part of UG, replaces NIC. It can be shown that it extends naturally to nontensed Ss and to nonsubject NPs (cf. Wehrli in preparation), thereby also replacing Opacity. But the formulation given here is sufficient for our present discussion.

LC constrains the operation of semantic interpretation rules, limiting their domain to local contexts when they affect subject interpretation. The grammars of specific languages may differ in the parameters defining locality. It has been noted by many linguists (e.g. Koster 1978, Rodman 1973, Rizzi 1978, Chomsky 1978) that languages tend to differ with respect to bounding nodes. Rather than specifying the parameters defining locality in the constraint itself, we assume that they are supplied by the grammar of each language, the unmarked case being that there are as many bounding nodes as there are possible domains of rule application in the language. (Cf. Morin 1974 for a clarification of the concept 'domain of rule application'.)

For the present discussion, we assume that S', at least, is bounding.

LC accounts not only for the limitations on WH-movement from subject position which were previously accounted for by filter (12) (but not by NIC), but also for the case of stylistic inversion, which was consistent with NIC (but not with filter (12)) and for deleted subjects in Spanish and Italian.

(34a) *Qui crois-tu que va venir?
(34b) Qui crois-tu qui va venir?
(34c) Creo que partio.
(34c') *Crois qu'est parti.
(34d) Où va la linguistique?
(34e) Où crois-tu que va la linguistique?
(34f) *Who do you think that saw Bill?

In those sentences which are grammatical, i.e. (34b,c,d,e), the subject is interpretable locally. In the case of Spanish (34c), the subject pronoun is present in LF (because of the independence of semantic interpretation rules and deletion rules). Example (34c') is out because subject pronoun deletion is not possible in this context in French. With WH-movement, though, local interpretation of the subject is possible only when a visible WH-phrase is present inside S', which is the case in (34b), but not in (34a).

In English, there is no such trace in the COMP of the embedded S'; therefore, local interpretation of its subject is impossible and (34f) is out.

Sentences (34d-e) are grammatical. Their subject has been moved within S' (by stylistic inversion). Local interpretation is thus possible.

The case of *that* deletion in English appears to be more problematic.

(35) Who do you think saw Bill?

Such sentences seem also possible in French and German (although less frequent than in English).

(36a) Qui crois-tu est venu?
(36b) Wer sagst du kommt heute abend.

However, as clearly shown by the German example, the subordinate clause is not actually embedded (its verb does not occur in final position). Both sentences are independent, one of them being a parenthetical. The same analysis can be extended to English. The structure of (35) would be (37), which is no longer a violation of LC: the subject of *saw* is locally interpretable, i.e. within S'_1.

(37) $[_{S'_1}$ who $[_{S'_2}$ do you think] saw Bill]

One could think that English is less restricted than other languages with respect to parentheticals; unfortunately, we cannot pursue that matter here. LC provides an explanation for the appearance in French of two WH-words, one in the matrix, the other in the embedded clause.

(38) [Qui crois-tu [qui est venu?]]

The presence of *qui* as a lexical trace of WH-movement in the subordinate clause permits it to avoid LC.

Finally, to account for English relatives, where the subject is interpretable only within the complex NP and not within the relative clause as shown in (39), it is necessary to add to

LC extension parameters specific to English. (Remember that relatives constitute an exception to filter (12).)

(39) $[_{NP}$ the man $[_{S'}$ that came]]

6.1 LC and NIC. It might seem, at first sight, that LC is nothing but a variant of NIC. As a matter of fact, there is a certain convergence between the two approaches, since both constraints are intended to restrict subjects of tensed clauses to a local interpretation. However, while LC does this directly, NIC is defined in terms of a complex theoretical machinery involving Case assignment, traces, and filters,[10] which is entirely superfluous and tends to create its own problems. Moreover, the two constraints are not empirically equivalent. As has been seen, sentences such as (40) cannot be ruled out by NIC.

(40) *Qui crois-tu que viendra?

The subject of *viendra* is not free in S' since, for Chomsky, the structure of (40) has to be (41).

(41) $[_{S'} [_{COMP} Qui_i]$ crois-tu $[_{S'}$ COMP t_i que]$[_{NP}$ e$]_i$ viendra]]

LC, on the other hand, blocks (40), which is assigned structure (42).

(42) $[_{S'} [_{COMP} Qui]$ crois-tu $[_{S'} [_{COMP} que]$ viendra.]]

The subject of *viendra* is not interpretable locally (i.e. within the embedded S') because *Qui* is part of the matrix S'. There is no trace in the embedded COMP (or in subject position of the embedded S'). Therefore the sentence is ruled out by LC, as opposed to (43), where there is an actual trace in the embedded COMP which allows local interpretation of the subject.

(43) Qui crois-tu $[_{S'} [_{COMP}$ qui viendra.]]

7. Conclusion. In this paper, we have introduced two restrictions concerning the subject of tensed clauses. The first, BC, restricts the interpretation of recoverability and is part of UG.

The Biuniqueness Condition formalizes the traditional grammarians' intuition of a correlation between richness of verbal inflection and optionality of the subject. That condition restricts the interpretation of RC when it comes to tensed sentence subjects. Moreover, it makes interesting predictions on the relationship between the weakening of the verbal flectional system and the obligatoriness of a subject.

The second, LC, also part of UG, expresses the property of boundedness in a direct way. LC constitutes a very general constraint on subject interpretation. It radically restricts the movements of subject NPs but, unlike NIC, it does not rely on the complex and sometimes even embarrassing system of Case or on the presence of traces at the level of surface structure. We have also shown that LC has clear empirical advantages over NIC and filter (12).

NOTES

1.   Infinitival clauses appear only as subordinates, a general property of natural languages which Chomsky and Lasnik (1977) can capture only through the use of language-specific filters, for example, *[NP to VP] or *[$_{S'}$ COMP NP], where S' is root. This property of infinitives follows from the base rules themselves if infinitives are actually VP-complements.   Cf. Wehrli and Morin (1978).
2.   These problems do not arise in Perlmutter's framework, where both relative *qui* and postposed subject constitute subjects.
3.   For Chomsky, this reformulation is intended to eliminate the redundancy between TSC and SSC.
4.   Traces in COMP are not marked for Case, as opposed to traces in S.
5.   Notice that, for the trace to be properly bound in (17c), stylistic inversion must have moved the subject *Jean* into a position where it c-commands t_i.   This constitutes a further problem which is avoided in our theory.
6.   This is the natural interpretation of filter (12), since traces are not distinguished from lexical NPs and it is sufficient for a structure to possess one proper analysis with respect to the structural description of a filter in order for the filter to apply and reject the structure.
7.   As is clear from our discussion, by verbal paradigm we mean a set of morphosemantic matrices where the only variable is person and number.
8.   Regular (i.e. biunique) paradigms could also have been recreated, resulting in an unmarked state of affairs.
9.   This hypothesis raises many interesting questions about the nature of subject clitics and their relation to the verb. Unfortunately, we cannot deal with these within the limits of this paper.
10.   Cf. Wehrli and Morin (1978) for a critical appraisal of that type of approach.

TREE-PRUNING AND ROMANCE SYNTAX

James S. Roberts
Georgetown University

Perhaps one of the most extensively discussed issues involved in Romance syntax has been the causitive construction. In French, Italian, and Spanish, this construction exhibits peculiar syntactic and semantic behavior that does not find an exact parallel in the other syntactic patterns of these languages. This paper considers data from French, but since the facts of causatives in other Romance languages are so similar, I expect that my analysis could be extended to them.

The causative construction in French involves the causative verb *faire* (*fare* in Italian, *hacer* in Spanish) in construction with another verb in its infinitive form, possibly followed by postverbal complements, as in (1)-(3).

(1) Marie fait manger le gâteau à son fils.
   'Marie has her son eat the cake.'
(2) Maria fa mangiare la torta a suo figlio.
(3) Maria hace comer la torta a su hijo.

The postverbal complements here are of the same type and occur in the same order as complements in a single clause. Compare, for example, the pattern of (1) with the noncausative (4), a simple one-clause sentence.

(4) Jean a montré ses photos à la famille après de dîner.
   'Jean showed his photographs to the family after dinner.'

In fact, the available evidence seems to support the analysis of causatives as a single clause in surface structure, with the verb *faire* serving as an auxiliary. Evidence of this comes from a host of syntactic data which show *faire* behaving in a manner exactly parallel to the other auxiliary verbs in single

clauses, *avoir* and *être*. In some cases, the *faire* + infinitive
construction group differs crucially from other verb + infinitive structures which involve two clauses. For example, Equi
and Raising verbs (such as *préférer* and *sembler*, respectively)
allow negation of the infinitive embedded under them with *ne*
... *pas* ((5b) and (6b)), as well as being susceptible of negation themselves ((5a) and (6a)).

(5a) Je ne préfère pas voyager tout seul.
'I do not prefer to travel alone.'
(5b) Je préfère ne pas voyager tout seul.
'I prefer not to travel alone.'

(6a) Serge ne semble pas être en retard ce soir.
'Serge does not seem to be late tonight.'
(6b) Serge semble ne pas être en retard ce soir.
'Serge seems not to be late tonight.'

Faire, on the other hand, does not allow both patterns. It
may be negated itself, as shown in (7a), but does not allow
the infinitive to be negated separately, as in (7b); in this it
follows the pattern of other auxiliaries, which do not allow
their main verb to be negated (as in (8)).

(7a) Je ne fais pas pleurer les enfants.
'I don't make the children cry.'
(7b) *Je fais ne pas pleurer les enfants.
'I make the children not cry.'

(8a) Je n'ai pas trouvé les gants perdus.
'I didn't find the lost gloves.'
(8b) *J'ai ne pas trouvé les gants perdus.

I attribute these data to the fact that (5) and (6) involve two
clauses, either of which may be negated, but (7) and (8) are
single clauses, and allow negation on the auxiliary only.
    Another piece of evidence for the single clause nature of
causatives in French comes from clitic placement. Pronominal
verbal complements appear as proclitics attached to the verb
of the clause in which they originate. Examples are given in
(9) and (10).

(9a) Je préfère le manger avec du beurre.
'I prefer to eat it with butter.'
(9b) *Je le préfère manger avec du beurre.

(10a) Suzanne semble en manger beaucoup.
'Suzanne seems to eat a lot of it.'
(10b) *Suzanne en semble manger beaucoup.

In (9) and (10), which involve two clauses, the clitics *le* and *en* originate as complements of the embedded verb *manger*. They attach to this lower verb, as seen in (9a) and (10a), and not to the verb of the higher clause (cf. (9b) and (10b)). In a single clause which involves an auxiliary, on the other hand, the clitic attaches to the auxiliary, and not to the main verb.

(11a) Je l'ai mangé dans la cuisine.
      'I ate it in the kitchen.'
(11b) *J'ai le mangé dans la cuisine.

Once again, the causative construction exhibits the pattern of (11), and not of the two-clause structures (9) and (10).

(12a) Hélène le fait manger à son enfant.
      'Hélène has her child eat it.'
(12b) *Hélène fait le manger à son enfant.

This shows again that the causative behaves like a single clause in surface structure, with *faire* having the status of an auxiliary. Additional evidence for the single clause nature of this construction is found in Aissen (1974b) and Roberts (forthcoming).

In addition to this evidence, though, another set of facts reveals that the construction should indeed be analyzed as two clauses in deep structure. Consider the following description. The logical subject of the infinitive in the surface construction is not related at all to the subject of the entire sentence. Instead, if the infinitive is an intransitive verb, its logical subject is found immediately following it; if it is transitive, the logical subject appears as a dative object.

(13) Le soleil fait disparaître les nuages.
     'The sun makes the clouds disappear.'
(14) Benoît fait laver son manteau au petit garçon.
     'Benoit makes the little boy wash his coat.'

This consideration suggests that the deep structure of causatives involves two clauses. The matrix clause contains the verb *faire*, while the embedded clause is that of the infinitive. Thus, corresponding to (13) and (14), there would be deep structures similar to (15) and (16), respectively.

(15) $_S$[le soleil fait $_S$[les nuages disparaître]]

(16) $_S$[Benoît fait $_S$[le petit garçon laver son manteau]]

The transformational machinery subsequently turns these structures into the appropriate sentences (13) and (14).

More formal arguments along this line can be constructed to support the bisentential source. For example, *rire* is an intransitive verb and may not take the subcategorization + __ NP.

(17) *Les enfants rient ces plaisanteries.
'The children laugh (at) these jokes.'

However, in the causative construction, an NP usually follows it.

(18) Le clown fait rire les enfants.
'The clown makes the children laugh.'

A deep structure similar to (15) would allow us to retain the subcategorization restriction, since the postverbal *les enfants* of (18) would originate as the embedded subject of *rire*, and no NP would follow the verb.

Selectional restrictions argue similarly. *Aboyer* 'to bark' requires that its subject be a dog, or something dog-like. When *aboyer* occurs in the causative construction, the 'dog-like' NP regularly follows the verb.

(19) Le bruit a fait aboyer le petit épagneul.
'The sound made the little spaniel bark.'

Again, the generalization about the subject of *aboyer* could be maintained if the postverbal *le petit épagneul* were generated as the subject of *aboyer* in deep structure.

The distribution of the reflexive/reciprocal clitic *se* also argues for a bisentential source for causatives. The account of clitic placement as I have sketched it here is complicated by the behavior of *se*, since this clitic may in some cases be attached to the infinitive in the causative construction, as well as to *faire*.

(20a) Jean se fait raser à son frère.
'Jean$_i$ has his brother shave him$_i$.'

(20b) Jean fait se raser son frère.
'Jean makes his brother$_i$ shave himself$_i$.'

This would suggest that *raser* was the verb of a clause distinct from that of *faire* at some stage of the derivation. *Se* could then attach to that verb without being forced to cliticize to *faire* after the two clauses are combined.

In the light of these and other considerations, I claim that the deep structures of (13) and (14) are (15) and (21), respectively.

(15) [le soleil fait _s[les nuages disparaître]]

(21) [Benoît fait _s[le petit garçon laver son manteau] au
petit garçon]

Structure (21) differs from the preliminary formulation in (16)
by the addition of the matrix (ethical) dative, *au petit garçon*.
Fuller justification of this structure is given in Roberts (forthcoming).[1] The transformation of Equi-NP Deletion erases the
embedded subject of (21) under identity with the matrix dative;
then a rule of *faire*-Attraction raises the embedded infinitive
of (15) and (21) into the matrix clause, thus combining the
two clauses into one.
Even so, there are some causative sentences in which we
cannot account for the surface order of constituents in this
way.

(22) Eve fait manger le fruit à Adam dans le jardin.
'Eve makes Adam eat the fruit in the garden.'

(23) Le général fait guillotiner le traître au bourreau après
la bataille.
'The general has the executioner guillotine the traitor
after the battle.'

Note that the order of constituents here reflects the typical
order in a simple clause (cf. (4)). The source structures
corresponding to these sentences would be (24)-(25).

(24) _s[Eve fait _s[Adam manger le fruit dans le jardin]
à Adam]

(25) _s[le général fait _s[le bourreau guillotiner le traître
après la bataille] au bourreau]

Application of the rules described would seem to generate the
ungrammatical (26)-(27).

(26) *Eve fait manger le fruit dans le jardin à Adam.
(27) *Le général fait guillotiner le traître après la
bataille au bourreau.

This problem has been encountered by other linguists seek-
ing to account for causatives, and they have sought to resolve
it in various ways. I would now like to show the inadequacies
of these proposals.
Kayne (1975) uses a deep structure for (22)-(23) that is
similar to (16) (i.e. it differs from our deep structure (25) in
the absence of the matrix dative). He accounts for the correct

surface order of the constituents in (22)-(23) by his rule of
faire-Infinitive, which is formulated to move the verb and the
direct object (if present) of the embedded clause up next to
faire. The preposition à is inserted before the embedded subject in case a direct object is present in the lower clause.
There are several problems with Kayne's rule, but I concentrate my objections here on the fact that the elements being
moved (verb and direct object) do not form a constituent.
Most linguists working in transformational syntax have assumed
that only constituents can be moved, in order to constrain the
admittedly great power of transformational rules. To admit of
a rule such as Kayne's would thus involve a great weakening
in the theory.

Aissen (1974b), following earlier work by Kayne, posits the
same deep structure, but her solution to the problem is different. The rule with which she accounts for causatives moves
only the embedded verb up into the matrix. Since this would
yield, for (28), the ungrammatical (29), she must posit another
rule to permute the accusative and dative objects, finally yielding the correct (30).

(28) $_S$[Eve fait $_S$[Adam manger le fruit dans le jardin]]

(29) *Eve fait manger à Adam le fruit dans le jardin.

(30) Eve fait manger le fruit à Adam dans le jardin.

In addition, Aissen suggests that the formulation of this
latter rule must be done transderivationally, to show the
parallel of the order of (30) with that of a base-generated
simple clause. It should be clear that this solution is no more
desirable than Kayne's. It introduces a new transformation
whose sole function is to patch up the results of her derivation. As well as being ad hoc, this rule is also transderi-
vational; admitting it in the grammar would again require an
unjustified increase in the power of transformations.

The solution to the ordering question that I propose avoids
the drawbacks of these analyses. Instead, it is seen as the
consequence of a general convention that hinges upon the reduction of syntactic structure by pruning. Such is the case
in the causative construction, since I have already shown that
its bisentential deep structure must be reduced into a single
clause on the surface. Thus, the embedded S node (at least)
must be deleted in the course of the derivation.

Since the transformational rules sometimes have the effect of
destroying the identity of clauses (and phrases), it is desirable to have a way of getting rid of the unwanted portion of
the structural tree that designates the original (but not derived) status of these elements. Ross (1967: 26) has proposed
a convention for tree-pruning which would have this very
effect.

(31) S-Pruning: Delete any embedded node S which does not branch (i.e. which does not immediately dominate at least two nodes).

This convention is to apply immediately when an embedded S node ceases to branch.

It is not clear that Ross' convention is adequate to handle all cases of S-pruning, however. For example, consider the derivations of (32) and (33).

(32) Jean fait partir Marie.
'Jean makes Marie leave.'

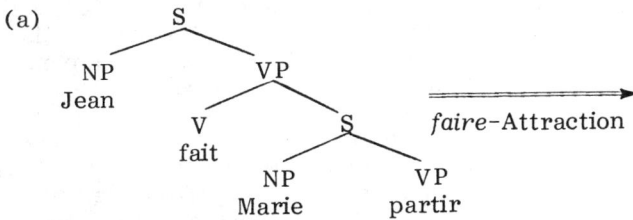

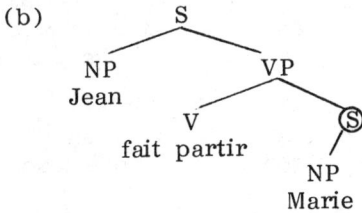

(a)

```
              S
           /     \
        NP        VP
        Jean     /   \
               V       S
              fait    / \        ⟹  faire-Attraction
                    NP   VP
                   Marie partir
```

(b)

```
              S
           /     \
        NP        VP
        Jean     /   \
               V       Ⓢ
           fait partir  \
                        NP
                       Marie
```

(33) L'hôte fait entrer les invités dans la salle.
'The host has the guests enter the room.'

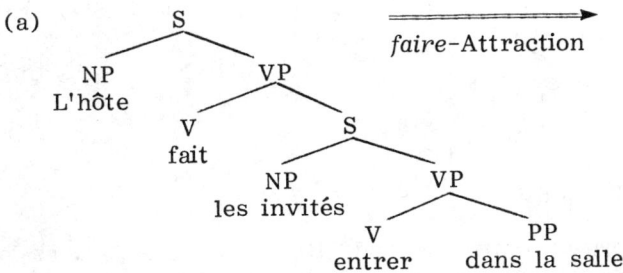

(a)

```
              S
           /     \
        NP        VP
       L'hôte    /   \            ⟹  faire-Attraction
               V       S
              fait    /  \
                    NP      VP
               les invités  /  \
                          V      PP
                        entrer  dans la salle
```

(b)

```
                    S
         ┌──────────┴──────┐
        NP                VP
      L'hôte        ┌──────┴───────┐
                    V            ⓢ
                fait entrer   ┌───┴──────┐
                             NP          VP
                         les invités     │
                                         PP
                                    dans la salle
```

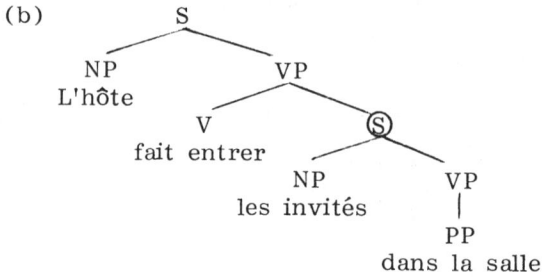

In both cases, clause reduction of the causatives is involved.
Principle (31) accounts for the pruning of S in (32), since
after the extraction of the verb by *faire*-Attraction, the embedded S node does not branch. However, the convention
cannot effect the needed pruning in (33) where, even after
faire-Attraction, the embedded S node still branches to NP
and VP. Thus, Ross' convention is too weak to handle the
data of French causatives. The chief problem here seems to
be that (31) places crucial emphasis simply on the fact that a
node branches, without considering what that node dominates.
   An alternative convention for pruning is the 'guillotine
principle' proposed by Kuroda in an unpublished 1965 paper,
referred to in Ross (1967:56). The essence of the principle
is given in (34).

> (34) A phrase node is pruned (i.e. deleted) when the head
> of the construction designated by that node label is
> removed.

This formulation fits in well with Emonds' (1976:12 ff.) base
restrictions, which give a principled definition of the head of
a construction within the $\bar{X}$ theory. The phrase node expansions which he allows (for NPs, VPs, APs, and PPs) are
shown in (35).

(35a) $H'' \rightarrow X_1 \; H_0 \; X_2$

(35b) $H' \rightarrow X_3 \; H_0 \; X_4$

(35c) $H'' \rightarrow PRO$

The Xs here are variables, and $H_0 = H$, H', or H'', as long
as H_0 does not have more primes than the H on the left side
of the arrow. With this definition, one can say that in (35a)
and (35b), H_0 is the head of the H'' or H'. Then, according
to principle (34), whenever that head is removed from the
construction, the phrase node (H'' or H') is pruned.
   This convention as stated does not deal directly with the
issue of S node pruning, since a clause is not usually considered an endocentric construction that would have a head.

However, Jackendoff (1977) has suggested that S is indeed an endocentric structure like the phrases mentioned earlier. In the $\bar{X}$ notation, he identifies S as V''', which expands as in (36).

(36) V''' → N''' M''' V''

In this rule, N''' = NP, V'' = VP, and M''' = auxiliary. By an extension of Emonds' rules (35), one can readily identify V'' as the head of V''' (= S).

If one now reexamines the data of the causative construction, one sees that Kuroda's convention (34), as clarified and augmented by the $\bar{X}$ theory, can adequately account for the necessary pruning. When the embedded infinitive is raised into the matrix by the rule of *faire*-Attraction, the embedded clause is left without its verb. This extraction occasions the pruning of the embedded VP node, and this pruning in turn triggers the pruning of the S (= V''') node, as required.

I am now prepared to examine an alternate and natural solution to the ordering dilemma in causatives. Along with the transformations of Equi and *faire*-Attraction and the pruning convention (34), I propose that convention (37) is also at work in the derivation of causatives.

(37) The Reordering Convention: Whenever a node X is pruned, the node Y that immediately dominated X before the pruning automatically reorders its immediate constituents (including its new constituents) in order to conform to the phrase structure (PS) rules for Y.

Let us consider the effect of this convention in the derivation of sentences such as (22)-(23). Using (22) as a representative example, one first notes the effect of the rules of Equi-NP Deletion and *faire*-Attraction.

(38a)

Equi-NP Deletion,
faire-Attraction

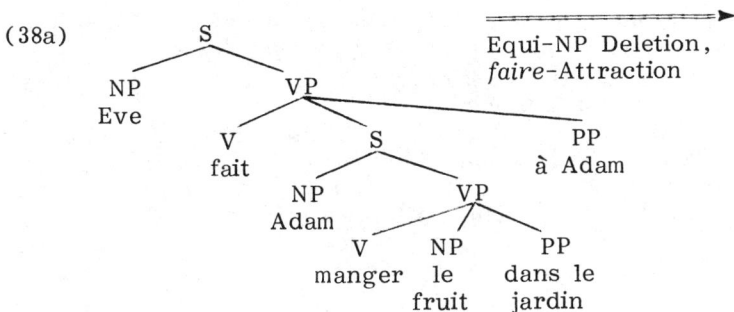

(38b)

```
                    S
          ┌─────────┴──────┐
        NP               VP
        Eve        ┌──────┼────────────┐
                   V      S            PP
                  fait    |          à Adam
                 manger   VP
                      ┌────┴────┐
                    NP         PP
                  le fruit   dans le
                             jardin
```

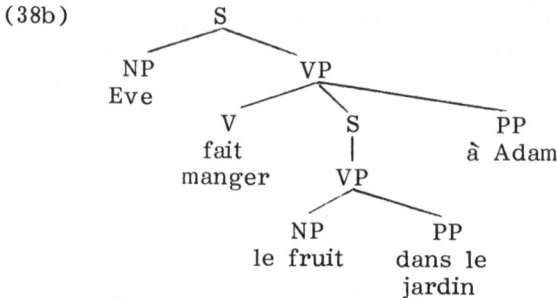

Note in (38b) that the embedded subject has been deleted under identity with the matrix dative, and that the embedded infinitive has been raised into the matrix clause. At this point, one finds that the embedded VP node has no head V, and so it must be deleted by pruning convention (34). This now leaves the embedded S node without its head VP, and so this S is pruned too. The resulting structure is shown in (39).

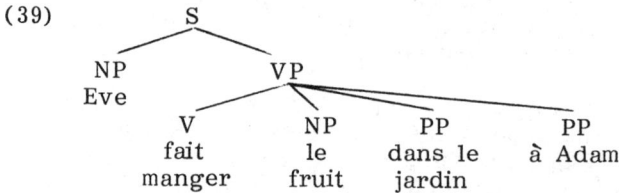

(39)

```
                    S
          ┌─────────┴──────┐
        NP               VP
        Eve       ┌───┬───┬──────────────┐
                  V   NP  PP             PP
                 fait le  dans le      à Adam
                manger fruit jardin
```

At this point, the Reordering Convention is applicable, calling for a reordering (if necessary) of the matrix VP node, the node that immediately dominated the pruned S. The PS-rule for VP is given in (40).[2]

(40) VP → V NP à NP PP ...

Since the verbal complements in the VP of (39) do not conform to the canonical order laid out in Rule (40), they must be reordered to reflect the PS-rule, by an interchange of the PPs *dans le jardin* and *à Adam*.

I should point out that the Reordering Convention applies in every instance of reduction of structure. However, in many cases the application will effect no change in the derived structure, when the constituents are already found in the order prescribed by the PS-rules. Such a vacuous application of the convention is illustrated in this derivation (cf. example (21)).

(41a) Benoît $_{VP}$[fait laver $_{NP}$[son manteau] $_{PP}$[au petit garçon]]] $\xrightarrow{(37)}$

(41b) Benoît fait laver son manteau au petit garçon.

The convention (37) that I have invoked to account for the necessary reordering of the postverbal complements thus serves to explain the data of (22)-(23), and prevents the generation of the ungrammatical sentences (26)-(27). But in order for this convention to be accepted as a universal principle of grammar, it must be shown that there is a similar need for such a principle in all cases of reduction of structure. Such independent evidence is available in other instances of structure reduction; I now consider other cases of clause reduction, the syntax of prenominal adjectives in English (and French), and the placement of the French quantifier *tous* in support of convention (37).

A number of languages have clause union processes similar to the causative construction of Romance. Jacaltec, a VSO language of Mexico and Guatemala, also has a causative construction which involves clause reduction. From the indications given in Craig (1977), a reordering similar to that of French is needed in the Jacaltec construction. Since the order of constituents in the construction is the same as that found in a single clause, the Reordering Convention accounts nicely for the facts.

Clitic Climbing in Romance languages is another case for which a syntactic clause union has been argued. This phenomenon is characterized by a pronominal clitic which climbs out of the clause in which it originated to attach to a higher verb, provided that it moves over an uninterrupted string of verbs. An example in Italian is given in (42).

(42) Lo voglio leggere.
'I want to read it.'

In this sentence *lo* is the deep structure object of *leggere*, but has moved up to cliticize to the higher verb *voglio*. Radford (1977) and Rizzi (1976), among others, have argued that the clauses of (42) have been united, with the original matrix verb serving as a syntactic auxiliary to the raised verb of the clause originally embedded. This clause reduction process suggests possibilities for testing the Reordering Convention. However, I have not been able to find any crucial examples of this type where reordering is necessary, and it may be that none exist. Napoli (1979) has argued that the matrix verb of the deep structure becomes a semantic as well as a syntactic auxiliary in cases of clitic climbing. She claims that this derived auxiliary verb is used to comment on another verb or clause, and thus does not allow any complements of its own. Reordering in cases of clause union typically involves adjustments among the complements of the two original clauses as they positioned in a single clause. Since the matrix verb in

the deep structure of clitic climbing sentences does not have
any complements of its own, reordering is never needed.

The second piece of independent evidence for the Reordering Convention comes from a different type of reduction in
structure--the derivation of prenominal adjectives. A traditional analysis, suggested by Smith (1961), calls for a deep
structure involving a relative clause which is reduced by a
deletion transformation.

(43a) $_{NP}$[the book$_S$[which is blue]]   WHIZ deletion ⟶

(43b) $_{NP}$[the book $_A$[blue]]

The relative clause is a postnominal complement of the NP *the
book*, and consists of a WH-word, a form of the copula *be*,
and an adjective (phrase). The rule of WHIZ deletion erases
the WH-word and the copula, leaving only the adjective behind, as in (43b). Subsequently, another rule is needed to
yield the correct result. This transformation, which has been
called Adjective Movement, moves the adjective into prenominal
position following the article, as seen in (43c).

(43c) $_{NP}$[the $_A$[blue] book]

Not all adjectives can be derived in this way, however.
There are some which can never appear after the copula, making a relative clause source for them, similar to (43a), im-
plausible. Instead, these adjectives appear only in the prenominal position occupied by *blue* in (43c). Witness this data,
as noted by Emonds (1976) and others.

(44a) a mere boy
(44b) *The boy is mere.

(45a) an utter failure
(45b) *Their failure was utter.

Other adjectives may appear both prenominally and post-
copularly, but allow an additional and markedly different meaning in the former position which is impossible after the copula.

(46a) the poor orphans (i.e. 'poverty-stricken', or
       'pitiable')
(46b) The orphans are poor. (i.e. 'poverty-stricken', but
       not 'pitiable')

The simplest way to generate adjectives like those of (44)-(46)
would be to provide for them directly in the phrase structure
rules. In the $\bar{X}$ notation, one would thus have the rules in (47).

(47a) N'' → Det   N'
(47b) N' → A   N

In this way, one can explain their failure to occur as post-verbal complements.

It is seen, then, that adjectives originate in (at least) two distinct places. Those that are generated in relative clauses are placed in prenominal position after the reduction of that relative clause. And it is precisely here that one might expect this proposal to be testable. The reduction of the relative clause (by WHIZ deletion) occasions the pruning of the VP and S nodes that are left without their respective heads. The Re-ordering Convention is applicable at this point, and its effect is shown in the derivation of (43), which is traced again here.

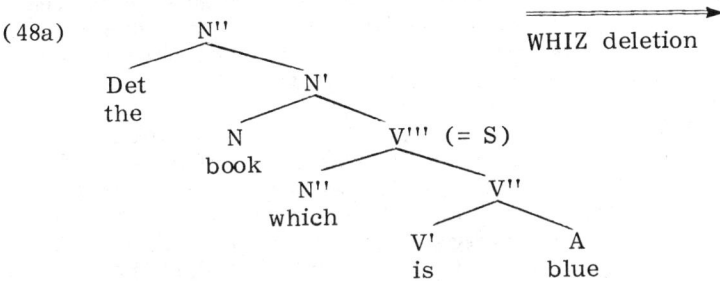

(48a)   WHIZ deletion

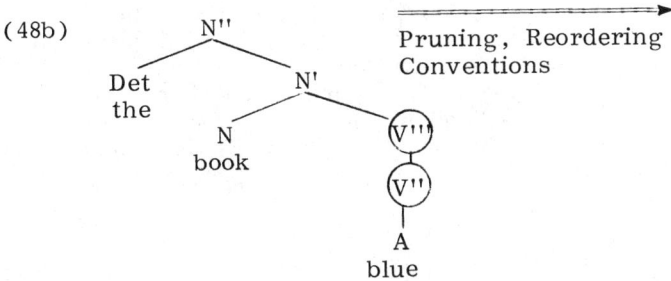

(48b)   Pruning, Reordering
                                Conventions

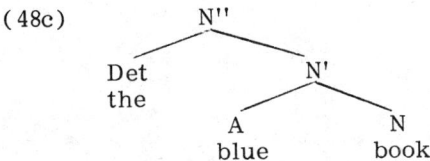

(48c)

In the structure of (48b), the V'' and V''' nodes are pruned. Convention (37) now calls for an examination and reordering (if necessary) of the N' node, the node which immediately dominated the pruned V'''. By comparing the PS-rule for N', given as (47b), with the structure of the tree

of (48b), it is seen that an interchange of the A and N is in
order, yielding finally the correct result of (48c).

It may now be observed that my account of this derivation
has greater explanatory power than the traditional analysis I
have outlined. Smith's rule of Adjective Movement is rather
ad hoc; it was posited just to take care of the order of the
adjective and noun after WHIZ deletion. There is no independent justification for such a rule. My explanation of the
derivation, on the other hand, eliminates completely the need
for the poorly motivated Adjective Movement rule. The same
reordering occurs in my account, but now it is seen as the result of a convention needed independently to readjust structures that have been reduced.

It may be objected that my account of the derivation of adjectives is unjustified. Since it is clear that some adjectives
must originate prenominally, why not generate all adjectives in
this position? There are at least a few reasons for deriving
some adjectives from relative clause sources, however, and
Smith (1961) mentions some. Napoli has pointed out to me two
that I consider here, one involving a semantic characteristic
and one involving a syntactic characteristic. The semantic
argument is that prenominal adjectives which have a corresponding relative clause (like (43) but not (44)) have both a
restrictive and nonrestrictive reading, just as relative clauses
with predicate adjectives do. But adjectives which have no
corresponding relative clause (like (44) but not (43)) do not
have this twofold reading. In (46), this contrast shows
nicely; only the 'poverty-stricken' reading has the possibility
of both restrictive and nonrestrictive interpretation.

As for the syntactic argument, it has often been observed
that prenominal APs must end in the head A (not in any
complement of the A), whereas postnominal APs may end in A
or in a complement of A. Now predicate adjectives may also
end in A or any complement of A. These facts are seen in
(49-(50).

(49a) a nice boy
(49b) a very nice boy
(49c) *a nice to talk to boy
(49d) a boy who is nice/very nice/nice to talk to

(50a) a book yellow with age
(50b) a book which is yellow with age

In the analysis I have proposed, all postnominal adjectivals are
generated by way of relative clause reduction (WHIZ deletion).
Prenominal adjectivals are either base generated in their surface position or moved there by way of the Reordering Convention after relative clause reduction leads to pruning. The
Reordering Convention is able to place APs in prenominal position only if an AP of that form could be base generated there.

Now we note that base-generated APs in prenominal position always end in A.

(51a) a mere boy (*a boy who is mere)
(51b) an impossible suspect (*a suspect who is impossible)
(51c) a very possible suspect (*a suspect who is very possible)
(51d) *an impossible to arrest suspect (a suspect who is impossible to arrest)

Thus, a relative clause reduction rule plus the Reordering Convention explains why prenominal APs, whether there is a corresponding relative clause or not, must end in A: the reason is that base-generated prenominal APs must end in A. Of course, no explanation (here or anywhere else in the literature) is offered for the fact that base-generated APs in prenominal position must end in A.

To summarize these facts, then, consider Table 1.

Table 1.

Base-generated adjectivals	Derived adjectivals
A. a mere boy	a yellow book
B. a very possible suspect	a very old widow
C. *a mere in experience boy	*a yellow with age book
D. *very someone	*interesting someone

In Table 1, the first column involves adjectivals that originate in relative clauses, while the second column involves adjectivals that are generated in their surface position. In the cases of one-word adjectives (A), adjectives with intensifiers (B), heavy adjectivals (C), and adjectives modifying pronouns (D), both the derived and the base-generated adjectivals display the same acceptability patterns. This is exactly what one would expect from the operation of the Reordering Convention, and gives significant confirmation of my approach. Whatever means is used to account for the base-generated prenominal adjectives accounts for the derived prenominal adjectives as well.

So far, I have been using English data for this argument supporting the Reordering Convention. The same argument can be reproduced in French, although crucial examples are not nearly as plentiful. The reason for this is that most adjectives are found in their surface position immediately after the reduction of the clause in which they originate, and the Reordering Convention would only apply vacuously. There are some cases, though, which involve a critical use of the convention.

Most adjectives in French are postnominal and would derive from reduced relative clauses, as in (52)-(53).

(52) l'homme (qui est) célèbre
'the man (who is) famous'

(53) la lecture (qui est) intéressante
'the reading (which is) interesting'

However, a few occur prenominally, and must be moved some-how from their postnominal source in relative clauses.[3]

(54a) sa soeur qui est jolie
'his sister who is pretty'
(54b) *sa soeur jolie
(54c) sa jolie soeur

This would be explained by the Reordering Convention if there were evidence that some adjectives must be generated prenominally in the PS-rules. And there are some such adjectives, e.g. *certain* 'particular'.

(55a) *un homme qui est certain
(55b) *un homme certain
(55c) un certain homme
'a particular man'

In this meaning of *certain*, the relative clause and postnominal uses of the adjective are impossible. Examples (55a) and (55b), which show this, actually are possible NPs. However, *certain* in these cases may not mean 'particular', but only 'sure', another completely separate meaning of the word. Thus, the phrase of (55c) must originate with the adjective base gener-ated before the noun. With this need for a prenominal A in the PS-rules established, I have justified the use of the Re-ordering Convention in accounting for the movement involved in the step from (54b) to (54c).

The last piece of evidence for the Reordering Convention that I consider concerns the behavior of French quantifiers such as *tous*. This quantifier may occur as a modifier of a postverbal noun, as in (56).

(56) Il a lu tous les manuscrits.
'He read all the manuscripts.'

If the element being modified is a clitic pronoun, the clitic is moved away to attach to the verb.

(57a) Il a lu $_{NP}[_Q[tous]_N[les]]$

(57b) Il les a lus $_{NP}[_Q[tous]]$

At this point, one finds that the object NP is left without its head noun, and so the NP node must be pruned.[4] This pruning makes the Reordering Convention applicable to the structure in question, as the Q *tous* is left directly dominated by the VP. It may very well be that the PS-rule for the VP does not specify any Q or QP; however, Bresnan (1973) has pointed out the parallels between QPs and APs, making it reasonable to examine instead the positions in the VP where adverbs are generated. Dubuisson (1974) has argued for base-generating (at least one class of) adverbs immediately after the verb, or the auxiliary if there is one. In the case of (57), where an auxiliary is present, such adverbs would be generated between *a* and *lus*, and it is to this position that the Q *tous* is moved.

(58) Il les a tous lus.
'He read them all.'

This movement is, of course, predicted by the Reordering Convention after the pruning of the NP node in (57b), given the parallels between quantifiers and adverbs. It should be noted that in addition to (58), there is also (59), in which *tous* does not seem to have moved from its original position of (57).

(59) Il les a lus tous.

This can be explained by further movement rules that apply to adverbs within a clause. Because the syntax of quantifiers and of adverbs is so similar, and because adverbs can appear in the position of *tous* is (59), one might claim that *tous* has been moved from its position in (58) by a generalized adverb movement rule.

There are still some questions which have not been answered with respect to the behavior of these quantifiers, but my analysis seems to be a reasonable approach. In particular, it simplifies the machinery used by Kayne (1975) in accounting for the data. He posits two transformational rules, Q-Postposing and Leftward-*tous*, which I have not needed. Instead, the value of the Reordering Convention is once again emphasized.

In the light of this evidence, I propose that the Reordering Convention (37) be added to the theory of grammar. This convention seems natural, since it allows the reduced, derived structure to assume the canonical form of the simpler structure as produced in the base. In many respects it can be seen to complement Emonds' Structure Preserving Hypothesis. Emonds (1976) has claimed that cyclic movement rules may only position elements in slots provided by the PS-rules. My convention likewise shows the importance of the PS-rules and their role in constraining the possible types of derivations.

NOTES

I wish especially to thank Donna Jo Napoli for many extensive discussions and helpful criticisms of this paper. Alexa McCray, Pam Bernstein, Nancy Yanofsky, and several others also provided comments from which I and the paper greatly benefited.

1. The difference between my deep structure (21) and the alternative deep structure (16), posited by many analysts, is not crucial to the issues of this paper. The facts that I consider here are a problem, regardless of the choice for deep structure.

2. The PS-rules probably do not specify individual lexical items such as the $\grave{a}$ in (40). The $\grave{a}$ NP phrase behaves syntactically as a PP, but I assume that there is some way of designating that it must precede any other PPs (perhaps by features). Similar problems arise in specifying the order of temporal and locative adverbs and PPs in the PS-rules.

3. These adjectives would have to be distinguished syntactically from the adjectives of (50)-(51), perhaps by means of subscripts as A_1 and A_2. Thus, the following discussion would deal only with the A_1 class and not with A_2.

4. This would be so if clitics do not have the same status as NPs and do not leave traces when they move, according to a suggestion made in Bordelois (1977).

EXPECTATION AND LOGICAL OPERATORS:
ADVERSATIVE CONJUNCTIONS IN ROMANCE LANGUAGES

Maria Manoliu-Manea
The University of California, Davis

0. Since the idea that no rigorous semantic description can be stated without symbolic logic has been widely accepted, conjunctions have been defined in terms of logical operators such as ET, VEL, implication, and negation. Despite the fact that there is a great deal of evidence that in natural languages there are only two logical operators functioning as coordinators (see Gazdar and Pullum 1976), i.e. ET and VEL, it is well known that the number of coordinate conjunctions exceeds the number of logical connectives.

In order to describe the difference between actualized conjunctions in natural languages, one also has to consider the logical relations between the connected terms or to combine ET or VEL with the negation. In the Romance area, it is worth mentioning Coseriu (1968), which accounted for the difference between the Latin copulative conjunctions in terms of logical equivalence; for example, Lat. -QUE occurs when the connected terms are logically equivalent (i.e. when the relation between them is such that when one is true, the other also must be true, and vice-versa), while AC does not imply such a logical relationship. Even in Romance traditional grammars, adversative conjunctions such as Rom. CI, Sp. SINO or Ptg. SENÃO were defined as requiring a negation in the first connected term. According to various logical descriptions, Fr. MAIS or Rom. DAR (the basic adversative conjunctions) correspond to the combination of ET and NON (see, for example, Kemeny, Snell, and Thompson 1965, Vasiliu 1970).

The purpose of this paper is to present some evidence supporting the hypothesis that, at least in Romance languages, logical operators and logical relations between the connected terms are not always able to explain the difference between conjunctions, and that several phenomena belonging to the

299

pragmatic level--such as expectation and various types of
speech acts--are to be considered.

1. Unlike presupposition or entailment, expectation does not
satisfy the criterion of uncontradictability. For example, a
complex sentence such as (1) has the expectation (2), since
(1) may be completed by a contradictory afterthought such as
... *but I am very happy anyway*, as (3) shows.

(1) If I could take a trip to Venus, I would be very happy.
(2) I am not very happy.
(3) If I could take a trip to Venus, I would be very happy,
    but I am very happy anyway.

The expectation is cancelled by the afterthought added in (3).
As Leech (1977:322) points out: 'Expectation relations are not
to be found in the abstract logical system of language, but
rather in the pragmatics of communication, along with thematic
ordering, information focus, etc.' The cancelled expectation
may be defined as the denied shared knowledge, i.e. 'what the
listener thinks to be true but the speaker denies'.[1] In this
sense, the expectation has meaning only in a very specific
kind of speech act called 'denial'. Whether negation always
expresses a denial or not, it is a different question which I
do not intend to answer in this paper. My purpose is to
examine the way in which cancelled expectation affects the
choice of conjunction.

Let us consider complex sentences in (4) and (5).

(4a) Sp. Ana no canta pero baila.
(4b) Rom. Ana nu cîntă dar dansează.
(4c) Fr. Anne ne chante pas mais elle danse.
     'Ann does not sing but she dances.'

(5a) Sp. Ana no canta sino baila.
(5b) Rom. Ana nu cîntă, ci dansează.
(5c) Fr. Anne ne chante pas, elle danse.
     'Ann does not sing, she dances.'

In both sets of sentences, the first term contains a propositional negation, but, despite the fact that both series of connectives are considered adversative conjunctions, nobody has
ever claimed that complex sentences such as (4) and (5) are
semantically equivalent.

According to current Romanian grammars (see Academia ...
1966), the adversative conjunctions DAR, CI, IAR represent
different degrees of intensity. As I have already pointed out
(Manoliu-Manea 1976), the 'Intensity hypothesis' is unable to
account for the constraints imposed on the choice of adversative conjunctions in Romanian.

(6a) *?Nu e măr, ci copac.
    'It is not an apple tree, it is a tree.'
(6b) Măr nu este, dar copac este.
    'It is not an apple tree, but it is a tree.'
(6c) *Nu e copac dar măr este.
    'It is not a tree, but it is an apple tree.'
(6d) *Nu este copac, ci măr.
    'It is not a tree, it is an apple tree.'

In my opinion, the difference in intensity is, in fact, an effet de sens due to the logical relations and different types of expectation involved.

1.1 Since adversative conjunctions are generally described as compounded of two logical operators (i.e. ET and NON) and negation is mainly considered a form expressing denial,[2] I first examine context-bound statements such as (7) through (9).

(7) - Am auzit că Ana cîntă şi dansează în acest spectacol.
    - Ana cîntă (e adevărat) dar nu dansează.
    'They say that Ann sings and dances in this show.'
    'Ann sings (it is true) but she does not dance.'

(8) - Am auzit că Ana cîntă la Operă (şi nu dansează astă seară).
    - Nu-i adevărat, Ana nu cîntă, ci dansează.
    'They say that Ann sings tonight at the Opera (and she does not dance).'
    'It is not true, she does not sing, she dances.'

(9) - Am auzit că Ana nu cîntă astă seară la Operă.
    - Nu cîntă, e adevărat, dar dansează.
    'They say that Ann does not sing tonight at the Opera.'
    'She does not sing, it is true, but she dances.'

If one writes p for 'Ann sings' and q for 'Ann dances', the logical structure of (7) could be stated as in (10).

(10) $-(p \cdot q) = (p \cdot -q)$

In other words, DAR denies the expectation $(p \cdot q)$ under the form $(p \cdot -q)$. As (9) shows, DAR can also deny the expectation $(-p \cdot -q)$, as $(-p \cdot q)$, as in (11).

(11) $-(-p \cdot -q) = (-p \cdot q)$.

CI also corresponds to ET, but in a different context, namely, when the expectation is $(p \cdot -q)$. The logical structure of (8) is to be stated as in (12).

(12) $-(p \cdot -q) = (-p \cdot q)$.

This description accounts for the fact that both DAR and CI can occur between a negative term and a positive one (as in (7) and (8)), but they differ as to the expectation and the way this expectation is denied: $(-p \cdot -q)$ versus $(p \cdot -q)$. The same type of logical relations can account for the semantic difference between Spanish PERO and SINO (cf. (4a) and (5a)) as well as for the difference between Fr. MAIS and zero-conjunction in (4c) and (5c). [3]

1.2 In order to express the large number of possible expectations and the possible forms of their denial, natural languages may combine two or more connectives and negations. For example, Rom. ŞI NU can deny the expectation $(-p \cdot q)$ as $(-p \cdot -q)$, as in (13a) or (13b).

(13a) – Am auzit că Ana nu va cînta, ci va dansa astă seară.
     – Nu-i adevărat, Ana nu va cînta, şi nu va dansa.
(13b) – Nu-i adevărat, Ana nici nu va cînta, şi nici nu va dansa astă seară.
     'I heard that Ann will not sing, she will dance to-night.'
     'It is not true, she will not sing and she will not dance tonight (either).'

The underlying logical structure of (13a-b) could be stated as in (14).

(14) $-(-p \cdot q) = (-p \cdot -q)$. [4]

The current transformational grammars of Romance languages do not account for the semantic difference between 'double conjunctions', such as Rom. ŞI ... ŞI, and the corresponding simple conjunctions (such as Rom. ŞI). In Vasiliu and Golopenţia (1972:82-83), the double conjunction is included in the Basic Phrase-Marker and the deletion of the conjunction before the first term is considered optional. [5] There is some evidence, however, that the double conjunction is not always equivalent to the one-term conjunction, as (15a) and (15b) show.

(15a) Au rămas de mici orfani, dar fratele cel mare a fost şi tată şi mamă pentru cel mic.
     'They very soon became orphans, but the elder son was both father and mother for the younger one.'
(15b) Au rămas de mici orfani, dar fratele cel mare a fost ?tată şi mamă pentru cel mic.

Example (15b) sounds less normal than (15a); the explanation is that ŞI ... ŞI denies an expectation ('if somebody is the father, he is supposed not to be the mother'), while ŞI is not supposed to deny any expectation.

2. The different constraints imposed upon the coordination in natural languages also are determined by what I would call 'the anomaly of the expectation'.
Compare, for example, (16) and (17).

(16) Acesta nu este măr, dar este copac (totuşi). (See (6b))
'This is not an apple tree, but it is a tree (however).'

(17) **Acesta nu este copac, dar este măr. (See (6c))
'This is not a tree, but it is an apple tree.'

Sentence (17) is unacceptable because it has an 'anomalous expectation': the anomaly of an expectation rests upon the violation of the logical relations that normally hold between the connected terms. In my case, the terms are: p = 'X is a tree' and q = 'X is an apple tree', and the normal logical relations between them are: (a) if something is an apple tree, then it is a tree; (b) if something is not a tree, then it cannot be an apple tree, either, that is: (a) $p \not\rightarrow q$ but $q \rightarrow p$; (b) $-p \rightarrow -q$; but (c) $-q \not\rightarrow -p$. The expectation required by the structure of Sentence (17) is $(-p \cdot -q)$, denied as $(-p \cdot q)$, but, as the logical expression (b) requests, non-p entails non-q; it means that $(-p \cdot q)$ must be an error, as it is always false. [6]

2.1 The type of expectation and the logical relations between the connected terms also are able to account for the unacceptability of (6a) and (6d).
In (6a), the cancelled expectation is 'It is an apple tree, it is not a tree', which is anomalous, as it violates logical relation (a).
In (6d), the expectation is normal: 'X is a tree and X is not an apple tree', but the operator CI denies it in a way that contradicts the logical relation between 'tree' and 'apple tree', i.e. relation (a).

2.2 I now examine another type of logical relationship, i.e. the one established between the terms of a nonbinary contrast.

(18) *Aceasta este piersică dar caisă.
'This is a peach but an apricot.'

Let us write p for 'X is a peach' and q for 'x is an apricot'. In (18), the expectation requested by the adversative operator would be $(p \cdot -q)$, denied as $(p \cdot q)$, i.e. $-(p \cdot -q) =$

304 / Maria Manoliu-Manea

(p · q). The strong inacceptability of a sentence such as (18) results from the violation of two rules.

First, (18) violates the relationship that holds between the terms of a multiple opposition, i.e. 'If x is p, then x is not q' (contraries) (see Lyons 1977, I:par. 9.3).

Second, the denial of the expectation (p · -q) as (p · q) is expressed in Romanian by ŞI ... ŞI and not by DAR, as in (19) (when talking about a special kind of fruit such as the French pêche-abricot).

(19) Este şi piersică şi caisă.

DAR occurs when the expectation is (p · q) or (-p · -q), which is not the case for (18).

An utterance such as (20) is, however, perfectly acceptable because it denies a statement such as (19), where both terms are positive (p · q), as (p · -q), and this is a normal semantic environment for DAR. [7]

(20) Aceasta este piersică, dar caisă nu este.
'This is a peach, but it is not an apricot.'

When connecting two terms of a nonbinary contrast, CI always produces well-formed sentences, since it denies the expectation (p · -q) as (-p · q), which is perfectly congruent with the relation between the terms in contrast, [8] as shown in (21).

(21) Aceasta nu este piersică, $\begin{cases} \text{ci caisă.} \\ \text{ci este caisă.} \end{cases}$
'This is not a peach, it is an apricot.'

2.3 I now consider the logical relations that hold between the terms of a gradable opposition, such as 'hate', 'indifference', and 'love'.

(22) I do not hate you, I love you.
(Rom.) Nu te urăsc, ci te iubesc.

(23) *I do not hate you, but I love you.
*Nu te urăsc, dar te iubesc.

If (22) is perfect, and (23) is unacceptable, a sentence such as (24) might be accepted if the context is extended by an utterance such as ... which is better than to be indifferent, in my opinion.

(24) I do not love you, but I hate you, which is better than to be indifferent, I think.
(Rom.) Nu te iubesc, dar te urăsc, ceea ce este mai bine decît să fiu indiferent, zic eu.

The explanation rests upon the sense relation between 'to be indifferent', 'to love', and 'to hate': (a) 'indifference' is normally preferred to 'hate'; (b) 'love' is usually considered better than 'indifference'. In (24), the usual expectation (a) is denied, while (23) would give expression to expectation (b). Compare (24) with the extended form of (23).

> (23a) *I do not hate you, but I love you, which is better than to be indifferent, I think.

Let us write p for 'I hate you', q for 'I love you', and z for 'I am indifferent'. The logical structure of (23) is: $-(-p \cdot -q \cdot (\text{better } q, z)) = (-p \cdot q \cdot (\text{better } q, z))$, while the logical structure of (24) is: $-(-q \cdot -p \cdot (\text{better } p, z)) = (-q \cdot p \cdot (\text{better } p, z))$. As I have already pointed out, DAR requests an expectation where all the terms are positive or all the terms are negative, which is not the case for (23). It might explain the weak acceptability of (23) and the acceptability of (24).

3. The type of semantic distinctions I have examined so far cannot be accounted for except in a logically formulated semantic component. The transfer of such differences to the syntactic component would result in a noneconomic and tautological device. For example, if one transferred these differences to the syntactic component, at the Base Phrase Marker level (in the way indicated by the hypothesis that introduces negation as a higher verb), Expression (11) and, consequently, sentences such as (4) would correlate with the deep structure in (25).

(25)

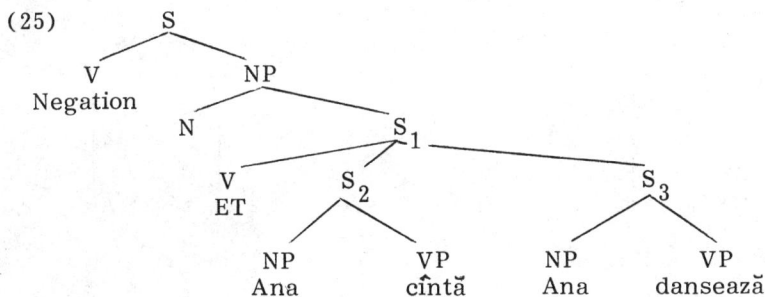

Expression (12) and, consequently, Sentence (5) could be accounted for by the deep structure (26).

Then one has to state an ad hoc condition which blocks Negation-Lowering into S_2 in (25) structures. The only way to state this constraint is to say that Neg-Lowering does not apply to the first S in a conjunction, if the connective (i.e. the first verb under negation) is represented by DAR (Sp. PERO) or Rom. ŞI (Sp. Y) (cf. Sentence 13); Neg-Lowering applies to both S_2 and S_3, when the connective is represented by CI (Sp. SINO).

(26)

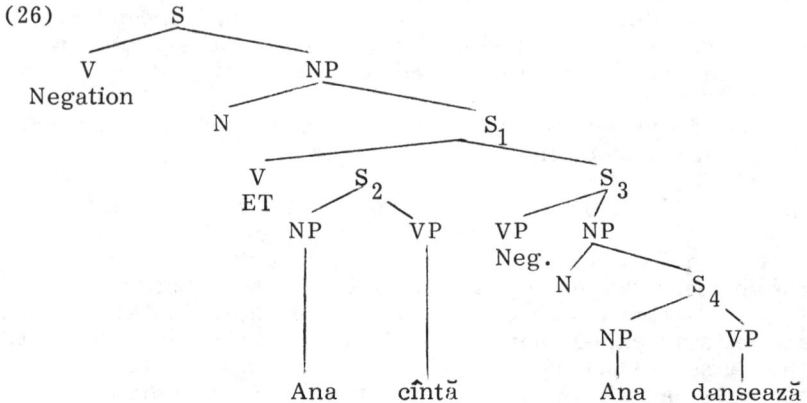

It means that the difference between DAR and CI has to be introduced as a constraint on Negation-Lowering. Then DAR and CI also have to be introduced as two different entries in the lexicon. If DAR and CI can be differentiated in the lexicon as resting upon different logical expressions, I see no reason to capture this difference in the syntactic component. Sentences (4) and (5) thus correspond to the same Base Phrase Marker, except for the interpretation assigned to the highest verb (see structure (27)).

(27)

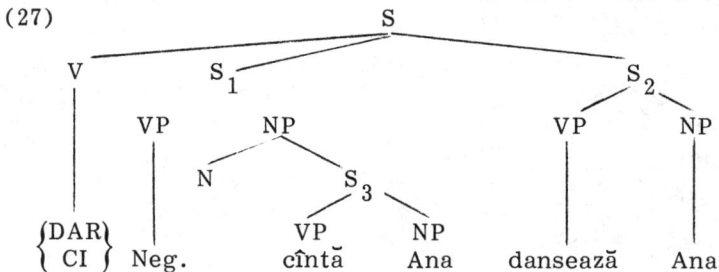

NOTES

1. I do not refer here to the various types of behavioral expectations presented in Grice (1975).
2. To deny that p holds is to reject p by means of a context-bound statement (Lyons 1977, II:771).
3. In Portuguese, SENÃO connects only two nouns.
4. ŞI NU can also deny the expectation (p · q) under the form (p · -q), as in (i).

(i) Ion doarme şi nu visează nimic.
'John is sleeping and he is not dreaming anything.'
(the expectation is that he is dreaming of something).

When ŞI NU expresses the relation (ii), i.e. $-(p \cdot q) = (p \cdot -q)$ it might be replaced by DAR.

(iii) Ion doarme dar nu visează nimic.

5. In their opinion, the basic rule is Coord → Conj. Correl. 'The phonological identity of Conj. with Correl. allows the optional deletion of one of them: *Ion citeşte şi Gheorghe citeşte* 'John is reading and George is reading' ... Such abbreviated surface structures opposes as neutral to the ones given above (i.e. *Şi Ion citeşte si Gheorge citeşte*) which we perceive as emphatic' (Vasiliu and Golopenţia 1972:83).
6. One of the fundamental requirements of communication is 'Do not say what you believe to be false' (see Grice 1975:46).
7. Gapping is blocked in this type of structure, as in (i).

(i) Aceasta este piersică dar $\begin{cases} \text{*caisă nu (a)} \\ \text{caisă nu-i (b)} \end{cases}$
'This is a peach, but it is not an apricot.'

8. Cf. (i) and (ii) (same meaning as (i).

(i) *Aceasta nu este piersică dar caisă.
'This is not a peach but an apricot.'
(ii) Aceasta piersică nu-i, dar caisă este.

Example (ii) is perfect because it denies the expectation 'this is not a peach nor an apricot', which is perfectly normal, since in a nonbinary contrast, 'if x is not p, it does not imply that it is q' (it might be c, or d, or something else, in the limits imposed by the number of the terms in opposition). Sentence (i) is unacceptable because of the gapping rule applied to (ii).

DELETION IN COORDINATE STRUCTURES IN PORTUGUESE

Mary A. Kato
Pontifícia Universidade Católica de São Paulo

1. Ross (1967, 1970) has proposed three rules to account for the reduction of the (a) forms in (1)-(3).

Left Conjunction Reduction (LCR):

(1a) *John plays* the piano and *John plays* the guitar.
(1b) *John plays* the piano and the guitar.

Right Conjunction Reduction (RCR):

(2a) John wrote a letter *to the newlyweds* and Peter sent a telegram *to the newly-weds.*
(2b) John wrote a letter, and Peter sent a telegram *to the newlyweds.*

Gapping:

(3a) John *plays* the piano and Peter *plays* the guitar.
(3b) John *plays* the piano and Peter, the guitar.

2. Tai (1969, 1971) and Kotsudas (1971) have proposed a single rule, Coordinate Deletion, for the three cases, using the argument that all cases obey the directionality principle: if the identical constituents are under left branches, deletion operates forward; if they are under right branches, it operates backward. Hankamer (1971, 1972) claims that there are two cases: forward deletion (Coordinate Deletion) and backward deletion (Delay). Hudson (1976), on the other hand, concedes that LCR, Gapping, and RCR are three separate phenomena in English, but he claims that these rules do not delete, but just raise constituents.

308

3. Coordinate structures can also be reduced by the rule of VP deletion, which is assumed by Ross (1967) and Hankamer (1971) to be a rule that deletes pro-forms rather than full VPs, being, therefore, subject to the well-known constraints of precedence and command postulated for pronominalization by Langacker (1969).

A simplified version of these constraints would say that pronominalization is not allowed to operate backwards into a nonsubordinate clause. This means that VP deletion is not restricted to coordination, as can be seen in Examples (4)-(5).

(4) John can play the fiddle well, and Bill can Ø too.
 (Ø = do so)

(5a) If John won't get rid of that anaconda, somebody else
 will Ø. (Ø = do it)
(5b) If John won't Ø, somebody else will get rid of that
 anaconda. (Ø = do it)

4. In this paper, I attempt to show that in Portuguese many cases that could be considered as instances of coordinate deletion are yielded, in fact, by rules with a wider scope than coordination like the aforementioned VP deletion. Only gapping remains as a rule exclusive of coordinate structures.

5. One dispute concerning coordination that has been constant in the literature is whether or not NPs, as well as other constituents, can appear conjoined in the base. As most linguists agree that, at least for NPs, there should be such possibility to account for sentences like (6), I assume that conjoined NPs appear as such in the deep structure.

(6) John and Bill are twins.

Sentences like (7), which, for some linguists, would result from conjunction reduction, are generated as simple sentences with compound NPs, and as such are not considered as cases of coordinate deletion.

(7) *João e Pedro* tomam chá à tarde.
 'John and Peter drink tea in the afternoon.'

(8) João toma *chá e café*.
 'John drinks tea and coffee.'

6. In Ross's analysis, when there are identical subjects there is a case of LCR. But this sort of redundancy can be eliminated either through pronominalization or deletion, as Example (9) shows.

(9a) *João* fala francês e *João* lê espanhol.
   'John speaks French and John reads Spanish.'
(9b) *João* fala francês e *ele* lê espanhol.
(9c) *João* fala francês e 0 espanhol.

In Portuguese there is a rule of Subject Pronoun Deletion
(SPD), applied after verb agreement, which does not necessarily require a coreferential NP in the sentence.[1]

(10) 0 Tomo chá todas as minhãs.
   '(I) drink tea every morning.'

(11) Eu me levanto cedo e 0 vou para cama tarde.
   'I get up early and 0 go to bed late.[2]

Furthermore, like the VP deletion discussed in Section 3, SPD
is not restricted to coordination and is also subject to the
general constraint on pronominalization.

(12) Pedro disse que 0 lê espanhol.
   'Peter said that (he) reads Spanish.'

(13a) Maria desmaiou quando 0 estava saindo da sala.
   'Mary fainted when (she) was leaving the room.'
(13b) Quando 0 estava saindo da sala, Maria desmaiou.
   'When (she) was leaving the room, Mary fainted.'

The SPD rule is, therefore, motivated independently of conjunction reduction.
   Portuguese presents further motivation to consider (8b) as
the result of Pronoun Deletion. When the shared element is
the object, there may be either backward deletion (RCR, or
Delay) or forward pronominalization.

(14a) Pedro cozinhou os mariscos e Maria comeu os mariscos.
   'Peter cooked the clams and Mary ate the clams.'
(14b) Pedro cozinhou 0, e Maria comeu os mariscos.
(14c) Pedro cozinhou os mariscos e Maria comeu-os.

But in child language and informal Brazilian Portuguese, one
may also have Object Pronoun Deletion.

(14d) Pedro cozinhou os mariscos e Maria comeu 0.

If one considers (14d) as an instance of coordinate deletion,
the directionality constraint would be violated: the shared
elements being under right branches, the deleted elements
should be the first, as in (14b). It is, therefore, more
reasonable to assume that (14d) derives through the rule of
Pronoun Deletion, which is not constrained to operate under
the directionality principle, though it can eventually obey it.

If Object Deletion is obtained through Pronoun Deletion, why should not Subject Deletion be?

Moreover, being such a productive rule in Portuguese, it would be very unreasonable to assume that the rule is constrained to apply only to subject pronouns of coordinate structures. The site of SPD in coordinate structures is that predicted by the directionality principle, but the reason for this fact is due to the constraint on the rule of pronominalization, which, as has been seen, is not allowed to operate backwards into a nonsubordinate clause.

A further point that one should bear in mind is that SPD does not require that the deleted items be functionally identical to its counterpart element as do RCR and Gapping. Example (15) illustrates this.

(15) Eu vi João quando ∅ caiu.
　　 'I saw John when (he) fell down.'
　　 (Object)　　(Subject)

SPD in coordinate structures is a specific case where such functional identity is observed and where the directionality principle is met. These aspects might have led linguists to include it as a case of conjunction reduction.

7. I now analyze a sentence which could be considered a case of a recursive application of LCR.

(16a) *João toma* café de manhã e *João toma* chá de tarde.
　　 'John has coffee in the morning and John has tea in
　　　　the afternoon.'
(16b) João *toma* café de manhã e *toma* chá de tarde.
(16c) João toma café de manhã e chá de tarde.

As with Example (8), the shared elements are the subject and the verb, but, contrary to it, the unshared elements are not noun modifiers and do not seem to form a single constituent, unless one assumes that an NP can have all the constituents of a VP and that the latter includes adverbials of time. With Hudson, on the other hand, one may assume that *café de manhã e chá de tarde* [3] cannot be generated as one constituent in the base as was done with *chá e café* in Example (8). As I have postulated the rule of SPD for subject deletion, (16b) can be derived without resorting to LCR. After SPD, however, a deletion rule is needed to erase the shared verb or verbal group. Examples of deletion of verbal group are given in (17), (18), and (19).

(17a) João *tem tomado* café de manhã e *tem tomado* chá de
　　　　'has had'　　　　　　　　　'has had'
　　 tarde.

(17b) João *tem tomado* café de manhã e chá de tarde.

(18a) João *nunca toma* café de manhã e *nunca toma* chá de
        'never has'   'never has'
        tarde.
(18b) João *nunca toma* café de manhã e chá de tarde.

(19a) João *quer tomar* café de manhã e *quer tomar* chá de
        'wants to have'   'wants to have'
        tarde.
(19b) João *quer tomar* café de manhã e chá de tarde.

This rule, which I call Verbal Deletion, or $\overline{V}$ Deletion, can be applied to subjectless sentences and clauses.

(20) Tome café de manhã e chá de tarde.
     'Drink coffee in the morning and tea in the afternoon.

(21) Tomar café de manhã e chá de tarde é o que vou fazer
     daqui para frente.
     'To drink coffee in the morning and tea in the after-
     noon is what (I) am going to do from now on.'

Verbal Deletion reduces a left peripheral verb group, but it is still not restricted to coordination, as shown in Example (22).

(22a) *João toma* mais café de manhã do que *ele toma* chá de
      tarde.
      'John drinks more coffee in the morning than he drinks
      tea in the afternoon.'
(22b) João *toma* mais café de manhã do que *toma* chá de
      tarde.
(22c) João toma mais café de manhã do que chá de tarde.

But Verbal Deletion has a narrower scope than Subject Pronoun Deletion, as it is applied only to coordinations and comparative constructions.

(23a) Se João toma café de manhã, então Ø toma chá de
      tarde.
      'If John drinks coffee in the morning then (he) drinks
      tea in the afternoon.'
(23b) *Se João toma café de manhã, então chá de tarde.

8. As was seen in Section 3, VP Deletion is analyzed as an instance of pro-form deletion, having the main properties of pronominalization[4]: (a) it is not restricted to coordination; (b) it can operate backwards if the deleted item is in a subordinate clause. I have noticed, however, that VP deletion

always leaves a verb behind, namely, the first one, be it an auxiliary or not.

Coordination:

(24) João não pode tomar chá de tarde, mas Pedro *pode* Ø.
     'John cannot have tea in the afternoon, but Peter can
     Ø.'

Relative Clause:

(25) Sigam-me aqueles que *quiserem* Ø.
     'Follow me, those who wish to Ø.'

Adverbial Clause:

(26) Você deve visitar a Torre Eiffel, se *conseguir* Ø.
     'You should visit the Eiffel Tower, if you can Ø.'

Hankamer has shown, however, that in comparative clauses there may be a deletion that erases all verbs, including the auxiliaries, as in (27).

(27) João tem estado mais cansado de que Pedro.
     'John has been more tired than Peter.'

He proposes, following Bresnan's (1971) analysis, that in comparatives there is a phenomenon similar to the deletion that occurs in relative clauses, the difference being that the identical elements are not nouns but adjectives (I would say verbs as well). [5]
But Hankamer's analysis does not account for a case of coordinate deletion in Portuguese which is similar to that of the comparatives in that no auxiliary is required in the remaining portion, but which is also dissimilar in that it requires two words in the reduced conjunct. [6]

(28) João sempre toma chá, e eu nunca Ø.
     'John always drinks tea, and I $\left\{ \begin{array}{l} \text{*never Ø} \\ \text{never do Ø} \end{array} \right\}$.'

(29) João toma chá, mas eu não Ø.
     '...   but I $\left\{ \begin{array}{l} \text{*not Ø} \\ \text{don't Ø} \end{array} \right\}$.'

(30) João toma chá, e Pedro também Ø.
     '...   and Peter $\left\{ \begin{array}{l} \text{*too Ø} \\ \text{does too} \end{array} \right\}$.'

I distinguish VP-pro-form deletion from this kind of deletion, calling them, respectively, VP-complement deletion and
VP-predicate deletion. The latter is constrained to operate
only on coordination and comparatives. See, for instance,
Examples (31) and (32).

(31a) Nós visitaremos a Torre Eiffel se eles visitarem a
        Torre Eiffel também.
        'We will visit the Eiffel Tower if they visit the
        Eiffel Tower too.
(31b) *Nós visitaremos a Torre Eiffel se eles também Ø.

(32a) Ontem, eu li o livro que você também leu.
        'Yesterday, I read the book that you also read.'
(32b) *Ontem, eu li o livro que você também Ø.

Although VP Deletion does not normally apply to relative
clauses in Portuguese, one may have a sentence such as (33).

(33a) Eu li o mesmo livro que você leu.
        'I've read the same book that you've read.'
(33b) Eu li o mesmo livro que você Ø.

What can be said here is that though the form of the embedded
sentence is that of a relative clause, the sentence as a whole
has the function of a comparative construction. The same can
be said of reduced coordinated structures like (34).

(34a) João leu este livro e eu também li este livro.
        'John has read this book and I also have read
        this book.'
(34b) João leu este livro e eu também Ø.

It seems, therefore, that functional aspects should be taken as
relevant variables to constrain or allow VP Deletion, but what
is important here is to show that this rule has a wider scope
than coordination.

9. The last case that needs attention is Right Conjunction
Reduction. Hudson (1976) has already pointed out that RCR
is not restricted to coordination. He gives examples of RCR
within an NP and in sentences with relative clauses such as
(35).

(35) It's interesting to compare the people who like with
        the people who dislike the power of the big unions.
        ((5c) p. 550)

For Hudson, the identical elements are simply raised to the
same position, being merged as a single constituent.

I would like to propose an alternative solution: I assume a process of clause embedding and deletion rather than raising. This process of embedding is motivated by the rule of appositive clause formation, which takes one conjunct of a coordination and places it within the main clause after the head, converting the identical element of the second conjunct into a relative pronoun. The phenomenon conventionally called RCR can be a symmetric process: the second clause is placed before the head and the identical element of the embedded clause is deleted. This would follow the relative clause formation of SOV languages like Japanese, in which relative clauses are embedded before the head and in which, instead of a relative pronoun, there is deletion. The following are some cases of Clause-Embedding Deletion in Portuguese.

Coordination:

(36) Eu direi, e Pedro negará, que Tonico é culpado.
    'I will say, and Peter will deny, that Tony is guilty.'

Figure 1.

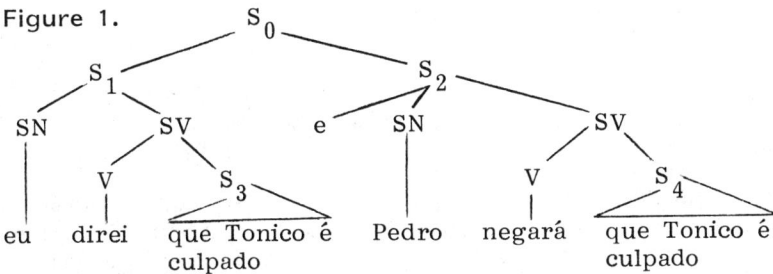

Figure 2.

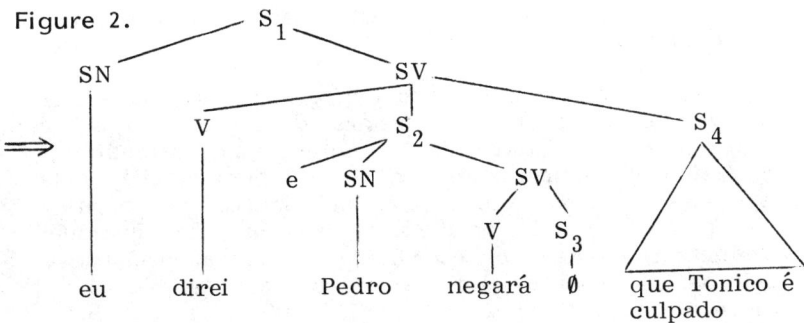

Notice that if S_2 is not embedded, the only possible output is (37).

(37) Eu direi que Tonico é culpado e Pedro negará (isso).
    'I'll say that Tonico is guilty and Peter will deny (it).'

On the other hand, after the embedding process, backward deletion of S3 is allowed because it is now in a subordinate clause.

Adverbial clause:

(38) Eu saberei, se me perguntarem, quem é o culpado.
'I'll know, if I am asked, who the culprit is.'

Relative clause:

(39) Os professores que exigiram Ø, conseguiram um aumento de remuneração.
'The teachers who demanded Ø, got a raise in their salaries.'

Appositive relative clause:

(40) João, que não havia pedido Ø, ganhou o maior pedaço de bolo.
'John, who hadn't asked for Ø, got the biggest piece of cake.'

The last case is very interesting, as the second conjunct in the underlying structure contains two identical elements: the first and the last. The first one becomes a relative pronoun and the last one is deleted.

It can be postulated thus that if the head is before the identical element in the embedded clause, this identical element has to be adjacent to the head; if the head is after the embedded clause, the shared element may be far from it, in case there is another head in the main clause placed before the other shared item.

10. I now summarize the content of this paper: (a) compound NPs were assumed to be generated as such in the base; (b) SPD deletes subjects in simple sentences, coordinations, and any kind of subordination; (c) VP-complement (VP) deletion operates on coordination, adverbial clauses, and relative clauses; (d) object and object clause deletion (right conjunction reduction) operates on coordinations, adverbial clauses, and relative clauses ((c) and (d) may be collapsed as a single phenomenon: right complement deletion); (e) the rule that deletes VP (predicate), leaving the subject, is applicable to coordinations and comparatives; (f) the rule that deletes the verb plus auxiliaries and/or preverbals ($\bar{V}$ Deletion), when in peripheral position, can be applied on coordinations and comparatives.

The conclusion is that 'gapping' is a rule peculiar to coordinate structures.

NOTES

1. Cases where coreferentiality is required were studied in Kato (1976) and Kato (1977).

2. It seems that the rule in English has to be constrained to apply only to coordination.

3. *Café da manhã* 'morning coffee' = 'breakfast' and *chá da tarde* 'afternoon tea' are, on the other side, perfect instances of a simple NP constituent.

4. Ross (1967) and Hankamer (1971) have studied other properties that are not of concern here.

5. Hankamer also distinguishes comparative deletion (21) from comparative reduction: *John is more tired than Peter is.* As the corresponding form in Portuguese is rather marginal, I am not concerned with it here. He also points out that unlike relative clauses, comparative clauses may or may not have a constituent identical to the head, in which case no deletion would occur: *John writes more radical pamphlets than Harry sells Cadillacs.*

6. I cannot accept Hudson's (1976) proposal that a sentence like (ii) should be derived by conjunct postposing of the basic for (i).

(i) (João e Pedro tomar chá)
(ii) João toma chá, e Pedro também.

First, the origin of the particle *too* cannot be explained, and second, I would say that the source for (28) would contain an internal contradiction within the second brackets.

(iii) ((João e eu)$_1$ (sempre e nunca)$_2$ (tomar chá))

I would rather support Harris' analysis (apud Hudson 1976) that (i) is the result of a rule that deletes everything except the subject and the word *too*.

(iv) (João tomar chá e Pedro tomar chá também)

Likewise, (iii) would derive from (v).

(v) ((João sempre toma chá) e (Pedro nunca tomar chá))

7. I have analyzed this problem in Kato (1978).

REFLEXIVE DELETION IN BRAZILIAN PORTUGUESE

Michael D. Kliffer
McMaster University

Consider these glosses:

John sat down.
Harry lay down.
They got married.
I remember.
He tires easily.
Get up!

If asked what these have in common as glosses, a linguist will probably answer 'obligatory reflexivity' if he knows their equivalents in most varieties of Romance. Portuguese, however, could omit the reflexive clitic in all six sentences. With *sentar, deitar, casar, lembrar, cansar,* and *levantar,* the optionality of the reflexive has become entrenched to the point where pedagogical grammars like Ellison (1971) present at least some of these verbs as being intransitive, i.e. reflexive-less. The spoken language is carrying this tendency even farther, so that reflexive deletion for some Brazilians has come to pervade the verb lexicon: one now hears *Eu não importo* 'I don't care' and *Eu não preocupo com isso* 'I'm not worried about that' in the major centres of Rio, São Paulo, Belo Horizonte, and Brasília.

Before going further into the data, I should clarify my use of the terms 'deletion', 'optionality', and 'reflexive'. For now, they are being used in a loose, pretheoretical way, without commitment to any model, transformational or otherwise. At most, 'deletion' carries diachronic, geographical, and sociolinguistic implications, in the sense that earlier stages of Portuguese, continental, and Brazilian periphery dialects, as well as formal styles, cannot dispense with the relfexive to the same extent as in the colloquial speech of central Brazil.

To say that the reflexive is optional with a certain verb is
likewise merely a pretheoretical, descriptive statement; it
should not be taken to imply that the reflexive is semantically
empty in the company of such a verb. Unless otherwise indicated, 'reflexive' is simply a time-honoured label for the form
se and other personal pronouns when the latter are coreferential with a verb's subject.

One additional caveat: in saying that reflexive deletion is
on the verge of becoming a productive phenomenon, I am not
claiming that the reflexive is disappearing. Quite the contrary, for it subsists at all formality levels, from erudite to
illiterate, and in every Brazilian region. Whether we are dealing with a notionally reflexive structure like (1) or an 'automatic' reflexive like (2), speakers from all social levels consistently put in the clitic with these particular verbs.

(1) Meu irmãozinho não gosta de se ver no espelho.
    'My little brother doesn't like to see himself in the
    mirror.'

(2) Eu me amarro.
    'I'm having a great time.' (slang)

In dictionaries, verbs of the sentar type are still entered as
'prenominal' in at least one of their uses and, indeed, some
less comprehensive or more conservative works class them as
exclusively reflexive (and/or transitive, of course).[1]

Broadly speaking, it is true that the more formal the register, the greater is the likelihood of reflexive retention, although this applies more to some verbs, e.g. casar, than to
others, e.g. sentar. During interviews with students of the
MOBRAL literacy program (see Lemle 1978), the illiterate and
semiliterate subjects exhibited interesting alternations with,
for instance, casar 'marry'.

(3) ...mas um dia eu pra mexê com a boca dela, eu disse:
    'Betinha, com quem você vai se casá?' Ela disse:
    'Eu vou casá com meu pai.'
    '...but one day just to kid around with her, I asked,
    "Betinha, who are you going to marry?" She said,
    "I'm going to marry my father."'

It is seen, then, that even if the Portuguese reflexive's range
is shrinking, it shows no more indication of disappearance than
its English counterpart, which underwent a similar retreat
centuries ago in regard to verbs like wash and dress.

I now present the bulk of the data. All the sentences were
recorded in May and June, 1978 in Rio and São Paulo, but I
first give those where the verb is subcategorized in the Novo
Aurélio dictionary (Buarque de Holanda Ferreira 1975) as either
'intransitivo' or 'pronominal'.

(4) A orelha destaca do diário.
'The tab sticks out of the register.'

(5) A lâmpada quebrou.
'The lamp broke.'

(6) A camisa desabotoou.
'The shirt came unbuttoned.'

(7) Se o aluno vai ganhar alimentação, acho que ele vai
desanimar.
'If the student is going to be given food, I think he's
going to be less motivated.' (Talking about a free
snack for MOBRAL students)

(8) Eu não acho de acordo que a pessoa não esforça tanto.
'I don't agree that a person shouldn't try so hard.'

(9) A água filtra na hora, quando passa.
'The water is filtered as soon as it goes through.'

(10) O Savoy Grill enche na hora do almoço.
'The S.G. fills up at lunchtime.'

(11) O Argentino quase que desmaiou quando o país dele
marcou o sexto gol.
'The Argentinian almost fainted when his country
scored the sixth goal.'

(12) Mas por que é que você afastou assim da gente?
'But why have you grown so distant from us?'

All these examples could add se without requiring us to
change the glosses, except that the reflexive, especially if
postposed to the verb, would make the sentence sound more
formal or literary. The same can be said for Sentences (13)
through (31), which are still unacceptable to many speakers,
presumably including the compilers to the Novo Aurélio. This
dictionary would require the verbs of (13)-(31) to be obligatorily 'pronominal' in the contexts given here.

(13) Paulo é subversivo porque decepcionou quando o Brasil
venceu a Itália.
'Paulo's a subversive because he was disappointed when
Brazil beat Italy.'

(14) O rádio estragou.
'The radio was damaged.'

(15) O cardaço soltou.
'The shoe lace came loose.'

(16) A camisa manchou.
'The shirt got stained.'

(17) Eu interesso muito pelo povo do lugar.
'I'm very interested in the people there.' (Said by a
Mineira teaching for the MOBRAL literacy program.)

(18) O povo também gosta de ir a festa e divertir.
'The people also like to go to parties and have a good
time.'

(19) A água esquenta rápido com chuveira elétrico.
'The water heats up fast with an electric shower unit.'

(20) Ele forma en julho.
'He graduates in July.'

(21) Eu aborreci com aquele pianista.
'I got bored with that pianist.'

(22) Meu irmão operou.
'My brother was operated on.'

(23) Ele escandalizou ao saber a notícia.
'He was appalled at the news.'

(24) Depois de falência, ele isolou do mundo.
'After his bankruptcy, he shut himself off from the
world.'

(25) Eu modifiquei bastante quando vim no Rio.
'I changed quite a bit when I came to Rio.'

(26) A gente limita a fazer dentro da realidade.
'We are limited to working within reality.'

(27) Você tem de arrepender do que fez.
'You better be sorry for what you did.'

(28) Gaba de ter amigos importantes.
'He boasts of having important friends.'

(29) Aquela dama pareceu com minha tia.
'That lady looked like my aunt.'

(30) Eu não atrevo a assistir numa Macumba.
'I don't dare attend a Macumba ritual.'

(31) Eu devo ausentar.
'I have to go away.'

Presenting these examples in separate groups along syntactic
or semantic lines would have masked the extensiveness of the
reflexive's retreat. Even the transitive/intransitive dichotomy
is of no account here: the smaller number of intransitive
examples, i.e. (11)-(12) and (27)-(31) indicates simply a relative scarcity of the *arrepender-se* type, rather than lower
applicability of *se*-deletion to intransitives. Lumping all the
examples together drives home the point that this process
occurs with an extremely wide semantic range of verb types.
Included are statives: (4), (7), (13), (17), (23), (24),
(26?), (29), (30); actions: (8), (12?), (18), (22), (28),
(31); and changes of state: (5), (9), (10), (11), (14), (15),
(16), (19), (21), (23), (27). Subjects may be animate or
inanimate (cf. (6) vs. (17)). Some verbs (e.g. (17) and
(24)) allow paraphrasing with *estar* and past participle, i.e.
Eu interesso entails *Eu estou interessado*. Others (e.g. (5),
(6), (14), (16), (21), (23), (24)) likewise have a *ficar* and
past participle analogue: *A lâmpada quebrou* corresponds to
A lâmpada ficou quebrada. Moreover, such semantic and
syntactic variety holds as much for the *Novo Aurélio*-approved
examples as for the innovative group.
The extent of reflexive deletion is actually greater than the
data so far suggest. Even where one would expect an 'indefinite' *se*, the speaker may provide only the verb in the third
person singular.

(32) No Brasil circula à direita.
'In Brasil people drive on the right.'

(33) Quando eu 'tava com a perna doendo, me encheu de
sabonete na clínica, melhorei na hora.
'When my foot was sore, they put soap all over me at
the clinic and I got better right away.'

(34) Uma servente estava lavando o banheiro e bateu na
porta e ela estava assustada.
'A servant was washing the bathroom and there was
a knock at the door and she was frightened.'

(35) Se ela começar esse ano, ela vai ter hora certa
porque lá na clínica deixa largar às seis.
'If she starts this year she'll have a fixed schedule
because at the clinic they let you off at six.'

(36) Nesse país sempre come arroz e feijão no almoço e
jantar.
'In this country people always eat rice and beans for
lunch and dinner.'

These examples are from semiliterate speakers, but the phenomenon extends to the written language as well. In classified ads one finds *Aluga apartamento* 'Apartment for rent' in addition to the standard *Aluga-se apartamento*. A sign on the motor covering of a bus is cited in (37).

(37) Não pode sentar nem colocar embrulho.
'One may not sit down or place packages here.'

Since I am dealing with a bare third person ending, the possibility exists that a subject like *você* 'you' or *a gente* 'we' is to be inferred, as in (38).

(38) Precisa de sol, tem, se não precisa tem também.[2]
'If you need sun, it's there; it you don't, it's still there.'

In lower class speech there is also a tendency for third person plurals (and, with some speakers, all verb endings) to reduce to simply a third person singular, so that an implies *eles* 'they' comes to be indistinguishable from an implied indefinite *se*.

(39) Quando tem qualquer coisa suja assim, depois que faz obras, ah eu não fico feliz enquanto não vejo aquilo limpo.
'Whenever there's something dirty after they've been working, I'm not happy until I see it's clean again.'

(40) É importante a época que planta também; tem planta que tem a época de plantá, senão não dá.
'The time when you plant is important too; some plants have a special time for planting, otherwise it's no good.'

Incidentally, it should be noted that the indefinite *se* seems confined more to higher registers and is thereby typically postposed to the verb: *aluga-se, procura-se*.

Just how productive is reflexive deletion? All the examples so far presented were actually noted, from Brazilians at all social levels and coming from states throughout the central area, from Bahia to São Paulo. I also recorded several verbs heard with a reflexive and then asked for judgments on the same sentences minus the reflexive. Some of the examples tested are given in (41)-(47).

(41) Por que as crianças nunca (se) comportam bem comigo?
'Why don't the kids ever behave with me?'

(42) Agora você pode (se) machucar só estando deitado na praia.
'Now you can get hurt just lying on the beach.'

(43) Eu não vou (me) adaptar ao modo de vida de São Paulo.
'I'm not going to adapt to the way of life in S.P.'

(44) Ela está (se) transformando em feiticeira.
'She's turning into a witch.'

(45) A mãe (se) empregou como doméstica.
'The mother found work as a domestic.'

(46) Aos 29 anos o operário (se) transferiu para o Rio.
'At 29, the worker transferred to Rio.'

(47) Ele tem amigos importantes na Igreja mas está (se)
integrando cada vez mais na Macumba.
'He has important friends in the Church, but he's
getting more and more involved in the Macumba
cult.'

The consensus among the half-dozen informants (three
Cariocas, and one each from São Paulo, Goiânia, and Belo
Horizonte) was that omitting the reflexive gives a colloquial,
substandard effect. This is similar to what occurs with verbs
long recognized as optionally reflexive, like *sentar* 'to sit'.
In Example (48), to delete *se* would render the metaphorical
sense of the verb incongruously prosaic.

(48) Uma angústia inaudita veio sentar-se na minha alma.
'A strange anguish came to dwell in my soul.'

The informants from Goiânia and Belo Horizonte were the ones
who objected least to deletion and, significantly, no one considered the missing reflexive in any of the examples in (41)-
(47) to be a mistake typical of a foreigner. On the other
hand, acquaintances from Porto Alegre and Belém judged not
only these sentences without *se* but even the extremely common
one in (49) as unacceptable, suggesting that deletion has yet
to reach the Brazilian periphery.

(49) Como é que chama?
'How do you say that?'

It would thus appear that the process under study is
bounded lexically as well as geographically. Having originated
in the colloquial domain, affecting high frequency items like
chamar 'call', *quebrar* 'break', *encher* 'fill', etc., *se*-deletion
still raises eyebrows when applied to more intellectual verbs
of the kind used in most of the examples in (41)-(47). As
linguistic innovations go, this is not surprising, since the
literary stratum is notorious for its resistance to just such
radical changes emanating from everyday speech.

The discussion has thus far gone little beyond description.[3] It is natural, however, to wonder to what extent reflexive deletion bears out previous analyses of se, especially as regards unity vs. homonymy in its syntactic and semantic make-up. Linguists have assumed that Portuguese, like other varieties of Romance, has several kinds of se, including 'intrinsic', 'pseudo-passive', and 'indefinite'. Azevedo (1980:76-77) derives the indefinite se and the notionally reflexive se from unrelated meanings, merging them postsemantically, i.e. transformationally. The effect is idiomatization: just as 'He kicked the bucket' fortuitously carries two readings, se just happens to be the garb assumed by both the indeterminate semantic actor and the 'true' reflexive pronoun.

Deletion, as has been seen, is less discriminating: it applies across the board, to notional reflexives (50), as well as indefinites (51), and intrinsic se (52).

(50) Ela lavou.
     'She washed herself.'

(51) No Brasil prefere cerveja.
     'In Brazil they prefer beer.'

(52) Ele arrependeu.
     'He was sorry.'

The pervasiveness of deletion suggests that the diverse reflexive uses mask a basic unity: instead of several homophonous ses, there may be only one.

Certainly, as regards form there is only one se. It is subject to no morphophonemic variation and for positioning with respect to the verb, it manifests the same register variations as other clitics like me, te, and nos. In assuming a form-meaning constancy, though, one finds that the unitary meaning is as elusive as the unitary form is apparent. In order to isolate the information that se would invariantly convey, I now proceed to discuss minimal and near-minimal pairs, where se contrasts with its absence. Space limitations prevent me from going beyond a first approximation; the data are of necessity selective, but, it is hoped, representative as well.

Consider these pairs.

(53a) João se vê.
      'John sees himself.' (reflexive)
(53b) João vê Mário.
      'John sees Mário.'

(54a) Elas se falam todo dia.
      'They speak to each other every day.' (reciprocal)
(54b) Elas me falam todo dia.
      'They speak to me every day.'

(55a) Vendeu-se aquela casa.
'That house was sold.' (indefinite)
(55b) O Henrique vendeu aquela casa.
'Henrique sold that house.'

Traditionally, such instances of *se* have been held to manifest
totally different meanings and certainly the glosses bolster
such an impression. There is, however, a common denomi-
nator: the sentences with *se* involve fewer participants. In
(55a), *se* conveys that the agent's identity is unknown or immaterial, while the reflexive and reciprocal examples restrict
the verbal process to the subject. [4]
The contrasts in (56)-(60) show that *se* may also establish
limits more abstract than the number of participants.

(56a) Ele se recuperou porque senão ia ser despedido.
'He recovered because otherwise he was going to be
fired.'
(56b) Sei lá quando ele vai recuperar.
'I have no idea when he's going to recover.'

(57a) O navio se derivou para o sul.
'The ship turned south.' (cit. *Novo Aurélio*)
(57b) O navio derivou para o sul.
'The ship turned south.'

(58a) O universitário prega-se nos estudos.
'The university student buries (lit. nails) himself
in his studies.' (cit. *Novo Aurélio*)
(58b) O corredor pregou apois alguns minutos.
'The runner collapsed after a few minutes.'
(cit. *Novo Aurélio*)

(59a) A política do governo abrandou-se inexplicavelmente.
'The government's policy softened inexplicably.'
(59b) A política do governo abrandou por causa das pressões
do exterior.
'The government's policy softened because of pressure
from abroad.'

(60a) A minha dor se aumentava com cada minuto.
'My grief was growing with each passing minute.'
(60b) A minha dor aumentou quando você me disse a verdade.
'My grief got worse when you told me the truth.'

The glosses suggest that these examples are semantically far
removed from reflexive, reciprocal, and indefinite uses. In
(56) and (57), *se* seems optional, since it appears to contribute
little or nothing to the sentence meaning; no wonder it has
been so often regarded as a semantically empty grammatical
formative. Yet if one looks more closely at each pair, a

pattern emerges. Example (56a) implies that the subject recovered because he wanted to, whereas in (56b), recovery
could be just something that will come along and happen
through circumstances beyond his control. Similarly, (57a)
has the ship deliberately veering south, but in (57b), it more
likely just went off course. Examples (56a) and (57a), in
other words, confine the verbal process by ascribing responsibility for it back to the subject. The (b) examples, lacking
se, are uncommitted vis-à-vis such responsibility; there may
be other factors involved.

In (58a) and (58b), the difference in verb glosses stems not
from any polysemy of *pregar*, but from the difference in the
subjects, as well as the presence vs. absence of *se*. The
same semantic effect applies as in the two previous pairs: *se*
brings the studying across as something done and decided by
the subject. Its absence in (58b) suggests there were other
factors involved in the runner's exhaustion: collapsing
normally entails physiological and/or external causes.

In (59) and (60), deliberateness is no longer an issue, since
the subjects are abstract NPs. Yet, *se* still sets up limits.
The *inexplicavelmente* of (59a) is a 'lubricator' for *se* because
the adverb rules out any perceptible cause. The policy moder-
ated and that is all the speaker claims to know. One would
consider *se* inappropriate in (59b) because pressure from
abroad is explicitly given as a factor behind the moderation.
Similarly, *com cada minuto* in (60a) gives incidental information
about the verbal process, but the *se* would exclude it from being a crucial factor. The pain was getting stronger on its
own, for no apparent reason. In (60b), the truth-telling
obviously triggered the increase in pain. As in (59b), the
process is not set up with the limits that *se* would impose.

The same contrast vis-a-vis limit-setting emerges even with
a verb like *casar* 'marry', which grammarians have long
claimed to be semantically constant whether *se* accompanies it
or not. The discourse Example (3) has the first occurrence
of *casâ* reflexive, where the question is implicitly one of intention: 'Who do you mean to marry?' The answer, without
se, is one of resignation: 'My father, because no one else
is available'. [5]

As the data have illustrated, the confines which *se* invariantly establishes are of diverse types. The limits may apply
to the number of participants, as with the reflexive, reciprocal, and indefinite uses, or they may be broader, pushing
motivation and responsibility back onto the subject, in addition to ruling out other influences or mitigating circumstances. [6]

How then could one reconcile the spreading reflexive deletion
described earlier with this proposed invariant meaning for *se*?
In all the minimal pairs presented, the sentences lacking *se*
did not necessarily rule out the limits which this clitic would
invariably convey. In other words, there is a Jakobsonian

marked/unmarked state of affairs. The *se* is marked for the
feature of limit-setting in that wherever the form occurs, this
feature accompanies it. Sentences without *se*, on the other
hand, are unmarked, i.e. uncommitted with respect to the feature. This is especially noticeable with verbs whose interpretation can radically alter if *se* is dropped. For example,
mudar-se is, at least in modern Portuguese, glossed as 'to
move (to another address)', whereas *mudar* usually translates
as 'to change'. Yet, the innovating dialects where reflexive
deletion is now rampant can use *mudar* in the sense of 'to
move' as well as 'to change'. The converse does not hold, as
mudar-se is still normally restricted to the interpretation of
'move'. Verbs where the shift in sense is less perceptible
likewise manifest a neutralness when unaccompanied by *se*.
In (57b), one is not told whether the change in course was
planned, but in (57a), the *se* confirms that it was. Unmarked-
ness for this feature of limit-setting also pertains to other
clitics which may be coreferential with the subject. Markedness theory is thus in complete accord with the morphological
facts, since only in the third person does a distinct form
exist for subject-clitic coreferentiality and *se* is the only
clitic marked for limit-setting.

To sum up, this paper has illustrated the growing Brazilian
trend towards dispensing with the so-called reflexive pronoun.
Reflexive deletion has long been a prominent trait of Portuguese, but only for a limited set of verbs. The colloquial
evidence from Rio, São Paulo, Minas Gerais, and Goiás suggests a radical spread of this tendency to verbs of widely
divergent semantic and syntactic properties. Deletion affects
indiscriminately every purported type of *se*, including its
reflexive, reciprocal, indefinite, and intrinsic uses, thus cast-
ing doubt on the long-held assumption that a plethora of separate meanings converge accidentally into a single form. Further data from both literary and colloquial registers pointed
to a constant meaning, tentatively characterized as 'limit-
setting', which links the seemingly disparate contextual variants of *se*.

Finally, the flexibility afforded by markedness theory enables one to appreciate how reflexive deletion does not have
to entail the demise of limit-setting. This is a beginning step
toward a theory of dynamic synchrony which would reconcile
the semantic invariant with inevitable chronological, regional,
and social variation.

NOTES

For allowing me access to their linguistic intuitions, I am
especially grateful to Antônio Gomes Lacerda, Paulo Brasil,
and Sebastião Votre. I would like to thank Anthony Naro for
arranging access to MOBRAL data and to all those at the
Centro de Documentação do MOBRAL in Rio who were

unfailingly helpful. Thanks also to Linda Waugh, whose comments greatly contributed to making sense of the data. This study was made possible through a 1978 grant from the Arts Research Board of McMaster University.
1. See, for example, Franco (1941).
2. In fact, many of the examples collected turned out to have *a gente* given one or two verbs before the verb under scrutiny arose, as is seen in this exchange between a Mineiro farmer and his MOBRAL teacher:

--A gente apanhava jaca de vez e banana.
--Ah, isso eu já fiz muito também.
--Cortava e escondia, fazia, cobria ela todinha sli.

'--We picked ripe jack fruit and bananas.'
'--Oh, I did that a lot too.'
'--We cut and hid it, we did it all and covered it up right
   there.'

3. One understandably wonders if reflexive deletion is akin to other syntactic phenomena such as object pronoun deletion, which Pires de Omena (1978) has subjected to variable rule analysis. Very briefly, she has demonstrated third person pronoun object suppression to be favoured if the NP referent is (1) inanimate, (2) unspecified, (3) also a direct object, (4) occurring in the directly preceding environment, and (5) limited to a single occurrence. Broadly speaking, the pronoun is left out when syntactic and semantic ambiguity are unlikely, a standard condition pertaining to anaphora. The discourse Example (3) with *casar* 'marry' would suggest the same holds true for reflexive deletion, i.e. with second mention the reflexive drops. However, the interviews done for Lemle (1978) fail to bear this out. Just as typical as (3) are examples such as:

(i) Ela tinha dô de num podê sentá nem deitá...é, ela já
    'tava doida pra se deitá.
    'She was uncomfortable because she couldn't sit down
    or lie down....yeah, she was desperate to lie down.'

(ii) Ela fêz a promessa pra se casá, ela se casô agora.
     'She promised to get married, so she's just gotten
     married.'

Apparently, the first mention is just as likely to lack the reflexive as the second, while the second mention may just as plausibly retain the reflexive. Clearly, something other than anaphora is at hand.
4. García (1975:59-74) posits a similar meaning for Spanish *se*, in addition to explaining how the reflexive, intrinsic, and indefinite uses stem from a single hypothesized meaning. Much

of her analysis would pertain to Portuguese as well, in spite
of obvious lexical differences.
5. Consider also (i)-(ii).

   (i) Ela ficô na solidão, viuva com 32 anos, nunca mais
       se casô, né?
     'She was alone, a widow at 32, and she never married
     again, you see?'

  (ii) Num tinha licença de nada, né? É...depois casô cum
       ele, ficô aquela vida de inferno.
     'She wasn't allowed to do anything, see? So...she
     married him afterward and her life was hell.'

Example (i) conveys a reluctance to marry, whereas (ii) presents marriage almost as something that happened to the subject, rather than something she did. The *se* in (i) implies
that it was the speaker's decision not to remarry, while its
absence in (ii) leaves open the possibility of other factors
affecting the verbal process. The same pattern is discernible
in the sentence examples of note 3.
6. This analysis owes much to the grammarian Bello, who
proposed a similar explanation for the sometimes reflexive
Spanish verbs *salir* 'leave', *entrar* 'enter', *estar* 'be', and
morir 'die'. He is right on the mark with statements like
'*Morirse* no es *morir*, sino acercarse a la muerte' ('*Morirse* is
not *morir* "to die", but rather to approach death') (Bello
1970:260).

CLITIC PLACEMENT FROM OLD TO MODERN ITALIAN: MORPHOLOGIZATION OF SYNTACTIC RULE

Dieter Wanner
University of Illinois, Urbana-Champaign

0. **Introduction.** To return to the rather well researched topic of Old Italian clitic placement, and to its only somewhat less extensively documented further evolution into Modern Italian, serves mainly a theoretical purpose. The evolution of clitic placement in Italian implies that syntactic change is not primarily guided by the parameters of syntactic naturalness, generality, and simplification; rather potential syntactic motivations remain unrealized and become replaced with localized morphosyntactic governance.

The initial description of the modern Italian clitic placement patterns presents the necessary mechanisms and background for a meaningful description of the historical dimension. Next, the thirteenth century steady-state of Florentine, embodying the closest realization of the Legge Tobler-Mussafia, provides the point of reference for a brief look at the possible origin of such a clitic placement system, and for its connection to the modern situation (stabilized essentially from the sixteenth century on).

1. **Modern Italian clitic placement.** The special clitic pronouns (cf. (1)) are characterized by their obligatory contiguity to a verb of their surface clause of occurrence. Cf. the difference between (2a) vs. (2b-c).

(1) 1st: mi, ci; 2nd: ti, vi; 3rd DO: lo, la, li, le;
      3rd IO: gli, le; 3rd refl.: si; gen.: ne; loc: ci, vi

(2a) Marisa no ha telefonato ancora <u>al suo avvocato</u>.
(2b) Marisa non <u>gli ha telefonato</u> ancora.
(2c) *Marisa non ha telefonato ancora <u>gli</u>.

Beyond this placement effect, clitics are also syntactically and phonologically attached to their host within the host-plus-clitic group, most prominently visible in the inseparability of the clitic(s) from the host. An adequate description requires two partially independent principles for achieving the appropriate surface placement patterns of clitics: (a) a syntactically governed principle of identification of, and placement of the clitics to, the host constituent within their surface clause of semantic pertinence; (b) linearization and attachment principles for syntactic and phonological integration of the clitic(s) into the group (encliticization/procliticization to the host word; phonetic rephrasing by lowering the word boundary thresholds). This is shown schematically in (3) (cf. also Selkirk 1972: Chapter 2).

(3a) placement   [Marisa   [ha telefonato]   ieri   gli]
                 S   v   v   S

$\Longrightarrow$ [Marisa   [{ ha telefonato, gli }] ieri]
               S   v   v   S

(3b) linearization $\begin{bmatrix} [\underline{gli}\ [\text{-ha}] \\ \text{v} \end{bmatrix}$ telefonato]
                               v   v
                         v

     attachment   [V ## <u>gli</u> # ha #(#) telefonato##]
                                                           V

The domain restriction to the surface clause is essential to prevent wrong structures such as (4b) from arising.

(4a) [Credeva [che Pia <u>ti</u> [avesse visto]]]
     S   S   V   V S S

(4b) *<u>Ti</u> credeva che Pia avesse visto.

As long as the surface clauses are all simple and tensed, the operation of placement is unproblematical. With verbal groups, however, some qualifications are needed; cf. their listing in (5) in terms of V_1 and V_2.

(5a) $[\text{aux}_1 - \text{ppl}_2]$ $\begin{cases} \text{ha telefonato:}\quad \text{compound tense of } V_2 \\ \text{fu ucciso:}\qquad\quad \text{passive voice of } V_2 \end{cases}$

(5b) $[\text{aspectual}_1 - \text{gerund}_2]$ sta leggendo: aspect of V_2

(5c)[1] $[\text{modal}_1 - \text{infinitive}_2]$ devo partire: modality + V_2

                                  mi fece venire: causation + V_2

(5d) $[V_1 [gerund_2]]$ partì piangendo: V_1 + concomitance of V_2

(5e)[1] $[V_1 [infinitive]]$ mi scrisse di continuare: VP complementation of V_1 by V_2

The meaning of V_1 becomes increasingly independent from (5a) to (5e). Only the types (5d-e) are able to support semantically constituents which could surface as clitics on either one (or both) of the verbs V_1 and V_2; the two verbs are effectively separated by clause boundaries as indicated. The syntactic placement principle thus identifies the whole verbal group as the host constituent for cases (5a-c); in (5d-e), the single verb (V_1 or V_2, depending on the semantic origin of the clitic constituent) is the host. Even disregarding for the moment the issue of actual linearization, clitics in structures (5a-c) do not occur uniformly: while in (5b-c) so-called 'clitic climbing' is optional, the 'aux + ppl' structure of (5a) demands such climbing; cf. (6a-c). On the other hand, climbing is properly excluded for the two-clause structures; cf. (6d-e).

Clitic on V_1	Clitic on V_2
(6a) me lo ha₁detto₂	= *ha₁ detto₂-me-lo)
(6b) lo sta preparando	= sta preparandolo
(6c) me lo vuole reglare	= vuole reglarmelo
(6d) si alzò	+ tenendosi al parapetto
(6e) la convincerò	+ a dirmelo

The particular linearization depends on the morphosyntactic identity of the verb form to which the clitic is attached. Specifically, enclisis occurs with all nonfinite verb forms (infinitive, gerund; past participle, present participle in absolute constructions) and with the (affirmative) imperative; all other verb forms/functions trigger proclisis; cf. (7).

(7) far-lo, facendo-lo fatto-lo, facente-lo; fa-llo, fate-lo, facciamo-lo; vs. lo faccio, lo facciamo (pres. ind.) etc.

This distribution explains the constant enclisis of the V_2-attached clitics in (6). If a V_1-attached clitic becomes enclitic, it is encliticized not to the verbal constituent identified by the placement principle, but only with regard to the verb-word to which it is attached; cf. (8).

	Proclisis	Enclisis

(8a) lo ha fatto   per averlo fatto (*per aver fattolo)
(8b) lo sta preparando   invece di starlo preparando
(8c) non te lo posso ripetere   per non potertelo ripetere

Syntactic placement operates thus in terms of the verbal
constituent; linearization/attachment in terms of a morphosyntactic item only.

Parallel to the indeterminacy in the host item resulting from
the constituent level placement in (5b-c), the linearization
principles produce a variation in the case of the negative imperative where both proclisis and enclisis are found; cf. (9).

	Affirmative	Negative enclitic	Negative proclitic
(9a)	dimmelo	non dirmelo	non me lo dire
(9b)	fatelo	non fatelo	non lo fate
(9c)	facciamolo	non facciamolo più	non lo facciamo più

Both enclisis and proclisis are acceptable, proclisis remaining
more normal.[2] The enclitic persistence of the clitics in the
negative forms is due to an extension of the morphosyntactic
environment of affirmative imperative to imperative simply; the
procliticizing force of the negation (cf. following for its motivation as a historical relic) is lost as the last vestige of a
syntactically and contextually based linearization principle in
Italian clitics, while the proclisis in the third column represents a survival of older conditions. The encliticization is
particularly compelling for 2 sg, where the verb form is
identical to the infinitive requiring as such constant enclisis.[3]

The arbitrary nature of these imperative linearizations is
revealed also from the curious fact that the formal command,
identical to the 3rd person present subjunctive forms, requires
proclisis whether affirmative or negative; cf. (10).

(10a) lo dica Lei   *dicalo Lei
      non lo dica Lei   *non dicalo Lei
(10b) se ne vadano Loro   *vadanosene Loro
      non se ne vadano Loro   *non vadanosene Loro

What seems to count is the morphosyntactic identity as sub-
junctives which exempts these forms (synchronically) from the
imperative treatment of progressive encliticization.

As against a naturally embedded syntactic placement principle, linearization is synchronically arbitrary. This arbitrariness has been increasing since the beginning of documented
Italian in the thirteenth century, while the placement principle remained unaltered as a syntactic rule.

2. Thirteenth century Florentine and the Legge Tobler-Mussafia.[4]

The most prominent manifest difference lies in the presence of a great number of enclitic linearizations with finite verb forms, and the possible procliticization with affirmative imperatives. But more important is the fact that clitic placement is unchanged so that the verb or verbal group is the supporting constituent. A careful check of the relevant sources and of a large number of suitable texts reveals that no change has occurred here with regard to the principle I have presented, to the extent that the topic of placement is not even recognized as potentially interesting in the previous literature.[5] However, the linearization principles, reinterpreted through the consensus reconstruction of the situation found in the sources, were less dependent on morphosyntactic categories and more responsive to the syntactic/structural configuration of the string in which the host plus clitic group occurred: clitics could not stand after a surface clause boundary, so that a clause-initial verb, regardless of its morphosyntactic shape, required enclitic linearization. Cf. the examples in (11), all with enclisis (class I of Mussafia 1886, Sorrento 1950, Ulleland 1960), vs. those in (12) with proclisis on the same type verb form, the difference being that in (12) some element (unstressed conjunction, negation, adverb, nominal constituent) intervenes between the clause boundary and the verb.

(11a) Ebeli Albizo (Schiaffini 1926:12)
(11b) Tiello credenza a me (Novellino 841) (In Segre and Marti (eds.))
(11c) Deone dare da l'ano innanzi (Castellani 1952:II.518)

(12a) (Avemmo una lettera) che nne mandaste per lo procuradore (C.II.594)
(12b) Non ti ramaricare (Nov.861)
(12c) Ben ci maraviglia noi molto (C.II.596)
(12d) Noi v'avemo iscritto (ibid.601)
(12e) Pro(venegi) ni ci vagliono oggi (ibid. 603)

The idealized syntactic configuration $[_S X [_S \#\#[_V V]_V Z]_S Y]_S$ for the identification of encliticizing environments is, however, extensively complemented by other contexts also triggering enclisis: after the paratactic conjunctions *e* and *ma* (but e.g. not *o*, *però*, *poi*, etc.), enclisis is obligatory (cf. (13) (class II of Mussafia 1886 etc.)); also with nonfinite verb forms, infinitive; gerund, participles (in absolute constructions) enclisis is required; cf. (14).

(13a) e dene pagare (Schaffini 1926:6)
(13b) ke Dio mantegna la nostra compagnia e avanzila (C.II.663)

(13c) Ma dico̱ti̱ che non ci sono (Nov.877)

(14a) e guardando̱si̱ di non mettervi alchuno danaio
(C.II.667)‾
(14b) ed allora debia sostene̱rsene̱ cum parola (ibid. 662)
(14c) Cotal morto, sì come usa̱to, facendo̱si̱ la spesa (ibid.
670)
(14d) nel quale luogo dato̱si̱ pace insieme[5] (S.92)

The enclisis with *e, ma,* and with nonfinite verb forms
cannot be comprehended as an extension of the syntactic
encliticization in clause-initial position. Even if *ma* as a
sentence/clause connector could be argued to stand outside
of the clause it introduces, a following proclitic pronoun
therefore wrongly standing next to clause boundaries, this
line of argumentation is blocked for *e*, which requires enclisis
regardless of whether it conjoins sentences, clauses, or sub-
clausal constituents; cf. (15).

(15a) vieni e mostra̱mi̱ la lancia (S.91)
(15b) sì si faccia e fa̱re si̱ debbia la chiamata loro (C.II.651)

Given that a negation preceding an otherwise clause-initial
verb is sufficient to stop the syntactic encliticization from
applying, the same negation (perhaps also the prepositional
complementizer) could be expected to have the same preventive
effect with infinitives, gerunds, participles, if one would want
to argue, for the sake of motivating the obligatory encliticization with such forms, that such nonfinite verb forms represent surface clause-initial verbs (resulting from Equi NP deletion or some other subject NP removal rule, on a more abstract level). But this clearly is not the case; cf. (16).

(16a) guardandosi [di non mettervi]   (C.II.667)
          S?   S̄?

(16b) siano tenuti [di farla̱ stare coperta]   (C.II.661)
          S?   S?

The inflexibility of the encliticization with nonfinite verbs is
identical to the modern conditions, so that already for thirteenth century Florentine the morphosyntactic conditioning of
some clitic linearization must be accepted. The unacceptability
of a string *e/ma + clitic + V*, however, is different from the
nonfinite encliticization in that the triggering factor here is a
lexical marking on the two particular items requiring removal
to enclisis of a following clitic.
Comparing it to Modern Italian, the imperative in Old Italian
behaves as an organic element of the syntactic configuration in
that its linearizations correspond directly to the requirements
of clause-initial encliticization, yielding the types: *aiutatemi*

in initial position, but *or m'aiutate, non m'aiutate* with an introductory element. The ultimate origin of the modern imperative clitic attachment is well recognizable here.

Only marginally different from the modern language are the clitic collocations with verbal groups. The cases of a single verbal constituent analysis for the two (or more) verbs are much more frequent, extending to verbs V_1 which are semantically independent; cf. (17). The frequent stylistic choice of preposing the second V_2 results then in the internal positioning of the clitic where either apparent enclisis to the nonfinite preceding V_2 may be recognized, or regular proclisis to the noninitial finite V_1; cf. (18). This configuration, eliminated from the written language only at the end of the last century, may be hypothesized to be connected with the now reduced, but once extensive 'clitic climbing' in contexts (5e), even though such a cohesion has not (yet) been documented.

(17a) il torneremo a vedere (S.155)
(17b) non ne credo avere peccato (Nov.135)

(18a) e fare si debbia (C.II.651)
(18b) ed essere vi potranno (ibid. 654)
(18c) ed esser vi potranno (ibid. 670)
(18d) e fare non si potrebbe (ibid. 657)

That the examples in (18) represent proclisis on V_1 derives from the observation that no amalgamated infinitive + clitic forms are found here (e.g. *vedello* from *veder-lo* from *verdere-lo*); the apocope *esserø* is not limited to clitic contexts. At the same time, this inversion seems to occur only where the clitics otherwise (without inversion) indicate through their attachment to V_1 that the verbal constituent is a single block (case (5c), not (5e)); this secondary internal positioning of clitics (from: clitic - V_1 + V_2 to V_2 (-) clitic - V_1) yields also a stabilization of clitic place independent of the syntactic context outside of the verbal group.

The main point of controversy in this clitic system is the variable or conditioned behavior of clitic linearization with a verb in sentence-internal, but (presumably) clause-initial position (Class III of Mussafia 1886 etc.). This does not regard subordinate clauses introduced by a conjunction since such a conjunction always operates to block the clause-initial encliticization; cf. (19). Asyndetic clauses on the same level of embedding and main clauses following an external element (term of address, extracted NP) indicate through the ensuing encliticization that they do not form part of the clauses in question; cf. (20).

(19a) uno che s'intenda di magisterio di lemgname
(C.II.652)

(19b) volemo che si faccia di quello cotale (C.II.655)

(20a) messere, piaccia vi di mandare in Pisa (Nov.864)
(20b) quelli la prese; andossene con essa (Nov.866)

But if the sentence-initial main clause is preceded by an adverbial tensed subordinate clause, by a relative clause, a gerund, or some other absolute construction, both enclisis and proclisis are found, with no valid principles to distinguish between one and the other linearization; the usage of the thirteenth century was already varying; cf. (21).

(21a) Papirio veggendo la voluntà della madre, si pensò
      una bella bugia. (Nov.856)
(21b) La gente, rallegrandosi, abbatéli la ventaglia dinanzi
      del viso. (Nov. 851)

The systematic interpretation of such cases is made very difficult by the ambiguity of the relevant examples and by their intonationally defective graphic rendition; cf. a longer discussion in Ulleland (1960) concerning the Novellino. However, to let one's analysis of clause constituency be guided by clitic linearization (Ulleland 1960:61) is circular and in view of the examples such as (21), nonempirical.[6] This question needs more study on less ambiguous materials (i.e. non-literary texts, which are, however, less varied). It appears that two linearization principles are competing, the clause-initial encliticization vs. the blocking of encliticization if some element (other than a lexically marked encliticizer) precedes the clitic-plus-verb group.

(22a) encliticization through [clit - V - X] analysis on the
     lower S-level   S   S

(22b) procliticization preserved as [[   ] clit - V - X];
                        S X X   S
     analysis on a higher S-level

On the whole, the thirteenth century Florentine dialect (the same would apply to any other Italian dialect of the same period) places clitics to the verbal constituent; it linearizes them according to a basic syntactic principle avoiding clause-initial clitics. Some morphosyntactic and lexical exception groups (plus accidental deviations) are partially stable but superimposed features make the syntactic basis of linearization opaque. The main instability derives from the ambiguous syntactic function of a sentence-initial subordinate clause (or reduced nontensed clause, i.e. class III) which can be interpreted as preceding the main clause, or as forming an element of the overall sentence. This ambiguity is directly created by the syntactically dependent linearization system itself. The linearization principles visible at this stage of Italian are by no means primitive (as might wrongly be implied in their appearance in the earliest recorded Italian texts); nor does it embody an ideally clear-cut, unspoiled situation. While its naturalness appears to be much higher than for its Modern Italian counterpart due to the syntactic dimension of governance, on a whole it remains equally heterogeneous.

3. **Potential predecessors of the Legge Tobler-Mussafia.** The fact that the earliest documented phase already shows a clitic distribution implying a partial dissolution of this very system, makes it interesting to try to find the hopefully ideal predecessors of the degraded rule, where all clitic linearizations, in complete parallel with their placement, would be syntactically conditioned, and thus interpretable as a 'natural syntactic rule', a motivated process. Any extant pre-thirteenth century Italian texts (mainly from Northern Italy, with a considerably shifted dialectal base) are, however, very fragmentary (twelfth century) or outright rarities of single-utterance length, starting with the documentary formulas of A.D. 960. As far as can be determined, their clitic system is identical (after the necessary adjustments for dialect provenience) to the one described for thirteenth century Florence.

Adding further time depth, there are numerous Latin documents from the previous centuries which might contain some concrete indication of an existing clitic placement and linearization system in the spoken Romance language of their time. Excluding as much less probable sources the documents from the ninth century on (due to the effects of the Carolingian reform on the increasingly correct latinity of the diplomatic language), this leaves mainly the *Codex diplomaticus longobardus* (Schiaparelli 1929-1933), which contains carefully edited dated texts. Errors should concern the Late Latin anaphoric pronouns (*is, hic*) and the demonstratives forming the etymological base for the Romance weak anaphoric pronouns (*me/mihi, te/tibi, nos/nobis, uos/uobis, ille, iste*), possibly the adverbial items *ibi, inde*, but all of them only to the extent that they represented noncontrastive, nondeictic, nonemphatic functions in the text. Of probing value would be instances where these originally nonclitic pronouns (therefore exempt from being obligatorily placed in the string) show collocations which cannot be accounted for in terms of (Late) Latin syntax. Since these stipulations are almost impossible to fulfill through the observation of occasional scribal inadvertencies, the next best observation should be congruence between actual Latin clitic place and its expected collocation according to the nascent Romance system of syntactically based clitic placement and linearization described earlier.

But the result is not convincing either: in line with the rather deviant non-Classical Latin standards embodied in

these texts, there are pronoun positions which differ from
classical expectations (e.g. postverbal sentence-final position,
as in (23a-b)), which are not Romance either. But in the
first place, the verb is not in its low-profile sentence-final or
'second position', with many initial positions and other shifts
becoming natural occurrences (cf. 23c-d)). But the ensuing
increased verb and (prospective) clitic juxtapositions are said
by Ramsden (1963:53-54) to be surprisingly high already for
the Itala (contested in Burger 1965); this judgment is decep-
tive here since the normal clauses containing such pronouns
are extremely poor in further elements which could potentially
separate the pronoun from the verb (cf. (23e-f)). Alongside
these reduced strings, typical Latin separation also appears
frequently (23g-h).

(23a) Ego respondi ei: (CDL:I:74)
(23b) ad ipsa ecclesia sanctificandum misit me ut ...
     (ibid. 72)
(23c) Misit me ad episcopo senese (ibid. 68)
(23d) et sum dedicavit B. episcopus (ibid. 71)
(23e) ut ipse me consagrare deuerit (ibid. 68)
(23f) W. Gastaldius mihi dicebat: (ibid. 64)
(23g) qui mihi de ipso sancto corpus patrocias dederunt
     (ibid. 72)
(23h) et mihi bene constat (ibid. 70)

A good number of these pronoun plus verb juxtapositions
actually go against the expected Romance linearization pattern
(e.g. 23a-b,d)). In addition, due to the nature of the texts
(documents of sale, affidavits, etc.) the deictic character of
the pronouns is always to be expected (depending on the
interpretation given), so that these Late Latin materials provide not only no substantial insight, but almost no hint of
the coming Romance clitic placement system.
  The same negative result obtains with other pre-Romance
texts, in particular the *Peregrinatio Aegeriae ad loca sancta*.
Ramsden (1963:54) recognizes a certain literary style explaining the pronominal classicity of the *Peregrinatio*. Classical
and colloquial Latin, of course, were subject to quite a different system where the stressed (emphatic, deictic, or contrastive) uses of these pronouns followed the free play of word
order of full constituents, the unstressed occurrences evidently becoming simple clitics (enclitic on a preceding strong
element, without implying a necessary forced collocation in the
string). Many times they turn into special clitics in second
position, i.e. actually changing to special clitics in second
position which are enclitic on the first strong element (cf.
Wackernagel 1892:406-407; Marouzeau 1949:67-69; Hofmann-
Szantyr 1972:398-401).

The Romance clitic system appears therefore as a *creatio ex nihilo*, an appearance which is definitely only a mirage caused by the imperfect tradition of linguistic materials. If the Longobard documents did not contain the effects of the new vulgar clitic system because it may not yet have been developed in the spoken Romance dialect, the later Latin charts could not let them show through because of increased purist Latin pressures blocking such Romance interferences. Yet there was hardly enough time for the process to develop gradually after the tenth century and arrive at the stage visible in thirteenth century Florentine and in the preceding non-Tuscan documents.[7] It is thus possible that the hypothesized ideal preliterary state of clitic collocation may never have existed, the surface manifest clitic placements always representing a heterogeneous collection of principles and free variation, with the thirteenth century system exhibiting an imperfect but stable steady state which was to last for a long time, even though it would gradually lose its syntactic dimension.

4. **Further evolution from the thirteenth century onward.**
The quasi-steady state of the thirteenth century nevertheless developed gradually away from its described syntactic conditioning of linearization. Clear indications of this evolution are already visible in the ambiguous treatment of the utterance-internal main clause beginning or continuation (class III). In the major figures of the fourteenth century (Dante, Petrarca, Boccaccio) the original conditions are fairly well preserved, but due to the extensive literary experimentation with language, clitic position became one possible variant of style or at least a feature available for manipulation according to need. The consequence was the addition of some encliticizations on finite verb forms outside of clause-initial position.

In particular, the prose of the *Decamerone* appears to be saturated with enclitics (roughly 1 in every 4 clitics, vs. much lower ratios of 1 in 6 to 1 in 10 in the thirteenth century). But this increase is not due to any change in the clitic linearizations; rather it is the consequence of Boccaccio's much more highly convoluted periodization, constructing long periods with the help of gerundial, participial, and infinitival constructions, all of which require enclisis. For the rest, absolute initial position always shows encliticization; a preceding *e, ma* normally induces encliticization; the nonfinite verbs always maintain enclitics. The imperative, which develops into a special problem, has been studied by Chiapelli (1953:4-7).

The excerpted materials clearly show that all of the imperatives (2sg, pl; 1pl; 3sg,pl = subjunctive) are in no way different from the other finite verb forms in Boccaccio since they obey the linearization rules exposed here; cf. (24). Only exceptional items go against these generalizations; cf. (26).

Significant is the preference for enclisis in class III situations; cf. (25).

(24a) ...e ditemi se vero è (6,8)
(24b) Comandatemi che io ... (10,10)
(24c) or mi bascia ben mille volte (8,7)
(24d) in tutto t'ingegna (7,9)
(24e) almeno un bicchier d'acqua mi fa' venire (8,7)

(25a) se vi piace narratemi i vostri accidenti (2,7)
(25b) e vestito che voi siete, recatevi in braccio vostro
      figlioccio (7,3)
(25c) come meglio puoi questa notte ti giaci (2,3) (rare)

(26a) Per che tacciansi i morditori (4,Intro)
(26b) e per ciò dillo sicuramente (1,1) (cf. (26c))
(26c) di ciò v'incresca (3,5)

Within the usage of Boccaccio, the difference between the two clitic linearizations in the imperative is clearly not a stylistic choice for purposes of emphasis (as Chiapelli argues); on the contrary, the (modern intuition of) emphasis given to the proclitic imperatives--always excluding here the negative forms which are invariably proclitic in Boccaccio due to the syntactic linearization condition--derives from the fact that they are proclitic due to the preposing of some constituent/ adverb etc. into prominent initial position: the stylistic/ emotive choice pertains to the overall construction of the sentence; the clitic position is then only a corollary.

Even in the fifteenth century a spontaneous prose text without any literary ambitions (the *Lettere* of Alessandra Macinghi Strozzi) still reveals the same part syntactic, part morphologized clitic linearization. It is only very rarely that some sentence-initial verb may show a proclitic pronoun (27a); *e/ma* occasionally admit proclisis (27b); subordinate clauses and gerundival/participial constructions preceding the main clause almost never lead to enclisis (27c); even an extracted NP occurs with proclisis (27d); for the imperatives, the observations about Boccaccio are still valid, the only difference being that the interplay between proclitic and enclitic environments is not dependent on much conscious stylistic choice. Finally, the nonfinite forms, especially the infinitive, are occasionally found with proclitic pronouns if the negation precedes the group (27e); this feature is typical of fifteenth and sixteenth century spontaneous language, e.g. the quotation from the *Principe* in (28), taken from Whitfield (1964:68), where the negative infinitives are proclitic, the affirmative ones enclitic (as opposed to invariable enclisis for both in the thirteenth century).

(27a) Ne darò libbre cinquanta (p. 25)
(27b) e te ne manderò (27)
(27c) Ora sentendo son giunti sani e a salvamento, m'hanno
      detto il caso intervenne loro (33)
(27d) La fanciulla d'Iacopo, che era con Filippo a Barzalona,
      l'aspetto ogni ora qui (31) (extracted NP)
(27e) per non mi fidare (26)

(28) Onde è da notare che, nel pigliare uno stato, debbe
     l'occupatore di esso discorrere tutte quelle offese
     che li è necessario fare, e tutte farle a un tratto,
     per non le avere a rinnovare ogni dì, e potere, non
     le innovando, assicurare li uomini e guadagnarseli
     con beneficargli (ch. viii)

As pointed out earlier, the natural syntactic treatment of
linearization with the nonfinite forms should be expected to
show parallelism between the collocational influence of the preceding negation and the introductory preposition (the preposition being the complementizer in the same way as *che* in
complement clauses, which causes regular proclisis); but it is
only the negation which requires the proclitic arrangement.
This points to the secondary, morphologized character of this
clitic linearization principle, which thus cannot be understood
as an extension of the thirteenth century syntactic system.
    Finally, the linearization system found in Cellini (*Vita*)
marks the point immediately preceding the modern state of
affairs. The utterance-initial prohibition against proclitics
is slowly giving way to many exceptions; variable at best is
the usage in the asyndetic main clauses; cf. (29). Class III
is regularly proclitic now; the nonfinite forms take proclitics
in negation, as for Machiavelli; and the imperatives have become stabilized with enclisis in the affirmative (Ulleland 1960:
62).

(29a) Riprese felice animo, mi rasciugò e confortò (I.85)
(29b) Aprendo la porta questa bestia ridendo mi si gittò
      al collo, abbracciommi e baciommi.[8]

(30a) Ora non c'è piu replica; speditegne voi ora! (I.135)
(30b) Solo contentatevi che io lo gusti (I.142)

It is evident that by Cellini's time the thirteenth century
system had ceased to operate in its syntactically anchored
dimension. The morphosyntactic dimension had become prominent, in that the behavior of the imperative can be understood diachronically as a generalization of its clause-initial
form (enclisis if affirmative, proclisis if negative), given that
this choice would represent the most normal use of the command form at a time when the sentence-initial position was
still visibly marked by enclisis (fifteenth century). In its

wake, the fixed enclitic grouping with the nonfinite verb forms
became subject to the same nonsyntactic variability introduced
by the negative particle (but not by the complementizer;
fifteenth and sixteenth centuries). Enclisis with other finite
verb forms always remained available in the sixteenth to nineteenth centuries as a stylistic choice carrying with it a solemn,
archaic tone. One conspicuous example is the quasi systematic
pattern of inverse linearization, the so-called 'imperativo
tragico' presented in Chiapelli (1953), in particular with reference to Alfieri (a non-Tuscan tragic poet known for contorted
word order); cf. (31).

(31a) E tutto sa, puniscami, s'io il merto (Merope 2,5)
(31b) State, e ci udite (Bruto Secondo, 4,2)
(31c) I vestimenti squarcinsi (Saul 2,2) (from Chiapelli
        1953:2)

The highly literary or even artificial nature of much of the
Tuscan texts between the sixteenth and early twentieth centuries is still reflected, for example, in Fornaciari (1882-1919:
455; from Whitfield 1964:64), where the then unnatural orders
of proclisis with nonfinite forms are recommended. The true
situation is much more evident in the celebrated subsequent
editions of I Promessi Sposi by A. Manzoni, of which the
second one (1840) represents a conscious linguistic reshaping
of the text into Tuscan norms, based on actual usage (of the
literary upper class in principle; cf. Migliorini 1960:611).
Here the imperatives become enclitic/proclitic according to
affirmation/negation; the subjunctive forms (3rd person polite
imperatives) retain proclisis throughout; the nonfinite verb
forms stabilize enclisis (cf. Whitfield 1964:69-70); Sorrento
1950:190-192).
    The final step is now almost completed in the increasing use--
according to the observations of Whitfield (1964:70-71), near
regularity--of the constant enclisis with nonsubjunctive imperatives, affirmative or negative; the imperative now is being
drawn into the pattern of the nonfinite verb forms. In the
same way, earlier in the fifteenth and sixteenth centuries,
the nonfinite forms followed the enclisis/proclisis pattern of a
newly de-syntacticized imperative clitic linearization, then a
phenomenon stemming from the dissolution of the thirteenth
century linearization system.

5. Conclusion. The point has been made repeatedly during
this presentation that the evolution from the thirteenth century
onward can only be reconstructed as a gradual reduction of
the syntactic motivation of the specific linearization procedures;
instead, morphosyntactic categories take their place. The relative arbitrariness of the morphosyntactic solution appears
clearly from the diachronic and modern variations encountered
with the imperative and the nonfinite forms, and also from the

loss of lexical exceptionality (*e/ma*), a trait which did not affect the system either before or after the event. The most likely development up to the thirteenth century will already have included some earlier reduction in the syntactic conditioning of linearization, in particular in the (class II) clauses with *e/ma*, given the idiosyncratic variations in the set of such items in each medieval Romance language. More extensive syntactic determination applied probably also for the internal main clause situation. But no ideal precursor stage can be evidenced; the thirteenth century situation may even represent the maximum of internal cohesion and syntactic motivation for clitic linearization.

The true syntactic generalization, rather transparently inherent in the thirteenth century Florentine clitic system, was dissolved in its further evolution, rather than consummated. The generally recognized special character of clitic elements, in particular their forced collocation in the surface string, suggests that automatic behavior of clitics should not be optional, present or absent according to accident or will; thus it is not expected to show extensive free variation or unmotivated exceptions. But such variation, exceptions, and loss of generalization are the reality of the Italian evolution. The same problem must be recognized for the other Romance languages known in their medieval phase, since none ever developed an ideal form of this shared set of linearization principles. This preponderance in diachronic evolutions of morphological criteria over the semantic-syntactic level points to the psychologically conscious word level (surface pairing of meaning and sound to express a concept or function). This level is known to play a role in the phonological evolution of language; cf. the so-called 'analogies' and paradigm adjustments, or preservation of a surface feature (stress location in Romance, cf. Wanner 1979).

If this is also the case for the syntactic domain, the status of broad, 'natural' generalizations, as understood in most present theoretical thinking, becomes precarious. They may thus turn out to be the accidental result of morphologically governed change, not its motivating force. A syntactically justified solution for clitic linearization would have been possible to different degrees of perfection (Old French almost reached such a stage), but the normal adjustments according to local surface patterns resulted in syntactically random change, as observed here. Both generalization and particularization occur in diachrony (thirteenth century partial syntactic linearization vs. later abolition of syntactic conditioning), but the occurrence of one or the other seems to be unpredictable at this point.

NOTES

Rsearch for this paper has been supported in part by funds
provided by the Research board of the University of Illinois.
I would like to thank Thomas D. Cravens for his active help
in the data collection. Given the limitations of the present
context, most of the documentary evidence can only be mentioned through reference; a comprehensive treatment of the
evolution of Italian clitics is in preparation.

1. The limits between the two classes (5c) and (5e) are not
clearly defined, not even on the ideolectal level: there are
verbs which varyingly/hesitatingly allow analysis according to
(5c) even though V_1 is semantically able to support a clitic
constituent (i.e. pointing to (5e)): *li continua a guardare*
and *continua a guardarli* may both be acceptable for a speaker.
This variation is connected to the diachronic fact that Old
Italian treated a great number of such constructions as belonging to (5c) vs. their present (exclusive or variable) analysis
as (5e).

2. Cf., however, the remarks in Whitfield (1964:68-71) and
G. Vallese (in a note at the end of Whitfield 1964:71-72),
postulating two parallel fully acceptable negative imperative
formations, of which the enclitic is said to be much more force-
ful as a command. Battaglia and Pernicone (1970:156) avoid
taking sides for 2sg, and do not even mention the use of
1pl, 2pl.

3. Italian has a further clitic pronoun, *loro* '3 pl dat. non-
refl.' which differs from the clitics of (1) in that it can occur
only in enclisis to the verbal constituent; i.e. following the
normal placement procedure, it is also linearized in terms of
this syntactic constituent analysis; cf. *lo ho detto loro, sta
scrivendo loro, posso scrivere loro; telefonò loro scusandosi,
per averlo detto loro.* Both types of clitics may cooccur in
enclisis so that *loro* is encliticized to the whole verbal expression, including any other clitics: per *dirlo loro.* This *loro*
is disregarded in the remainder since it did not change its
behavior at any time during the recorded history, always
representing the externally encliticized element of the verbal
expression. As soon as it assumes the form *lo* or *lor* (known
in medieval texts (e.g. Boccaccio, *Decamerone*) and dialectally
in W, S Toscana, Umbria, it becomes regularly proclitic like
the homophonous *lo* '3 sg m acc.'. Cf. Castellani 1956:29-30:
lo fuste data etc.

4. According to Tobler (1875-1912 and 1889), reporting
the phenomenon for Old French; and Mussafia (1886, 1898),
extending it to Italian. The most complete treatments of this
phenomenon are now in Schiaffini (1926:275-283); Sorrento
(1950:139-201); Ulleland (1960 with further bibliography);
Rohlfs (1968:170-176); Tekavčić (1972:255-258); on a Romance
perspective, cf. also Ramsden (1963). In addition, many detailed observations and data collections have been coming from

the group around Castellani, editing and excerpting the
thirteenth and fourteenth century original texts of Central
Italy; cf., for example, *Studi di Filologia Italiana*, passim
from 1952 (Vol. 13) onwards.

5. These rules are not without erratic exceptions; against
hundreds of encliticizations after *e, ma*, singular procliticiza-
tions do occur, e.g. *e si legga la somma* (C.II.660); cf. also
Ulleland (1960) passim. It is only where they become much
more numerous that they invalidate an exclusivistic interpretation.

6. There are certainly statistical regularities of the type
that after a relative clause, the main clause-initial verb carries
proclitic pronouns, rather than enclitic ones (e.g. 9 proclitic
vs. 1 enclitic cases in the Novellino, according to Ulleland
1960:58-59), the gerund (illustrated in (21)) exhibiting an
approximately even split between proclisis and enclisis (55-57).
In the same way as the imperative vacillations of Modern
Italian, these variations indicate ongoing change in the system.
Further research will need to concentrate on the syntactic and
semantic structures involved in the various utterance-internal
but clause-initial verb-plus-clitic joinings. This must not go
in the direction of Ramsden (1963:55-103), where 13 categories
are distinguished for clitic linearization, all exclusively based
on the preceding element (but varying between surface and
more abstract levels, without any justification); this prolifer-
ation only serves to obscure the issue, as becomes clear if
the categories are compared to the corresponding four cases
distinguished in Mussafia (1886), Sorrento (1950), Ulleland
(1960). Ulleland fails, however, in his purely impressionistic
categorization (conceptually and in its application) of the
syntactic/semantic values by which he tries to distinguish,
for example, various uses of the gerund. There is room for
improvement of the range of syntactic conditioning, but it is
not possible to resolve all variation in this syntactic analysis,
given the data; cf., however, Note 8.

7. The parallel French evolution, starting with Romance
texts in the tenth century, does not help to fill in the gap
either. The first Romance texts already have a perfect clitic
system (e.g. Cantilène de Ste. Eulalie), while no precursor
systems (in Latin documents, or e.g. in Gregorius Turensis)
have been reported to exist. Given the extreme parallelism
in the clitic linearizations between the medieval Romance languages (cf. the legge Tobler-Mussafia for French and Italian,
as one telling expression), a long developmental delay between
French and Italian would imply a common root of this clitic
system in some invariant components of pre-French and pre-
Italian Latin vernacular, a constellation of linguistic features
which again has not yet been successfully identified.

This does not mean that there were no differences between
the languages; for example, the enclisis after *e, ma* is language specific to Italian; enclisis with the infinitive in its

exclusiveness is Italian; French shows extensive proclisis to the infinitive, in part due to the necessary stressedness of the group-final pronoun (*fet-sói li rois* vs. *fet-se-íl* cf. Foulet 1924:58-61).

For these reasons, and because of the general inadmissibility of overly schematic (and speculative) treatments of word order (in the style of SVO, etc. discussions or as a *pater me videt* rhythmical-pattern-plus-SVO argument), the long and heated debates about (comprehensive) enclisis (Meyer-Lübke 1897) vs. proclisis (Lerch 1940) vs. some other generalized characterization (i.e. the 'ideal solution' from above, or Melander (1935-1936) in between Meyer-Lübke and Lerch) appears nonempirical and gratuitous. Especially for French, it is essential to distinguish between syntactic attachment (cliticization as such) and phonological adjustment (special clitic sandhi) to the phonetic string which may be extended beyond the immediate domain of the syntactic bond. These complex issues await some factual new contributions.

8. In spite of Ulleland's mockery (1960:63) of attempts to distinguish these two constructions, it should be pointed out that they are different: Example (29a) shows conjunction reduction making proclisis necessary; cf. the certainly ungrammatical **rasciugòmmi e confortò*; rather the repetition of the clitic would be necessary, as in (25b). The examples are taken from Ulleland (1960).

MISSING REFLEXIVES IN ITALIAN

Mario Saltarelli
University of Illinois

0. Introduction. In French (1) and Spanish (2), the appearance of reflexive pronouns in raised complement constructions is possible for 'at least some speakers'. In Italian (3), on the other hand, reflexive pronouns are categorically excluded from such constructions.

(1) Cela a fait se tuer Jean-Jacques. (Kayne 1975:214)
    'That made Jean-Jacques kill himself.'

(2) El golpe hizo caerse a Juan. (Aissen 1974a:351)
    'The blow made Juan fall down.'

(3) Gianni fece lavar(*se) Piero.
    'Gianni made Piero wash himself.'

In (1)-(3), there are typical cases of Romance raised complement constructions occurring with causative matrix verbs like French *faire*, Spanish *hacer*, and Italian *fare*. It is claimed that these constructions are single clauses on the surface. It is also hypothesized that the infinitival phrases *se tuer Jean-Jacques, caerse a Juan, lavar(*si) Piero* are derived from underlying sentential complement structures through a rule of Verb Raising (Aissen 1974a), or Clause Union (Perlmutter and Postal 1974), or Clause Reduction (Perlmutter and Aissen 1976), or an equivalent transformational or relational process. The process involves the raising of the complement verb to the function of main verb of the higher clause. As a consequence, the causative assumes an auxiliary-like function and the underlying complement phrases (*Jean-Jacques, Juan, Piero*) are relationally readjusted as dependents of the higher clause on the basis of an extended Keenan-Comrie hierarchy (Saltarelli 1979). Thus, Romance languages exhibit single-clause periphrastic causative constructions which are derived from underlying bisentential structures through complement raising. Whether this analysis is synchronically justified is still a matter of debate; diachronically, the derivational analysis is consistent with the evolution from sentential complement to accusative-infinitive to infinitive constructions (Saltarelli 1976, 1979; Pepicello 1979).

This paper seeks a grammatical explanation for the instability in the occurrence of the reflexive pronoun *se/si* in raised complements like (1)-(3). Without elaborations or quantitative support, Kayne (1975) and Aissen (1974a) admit the fleeting nature of the reflexive pronoun in French and Spanish but avoid the pertinent theoretical issue by stating that for at least some speakers the reflexive pronoun does occur. The facts of Italian, however, do not lend themselves to this convenient solution, since under no circumstances can the reflexive pronoun *si* appear in sentences like (3).

In review, the distribution of reflexive pronouns in Modern Romance, defined in terms of a reflexivization process, is as follows. Reflexive pronouns appear in all tensed clauses, regardless of whether they are main or complement clauses. Reflexive pronouns also appear in accusative-infinitive complement clauses, derived through a Subject to Object (accusative) Raising rule. In infinitival causative complement clauses of the type (1)-(3), the reflexive pronoun which is anaphoric with the logical subject of the lower clause (i.e. *Jean-Jacques, Juan, Piero*) may not appear in Italian; in French and Spanish, however, the reflexive may appear under conditions which have resisted an explicit definition.

The theoretical issue involved in a description of missing reflexives in Italian, as well as fleeting reflexives in French and Spanish, is the following. Since a pronoun-generating reflexivization process applies in all tensed clauses as well as in accusative-infinitive clauses derived through the rule of Subject to Object Raising, what is grammatically peculiar to infinitival causative clauses derived through a rule like Verb Raising which might account for the absence of reflexive pronouns in Italian and possibly explain their fleeting nature in French and Spanish?

An account of the facts is available in terms of the interaction between Verb Raising and Reflexivization. The precyclic hypothesis of Verb Raising weakly proposed by Aissen (1974a) would prevent Reflexivization, a cyclic rule, from applying to the underlying sentential complement of causative constructions. The precyclic hypothesis implies that cyclic rules do not apply in causative complement structures. But this prediction is wrong, since there is at least one cyclic rule, i.e. the passive, as evidenced in French *faire...par* constructions (Kayne 1975:235), which applies to the complement of causative verbs. Furthermore, although the order hypothesis might have accounted for missing reflexives in

Italian, it would not have offered any explanation for the
fleeting reflexives in French and Spanish. The analysis
which is proposed in this paper, while assuming a bisentential
source for infinitival causative clauses, posits a version of
Clause Union which accounts for missing reflexives without
appeal to cyclic order constraints. Fleeting reflexives find a
synchronically and diachronically justified explanation on the
basis of the interaction of Clause Union and Subject to Object
Raising.

1. **Fleeting lower clause reflexives in French and Spanish.**
That reflexive pronouns in sentences like (1) and (2) appear
'for at least some speakers' (Aissen 1974a, Kayne 1975) is an
imprecise statement of the actual usage. If it were the case
that the community of speakers could be homogeneously distinguished into users and nonusers of reflexives on a regional,
social, or other basis, then one could consider the variation
due to coexisting grammars. But this is not the case. I show
that the presence or absence of the reflexive is the result of
alternate derivational paths possible within the grammar of
French and Spanish, but not within the grammar of Italian.
The variation observed in French and Spanish exists within
the grammar of the individual speaker, and carries no implications of grammaticality. The case of the fleeting reflexive
has mystified French academicians, writers, and grammarians
since the sixteenth century. Statements found in contemporary
manuals are vague and often contradictory, with little quantitative evidence. Grevisse (1953:467) writes that after the semi-
auxiliary *faire*, the reflexive pronoun is often omitted. Also,
it is often omitted after *envoyer, laisser, mener, emmener.*
In these cases, however, the omission is never obligatory.

(4a) Nous essayons de le faire s'asseoir.
    'We tried to make him sit down.'
(4b) Tout à coup me fait retourner.
    'Suddenly he made me go back.'
(4c) Le bruit de la serrure le fit se lever.
    'The lock's noise made him get up.'

Grevisse's norm prescribes further that in Modern French
'logical' or true reflexives (cf. (1)) are only exceptionally
omitted. But norms are in disagreement, as one can find in
other manuals (for example, Fraser et al. 1942:292) that the
infinitive of certain verbs such as *s'asseoir, se souvenir, se
taire* regularly omit *se* when preceded by *faire*.
An informal empirical study of native speakers' responses
gave still different results. A questionnaire containing sentences from Grevisse was submitted by Camille Kennedy to a
group of native graduate students and teachers of French.
The results are summarized as follows. With *faire*-infinitive,
the sentences were equally accepted with or without the

reflexive. The reflexive was slightly more popular with *se
sauver*, *s'en aller*, less popular with *s'asseoir*. With *laisser*-
infinitive, the reflexive type only was accepted with *se
coucher*, *se promener*; with *s'echapper*, on the other hand,
there was some variation.

The historical situation in French is traced in Gougenheim
(1929:349, III). Since the Middle Ages, the reflexive pronoun
has been generally absent when it precedes or follows the
faire/laisser-infinitive construction. The reflexive pronoun is
present if the antecedent is between the causative and the
infinitive. The latter type of structure is, in my theory,
derived through Subject to Object Raising, whereas the former
is derived through Clause Union or Verb Raising. Gougenheim
observes that since the seventeenth century, there has been
a tendency on the part of grammarians to reintroduce the reflexive in Clause Union *faire*-infinitive constructions. This
tendency is especially evident in nineteenth century authors
in contrast with the popular language.

In Spanish, the fleeting reflexive is not as richly described
as in French. An informal study of Spanish speakers, however, gave results qualitatively similar to those obtained for
French. The variation occurs with 'logical' reflexives (5c-d)
as well as with pseudoreflexives (5a-b), (2).

(5a) Hice arrodillar(se) a Juan.
     'I made Juan kneel down.'
(5b) La condena no hizo arrepentir(se) al ladrón.
     'The sentence did not make the thief repent.'
(5c) La madre hizo lavar(se) al [a su] hijo.
     'The mother made [her] son wash (himself).'
(5d) La culpa hizo matar(se)/suicidar(se) a Juan.
     'Guilt made Juan kill himself/commit suicide.'

As in French, Spanish speakers accept the sentence with or
without the reflexive pronoun, without any implications of
grammaticality. A very noticeable difference among speakers
is found in their preference for the reflexivized versus the
unreflexivized variant. The preference appears to be consistent on an individual basis. No syntactic, social, or
regional patterns were discovered. Although a comprehensive
quantitative study of variation is necessary in order to better
understand the empirical nature of the fleeting reflexive in
French and Spanish, I feel sufficiently confident that one is
dealing with a phenomenon resulting from alternate derivational
paths possible within the same grammar. It is not the case,
I claim, that the observed variation is due to separate grammars in a state of coexistence, as implied in the descriptive
solution adopted in Aissen (1974a) and Kayne (1975).

The single-grammar analysis of the fleeting reflexive in
French and Spanish leads to the question of the missing reflexive in Italian. What is the difference in the syntax of

French and Spanish vis-à-vis the syntax of Italian which might explain the ungrammaticality of the reflexive in *fare*-infinitive constructions (3)?

2. Missing lower clause reflexives in Italian. In contrast with French and Spanish, in Italian the presence of a lower clause reflexive pronoun renders the sentence unequivocally ungrammatical. In (6)-(10), the phenomenon is illustrated for the relevant syntactic constructions.

(6a) Gianni fece sì che Piero si lavasse.
(6b) Gianni fece lavar(*si) Piero.
'Gianni made Piero wash himself.'

(7a) Gianni fece sì che Piero si mettesse il pigiama.
(7b) Gianni fece metter(*si) il pigiama a Piero.
'Gianni made Piero$_i$ put on his$_i$ pyjamas.'

(8a) La polizia fece sì che il detenuto si uccidesse/
    suicidasse.
(8b) La polizia fece uccider(*si)/suicidar(*si) il detenuto.
'The police made the prisoner kill himself/commit
    suicide.'

(9a) Gianni fece sì che Piero e Maria si conoscessero.
(9b) Gianni fece conoscer(*si) Piero e Maria.
'Gianni made/had Piero and Maria meet (each other).'

(10a) Piero fece sì che i genitori si svegliassero.
(10b) Piero fece svegliar(*si) i genitori.
'Piero$_i$ made his$_i$ parents wake up.'

Each item gives the two types of complements that can be embedded under the causative verb *fare*: (a) the sentential/tensed complement, e.g. *che Piero si lavasse* (6a), and (b) the reduced/infinitival complement *lavar(*si) Piero* (6b). It is important to note that the accusative-infinitive construction, *Gianni fece Piero lavar(*si)*, is not possible in Italian, with or without the reflexive pronoun.
It should be noted, furthermore, that (a) and (b) are not necessarily derivationally related. The (a) variant is a learned form of the Classical Latin causative *facere ut*, borrowed as *far sì*. Only (b) represents the popular development. In this paper I use the two forms to illustrate the behavior of reflexive pronouns in causative complementation. Observe that in the sentential (a) variant, the reflexive pronoun *si*, whose antecedent is the subject of the lower clause, must be present. Such a pronoun must not be present in the infinitival (b) variant. Example (6) is a case of logical or true reflexive. The antecedent of the lower clause reflexive pronoun functions

as subject in (6a), but as direct object in (6b). Note also
that in (6b), as in all Clause Union or Verb Raised complements, the antecedent *Piero* follows the verb and, consequently, the reflexive anaphor *si*. In (7b), the logical subject of the lower clause functions as indirect object in accordance with the relational characteristics of Clause Union constructions. In (8b), one can see that even intrinsically reflexive verbs such as *suicidarsi* 'to commit suicide' must omit
the reflexive pronoun in raised causative complements. Re-
ciprocals (9b) and pseudoreflexives (10b) are also missing
from such constructions.

In (6)-(10), the missing reflexive is a lower clause constituent in a construction which has undergone Clause Union.
Clause Union, however, does not fully characterize the distribution of the missing reflexive. In fact, in (11), there is a
case of a lower clause constituent *gli* 'to him' (11a), which
appears as a reflexive pronoun *si/se* in its raised complement
variant.

(11a) Gianni$_j$ fece sì che gli$_i$ scrivessero una cartolina.
(11b) Gianni si fece scrivere una cartolina.
(11c) Gianni se la fece scrivere.
     'Gianni$_i$ had someone write him$_i$ a card.'

It should be noted that in equivalent French and Spanish constructions, the reflexive pronoun is also obligatory: *Jean se
fera laver les mains par Marie* 'Jean$_i$ will have Marie wash his$_i$
hands'; *María se hizo arruinar por Juan* 'María$_i$ let Juan
ruin her$_i$'.

The difference between (6)-(10) and (11) is in the controller.
In the latter, the controller *Gianni* is in the higher clause,
whereas in the former set of sentences, the nominal controlling
reflexivization is a constituent of the lower clause. Thus, in
(11), the conditions for reflexivization are met only after the
constituent *gli* (11a) is raised through Clause Union (11b)-
(11c). It is significant, then, to distinguish between reflexivization as a lower clause versus higher clause phenomenon.
Fleeting and missing reflexives concern lower clause reflexivization, in which the controller is a lower clause constituent.

The syntactic behavior of lower clause reflexive pronouns
differs from that of higher clause reflexives. Higher clause
reflexives are promoted to the position occupied by clitic pronouns. In Italian, this position is before the causative in
fare-infinitive constructions (11b), (11c). This follows from
the assumption that Clause Union reduces bisentential structures into single-clause surface constructions. In contrast to
higher clause reflexives, lower clause reflexives observed in
French and Spanish are syntactically 'frozen' to the lower
verb. In Italian (11b), French (14a), and Spanish (12a),
the normal position for higher clause reflexives is immediately
before the causative.

(12a) María se hizo arruinar por Juan.
(12b) ?María hizo arruinarse por Juan.
   'Maria let Juan ruin her.'

(13a) El golpe hizo caerse a Juan.
(13b) *El golpe se hizo caer a Juan.
   'The blow made Juan fall down.'

(14a) Jean se fera laver les mains par Marie.
(14b) ?Jean fera se laver les mains par Marie.
   'Jean$_i$ will have Marie wash his$_i$ hands.'

(15a) Cela a fait se tuer Jean-Jacques.
(15b) *Cela s'a fait tuer Jean-Jacques.
   'That made Jean-Jacques kill himself.'

This is the position for other clitic pronouns as well, as one can see in (11c), where *la* is the clitic pronoun form of *una cartolina* 'a card'.

Lower clause reflexives, on the other hand, cannot advance to the precausative clitic position (13b), (15c), as other lower clause pronouns can in raised complement constructions. The 'frozen' behavior of the lower clause reflexive pronoun appearing in French and Spanish may indicate that it is a chômeur, no longer bearing a syntactically viable relational category.

   3. **Transitive and intransitive reflexives.** Although reflexive pronouns behave in the same manner in terms of the syntactic characteristics which I have considered so far, their underlying and derivational source is not uniform. There is evidence that a distinction must be made between at least two types of reflexives: 'logical' and 'pseudo or pronominal verb' reflexives. In addition to the semantic arguments that can be mustered in support of this distinction, the former type has surface characteristics of transitive constructions, whereas the latter has the features of intransitive constructions. The significant coding properties which support this distinction are Auxiliary Selection and Gender/Number Agreement. Consider (16) and (17).

(16ai) Maria si è vista alla TV.
(16aii) *Maria si ha visto alla TV.
(16bi) Maria ha visto sè stessa alla TV.
(16bii) *Maria è vista sè stessa alla TV.
   'Maria saw herself on television.'

(17ai) Maria si è allontanata.
(17aii) *Maria si ha allontanato.
(17bi) *Maria ha allontanato sè stessa.
(17bii) *Maria è allontanata sè stessa.
   'Maria went away.'

In Italian, reflexive pronouns have a strong or stressed variable form *sè stessa/o* and a weak or unstressed invariable form *si*. The auxiliary verbs are *essere* 'be' or *avere* 'have'. The latter is selected with transitive verbs; the former with intransitive, in general. Logical reflexives exhibit a weak form (16a) and a strong form (16b) of the reflexive. Pseudo-reflexives, on the other hand, do not have a strong reflexive construction as a grammatical possibility (17b). Accordingly, logical reflexives are analyzed as underlying transitives, i.e. with an underlying subject and object, whereas pseudo-reflexives are underlying intransitives, i.e. without object.

This solution explains the nonoccurrence of (17b). If pseudoreflexives are underlyingly intransitive, then the selection of the auxiliary *è* and the participial form *allontanata* (17ai) as opposed to (17aii), is straightforward. The rule which generates the reflexive pronoun in (17) cannot be the same as the rule which yields the reflexive pronoun in logical reflexives (16). Pseudoreflexives are adequately derived through a Subject Copy rule which inserts a reflexive pronoun with the coreferential properties of the subject. The rule is triggered by a subset of lexical verbs. This rule is in essence a characterization of the traditional concept of 'pronominal' verb, i.e. there are some verbs which require an obligatory reflexive pronoun. There is no other way to account for the peculiar appearance of the pronouns in the Romance equivalent of 'to have': Italian *andarsene*, French *s'en aller*, Spanish *irse*. The operation of the Subject Copy rule is illustrated in (18).

(18ai) [Maria AUX allontan-REFL]
(18aii) Maria si è allontanata. SUBJECT COPY, AUX SEL, AGR
'Mary went away.'
(18bi) [Gianni AUX fare [Maria AUX allontan-REFL]]
(18bii) Gianni fece allontanare Maria. CLAUSE UNION
'Gianni made Mary go away.' *SUBJECT COPY, AUX
SEL, AGR

In main/tensed clauses (18a), the source structure has a single (subject) nominal. The verb *allontanare* is lexically marked to trigger the Subject Copy rule which inserts the coreferential reflexive anaphor *si*. The auxiliary *essere* and participial agreement are a consequence of the same intransitive structure. In (18b), the pseudoreflexive structure functions as the complement of a causative matrix (18b), which triggers Clause Union.

As a result of this rule, the lower verb becomes the higher verb and the lower subject, i.e. *Maria*, is now the direct object of *fece allontanare*. By definition, then, Clause Union renders the derivation insensitive to Subject Copy. Furthermore, Clause Union is by definition a 'transitivizing'/object-creating rule, which explains the selection of *avere* as the auxiliary of causative constructions: *Gianni ha/*è fatto allontanare Maria* 'Gianni has made Mary go away'. In conclusion, the absence of lower clause pseudoreflexives in raised complements is explained as a consequence of the operation of Clause Union on underlying intransitive-reflexive constructions.

4. Transitive reflexives, Clause Union, and Antipassive.

In Section 3, I pointed out that logical or true reflexives (16) differ from pseudoreflexives (17) in that the former exhibit a strong form of the reflexive pronoun: *sè (stessa)* (16b). Any theory of reflexivization must assume that logical reflexive constructions have an object at some point in their derivation. Example (16b) is, in fact, not just a marginal variant of (16a). There are cases (19) in which the strong form is the preferred, if not the only, possibility.

(19ai) Tu, pensa a te (stesso).
(19aii) *Tu, pensati.
    'You, mind your own business.'
(19bi) Maria non ha una gran stima di sè stessa.
(19bii) *Maria non si ha una gran stima.
    'Maria doesn't think much of herself.'

There are at least two theories of reflexivization which are consistent with the facts, as illustrated in (20).

(20a) Single-nominal with double relational value:

  i. [Gianni fece [Piero-1,2 lavare]]
  ii. Gianni fece lavare Piero-2 Clause Union
                        *Reflexivization

(20b) Bi-nominal coreferential with distinct relational value:

  i. [Gianni fece [Piero-1 lavare Piero-2]
  ii. *Gianni fece lavare Piero-2 a Piero-3 Clause Union
                        *Reflexivization

Example (20a) is the theory apparently accepted in the relational framework now being developed by Postal, Perlmutter, and Johnson. This theory of reflexivization generates reflexives in tensed clauses: *Piero si è lavato* 'Gianni washed himself'. In Clause Union constructions, the conditions for Reflexivization are not met; hence the absence of logical reflexives in raised complements. One drawback of the single-nominal theory is that it does not allow for the strong/weak form of the reflexive as an underlying distinction. A more serious weakness of the single-nominal reflexivization is that it does not eliminate the need for bi-nominal reflexivization. Derived reflexives (11b) can only be accounted for by an underlying bi-nominal coreferential structure. Thus, the grammar of Italian would be more complex by having two distinct sources and rules for logical reflexivization.

The question which presents itself now is the following: is the single-nominal reflexivization such a highly valued characterization of missing reflexives as to warrant the additional complication in the grammar? Clearly, the bi-nominal solution (20b), in essence equivalent to Aissen's analysis (1974a), yields the wrong derivations in the standard definition of Clause Union (21). However, an extended version of the relational consequences of Clause Union (22) accounts correctly for missing reflexives through the independently motivated binominal reflexivization, thus eliminating the need for the single-nominal type of reflexivization rule. The extensions suggested in (22) incorporate the uniqueness condition on surface structure which obtains for Romance.

(21) The subject of intransitive complements becomes direct object, whereas the subject of transitive complements becomes indirect object (Aissen and Perlmutter 1976).

Extended Keenan-Comrie case demotion (Saltarelli 1979).
(22a) Complement Subject = $\emptyset$ > S > DO > IO > AG
(22bi) CS = $\emptyset$ if indefinite or coreferential with lower case NP
(22bii) CS = S if there is no subject
(22biii) CS = DO if there is a subject
(22biv) CS = IO if there is a subject and a direct object
(22bv) CS = AG if there is a subject, a direct object, and an indirect object

This condition, articulated in (22bi), stipulates that the complement subject is deleted if coreferential with a lower case noun phrase. The ungrammaticality of the derivation (20bii) is the result of not having realized that a form of Equivalent Noun Phrase Deletion applies also in the case of raised infinitival complements. I am not going to discuss (22bv), as it is not directly relevant to reflexivization.

There is evidence, then, in support of bi-nominal reflexivization as an adequate theory accounting for missing logical reflexives in Clause Union constructions. What I have not explained about transitive reflexives is why the weak *si* form of the sentence (16a) requires the auxiliary *essere*, just like intransitive reflexives (17a). Are weak transitive logical reflexives superficially intransitive? Evidence for this detransitivizing or antipassive phenomenon in Romance comes from the behavior of the complement subject in causative constructions. The subject of logical reflexive complements embedded under causatives surfaces as a direct object (1) and (3). If *se* in (1) functioned as a direct object, then *Jean-Jacques* should have surfaced as an indirect object, in accordance with the uniqueness condition embodied in (21)-(22). Romance, then, would have a rule similar to Antipassive (cf.

Postal 1977), which detransitivizes weak/unstressed logical
reflexive constructions by making the object a chômeur.
This hypothesis explains the auxiliary selection as well as
the relational behavior in raised complements. Further support for the chômeur nature of fleeting lower clause reflexives
comes from their insensitivity to clitic promotion (13b), (15b).

5. **Clause Union, Subject to Object Raising, and the fleeting reflexives.** The analysis proposed in Section 4 accounts
for the absence of reflexive pronouns. This is sufficient for
Italian but not for French and Spanish, where reflexive pronouns, as has been seen, may appear in raised complements.
The difference, I claim, is to be found in the present-day
stage of syntactic development in which Italian, French, and
Spanish find themselves. With causative matrices, French and
Spanish exhibit a Subject to Object raised complement in competition with Clause Union complements. There is evidence that
Clause Union is winning out in Modern French, whereas in Old
French, Subject to Object Raising was more common. The
taking over of Clause Union is more rapid with *faire* than with
laisser matrices. Thus, **il a fait Jean partir* would have been
grammatical in the syntax of Old French. *Il a laissé Jean
partir*, on the other hand, is in competition with *il a laissé
partir Jean*, according to Gougenheim (1929). In Spanish,
the present-day situation with respect to *hacer* and *dejar* is
analogous to that of French. But in Italian, there is no trace
of Subject to Object raised complements with either *fare* or
with *lasciare*. Clause Union types only are found.
The genesis of Clause Union can be detected in Late Latin
texts between the sixth and the eighth century, as a final
consequence of an initially phonetic reanalysis (Saltarelli 1979).
Clause Union constructions are historically an evolution of Subject to Object raised constructions or a reanalysis in which the
rule of Clause Union operates directly on the underlying representation. If the former is the case, one ends up with the
reflexive pronoun in surface structure. In the latter case,
the reflexive pronoun does not appear, in accordance with the
theory proposed in Section 4. This double possibility in the
evolution explains the fleeting nature of the reflexive pronoun.
As an illustration in terms of syntactically derived structures,
consider (23). Structure (23a) is the underlying causative
representation whose complement is a bi-nominal coreferential
structure (cf. (20b)).

(23a)   [cela a fait [Pierre-1 tuer Pierre-2]]
(23b)   [cela a fait [que Pierre se tue]]   REFLEXIVIZATION
(23c)   *[cela a fait Pierre [se tuer]]   SUBJECT RAISING,
      REFLEXIVIZATION
(23d)   [cela a fait se tuer Pierre]   SUBJECT RAISING,
      REFLEXIVIZATION, CLAUSE UNION
(23e)   [cela a fait tuer Pierre]   CLAUSE UNION

Structure (23b) is derived from (23a) through Reflexivization only. Structure (23c) is the result of Subject to Object Raising; i.e. *Pierre*, the subject of *tuer*, functions now as the direct object of the higher verb *a fait*. In this type of infinitival constructions, Reflexivization is obligatory. Structure (23d) is the construction for which this section provides an explanation. Structure (23d) results from the application of Clause Union to Subject Raised constructions like (23c), providing then a derivational account for the presence of reflexive pronouns in Clause Union constructions. Structure (23e) results from the application of Clause Union to (23a); hence the absence of reflexives.

Given the single-grammar hypothesis of the fleeting reflexive (cf. Section 1), Clause Union applies to two derivational sources: the underlying structure (23a) or the intermediate Subject to Object raised structure (23c). The double derivational path justifies the speaker's undecided grammaticality response. The user has available two possible strategies of production which follow from the same grammar. Note that the double derivational path type of syntactic variation is not the type of variation defined in the Labovian concept of variable rule (Labov 1969; cf. also Rousseau and Sankoff 1978). It is not a question of the probabilistic application of a rule. Clause Union applies to all causative-infinitive constructions. The variation in linguistic structures evidenced by the fleeting reflexive describes a chronological stage of the syntax in which two rules, Subject to Object Raising and Clause Union, are in competition.

One can speculate that such stages are not stable conditions in grammars, as suggested by the history of French. Gougenheim's study (1929) indicates that Clause Union is generalizing at the expenses of Subject to Object Raising. The evolutionary process moves by clearly defined lexical classes. Whereas in Old French, Subject Raising as well as Clause Union could apply to the complement of *faire* and *laisser*, today *faire* is restricted to Clause Union complements. In Modern Castilian an analogous situation is found. There seems to have been a sociological effort by the learned community to maintain Subject to Object Raising, in contrast with the popular development. The French Academy in 1694 gives *faire en aller* as a sanction of the popular usage. But the writers of the eighteenth and nineteenth centuries tend to put the reflexive pronoun back in, *faire s'asseoir*, owing to the 'purism' or logical rigor of authors like Chateaubriand (Gougenheim 1929: 354-355).

Assuming that the derivational hypothesis (23) is correct for French and Spanish, a final question must be answered: how different must the derivational sequence (23) be to account for the fact that in Italian the reflexive pronoun never appears in causative-infinitive constructions? The answer should now be obvious. The Italian version of (23) does not include the intermediate derivational structure (23c) on which Clause Union can apply. In other words, there is only one source for Italian causative-infinitive construction (23a). That this is a reasonable hypothesis is supported by the fact that Subject to Object raised complements of either causative verb are not grammatical: *Gianni fece/lasciò Maria lavarsi. Clause Union complements only are possible: *Gianni fece/lasciò lavare Maria 'Gianni made/let Mary wash (herself).'

In conclusion, the grammatical explanation for the missing reflexive in Italian and the fleeting reflexive in French and Spanish is the following. The syntax of French and Spanish has Subject to Object Raising and Clause Union as competing rules for causative complementation. The syntax of Italian, on the other hand, has Clause Union only.

REFERENCES

Academia R.S. România. 1963. Gramatica limbii române. I-II. 2nd ed. revised and augmented. Bucharest: Editura Academiei R.S. România.

Adjukiewicz, K. 1928. Główne zasady metodolog. Nauk i lokiki formalnej. Warsaw.

Agren, John. 1973. Étude sur quelques liaisons facultataires dans le français de conversation radiophonique. Studia romanica upsaliensia, 10. Uppsala: Uppsala University.

Aissen, J. 1974a. Verb raising. Linguistic Inquiry 5.325-366.

Aissen, J. 1974b. The syntax of causative constructions. Ph.D. dissertation. Harvard University.

Aissen, Judith, and David Perlmutter. 1976. Clause reduction in Spanish. Berkeley Linguistic Society 2.1-30.

Anderson, Shannon L. 1975. On the syntax of liaison. The French Review 48.848-855.

Anderson, Stephen R. 1974. The organization of phonology. New York-London: Academic Press.

Arnaud, A., and P. Nicole. 1662. La logique, ou l'art de penser. Paris: Flammar.

Ashby, William J. 1975. The rhythmic group, liaison, nouns and verbs of French. Studia linguistica 29.110-116.

Ashby, William J. 1977. The status of the negative morpheme ne, in the French of Tours. Unpublished paper read at the Annual Meeting of the Linguistic Society of America, Chicago.

Atkinson, James C. 1973. The two forms of subject inversion in modern French. The Hague: Mouton.

Azevedo, Milton. 1980. Passive sentences in English and Portuguese. Washington, D.C.: Georgetown University Press.

Babby, Leonard H. 1978. Negation and subject case selection in existential sentences: Evidence from Russian. Bloomington: Indiana University Linguistics Club.

Babby, Leonard H. 1979. Word order, case, and negation in Russian essential sentences. Cornell University MS.

362

Bach, Emmon. 1968. Nouns and noun phrases. In: Universals in linguistic theory. Edited by Emmon Bach and Robert Harms. New York: Holt, Rinehart and Winston. 91-124.

Badía Margarit, Antonio. 1951. Gramática histórica catalana. Barcelona: Editorial Noguer.

Badía Margarit, Antonio. 1962. Gramática catalana. Madrid: Editorial Gredos.

Baker, Carl Leroy. 1970. Notes on the description of English questions: The role of an abstract question morpheme. Foundations of Language 6.197-219.

Baltin, M. 1978a. PP as a bounding node. Paper read at the Eighth Annual Meeting of the Northeastern Linguistic Society, Amherst, Mass.

Baltin, M. 1978b. Toward a theory of movement rules. Unpublished doctoral dissertation. MIT.

Baltaglia, S., and V. Pernicone. 1970. Grammatica Italiana. Turin: Loescher.

Barbosa, Jorge Morais. 1965. Études de phonologie portugaise. Lisbon: Bertrand.

Bell, A., and J. Hooper. 1978. Issues and evidence in syllabic phonology. In: Syllables and segments. Edited by A. Bell and J. Hooper. New York: North-Holland Publishing Co. 3-22.

Bello, Andrés. 1970. Gramática de la lengua castellana. 8th ed. Buenos Aires: Sopena.

Bentivoglio, Paola. 1976. Queísmo y dequeísmo en el habla culta de Caracas. In: 1975 Colloquium on Hispanic Linguistics. Edited by Frances M. Aid, Melvyn C. Resnick, and Bohdan Saciuk. Washington, D.C.: Georgetown University Press. 1-18.

Bjarkman, Peter C. 1975. Towards a proper conception of processes in natural phonology. In: Papers from the Eleventh Regional Meeting, Chicago Linguistic Society. Edited by Robin E. Grossman, L. James San, and Timothy J. Vance. Chicago: Chicago Linguistic Society. 60-72.

Bjarkman, Peter C. 1976. Natural phonology and loanword phonology. Unpublished doctoral dissertation. University of Florida.

Bjarkman, Peter C. 1977. The role of autonomous phonetics in natural phonology. In: Current issues in the phonetic sciences. Edited by Patricia Hollien. Amsterdam: John Benjamins.

Bjarkman, Peter C. 1978. Reassessment of the role of natural phonology in the analysis of Cuban Spanish. Paper read at the 93rd Annual Convention of the Modern Language Association of America, New York.

Blinkenberg, A. 1968. Le problème de l'accord en français moderne. Copenhagen: Munksgaard.

Boër, Steven E. 1978. Toward a theory of indirect question clauses. Linguistics and Philosophy 2.3:307-345.

Bolinger, Dwight L. 1967. Adjectives in English: Attribution and predication. Lingua 18.1-34.
Bolinger, Dwight L. 1977. Meaning and form. London: Longmans.
Bonnard, H. 1961. Le système des pronoms *qui, que* et *quoi* en français. Français Moderne 29.169-182, 241-251.
Bordelois, I. 1977. Animacy or subjecthood: Clitic movement and romance causitives. In: Contemporary studies in Romance linguistics. Edited by M. Suñer. Washington, D.C.: Georgetown University Press. 18-40.
Brakel, A. 1977. Unpublished paper from the Colloquium on Romance Linguistics, University of Illinois.
Brame, Michael, and Ivonne Bordelois. 1973. Vocalic alternations in Spanish. Linguistic Inquiry 4.111-168.
Brame, Michael. 1974. The cycle in phonology: Evidence from Palestinian, Maltese, and Spanish. Linguistic Inquiry 5.39-60.
Brame, Michael. 1976. Conjectures and refutations in syntax and semantics. Amsterdam: Elsevier North-Holland.
Brame, Michael. 1978. Base generated syntax. Seattle: Noit Amrofer.
Breivik, Leiv. 1975. The use and non-use of existential *there* in present-day English. Forum Linguisticum 7.57-103.
Bresnan, J. 1971. On a non-source for comparatives. Linguistic Inquiry 2.117-124.
Bresnan, J. 1973. Syntax of the comparative clause construction in English. Linguistic Inquiry 4.275-343.
Bresnan, J. 1975. Comparative deletion and constraints on transformations. Linguistic Analysis 1.25-74.
Bresnan, J. 1976a. On the form and functions of transformations. Linguistic Inquiry 7.3-40.
Bresnan J. 1976b. Evidence for a theory of unbounded transformations. Linguistic Analysis 2.353-394.
Bresnan, J. 1977. Variables in the theory of transformations. In: Formal syntax. Edited by P. W. Culicover et al. New York-London: Academic Press. 157-196.
Bresnan, J. 1978. A realistic transformational grammar. In: Linguistic theory and psychological reality. Edited by M. Halle et al. Cambridge, Mass.: MIT Press. 1-59.
Bresnan, J., and Jane Grimshaw. 1978. The syntax of free relatives in English. Linguistic Inquiry 9.331-391.
Brown, W., and B. Vattuone. 1975. Theme-rheme structure and Zenéyze clitics. Linguistic Inquiry 6.1:136-140.
Bruneau, Charles. 1926. Enquête linguistique sur les patois d'Ardennes. Vol. 2. Paris: Honoré Champion.
Brunot, F. 1905. La pensée et la langue. Paris: Masson.
Buarque de Holanda Ferreira, Aurélio. 1975. Nova dicionário da língua Portuguesa. Rio de Janeiro: Nova Fronteira.
Bull, William. 1943. Related functions of *haber* and *estar*. Modern Language Journal 27.119-123.

Bull, William. 1954. Spanish adjective position: The theory of valence classes. Hispania 37.32-38.

Bull, William. 1965. Spanish for teachers: Applied linguistics. New York: Ronald Press.

Burger, A. 1965. Review of: Ramsden (1963). Vox Romanica 24.136-138.

Carnap, Rudolf. 1934. Logische Syntax der Sprache. Vienna: Julius Springer.

Casagrande, Jean. 1973. Gliding and diphthongization in French. Paper read at the Winter Meeting of the Linguistic Society of America, San Diego.

Casagrande, Jean. 1975. Fossilization in French syntax. In: Diachronic studies in Romance linguistics. Edited by M. Saltarelli and D. Wanner. The Hague: Mouton.

Casagrande, Jean. (forthcoming a.) La survivance en français moderne des i et u du latin classique. Proceedings of the Fourteenth International Congress on Romance Linguistics and Philology, Naples.

Casagrande, Jean. (forthcoming b.) The sound system of French. New York: John Wiley.

Castellani, A. 1952. Nuovi testi fiorentini del Dugento. Florence: Sansoni (2 vols.).

Castellani, A. 1956. Testi sangimignanesi. Florence: Sansoni.

Castillo, Carlos, and Otto F. Bond. 1972. University of Chicago Spanish Dictionary. 2nd ed. Chicago: The University of Chicago Press.

Cellini, B. 1962. La vita. Edited by B. Maier. Novara: 1st Geografico Agostini.

Chafe, Wallace L. 1974. Language and consciousness. Lg. 50.111-133.

Chafe, Wallace L. 1976. Giveness, contrastiveness, definiteness, subjects, topics and points of view. In: Subject and topic. Edited by Charles Li. New York-London: Academic Press. 25-56.

Chao, Y.-R. 1963. The non-uniqueness of phonemic solutions of phonetic systems. In: Readings in linguistics. Edited by Martin Joos. New York: American Council of Learned Societies. 38-54.

Chiapelli, F. 1953. Note sull' imperativo tragico in italiano. Lingua Nostra 1.4.1-8.

Chinchor, Nancy. 1978. On the treatment of Mongolian vowel harmony. Paper presented at the Ninth Annual North East Linguistics Society, New York City.

Chomsky, N. 1955. The logical structure of linguistic theory. New York: Plenum (1975).

Chomsky, N. 1957. Syntactic structures. The Hague: Mouton.

Chomsky, N. 1970. Remarks on nominalizations. In: Readings in English transformational grammar. Edited by

R. Jacobs and P. S. Rosenbaum. Washington, D.C.:
Georgetown University Press. 184-221.

Chomsky, N. 1973. Conditions on transformations. In: A
Festschrift for Morris Halle. Edited by S. R. Anderson and
P. Kiparsky. New York: Holt, Rinehart and Winston.

Chomsky, N. 1976. Conditions on rules of grammar. Linguistic Analysis 2.303-351.

Chomsky, N. 1977. On WH-movement. In: Formal syntax.
Edited by P. W. Culicover et al. New York-London:
Academic Press. 71-132.

Chomsky, N. 1978. On binding. Unpublished MS. MIT.

Chomsky, N., and H. Lasnik. 1977. Filters and control.
Linguistic Inquiry 8.425-504.

Chomsky, N., and M. Halle. 1968. The sound pattern of
English. New York: Harper and Row.

Clements, G. N. 1976. Vowel harmony in non-linear generative phonology: The autosegmental theory. Unpublished
manuscript, Harvard University.

Cochet, E. 1933. Le patois de Gondecourt: Grammaire et
lexique. Paris: E. Droz.

Colasuonno, Giovanni. 1976. Grammatica e lessico etimologico
del dialetto di Grumo Appula con 628 proverbi e modi di dire.
Cassano Murge (Bari): Tipografica Meridionale.

Comrie, B. 1976. Aspect. Cambridge: Cambridge University
Press.

Contreras, H. 1973. Spanish non-anaphoric lo. Linguistics
111.5-30.

Contreras, H. 1976. A theory of word order with special
reference to Spanish. Amsterdam: North-Holland.

Coseriu, Eugenio. 1968. Coordinación latina y coordinación
románica. In: Actas del III Congreso español de estudios
clásicos. Madrid: CSIC.

Craig, C. 1977. The structure of Jacaltec. Austin: University of Texas Press.

Cressey, William W. 1966. A transformational analysis of the
relative clause in urban Mexican Spanish. Unpublished
doctoral dissertation. University of Illinois.

Cressey, William W. 1974. Homorganic in generative phonology.
Papers in Linguistics 7.69-81.

Cressey, William W. 1978. Spanish phonology and morphology:
A generative view. Washington, D.C.: Georgetown University Press.

Cuervo, Rufino José. 1895. Los casos enclíticos y proclíticos
de pronombre de tercera persona en castellano. Romania
24.95-244.

D'Ambra, Raffaele. 1873. Vocabolario napolitano-toscano
domestico di arti e mestieri. Napoli: Chiurazzi.

Daoust-Blais, Denise, and Monique Lemieux-Nieger. 1979.
/tUt/ en français de Québec. Cahier de Linguistique.
9.73-121.

Delattre, Pierre. 1947. La liaison en français, tendences et
classifications. The French Review 21.148-157.

Delattre, Pierre. 1951. Principes de phonétique française à l'usage des étudiants anglo-américains. Middlebury: Ecole française d'été.
Delattre, Pierre. 1955. Les facteurs de la liaison facultative en français. The French Review 29.42-49.
Dell, François, and Elizabeth Selkirk. 1978. On morphologically governed vowel alternation in French. Studies in European Linguistics. Cambridge, Mass.: MIT Press.
Demonte, V. 1978. Semántica y sintaxis de las construcciones con *ser* y *estar*. To appear in: Revista Española de Lingüística.
Dinnsen, Daniel A. 1978. Phonological rules and phonetic explanation. Bloomington: Indiana University Linguistics Club.
Dinnsen, Daniel A. 1979a. Atomic phonology. In: Current approaches to phonological theory. Edited by Daniel A. Dinnsen. Bloomington: Indiana University Press.
Dinnsen, Daniel A. 1979b. Current approaches to phonological theory. Bloomington: Indiana University Press.
Dubuisson, C. 1974. Le système adverbial français. Recherches Linguistiques à Montréal 2.67-91.
Dubuisson, C. 1979. Y a-t-il une transformation d'inversion du SN sujet en français? Paper presented at the Colloque de Vincennes.
Dubuisson, C., and J. Goldsmith. 1976. A propos de l'inversion du clitique sujet en français. In: Papers from the Sixth Meeting of the Northeastern Linguistics Society. Montréal Working Papers in Linguistics. 6.103-112.
Elcock, William Dennis. 1938. De quelques affinités phonétiques entre l'aragonais et le béarnais. Paris: E. Droz.
Ellison, Fred P., and Francisco Gomes de Matos. 1971. Modern Portuguese. New York: Knopf.
Emonds, Joseph. 1976. A transformational approach to English syntax. New York-London: Academic Press.
Fabra, Pompeyo. 1912. Gramática de la lengua catalana. Barcelona: Masso Casas y Ca.
Fasold, Ralph W. 1978. Language variation and linguistic competence. In: Linguistic variation, models and methods. Edited by David Sankoff. New York-London: Academic Press. 85-95.
Fauconnier, G. 1973. Cyclic attraction into networks of coreference. Lg. 49.1-18.
Fernández, Salvador. 1950. Gramática española. Madrid: Revista de Occidente.
Fodor, J. D. 1978. Parsing strategies and constraints on transformations. Linguistic Inquiry 9.427-473.
Foley, James. 1967. Spanish plural formation. Lg. 43.486-493.
Fornaciari, R. 1919. Sintassi italiana dell'uso moderno. Florence: Sansoni.

Fouché, P. 1967. Le verbe français: Étude morphologique. Paris: Klincksieck.

Foulet, L. 1924. L'accent tonique et l'ordre des mots: Formes faibles du pronom personnel après le verbe. Romania 50.54-93.

Foulet, L. 1928. Petite syntaxe de l'ancien français. Paris: H. Champion.

Franco, Alvaro. 1940. Dicionario inglês-português e portugues-inglês. Porto Alegre: Globo.

Fraser, W. H., J. Squair, and C. Parker. 1942. French composition and reference grammar. Boston: Heath.

Frei, H. 1929. La grammaire des fautes. Paris: Paul Geuthner.

García, Erica. 1975. The role of theory in linguistic analysis. Amsterdam: North Holland.

García Márquez, Gabriel. 1975. El otoño del patriarca. Buenos Aires: Editorial Sudamericana.

Gazdar, G., and G. K. Puthum. 1976. Truth-functional connectives in natural language. Papers from the Twelfth Regional Meeting, Chicago Linguistic Society. Chicago: Chicago Linguistic Society. 220-234.

Gili y Gaya, S. 1961. Curso superior de sintaxis española. 9th ed. Barcelona: Bibliograph.

Girard, Jocelyn. 1977. La syntaxe de l'exclamation en français. Thèse de 3e cycle. Université de Paris à Vincennes VIII. Vincennes, Paris.

Givón, T. 1975a. Focus in the scope of assertion: Some Bantu evidence. Studies in African Linguistics 6.2.

Givón, T. 1975b. Negation in language: Pragmatics, function, ontology. Working Papers on Language Universals 18.59-116.

Goldsmith, John. 1975. An autosegmental typology of tone. In: Proceedings of the Fifth North East Linguistics Society. Edited by E. Kaisse and J. Hankamer. Cambridge, Mass.: Harvard University. 172-182.

Goldsmith, John. 1976a. An overview of autosegmental phonology. Linguistic Analysis 2.23-68.

Goldsmith, John. 1976b. Autosegmental phonology. Doctoral dissertation. MIT. New York: Garland Press (1979).

Goldsmith, John. 1977. Complementizers and the status of root sentences. Proceedings of the North East Linguistic Society. Amherst, Mass.

Goldsmith, John. 1978. Que c'est quoi? Que c'est QUOI. Recherches linguistiques à Montréal.

Goldsmith, John. 1979. The aims of autosegmental phonology. In: Current approaches to phonological theory. Edited by D. Dinnsen. Bloomington: Indiana University Press.

Gonçalves Viana, Aniceto dos Reis. 1886. Exposição da pronúncia normal portuguesa para uso de nacionais e estrangeiros. Porto: Tipográfia Occidental.

Gonçalves Viana, Aniceto dos Reis. 1903. Portugais. Phonétique et phonologie. Morphologie. Textes. Leipzig: B. G. Teubner.

Gougenheim, Georges. 1929. Étude sur les périphrases verbales de la langue française. Paris: Les Belles Lettres.

Gougenheim, Georges. 1970. L'emploi des pronoms interrogatifs *que* et *quoi* devant l'infinitif. In: Études de grammaire et de vocabulaire français. Paris: Editions Picard.

Grevisse, M. 1953. Le bon usage. 5th ed. Gembloux: Duculot.

Grevisse, M. 1964. Le bon usage. 8th ed. Gembloux: Duculot.

Grice, H. P. 1975. Logic and conversation. In: Syntax and semantics. Vol. 3. Speech acts. Edited by Cole and Morgan. New York-London: Academic Press.

Grimshaw, J. 1977. English WH-constructions and the theory of grammar. Unpublished doctoral dissertation. University of Massachusetts.

Gross, Maurice. 1968. Grammaire transformationelle du français: Syntaxe du verbe. Paris: Larousse.

Guitart, Jorge M. 1976. Markedness and a Cuban dialect of Spanish. Washington, D.C.: Georgetown University Press.

Guitart, Jorge M. 1977. Aspectos del consonantismo habanero: Reexamen descriptivo. Paper presented at the Spanish-American Dialectology Special Session, 92nd Annual Convention of Modern Language Association of America, Chicago.

Guitart, Jorge M. 1978. ¿Cuán autónoma es la fonología natural del español cubano de Miami? Paper presented at the Third Annual Symposium on the Dialectology of Carribean Spanish, Florida International University, Miami.

Gundel, J. K. 1977. Role of topic and comment in linguistic theory. Bloomington: Indiana University Linguistics Club.

Haase, A. 1969. Syntaxe francaise du XVIIe siècle. Paris: Delagrave.

Hadlich, Roger L. 1971. A transformational grammar of Spanish. Englewood Cliffs, N.J.: Prentice-Hall.

Hall, R. A. Jr. 1972. Neuters, mass nouns, and the ablative in Romance. In: Readings in Romance linguistics. Edited by James M. Anderson and Jo Ann Creore. The Hague: Mouton.

Halle, Morris. 1959. The sound pattern of Russian. The Hague: Mouton.

Halle, Morris. 1971. English stress. New York: Harper and Row.

Halliday, M. A. K. 1967. Notes on transitivity and theme in English, Part 2. Journal of Linguistics 3.199-244.

Hammond, Robert M. 1976a. Some theoretical implications from rapid speech phenomena in Miami-Cuban Spanish. Unpublished doctoral dissertation. University of Florida.

Hammond, Robert M. 1976b. Phonemic restructuring of voiced
obstruents in Miami-Cuban Spanish. In: 1975 colloquium on
Hispanic linguistics. Edited by Frances M. Aid et al.
Washington, D.C.: Georgetown University Press. 42-51.
Hankamer, J. 1971. Constraints on deletion in syntax.
Unpublished doctoral dissertation. Yale University.
Hanssen, F. 1913. Gramática histórica de la lengua
castellana. Halle: M. Niemeyer.
Harman, Gilbert. 1975. If and modus ponens. Bloomington:
Indiana University Linguistics Club.
Harms, Robert T. 1968. Introduction to phonological theory.
Englewood Cliffs, N.J.: Prentice-Hall.
Harris, James. 1969. Spanish phonology. Cambridge, Mass.:
MIT Press.
Harris, James. 1975. Stress assignment rules in Spanish.
In: 1974 colloquium on Spanish and Portuguese linguistics.
Edited by W. G. Milan, J. J. Staczek, and J. C. Zamora.
Washington, D.C.: Georgetown University Press.
Hart, George. 1978. Nasality and the organization of auto-
segmental phonology. Unpublished MS. Indiana University.
Hausser, Roland, and D. Zaefferer. 1979. Questions and
answers in a context Montague grammar. In: Formal
semantics and pragmatics for natural language. Edited by
Guenther, Franz, and Schmidt. Dordrecht: D. Reidel.
Himtikka, Jaako. 1962. Knowledge and belief: An introduc-
tion to the logic of two notions. Ithaca: Cornell University
Press.
Hirschbühler, Paul. 1976. Observations sur l'emploi du
principe du A-sur-A relativisé en français. Rapport de
Recherche 2. In: Les constraints sur les règles. Edited
by Philippe Barbaud. University of Quebec at Montréal.
Hirschbühler, Paul. 1976. Two analyses of free relatives in
French. Recherches linguistiques à Montréal 6.137-152.
Hirschbühler, Paul. 1978. The syntax and semantics of WH-
constructions. Amherst: University of Massachusetts
Press.
Hofmann, J. B., and A. Szantyr. 1972. Lateinische Syntax
und Stylistik. München: Beck.
Hooper, Joan. 1972. The syllable in phonological theory.
Lg. 28.525-540.
Houlihan, K., and G. Iverson. 1979. Functionally constrained
phonology. In: Current approaches to phonological theory.
Edited by Daniel A. Dinnsen. Bloomington: Indiana Uni-
versity Press. 50-73.
Hudson, Richard A. 1976. Arguments for a non-transforma-
tional grammar. Chicago: University of Chicago Press.
Hudson, Richard A. 1976. Conjunction reduction, gapping
and right-node raising. Lg. 52.535-562.
Huguet, Edmond. 1962. Dictionnaire de la langue française
du XVIIe siècle, I-VII. Paris: Didier.

Huot, Hélène. 1974. Les relatives parenthétiques. In: Actes du Colloque Franco-Allemand de Grammaire Transformationelle. Edited by Rohrer and, Nicolas Ruwet. Tübingen: Niemeyer.

Hust, Joel. 1976. A lexical approach to the unpassive construction in English. Unpublished doctoral dissertation. University of Washington.

Hyman, Larry M. 1975. Phonology: Theory and analysis. New York: Holt, Rinehart and Winston.

Iverson, Gregory. 1974. Ordering constraints in phonology. Unpublished doctoral dissertation. University of Minnesota.

Iverson, Gregory. 1978. The functional determination of phonological rule interactions. Bloomington: Indiana University Linguistics Club.

Jackendoff, Ray. 1972. Semantic interpretation in generative grammar. Cambridge, Mass.: MIT Press.

Jackendoff, Ray. 1977. X̄ syntax: A study of phrase structure. Cambridge, Mass.: MIT Press.

Jaeger, Jeri Y. 1978. Speech aerodynamics and phonological universals. Report of the Phonology Lab 2.12-30. Berkeley.

Jenkins, L. 1975. The English essential. Linguistische Arbeiten 12. Tübingen: Max Niemeyer Verlag.

Jespersen, O. 1924. The philosophy of grammar. London: Allen and Unwin.

Jespersen, O. 1927. A modern English grammar on historical principles, Part III. London: Allen and Unwin.

Jakobson, Roman. 1939. Signe zéro. Mélanges Bally. Geneva: Georg. 143-152.

Kahn, Dan. 1975. Syllable-based generalizations in phonology. Unpublished doctoral dissertation. MIT.

Kato, M. A. 1976. A elisão do pronome sujeito em Português e a hipótese do discurso directo de Kuno. Il Encontro Nacional de Linguística, PUC-RJ. 85-90.

Kato, M. A. 1977. Restrições à regra da omissão do pronome pessoal sujeito em Português. Il Encontro Nacional de Linguística, PUC-RJ. 67-76.

Kato, M. A. 1978. Restrições à regra de elipse verbal. Paper presented at the 30th Annual Meeting of SBPC, USP, São Paulo.

Kaye, Jonathan D. 1979. On the alleged correlation of markedness and rule-function. In: Current approaches to phonological theory. Edited by Daniel A. Dinnsen. Bloomington: Indiana University Press.

Kaye, Jonathan D., and Jean-Yves Morin. 1979. The syntactic bases for French liaison. Unpublished MS. Montréal.

Kayne, Richard. 1974. French relative 'que'. In: Current studies in Romance linguistics. Edited by M. Luján and F. Hensey. Washington, D.C.: Georgetown University Press. 255-299.

Kayne, Richard. 1975. French syntax: The transformational cycle. Cambridge, Mass.: MIT Press.

Kayne, Richard. 1976. Il relativo francese 'que'. Rivista di Gramatica Generativa 1.3. 59-111.
Kayne, Richard, and J. Y. Pollock. 1978. Stylistic inversion, successive cyclicity and move NP in French. Linguistic Inquiry 9.4:595-621.
Keenan, Edward L. 1972a. Relative clause formation in Malagasy. In: The Chicago which hunt. Edited by Paul Peranteau et al. Chicago: Chicago Linguistic Society. 169-189.
Keenan, Edward L. 1972b. On semantically based grammar. Linguistic Inquiry 3.413-460.
Keenan, Edward L. 1976. Towards a universal definition of subject. In: Subject and topic. Edited by C. N. Li. New York-London: Academic Press.
Keenan, Edward L., and B. Comrie. 1977. Noun phrase accessibility and universal grammar. Linguistic Inquiry 8.63-99.
Kemeney, J. C., J. L. Snell, and G. L. Thompson. 1965. Algèbre moderne et activités humaines. French translation, M.C. Loyau. Paris: Didier.
Kemp, William. 1977. Noun phrase questions and the question of movement rules. In: Papers from the Thirteenth Regional Meeting, Chicago Linguistic Society. Edited by Beach, Fox, and Philosoph. Chicago: Chicago Linguistic Society. 198-212.
Kemp, William. 1979. On that that that that became that which which became what. Papers from the Fifteenth Regional Meeting, Chicago Linguistic Society. Edited by William F. Hanks et al. Chicago: Chicago Linguistic Society.
Keniston, H. 1937. The syntax of Castillian prose. Chicago: University of Chicago Press.
Kimball, J. P. 1973. The grammar of existence. In: Papers from the Ninth Regional Meeting, Chicago Linguistic Society. Chicago: Chicago Linguistic Society. 262-270.
Kimball, J. P. 1973. Seven principles of surface structure parsing. Cognition 2.7-24.
Kiparsky, Paul. 1976. Abstractness, opacity and global rules. In: The application and ordering of grammatical rules. Edited by A. Koutsoudas. The Hague: Mouton. 160-188.
Klausenburger, Jurgen. 1978. French linking phenomena. Lg. 54.21-40.
Klein, Flora. 1979. Pragmatic and sociolinguistic bias in semantic change. Paper presented at the Fourth International Congress of Historical Linguistics. Stanford University.
Klein, Flora. (forthcoming) Factores sociales en algunas diferencias lingüísticas en Castilla la Vieja. Revista de Sociología.
Koster, J. 1978. Conditions, empty nodes and markedness. Linguistic Inquiry 9.551-593.

Koutsudas, A. 1971. Gapping, conjunction reduction and coordinate deletion. Foundations of Language 7.37-86.

Koutsudas, A., G. Sanders, and C. Noll. 1974. The application of phonological rules. Lg. 50.1-28.

Kuno, Susimo. 1974. The position of relative clauses and conjunctions. Linguistic Inquiry 5.117-136.

Kuroda, S. Y. 1968. English relativization and certain related problems. Lg. 44.244-266.

Labov, William. 1969. Contraction, deletion, and inherent variability of the English copula. Lg. 45.715-762.

Labov, William. 1972. Sociolinguistic patterns. Philadelphia: University of Pennsylvania Press.

Ladefoged, Peter. 1975. A course in phonetics. New York: Harcourt Brace, Jovanovich.

Lakoff, George. 1966. Stative adjectives and verbs in English. In: Mathematical linguistics and automatic translation, Report NSF-17. Harvard University Computation Laboratory.

Lakoff, George. 1970. Irregularity in syntax. New York: Holt.

Lakoff, George. 1971. On generative semantics. In: Semantics: An interdisciplinary reader in philosophy, linguistics and psychology. Edited by D. Steinberg and L. A. Jakobovitz. Cambridge: Cambridge University Press. 232-296.

Langacker, R. 1969. On pronominalization and the chain of command. In: Modern studies in English. Edited by D. Reibel and S. Shane. Englewood Cliffs, N.J.: Prentice-Hall. 160-186.

Langacker, R. 1972. French interrogatives revisited. In: Generative studies in Romance languages. Edited by J. Casagrande and B. Saciuk. Rowley, Mass.: Newbury House. 36-69.

Lapesa, Rafael. 1950. Historia de la lengua española. Cuarta edición corregida y aumentada. New York: Las Américas.

Lapesa, Rafael. 1968. Sobre los orígenes y evolución del leísmo, laísmo y loísmo. In: Festschrift Walter von Wartburg. Edited by K. Baldinger. Tübingen: Neimeyer. 523-551.

Leech, G. 1977. Semantics. Middlesex-New York: Penguin Books.

Lefebvre, C., and R. Fournier. 1978. Les relatives en français de Montréal. Cahier de linguistique 8: Syntax et sémantique du français. 273-294.

Le Maistre, Frank. 1966. Dictionnaire Jersiais-Français. Jersey: Don Balleine Trust.

Lemle, Miriam, and Anthony J. Naro. 1978. Competências básicas do Português. Rio de Janeiro: Mobral.

Lerch, E. 1940. Proklise oder Enklise der alfranzösischen Objektspronomen. Zeitschrift für romanische Philologie 60.417-501.

Li Fang-Kuei. 1946. Chipewyan. Linguistic structures of native America (Viking Fund Publications in Anthropology, Number 6). New York: The Viking Fund.

Liberman, Mark. 1974. The intonational system of English. Unpublished doctoral dissertation. MIT.

Liberman, Mark, and Alan Prince. 1977. On stress and linguistic rhythm. Linguistic Inquiry 8.249-336.

Lindsay, W. M. 1894. The Latin language. Oxford: Clarendon.

Linell, Per. 1977. Morphophonology as part of morphology. In: Phonologica 1976. Edited by Wolfgang U. Dressler and Oskar E. Pfeiffer. Innsbruck: Innsbrucker Beitrage zur Sprachwissenschaft. 9-20.

Lloyd, Richard J. 1908. Northern English. Phonetics. Grammar. Texts. 2nd ed. Leipzig: B. G. Teubner.

López del Castillo, L. 1976. Lengua standard i nivells de Llenguatge. Barcelona: Editorial Laia.

Lowenstamm, Jean. 1977. Relative clauses in Yiddish: A case for movement. Linguistic Analysis 2.197-216.

Lozano, María del Carmen. 1978. Stop and spirant alternations: Fortition and spirantization processes in Spanish phonology. Bloomington: Indiana University Linguistics Club.

Luján, Marta. 1972. Adjectives in Spanish. Unpublished doctoral dissertation. University of Texas.

Luján, Marta. 1972. On the so-called neuter article in Spanish. In: Generative studies in Romance languages. Edited by Jean Casagrande and B. Saciuk. Rowley, Mass.: Newbury House. 139-161.

Luján, Marta. 1974a. Adverbial adjectives in Spanish. Paper presented at the 1974 Colloquium on Hispanic Linguistics, Amherst, Mass.

Luján, Marta. 1974b. Prenominal adjectives in Spanish predicates. In: Linguistic studies in Romance languages. Edited by R. J. Campbell, M. G. Goldin, and M. C. Wang. Washington, D.C.: Georgetown University Press.

Luján, Marta. 1979. Sintaxis y semántica del adjetivo. Madrid: Ediciones Cátedra.

Lyons, J. 1968. Introduction to theoretical linguistics. Cambridge: Cambridge University Press.

Lyons, J. 1977. Semantics. I-II. Cambridge: Cambridge University Press.

Macinzki Strozzi, A. 1914. Lettere. Edited by G. Papini. Sanciano: Carabba.

Malécot, André. 1975. French liaison as a function of grammatical, phonetic and paralinguistic variables. Phonetica 32.161-179.

Malmberg, Bertil. 1955. Estudios de fonética hispánica. Madrid: Instituto Miguel de Cervantes.

Manoliu-Manea, Maria. 1976. I don't hate you, I love you: Adversative conjunctions in a Romanian-English contrastive grammar. In: Papers from the Third International Conference on Contrastive Grammar. Edited by D. Chitoran. Bucharest: The University Press. 156-168.

Manoliu-Manea, Maria. 1978. ITI CUMPAR CE PAPUSA VREI. Le défini dans une grammaire transformationnelle du roumain. Revue Romåne 13.47-62.

Maratsos, Michael. 1978. New models in linguistics and language acquisition. In: Linguistic theory and psychological reality. Edited by M. Halle, J. Bresnan, and G. A. Miller. Cambridge, Mass.: MIT Press.

Mariner, Sebastian. 1973. Situación del neutro románico en la oposición genérica. Revista española de lingüística 3.23-38.

Marouzeau, J. 1949. L'ordre des mots dans la langue latine. III. Les articulations de l'énoncé. Paris: Les Belles Lettres.

Martinet, André. 1958. C'est jeuli, le Mareuc. Romance Philology 2.345-355.

Mascaró, Joan. 1978. Catalan phonology and the phonological cycle. Bloomington: Indiana University Linguistics Club.

Melander, J. 1935-1936. Enklise oder Proklise des tonlosen Objektspronomen im Altfranzösischen. Studia Neophilologica 8.45-60.

Melillo, Michele. 1955a. Atlante fonetico lucano. Roma: Arti Grafiche S. Marcello.

Melillo, Michele. 1955b. Atlante fonetico pugliese. Roma: Arti Grafiche S. Marcello.

Menéndez Pidal, Ramón. 1950. Orígenes del español. Madrid: Espasa-Calpe.

Merlo, Clemente. 1909. Note italiane centro-meridionali. Revue de dialectologie romane 1.240-262.

Meyer-Lubke, W. 1897. Zur Stellung der tonlosen Objektspronomina. Zeitschrift für romanische Philologie 21.313-334.

Mizliorini, B. 1960. Storia della lingua italiana. Florence: Sansoni.

Milner, Jean Claude. 1977. De quelques restrictions limitant le mouvement de qu-. Unpublished MS. Université de Paris.

Milsark, G. L. 1977. Toward an explanation of certain peculiarities of the existential construction in English. Linguistic Analysis 3.1-29.

Moignet, Gérard. 1974. Le système du paradigme qui/que/quoi. In: Études de psychosystématique française. Paris: Klincksieck.

Moignet, Gérard. 1976. Grammaire de l'ancien français. Paris: Klincksieck.

Morin, J. Y. 1974. Aspects méthodologiques du monde d'application des règles syntaxiques: du cycle. Unpublished doctoral dissertation. McGill University.

Mussafia, A. 1886. Una particolarità sintattica della lingua italiana dei primi secoli. In: Miscellanea di filologia e linguistica in memoria di N. Caix e U.A. Canello. Florence.

Mussafia, A. 1898. Enclisi o prodisis del pronome personale atono qual aggeto. Romania 27.145-149.

Napoli, D. 1979. The notion 'semantic auxiliary': Clitic climbing in Italian. Unpublished MS. Georgetown University.

Navas Ruiz, R. 1963. Ser y estar, estudio sobre el sistema atributivo del español. Salamanca: Acta Salmanticencia. Filosofía y Letras, Tomo XVII.

Neu, Helene. 1978. French liaison: A statistical analysis of variation. Paper presented at the Michigan Academy.

Nyrop, K. 1925. Grammaire historique de la langue française. Copenhague: Guldendalske Boghandel Nordisk Forlag.

Obenauer, Hans. 1976. Études de syntaxe intérrogative du français: Quoi, combien et le complémenteur. Tübingen: Max Niemeyer.

Obenauer, Hans. 1977. Syntaxe et interprétation: Que interrogatif. Le français moderne 4.305-340.

Obenauer, Hans. 1978. A-sur-A et les variables catégorielles: Comment formuler les transformations transcatégorielles. Cahiers linguistiques de l'Université de Québec 8.377-406.

Otheguy, Ricardo. 1977. The meaning of Spanish el, la, lo. Unpublished doctoral dissertation. City University of New York.

Otheguy, Ricardo. 1978. A semantic analysis of the difference between el, la, and lo. Contemporary studies in Romance linguistics. Edited by M. Suñer. Washington, D.C.: Georgetown University Press. 241-257.

Penny, Ralph J. 1970. El habla pasiega. London: Tamesis.

Pepicello, W. J. (to appear) The development of accusative-infinitive constructions. Paper read at the Fourth International Conference on Historical Linguistics, Stanford, California.

Peregrinatio Aetheriae. Silviae vel potium Aetheriae peregrinatio ad loca sancta. Edited by W. Heraeus. Heidelberg: Winter.

Perlmutter, D. 1970. On the article of English. In: Progress in linguistics. Edited by M. Bierwisch and K. E. Heidolph. The Hague: Mouton. 233-248.

Perlmutter, D. 1971. Deep and surface structure constraints in syntax. New York: Holt.

Perlmutter, D. 1972. Evidence for shadow pronouns in French relativization. The Chicago which hunt. Chicago: Chicago Linguistic Society. 73-105.

Perlmutter, D. 1978. Studies in relational grammar. Unpublished MS. University of California, San Diego.

Pires de Omena, Nelize. 1978. Pronome pessoal de terceira pessoa: Suas formas variantes em função acusativa.

Unpublished M.A. thesis. Pontifícia Universidade Católica, Rio de Janeiro.

Postal, Paul. 1977. Antipassive in French. Proceedings of the Seventh Annual Meeting of the North East Linguistic Society. Cambridge, Mass.: Department of Linguistics, MIT. 275-314.

Postal, Paul, and David Perlmutter. 1974. Unofficial notes on relational grammar from the Summer Linguistics Institute, Amherst, Mass. Unpublished MS.

Querido, A. 1976. The semantics of copulative constructions in Portuguese. In: Current studies in Romance linguistics. Edited by M. Luján and F. Hensey. Washington, D.C.: Georgetown University Press. 343-366.

Quicoli, C. 1976. Missing subjects in Portuguese. In: Current studies in Romance linguistics. Edited by M. Luján and F. Hensey. Washington, D.C.: Georgetown University Press. 100-143.

Radford, A. 1977. Italian syntax: Transformational and relational grammar. New York: Cambridge University Press.

Ramsden, H. 1963. Weak-pronoun position in the early Romance languages. Manchester: University Press.

Ramsey, M. 1956. A textbook of modern Spanish. New York: Holt, Rinehart and Winston.

Real Academia Española. 1973. Esbozo de una nueva gramática de la lengua española. Madrid: Espasa-Calpe.

Real Academia Española. 1974. Esbozo de una nueva gramática de la lengua española. Madrid: Espasa-Calpe.

Remache, L. 1960. Syntaxe du parler wallon. Paris: Les Belles Lettres.

Renchon, Hector. 1967. Études de syntaxe descriptive II. La syntaxe de l'interrogation. Bruxelles: Palais des Académies.

Van Riemskijk, Henk C. 1978. On 'matching effects' in free relatives. Paper presented at the 53rd Annual Meeting of the Linguistic Society of America, Boston.

Ringo, Elbert W. 1954. The position of the noun modifier in colloquial Spanish. In: Descriptive studies in Spanish grammar. Edited by H. R. Kahane and A. Pietrangeli. Urbana, Ill.: University of Illinois Press.

Rissel, Dorothy A. 1976. An investigation of world view as manifested in a portion of the lexicon in a bilingual/bicultural situation: Spanish-English. Unpublished doctoral dissertation. State University of New York, Buffalo.

Rivero, M. L. 1978a. On left-dislocation and topicalization in Spanish. Unpublished MS. University of Ottawa.

Rivero, M. L. 1978b. Theoretical implications of the syntax of left-branch modifiers in Spanish. Unpublished MS. University of Ottawa.

Rizzi, L. 1976. Ristrutturazione. Rivista de grammatica generativa 1.1-54.

Rizzi, L. 1978. Violations of the WH-island constraint in Italian and the subjacency condition. Pisa: Scuola Normale Superiore.

Roberts, J. (forthcoming) Causatives and the syntax of French.

Roca Pons, J. 1958. Estudios sobre perífrasis verbales del español. Revista de filología española.

Rochmont, M. S. 1978. A theory of stylistic rules in English. Unpublished doctoral dissertation. University of Massachusetts.

Rodman, R. 1973. The study of fuzzy islands within the framework of transformational generative grammar. Unpublished doctoral dissertation. UCLA.

Roldán, M. 1974. Toward a semantic characterization of *ser* and *estar*. Hispania 57.68-75.

Rohlfs, Gerhard. 1949. Historische Grammatik der italienischen Sprache. Band 1: Lautlehre. Bern: A. Francke.

Rohlfs, Gerhard. 1968. Grammatica storica della lingua italiana e dei suoi dialetti. II: Morfologia. Turin: Einaudi.

Rosoff, Gary H. 1973. A study of liaison in extemporaneous Montreal French speech. Unpublished doctoral dissertation. Columbia University.

Ross, J. R. 1967. Constraints on variables in syntax. Indiana Linguistics Club.

Ross, J. R. 1970. Gapping and the order of constituents. In: Progress in linguistics. Edited by M. Bierwisch and K. E. Heidolph. The Hague: Mouton. 249-259.

Rousseau, Pascale, and David Sankoff. 1978. Advances in variable rule methodology. In: Linguistic variation: Models and methods. Edited by D. Sankoff. New York-London: Academic Press. 57-69.

Sag, Ivan. 1977. Deletion and logical form. Bloomington: Indiana University Linguistics Club.

Saltarelli, Mario. 1970. Spanish plural formation: Apocope or epenthesis? Lg. 46.89-96.

Saltarelli, Mario. 1976. Accusativus cum infinitivo. In: Current studies in Romance linguistics. Edited by M. Luján and F. Hensey. Washington, D.C.: Georgetown University Press. 88-99.

Saltarelli, Mario. (in press) Complement subject deletion and infinitive formation in Italian. In: Essays in contemporary Romance linguistics: Proceedings of the Eighth Linguistic Symposium on Romance Languages, 1978. Edited by F. Nuessel. Rowley, Mass.: Newbury House.

Saltarelli, Mario. (in press) Syntactic diffusion. In: Papers from the Fourth International Conference on Historical Linguistics. 1979. Edited by E. Traugott, R. LaBrum, and S. Shepard. Amsterdam: John Benjamin BV.

Sanders, G. 1979. Equational phonology. In: Current approaches to phonological theory. Edited by Daniel A. Dinnsen. Bloomington: Indiana University Press.

Schachter, P. 1973. Focus and relativization. Lg. 49.19-46.

Schane, Sanford A. 1968. French phonology and morphology. Cambridge, Mass.: MIT Press.

Schane, Sanford A. 1972. How abstract is French phonology? In: Generative studies in Romance languages. Edited by J. Casagrande and Bohdan Saciuk. Rowley, Mass.: Newbury House. 340-352.

Schane, Sanford A. 1973. Generative phonology. Englewood Cliffs, N.J.: Prentice-Hall.

Schane, Sanford A. 1976. Truncation and stress in Spanish. In: Current studies in Romance linguistics. Edited by M. Luján and F. Hensey. Washington, D.C.: Georgetown University Press. 50-62.

Schiaffini, A. 1926. Testi fiorentini del duecento e dei primi del trecento. Florence: Sansoni.

Schiaparelli, L. 1929-1933. Codice diplomatico longobardo. 2 vols. Rome: Tipografia del senato.

Segre, C., and M. Marti, eds. La letteratura italiana. Storia e testi. Vol. 3. Milano: Ricciardi. 793-882.

Selkirk, Elizabeth. 1972. The phrase phonology of English and French. Unpublished doctoral dissertation. MIT.

Sievers, E. 1893. Grundzüge der Phonetik. Leipzig: Breitkopf and Hartel.

Smith, C. 1961. A class of complex modifiers in English. Lg. 37.342-365.

Smith, C. 1964. Determiners and relative clauses in a generative grammar of English. Lg. 40.37-52.

Sorrento, L. 1950. Sintassi romanza. Richerche e prospettive. Varese-Milano: Cisalpino.

Stahlke, Herbert. 1976. Which that. Lg. 53.584-610.

Stampe, David L. 1973. A dissertation on natural phonology. Unpublished doctoral dissertation. University of Chicago.

Stockwell, R., J. Bowen, and J. Martin. 1965. The grammatical structures of English and Spanish. New York: Holt, Rinehart and Winston.

Suñer, Margaret. 1975. Spanish adverbs: Support for the phonological cycle? Linguistic Inquiry 6.602-605.

Suñer, Margaret. (in preparation) Spanish existential sentences.

Tagliavini, Carlo. 1969. Le origini delle lingue neolatine. Introduzione alla filologia romanza. Bologna: Pàtron.

Tai, James H. Y. 1969. Coordination reduction. Unpublished doctoral dissertation. Indiana University.

Tai, James H. Y. 1971. Identity deletion and regrouping in coordinate structures. In: Papers from the Seventh Regional Meeting, Chicago Linguistic Society. Chicago: Chicago Linguistic Society. 264-274.

380 / References

Tekavčić, P. 1972. Grammatica storica dell'italiano. II:
Morfosintassi. Bologna: Il Mulino.
Tobler, A. 1875-1912. Review of: J. Le Coultre, De l'ordre
des mots dans Chrétien des Troyes. Vermischte Beiträge
zur französischen Grammatik 5.395-414. Leipzig: Hirzel.
Tobler, A. 1886. Vermischte Beiträge zur französischen
Grammatik. Leipzig: Hirzel.
Tobler, A. 1889. Vermischte Beiträge zur französischen
Grammatik, Neue Folge, #10. Zeitschrift für romanische
Philologie 13.186-191.
Tranel, Bernard. 1977a. On the elision of [i] in French
qui. French Studies in French Linguistics I-1.53-74.
Tranel, Bernard. 1977b. French quoi. Unpublished manu-
script, University of California, Irvine.
Trubetzkoy, N. S. 1939. Grundzüge der Phonologie.
Traveaux du cercle linguistique de Prague 7.5-261.
Ulleland, M. 1960. Alcune osservazioni sulla legge Tobler-
Mussafia. Studia Neophilologica 32.53-79.
Vasiliu, Emanuel. 1970. Elemente de teorie semantica a
limbilor naturale. Bucharest: Editura Academiei R. S.
Romãnia.
Vendler, Zeno. 1968. Adjectives and nominalizations. The
Hague: Mouton.
Vennemann, Theo. 1972. Rule inversion. Lingua 29-209-242.
Vergnaud, R. 1974. French relative clauses. Unpublished
doctoral dissertation. MIT.
Vox Diccionari Manual Castellà-Català, Català-Castellà.
Barcelona: Bibliograf, S. A.
Wackernagel, J. 1892. Über ein Gesetz der indogermanischen
Wortstellung. Indogermanische Forschungen 1.333-436.
Walsh, T. 1977. On the necessity of rule ordering in natural
generative phonology. Paper presented at the Seventh
Linguistic Symposium on Romance Linguistics. Cornell
University.
Wanner, D. 1979. Die Bewahrung der lateinischen
Haupttonstelle in Romanischen. Vox Romanica 38.
Waugh, Daniel C. 1979. Micaelense phonetics. Unpublished
B.A. thesis. Harvard University.
Waugh, Linda R. 1976a. Lexical meaning: The prepositions
en and dans in French. Lingua 39.69-118.
Waugh, Linda R. 1976b. Roman Jakobson's science of lan-
guage. Lisse: Peter de Ridder.
Waugh, Linda R. 1976c. The semantics and paradigmatics of
word order. Lg. 52.82-107.
Wehrli, E. (forthcoming) Compléments-VP, implications
théoriques. Unpublished MS. McGill University.
Wehrli, E., and J. Y. Morin. 1978. WH-movement in VP.
Paper read at the Tenth Annual Meeting of the Northeast
Linguistic Society.

Wheeler, Max W. 1974. Pronunciation and spelling. In: Introductory Catalan grammar. Edited by Joan Gili. Oxford: Dolphin Book Co.

Whitfield, J. H. 1964. In margine alla legge Tobler-Mussafia: La proclisi della negative. Le parole et le idée 6.61-72.

Williams, E. S. 1977. Discourse and logical form. Linguistic Inquiry 8.101-140.

Williams, E. S. 1978. Across-the-board rule application. Linguistic Inquiry 9.31-44.

Winter, Werner. 1965. Transformations without kernels? Lg. 41.484-489.

Wise, Claude M. 1957. Applied phonetics. Englewood Cliffs, N.J.: Prentice-Hall.

Woisteschlaeger, E. 1976. On how useful a construct the left branch condition is. In: Papers presented at the Sixth Annual Meeting of the Northeastern Linguistic Society. Montreal Working Papers in Linguistics 6.251-258.

Woolford, Ellen. 1978. Free relatives and other base generated WLT constructions. In: Papers presented at the Fourteenth Regional Meeting, Chicago Linguistic Society. Edited by Donna Farkas et al. Chicago: Chicago Linguistic Society. 482-490.

Yates, Alan. 1975. Teach yourself Catalan. London: Hodder and Stoughton.

Zamora Vicente, Alonso. 1974. Dialectología española. Madrid: Gredos.